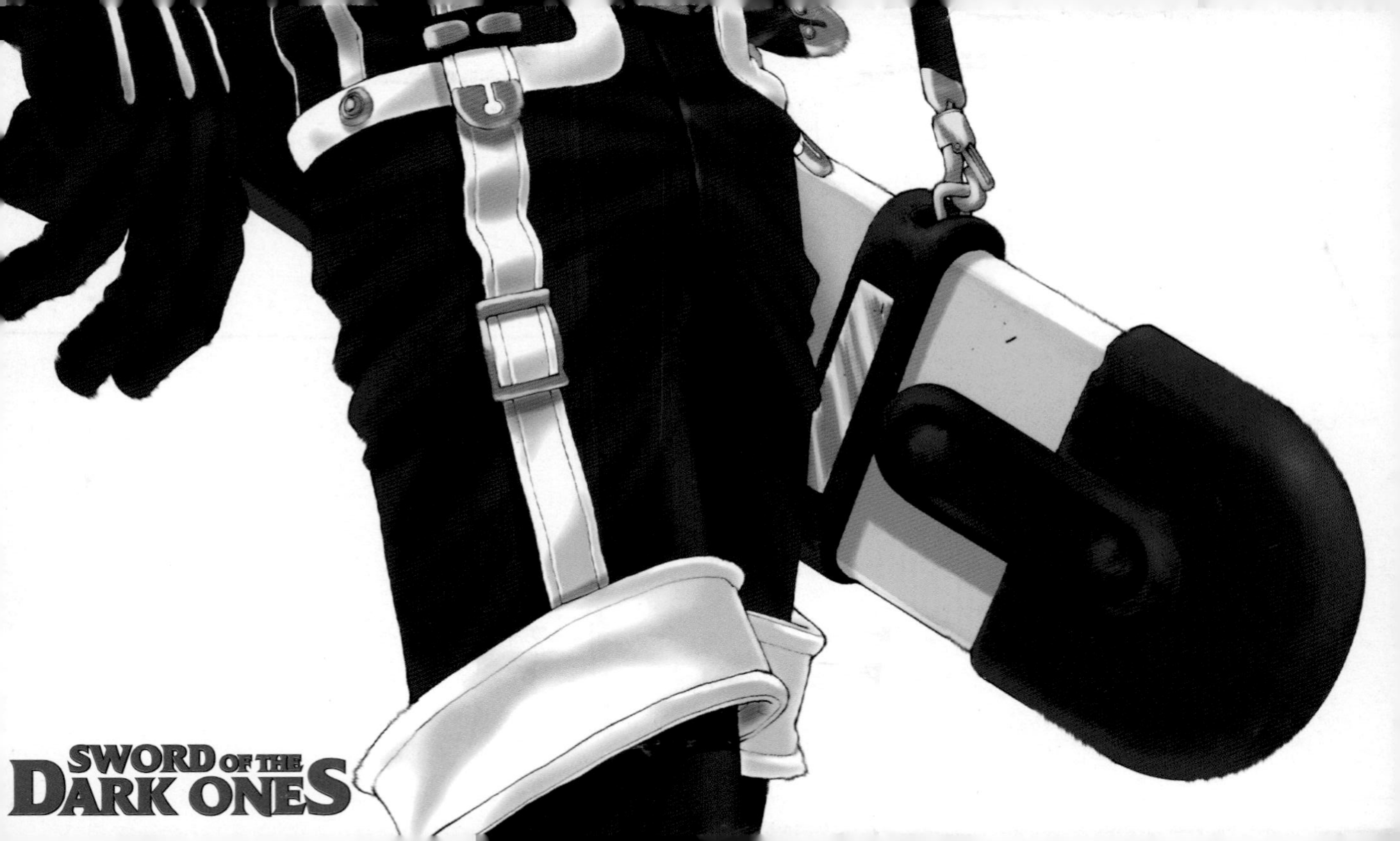
SWORD OF THE
DARK ONES

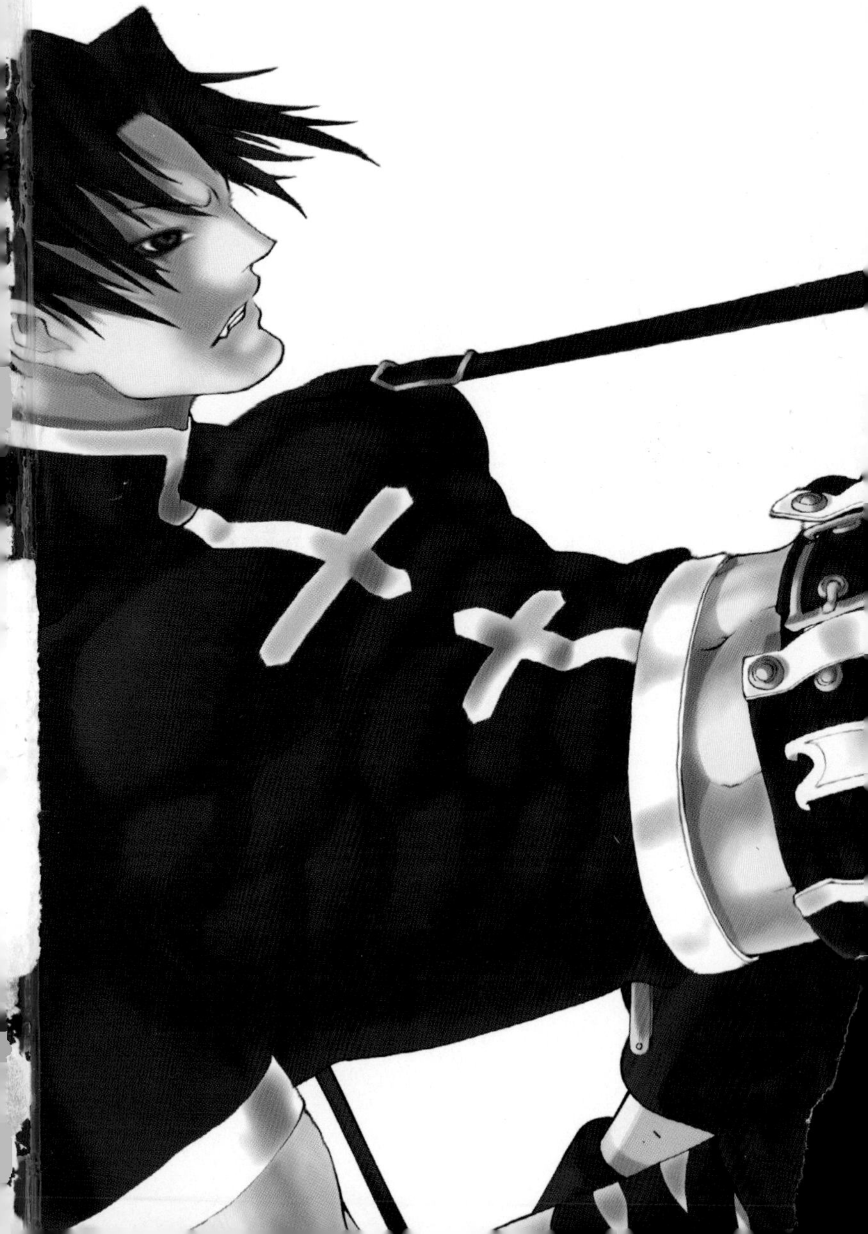

THE DARK ONES

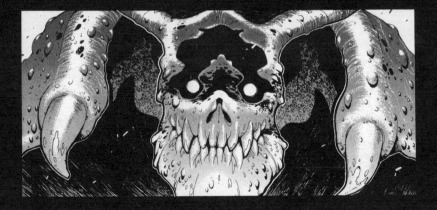

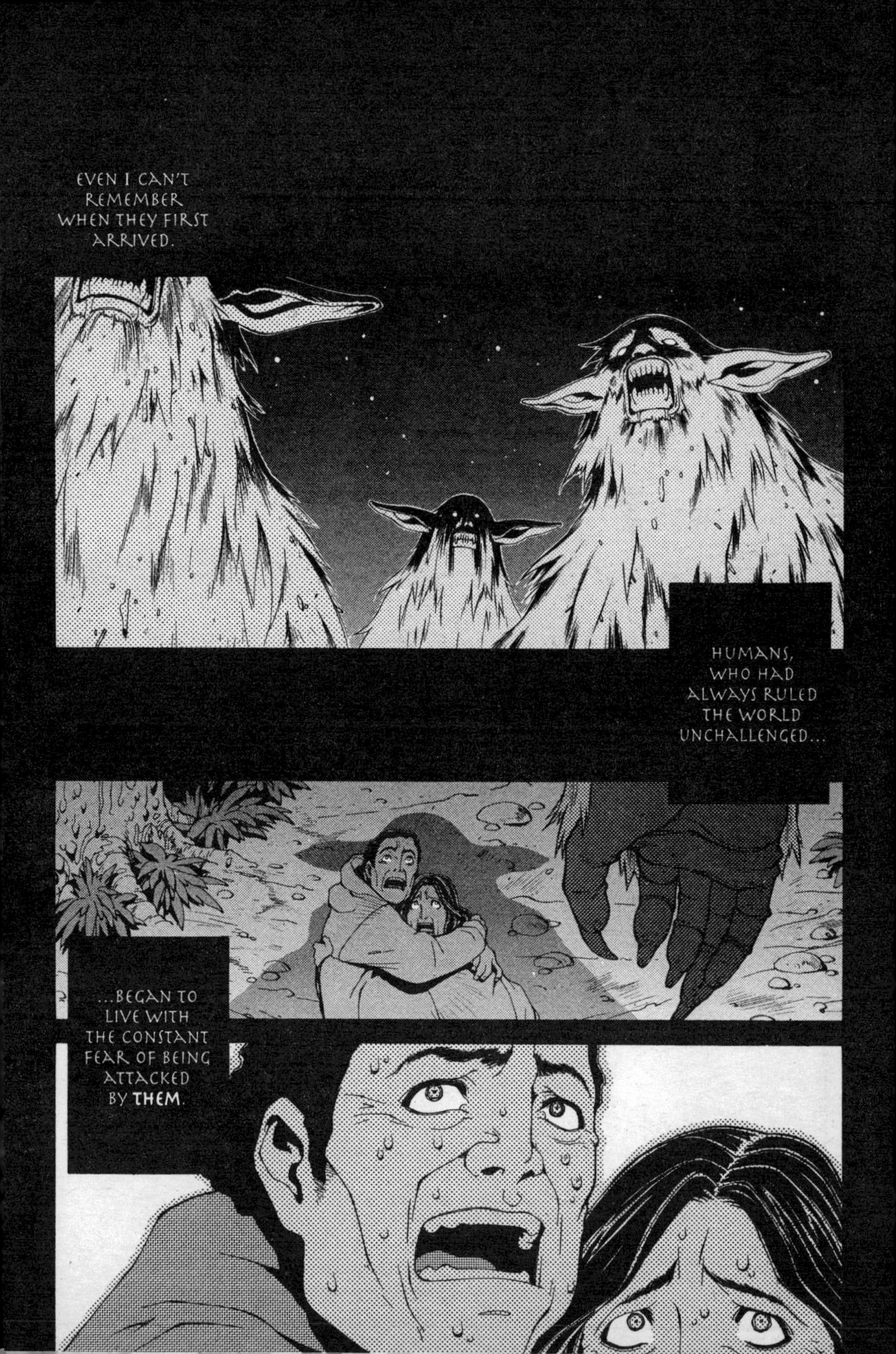
EVEN I CAN'T REMEMBER WHEN THEY FIRST ARRIVED.
HUMANS, WHO HAD ALWAYS RULED THE WORLD UNCHALLENGED...
...BEGAN TO LIVE WITH THE CONSTANT FEAR OF BEING ATTACKED BY **THEM**.

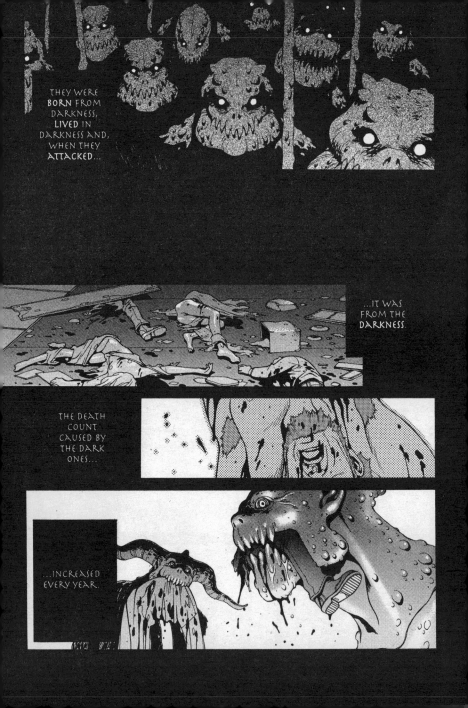

THEY WERE **BORN** FROM DARKNESS, **LIVED** IN DARKNESS AND, WHEN THEY **ATTACKED**...

...IT WAS FROM THE **DARKNESS**.

THE DEATH COUNT CAUSED BY THE DARK ONES...

...INCREASED EVERY YEAR.

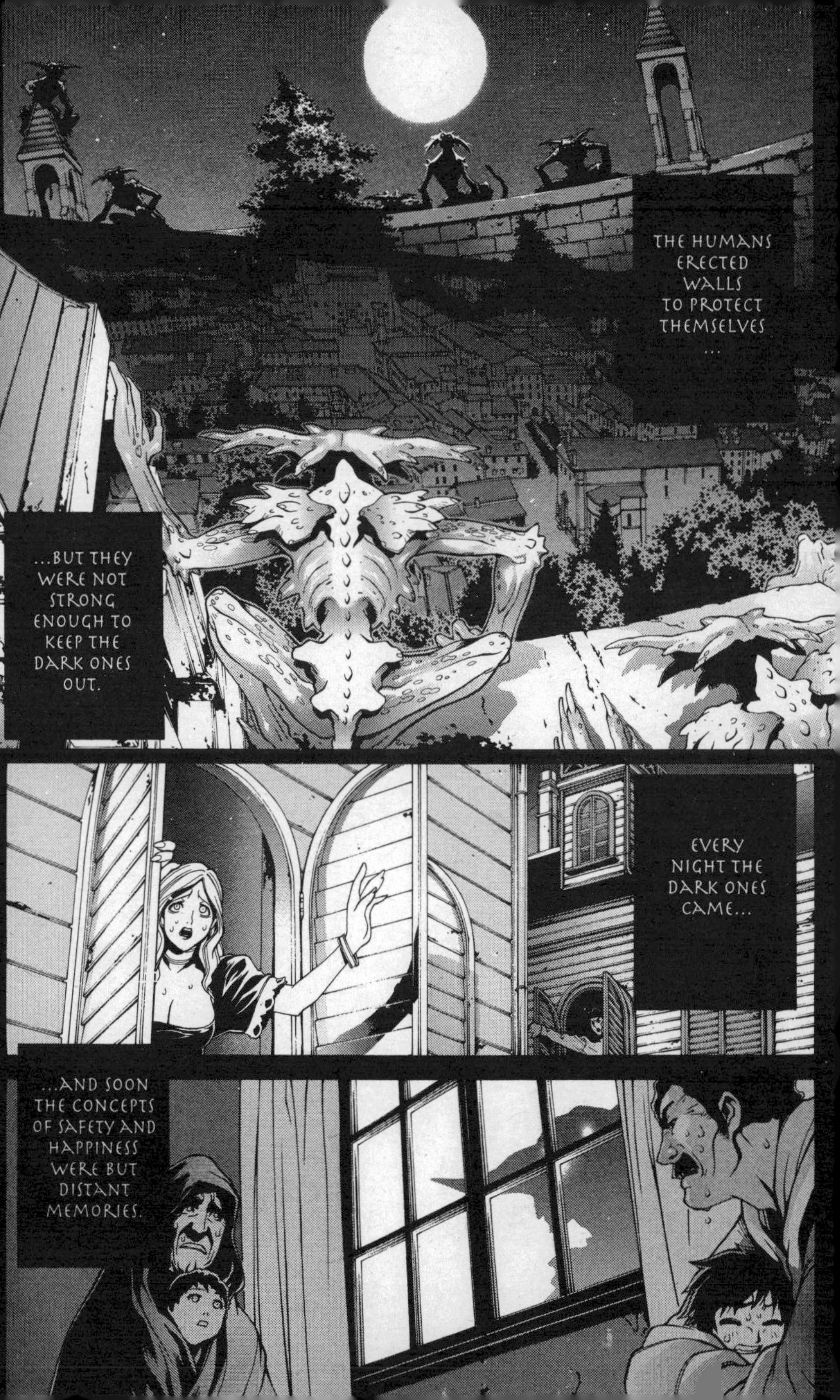
THE HUMANS ERECTED WALLS TO PROTECT THEMSELVES ...
...BUT THEY WERE NOT STRONG ENOUGH TO KEEP THE DARK ONES OUT.
EVERY NIGHT THE DARK ONES CAME...
...AND SOON THE CONCEPTS OF SAFETY AND HAPPINESS WERE BUT DISTANT MEMORIES.

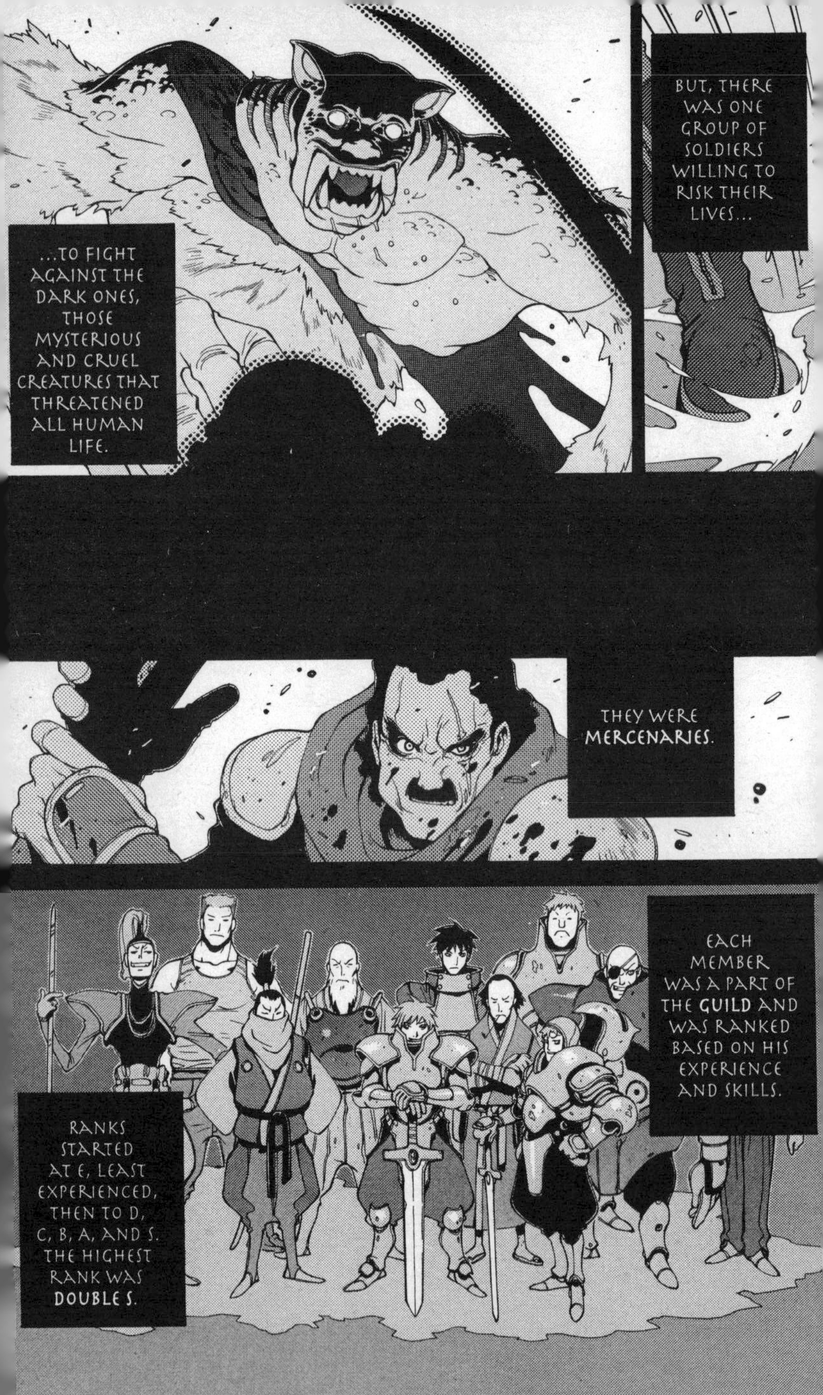
BUT, THERE WAS ONE GROUP OF SOLDIERS WILLING TO RISK THEIR LIVES...
...TO FIGHT AGAINST THE DARK ONES, THOSE MYSTERIOUS AND CRUEL CREATURES THAT THREATENED ALL HUMAN LIFE.
THEY WERE **MERCENARIES**.
EACH MEMBER WAS A PART OF THE **GUILD** AND WAS RANKED BASED ON HIS EXPERIENCE AND SKILLS.
RANKS STARTED AT E, LEAST EXPERIENCED, THEN TO D, C, B, A, AND S. THE HIGHEST RANK WAS **DOUBLE S**.

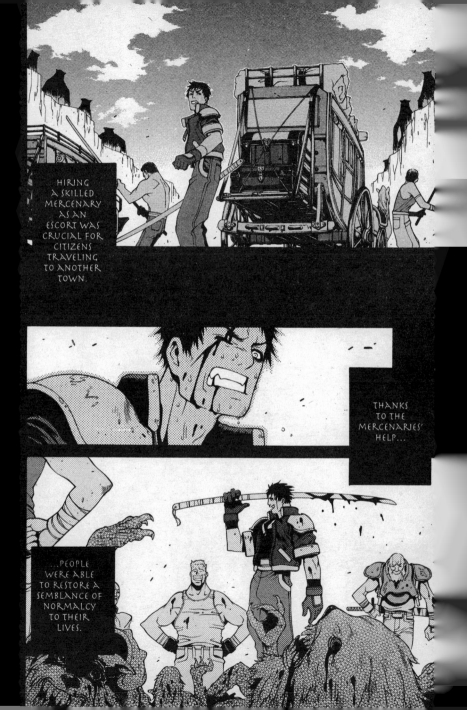

HIRING
A SKILLED
MERCENARY
AS AN
ESCORT WAS
CRUCIAL FOR
CITIZENS
TRAVELING
TO ANOTHER
TOWN.

THANKS
TO THE
MERCENARIES'
HELP...

...PEOPLE
WERE ABLE
TO RESTORE A
SEMBLANCE OF
NORMALCY
TO THEIR
LIVES.

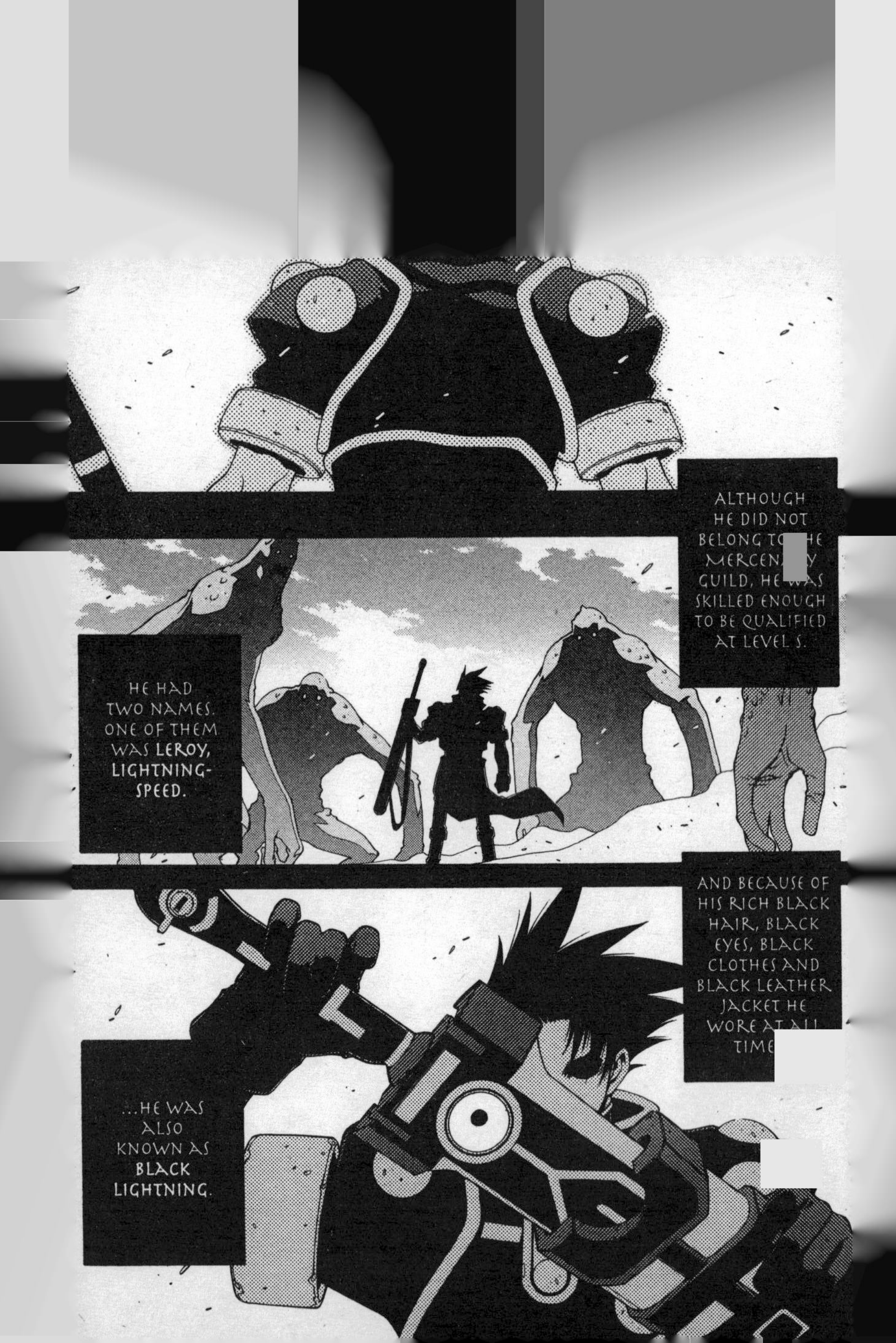
ALTHOUGH HE DID NOT BELONG TO THE MERCENARY GUILD, HE WAS SKILLED ENOUGH TO BE QUALIFIED AT LEVEL S.
HE HAD TWO NAMES. ONE OF THEM WAS **LEROY, LIGHTNING-SPEED.**
AND BECAUSE OF HIS RICH BLACK HAIR, BLACK EYES, BLACK CLOTHES AND BLACK LEATHER JACKET HE WORE AT ALL TIME
...HE WAS ALSO KNOWN AS **BLACK LIGHTNING.**

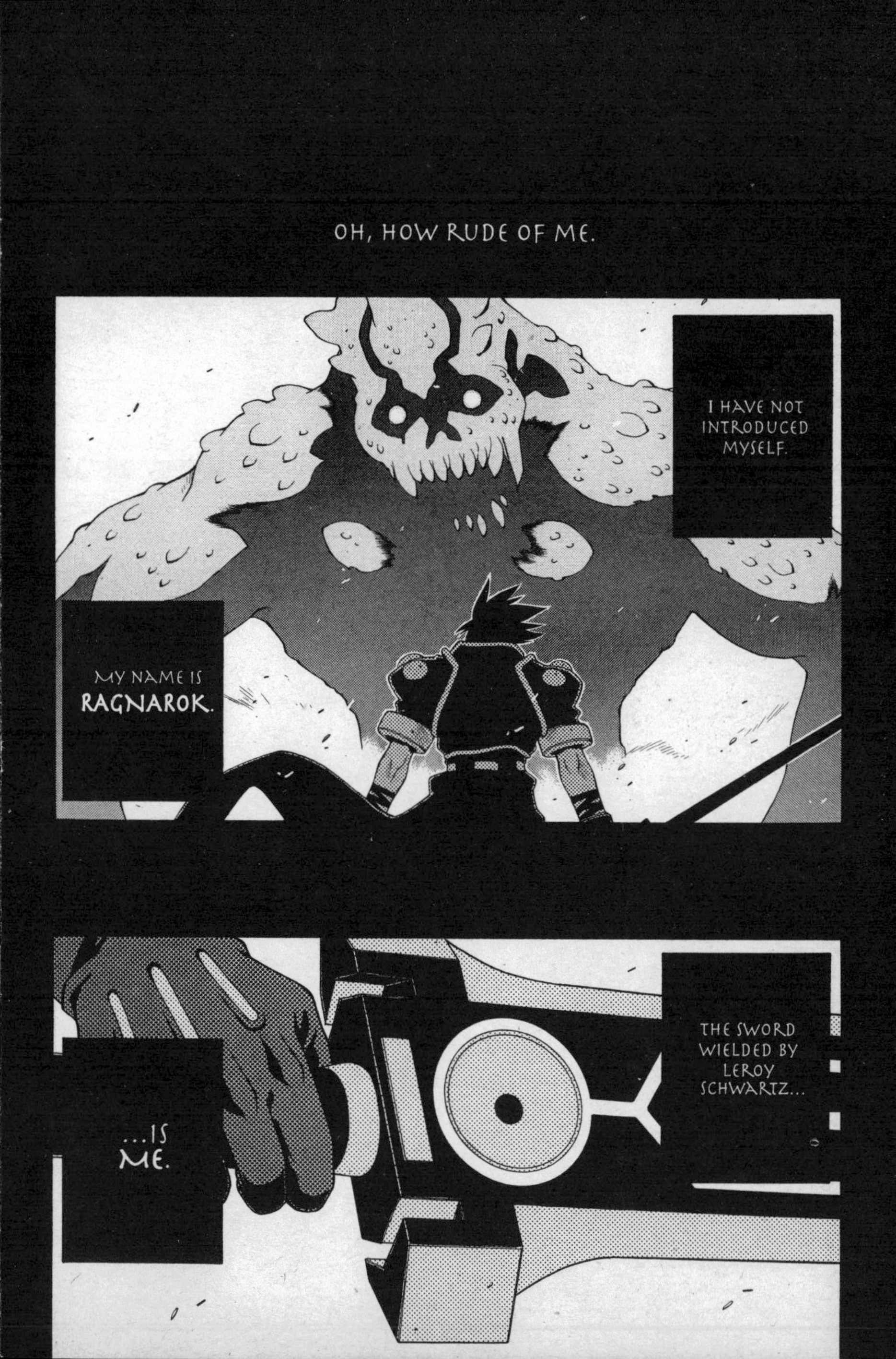
OH, HOW RUDE OF ME.
I HAVE NOT INTRODUCED MYSELF.
MY NAME IS RAGNAROK.
THE SWORD WIELDED BY LEROY SCHWARTZ...
...IS ME.

SWORD OF THE DARK ONES

1

BY KOTOBUKI TSUKASA

FROM A STORY BY YASUI KENTARO
DESIGN BY TASA

CONTENTS

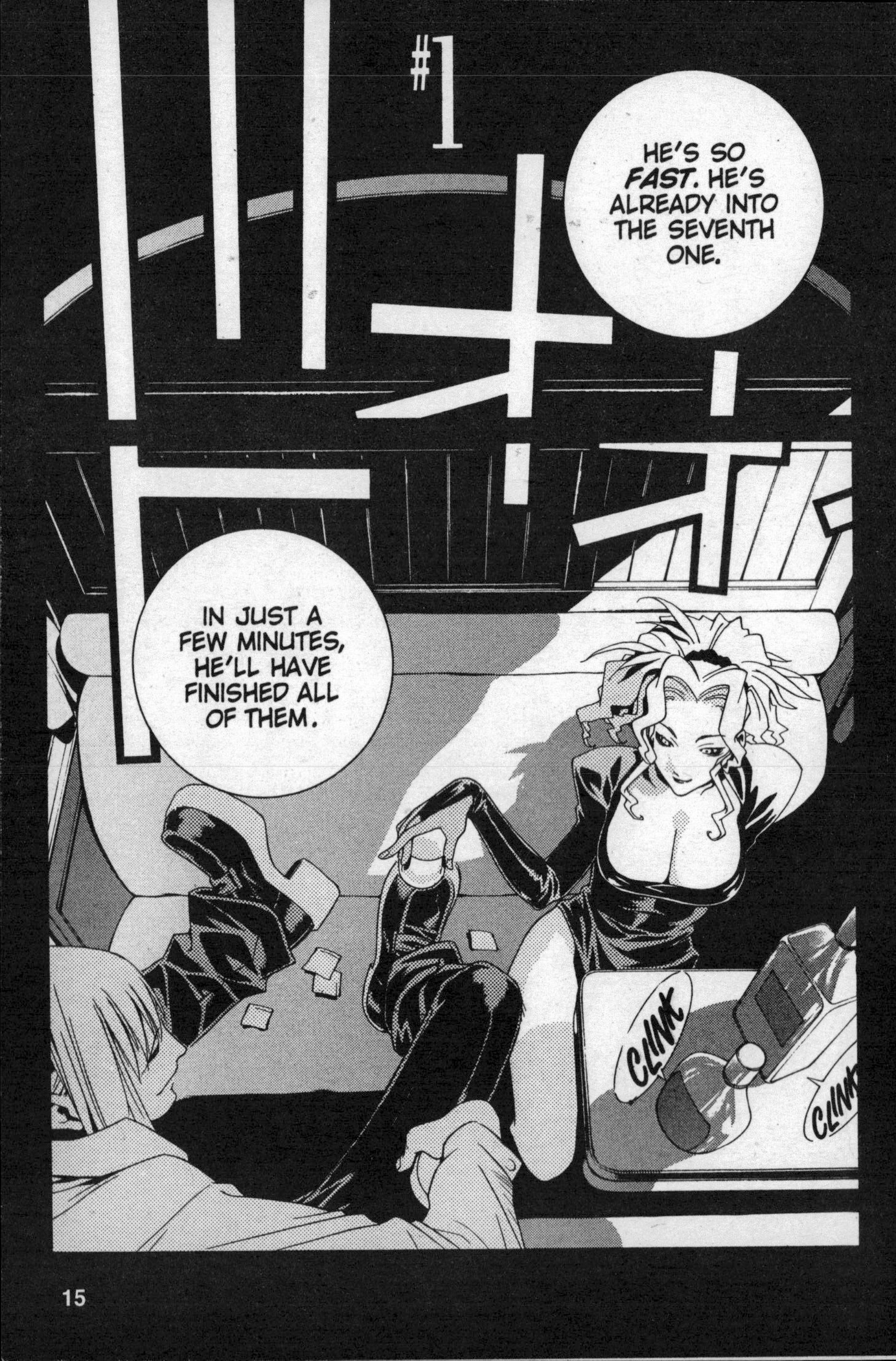
#1
HE'S SO FAST. HE'S ALREADY INTO THE SEVENTH ONE.
IN JUST A FEW MINUTES, HE'LL HAVE FINISHED ALL OF THEM.
CLINK
CLINK

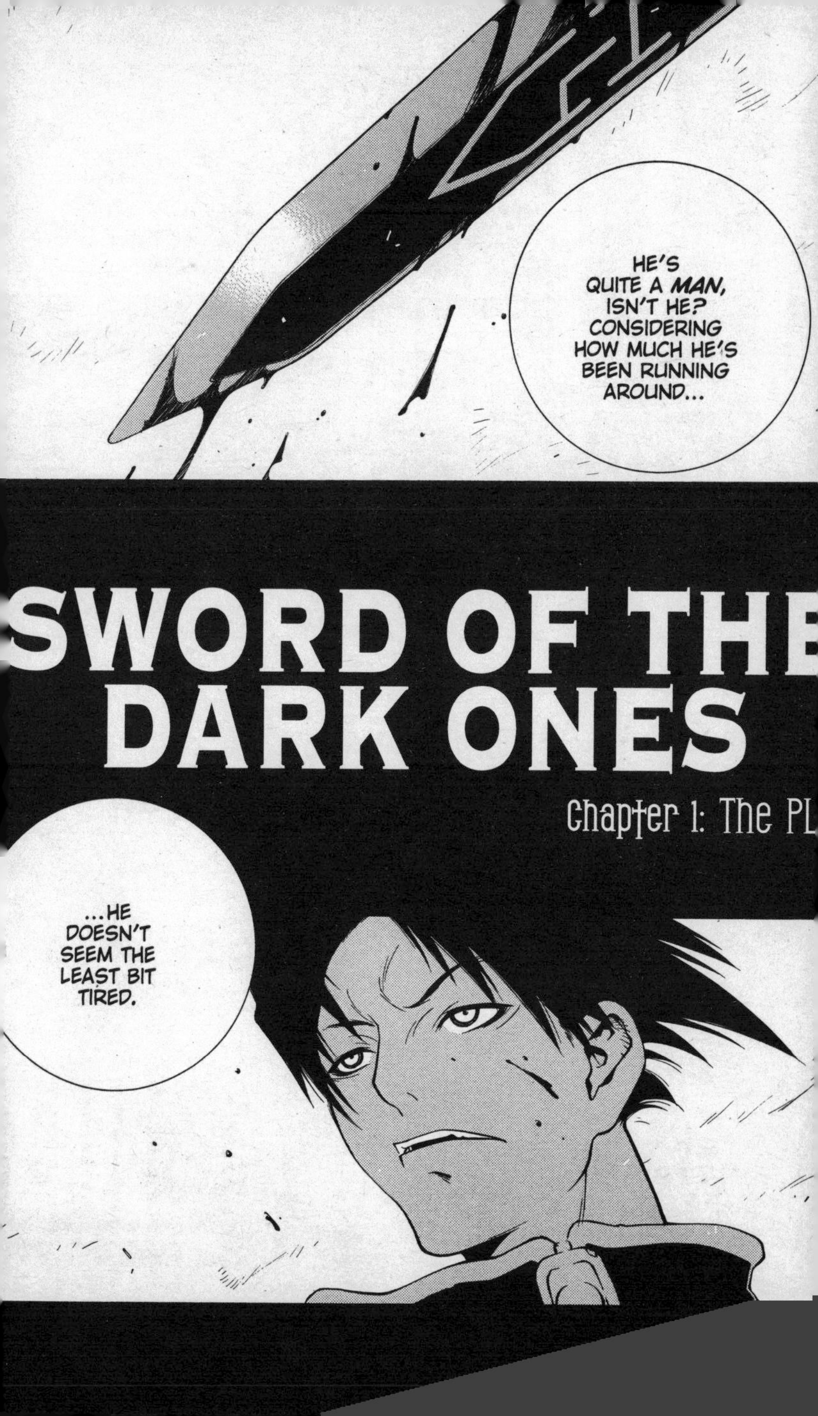
HE'S QUITE A *MAN*, ISN'T HE? CONSIDERING HOW MUCH HE'S BEEN RUNNING AROUND...
SWORD OF THE DARK ONES
Chapter 1: The PL
...HE DOESN'T SEEM THE LEAST BIT TIRED.

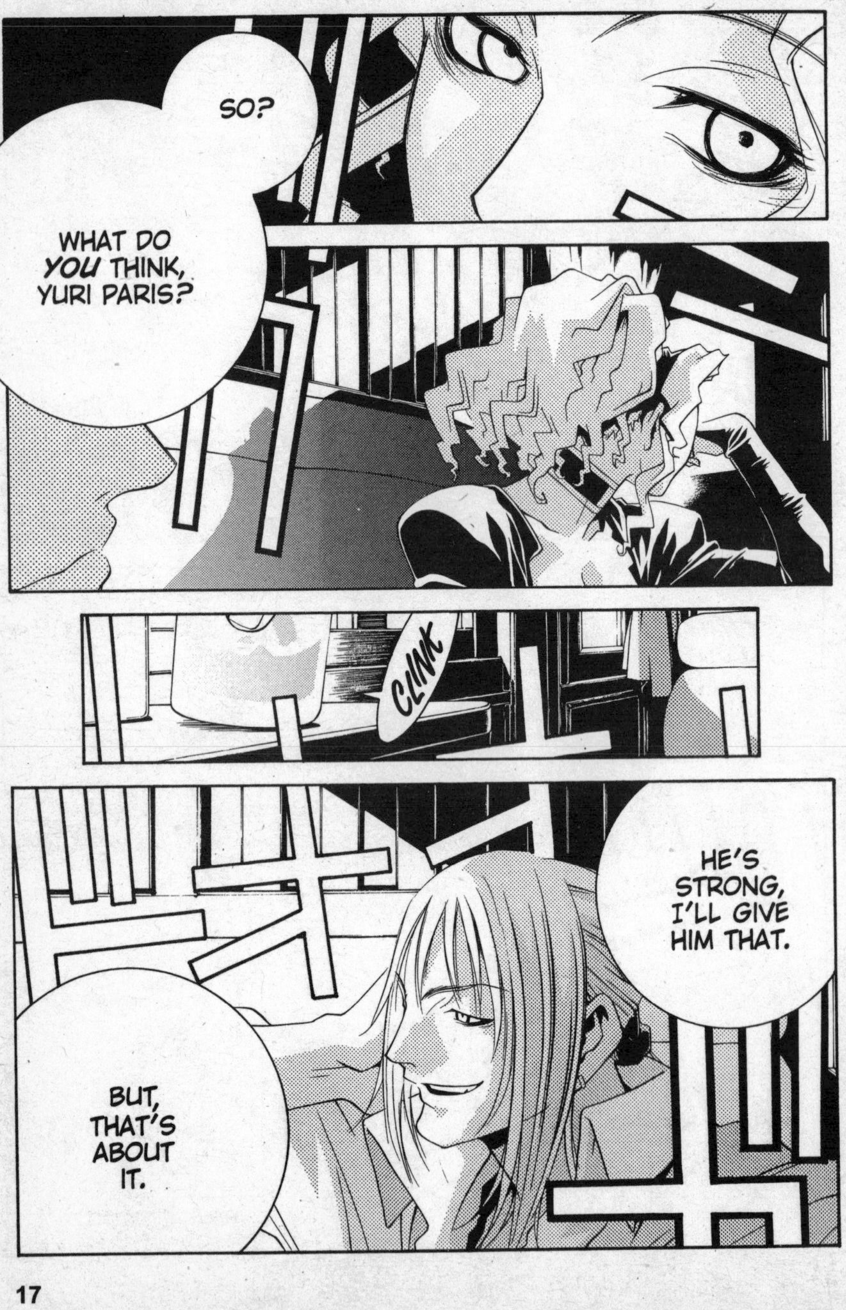
SO?
WHAT DO *YOU* THINK, YURI PARIS?
CLINK
HE'S STRONG, I'LL GIVE HIM THAT.
BUT, THAT'S ABOUT IT.

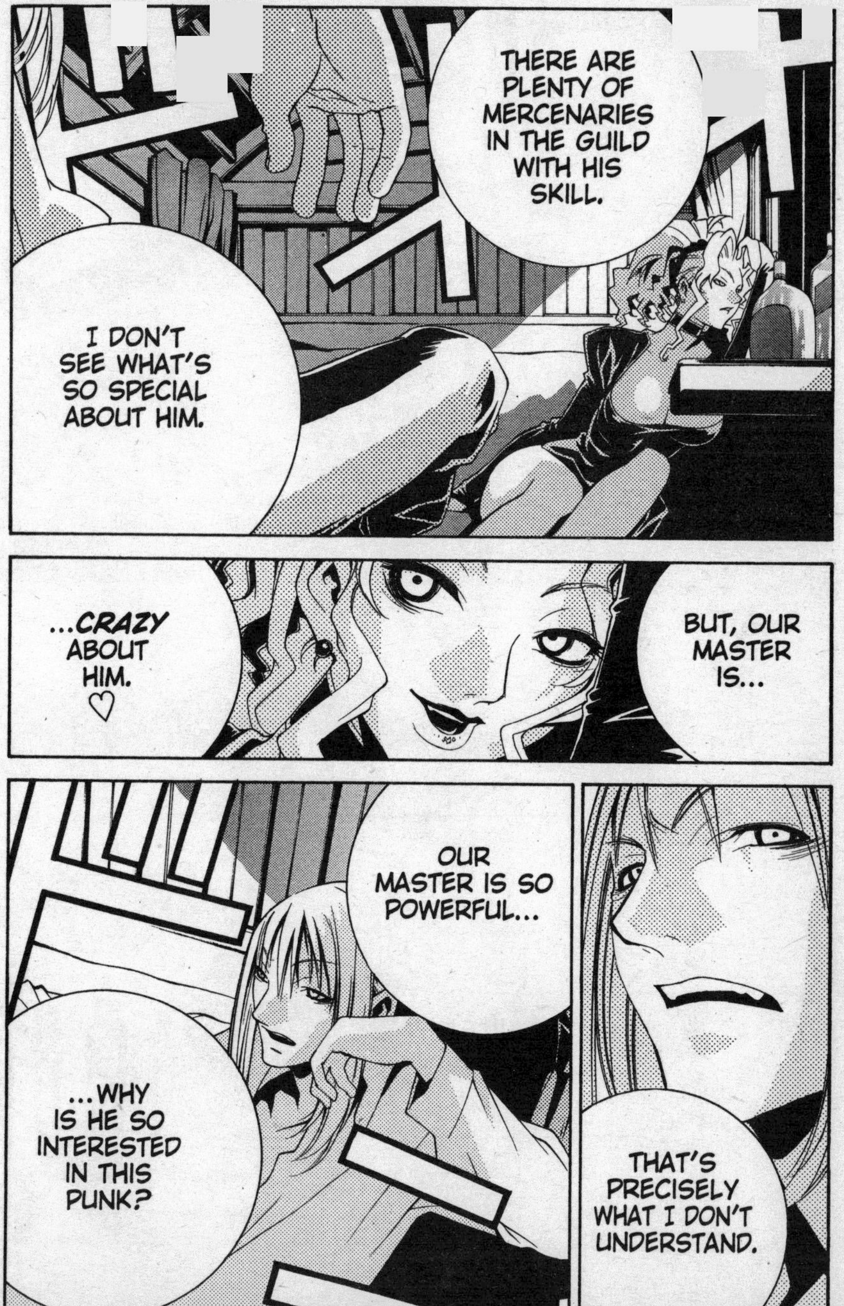
THERE ARE PLENTY OF MERCENARIES IN THE GUILD WITH HIS SKILL.
I DON'T SEE WHAT'S SO SPECIAL ABOUT HIM.
BUT, OUR MASTER IS...
...*CRAZY* ABOUT HIM. ♡
THAT'S PRECISELY WHAT I DON'T UNDERSTAND.
OUR MASTER IS SO POWERFUL...
...WHY IS HE SO INTERESTED IN THIS PUNK?

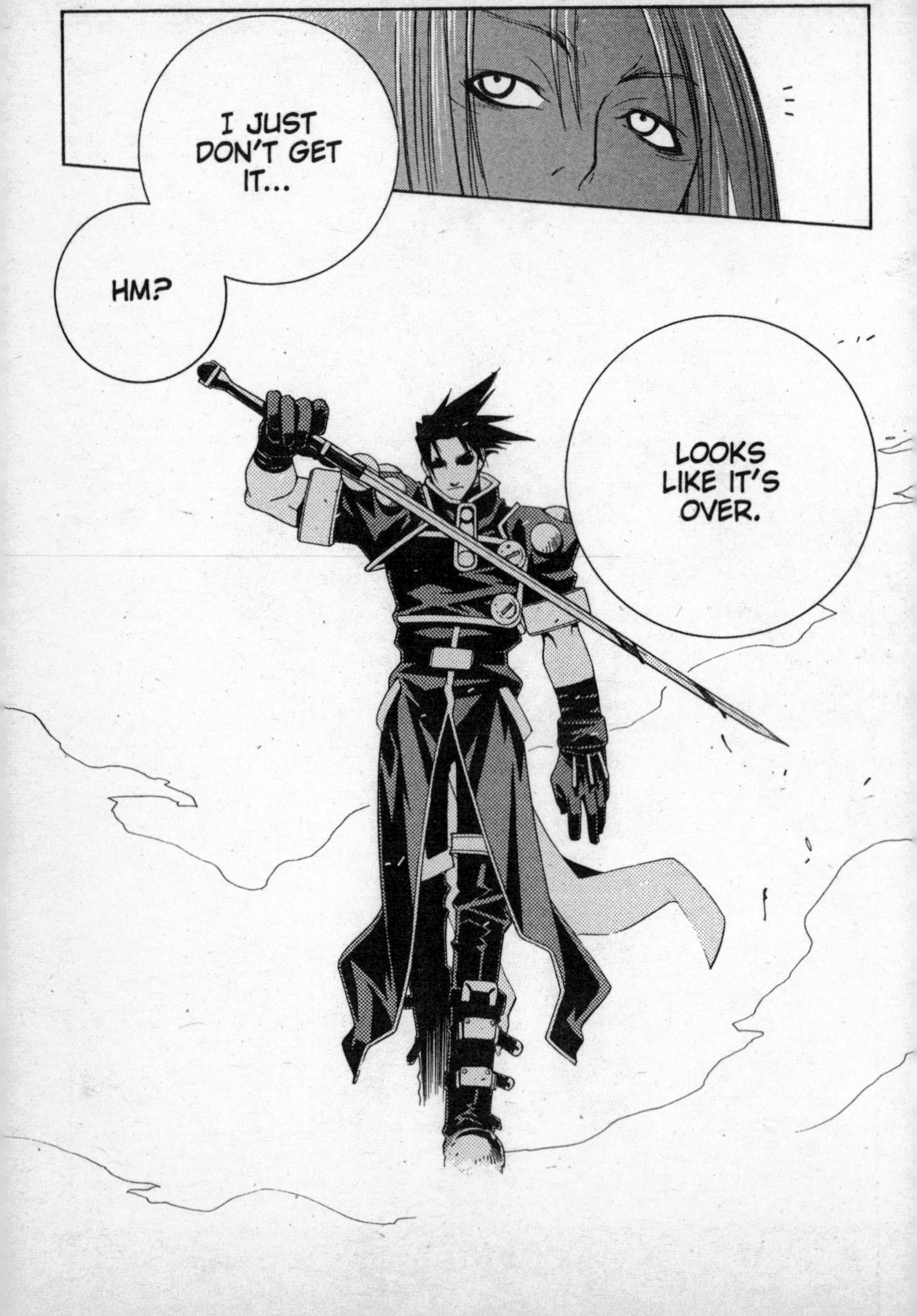
I JUST DON'T GET IT...
HM?
LOOKS LIKE IT'S OVER.

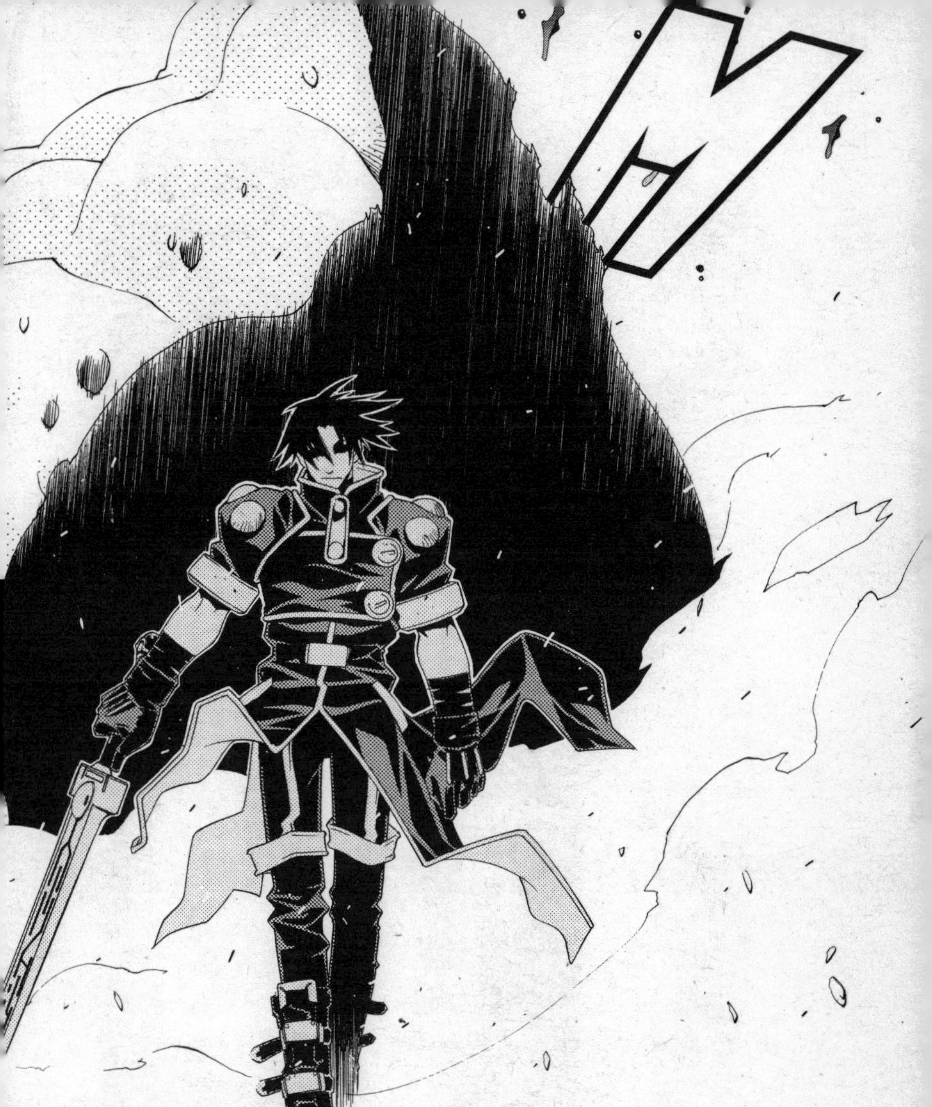

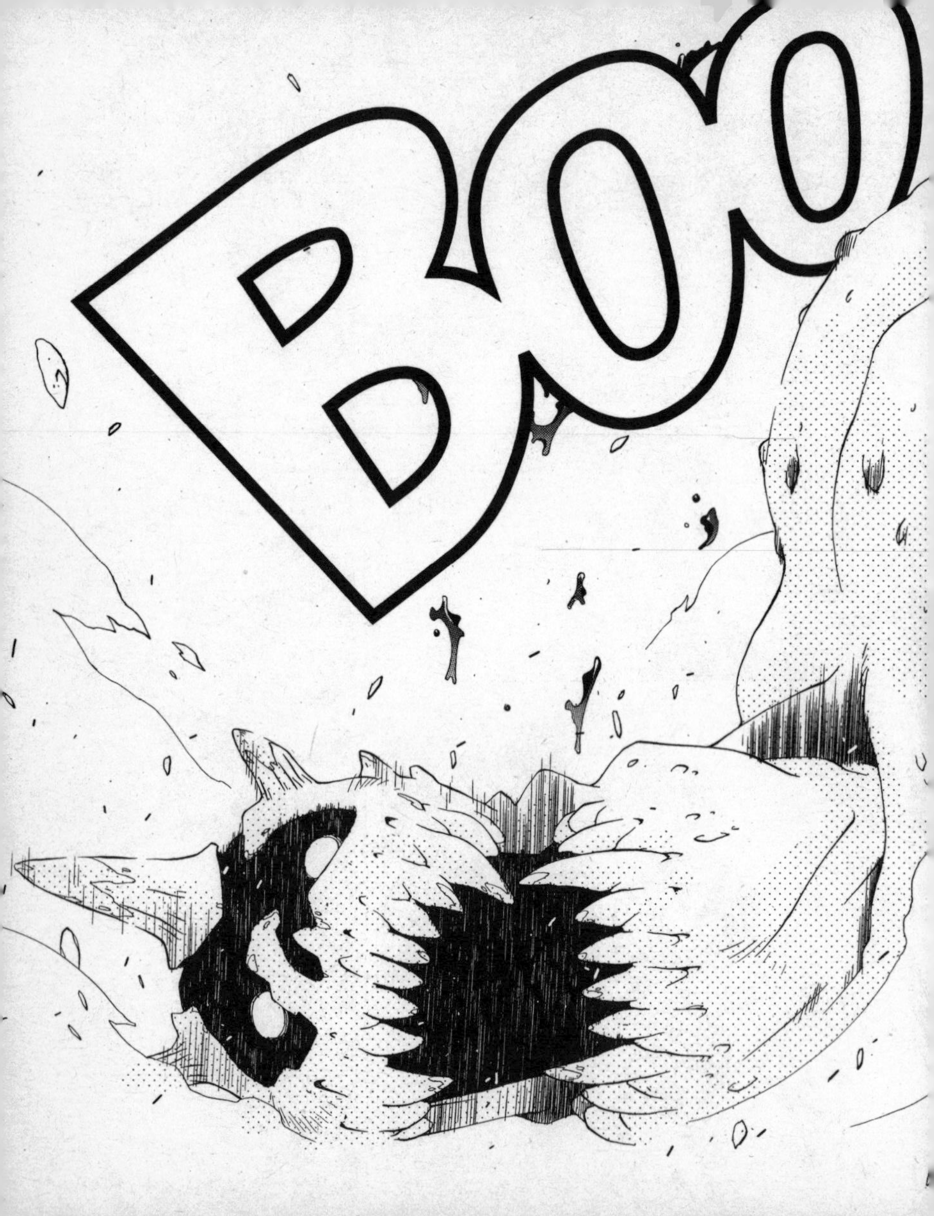
BOOO

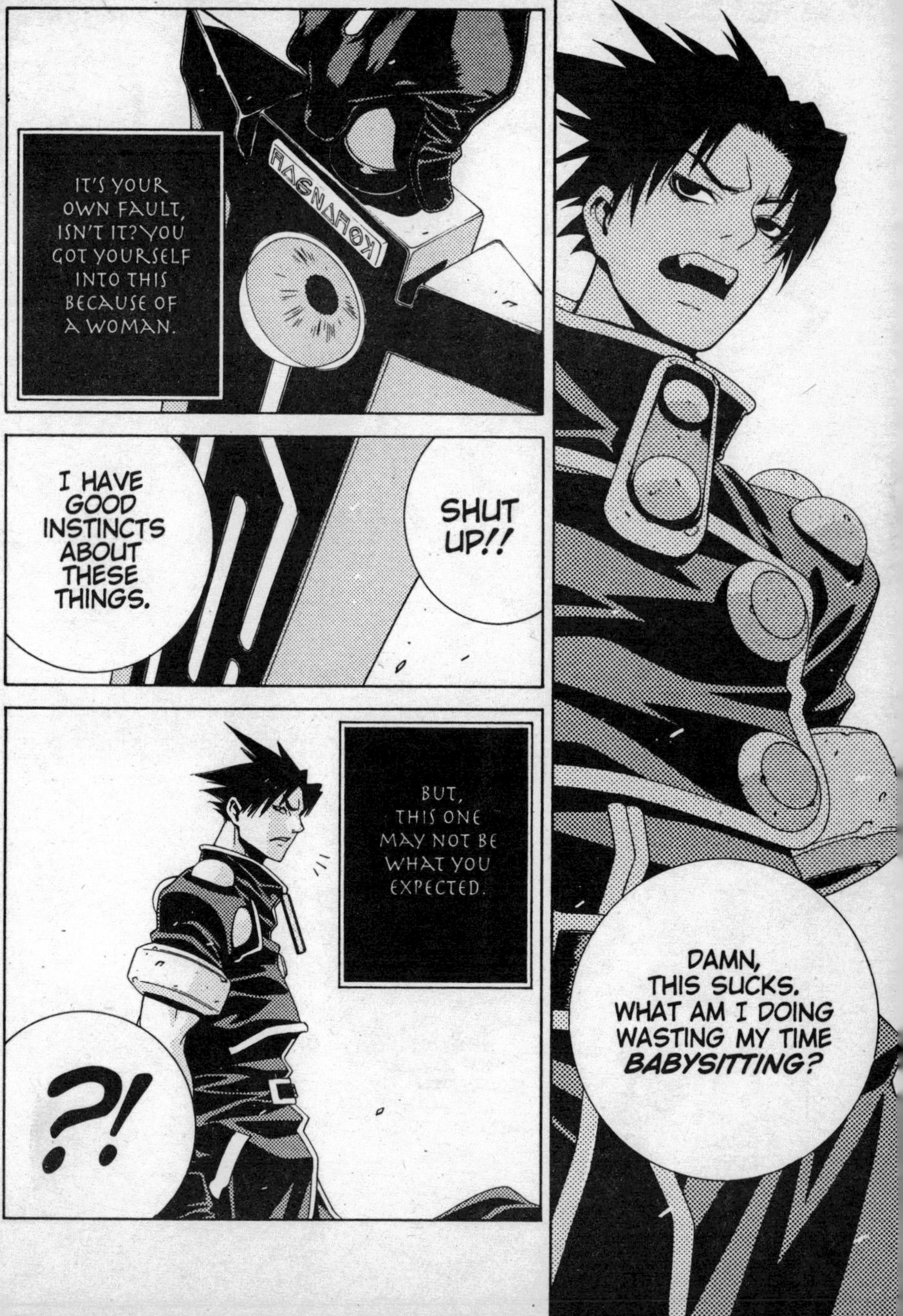
DAMN, THIS SUCKS. WHAT AM I DOING WASTING MY TIME *BABYSITTING?*
IT'S YOUR OWN FAULT, ISN'T IT? YOU GOT YOURSELF INTO THIS BECAUSE OF A WOMAN.
SHUT UP!!
I HAVE GOOD INSTINCTS ABOUT THESE THINGS.
BUT, THIS ONE MAY NOT BE WHAT YOU EXPECTED.
?!

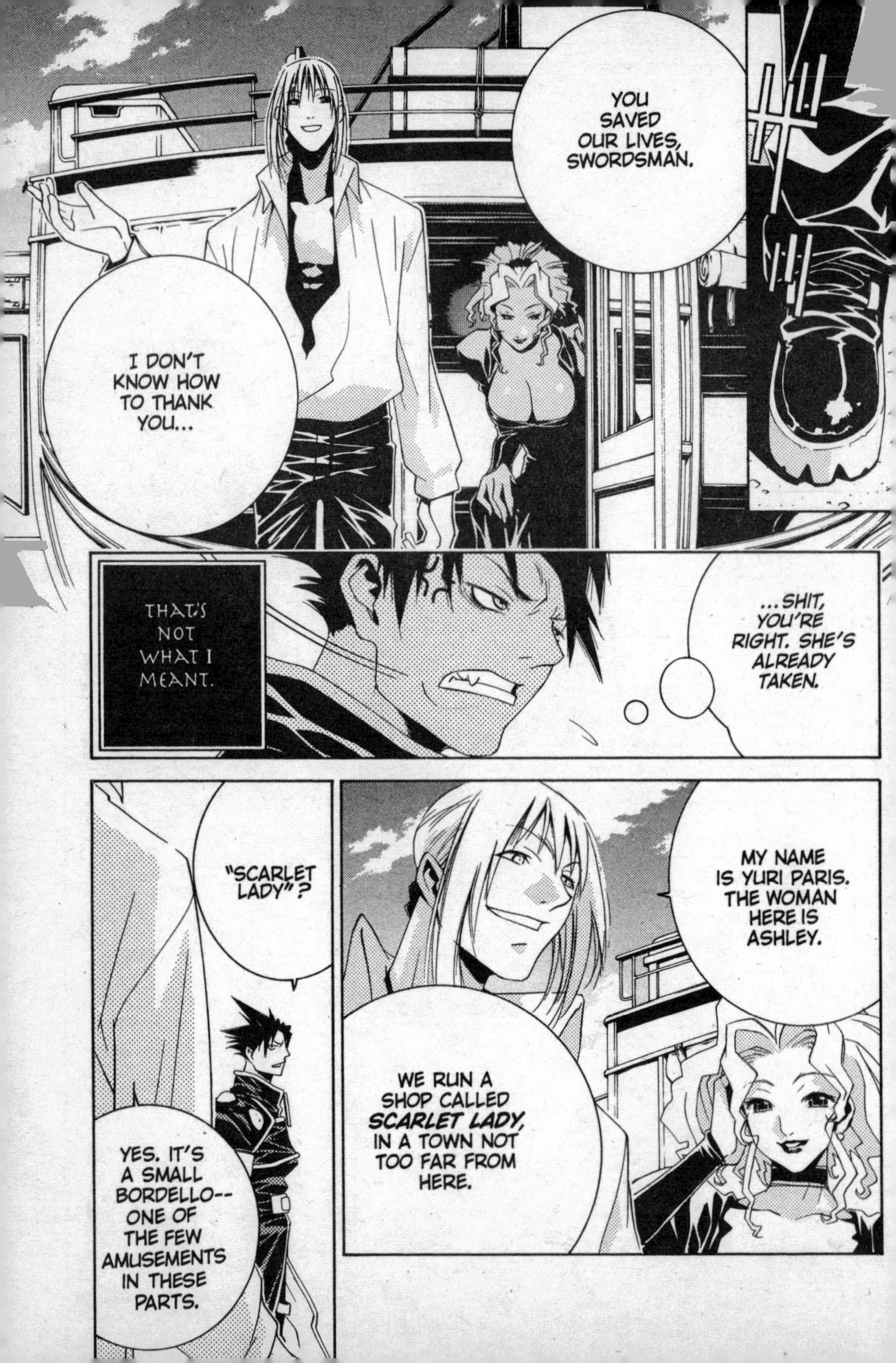
YOU SAVED OUR LIVES, SWORDSMAN.
I DON'T KNOW HOW TO THANK YOU...
...SHIT, YOU'RE RIGHT. SHE'S ALREADY TAKEN.
THAT'S NOT WHAT I MEANT.
MY NAME IS YURI PARIS. THE WOMAN HERE IS ASHLEY.
WE RUN A SHOP CALLED *SCARLET LADY,* IN A TOWN NOT TOO FAR FROM HERE.
"SCARLET LADY"?
YES. IT'S A SMALL BORDELLO-- ONE OF THE FEW AMUSEMENTS IN THESE PARTS.

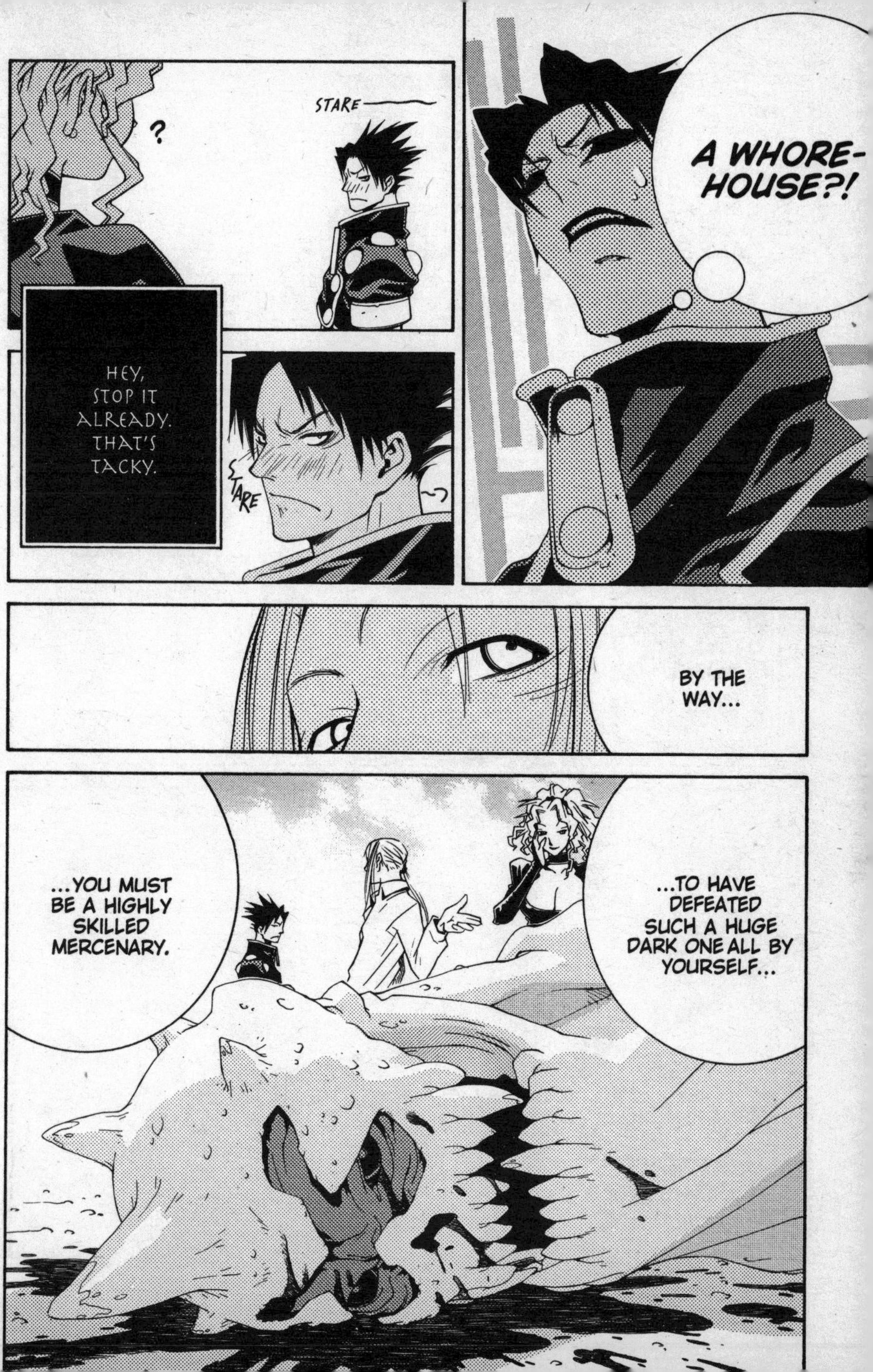
A WHORE-HOUSE?!
STARE
?
HEY, STOP IT ALREADY. THAT'S TACKY.
STARE
BY THE WAY...
...TO HAVE DEFEATED SUCH A HUGE DARK ONE ALL BY YOURSELF...
...YOU MUST BE A HIGHLY SKILLED MERCENARY.

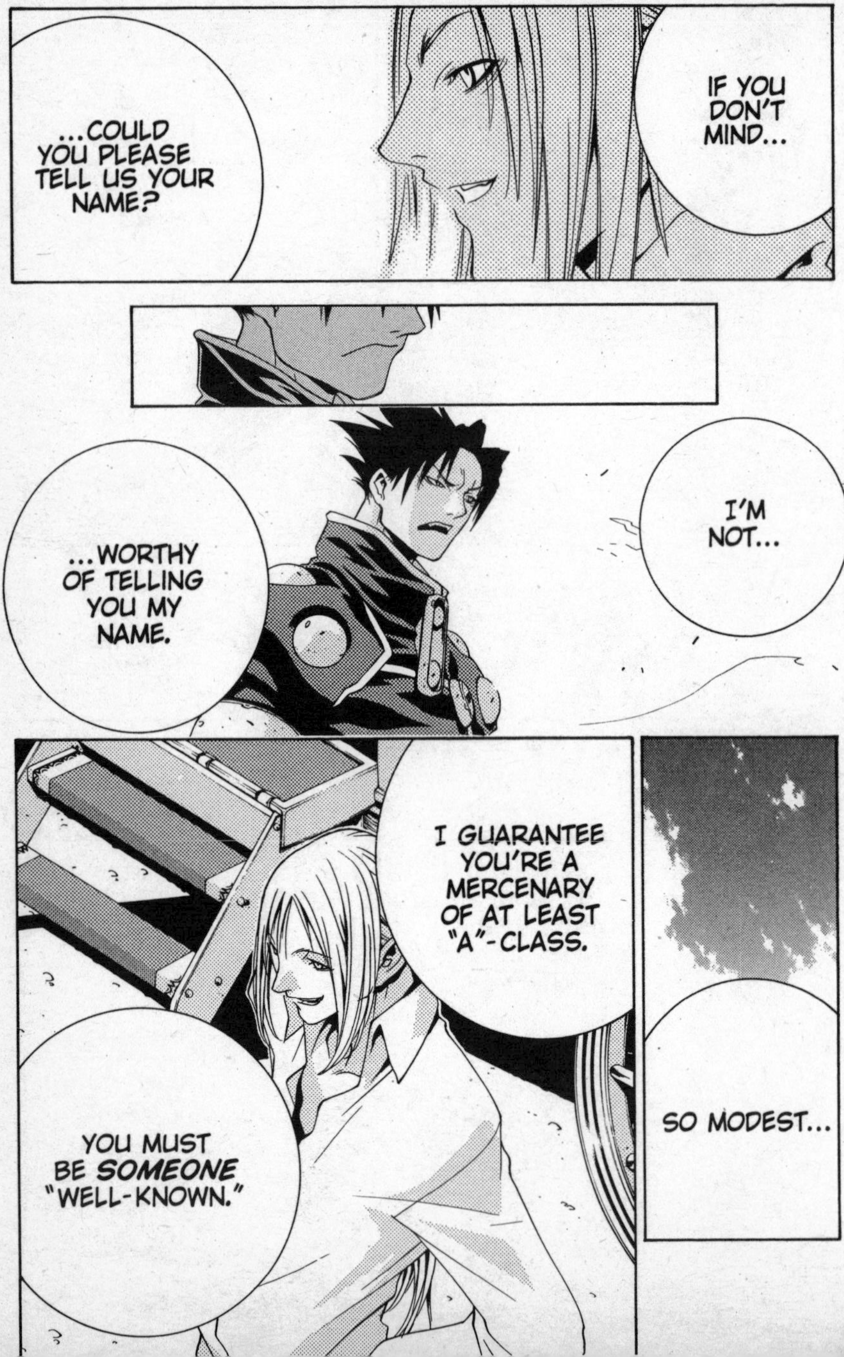
IF YOU DON'T MIND...
...COULD YOU PLEASE TELL US YOUR NAME?
I'M NOT...
...WORTHY OF TELLING YOU MY NAME.
SO MODEST...
I GUARANTEE YOU'RE A MERCENARY OF AT LEAST "A"-CLASS.
YOU MUST BE *SOMEONE* "WELL-KNOWN."

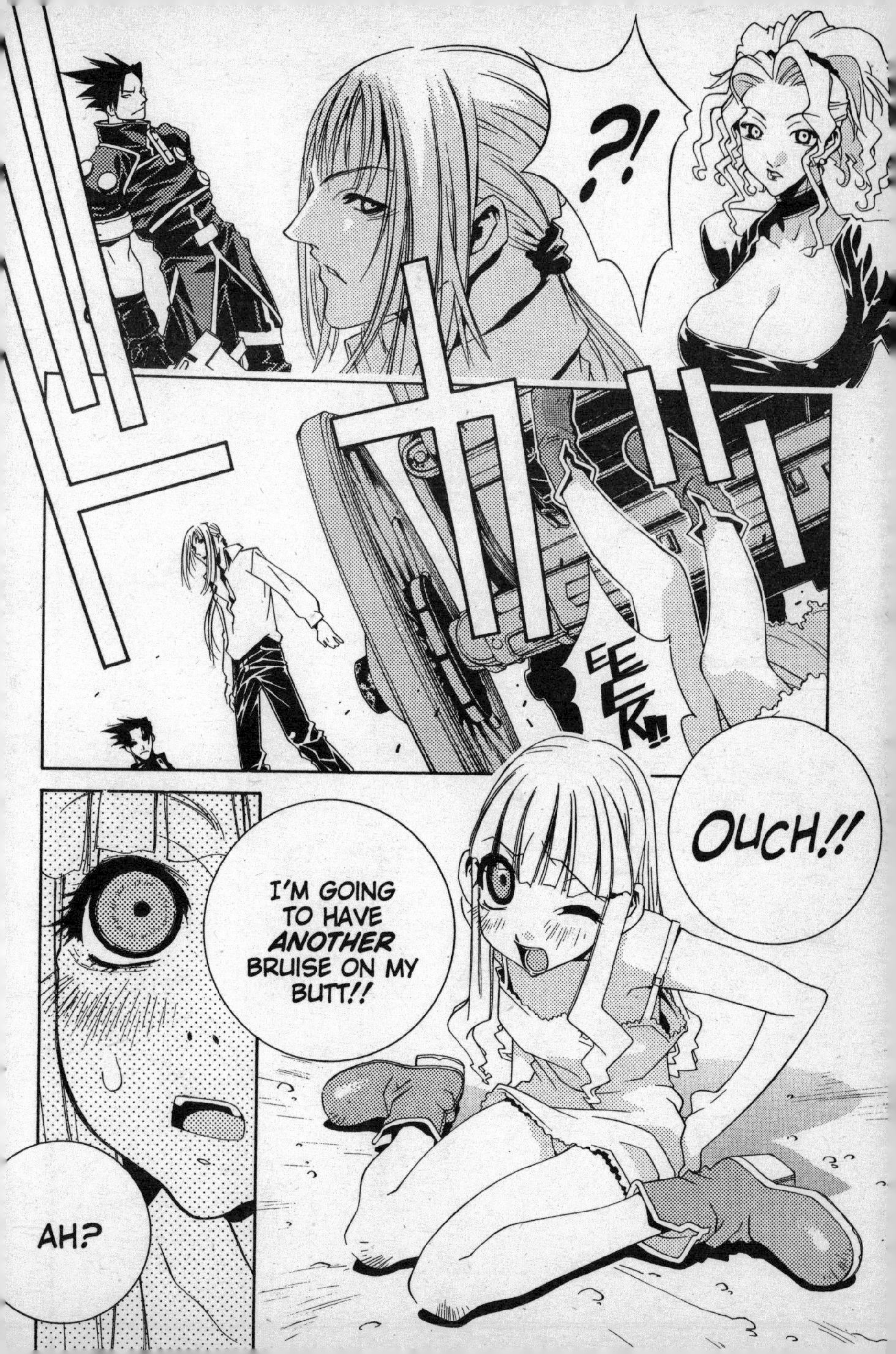
?!
EEEK!!
OUCH!!
I'M GOING TO HAVE *ANOTHER* BRUISE ON MY BUTT!!
AH?

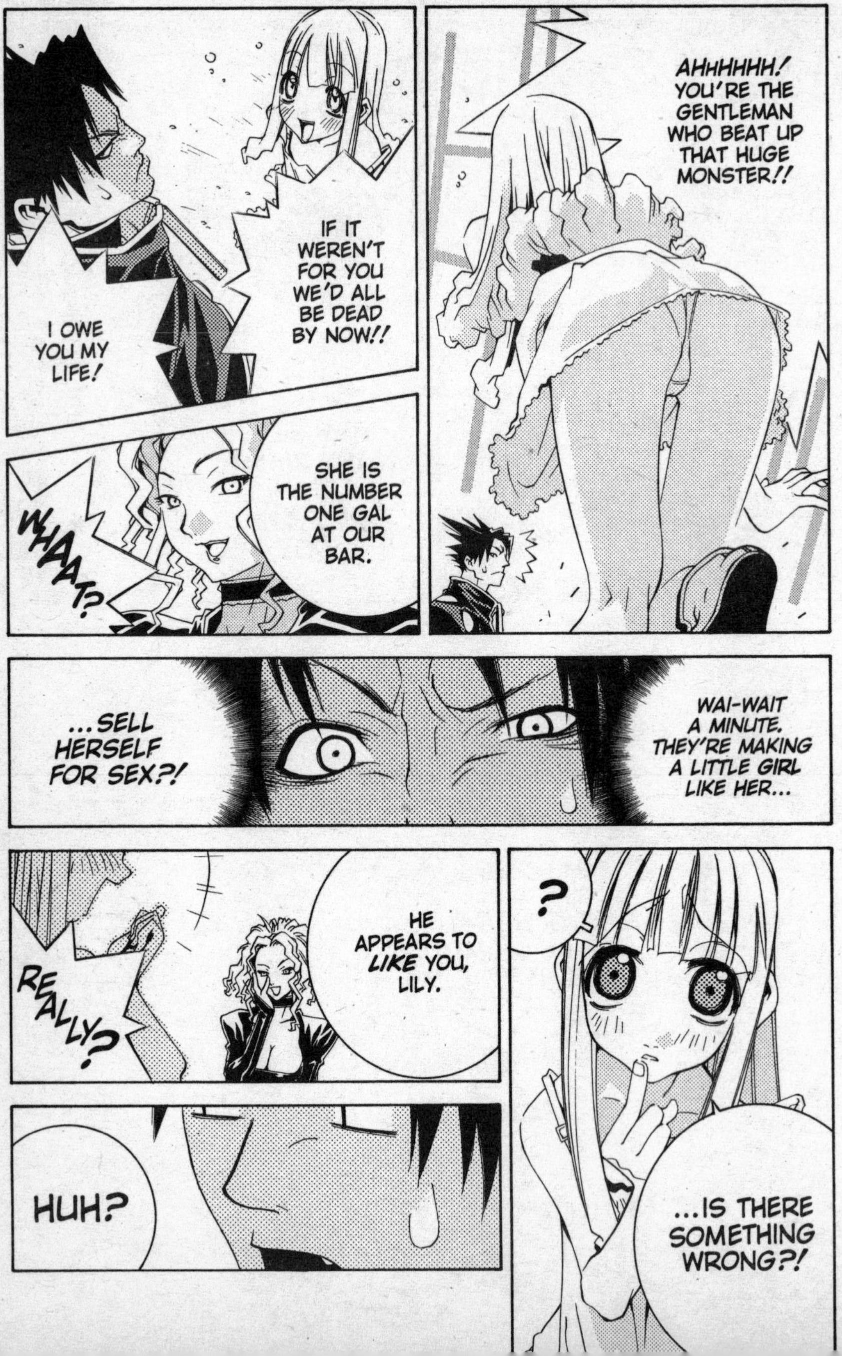
AHHHHHH! YOU'RE THE GENTLEMAN WHO BEAT UP THAT HUGE MONSTER!!
IF IT WEREN'T FOR YOU WE'D ALL BE DEAD BY NOW!!
I OWE YOU MY LIFE!
SHE IS THE NUMBER ONE GAL AT OUR BAR.
WHAAAT?
WAI-WAIT A MINUTE. THEY'RE MAKING A LITTLE GIRL LIKE HER...
...SELL HERSELF FOR SEX?!
?
...IS THERE SOMETHING WRONG?!
HE APPEARS TO LIKE YOU, LILY.
REALLY?
HUH?

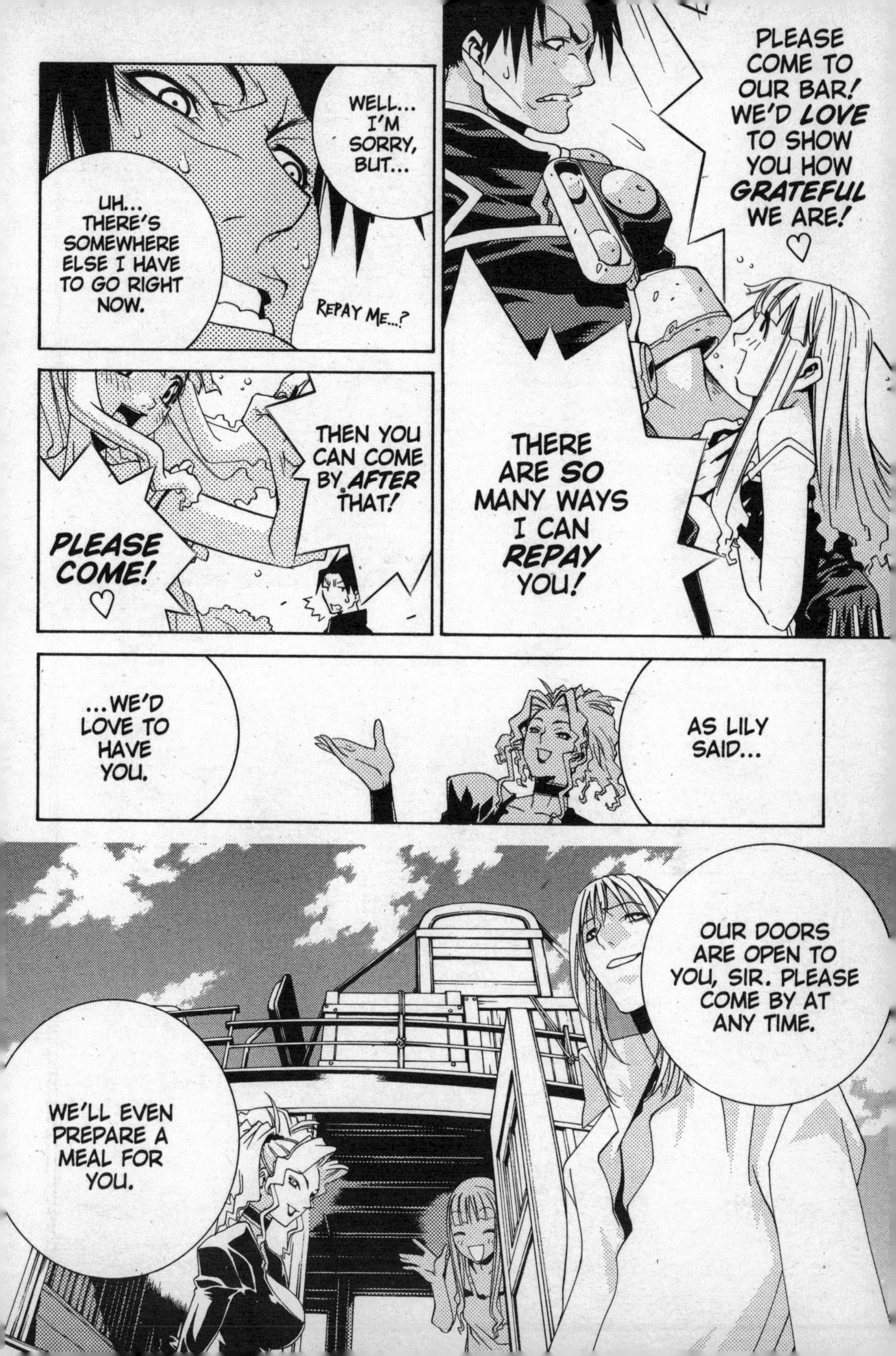

PLEASE COME TO OUR BAR! WE'D *LOVE* TO SHOW YOU HOW *GRATEFUL* WE ARE! ♥
THERE ARE *SO* MANY WAYS I CAN *REPAY* YOU!
WELL... I'M SORRY, BUT...
REPAY ME...?
UH... THERE'S SOMEWHERE ELSE I HAVE TO GO RIGHT NOW.
THEN YOU CAN COME BY *AFTER* THAT!
PLEASE COME! ♥
AS LILY SAID...
...WE'D LOVE TO HAVE YOU.
OUR DOORS ARE OPEN TO YOU, SIR. PLEASE COME BY AT ANY TIME.
WE'LL EVEN PREPARE A MEAL FOR YOU.

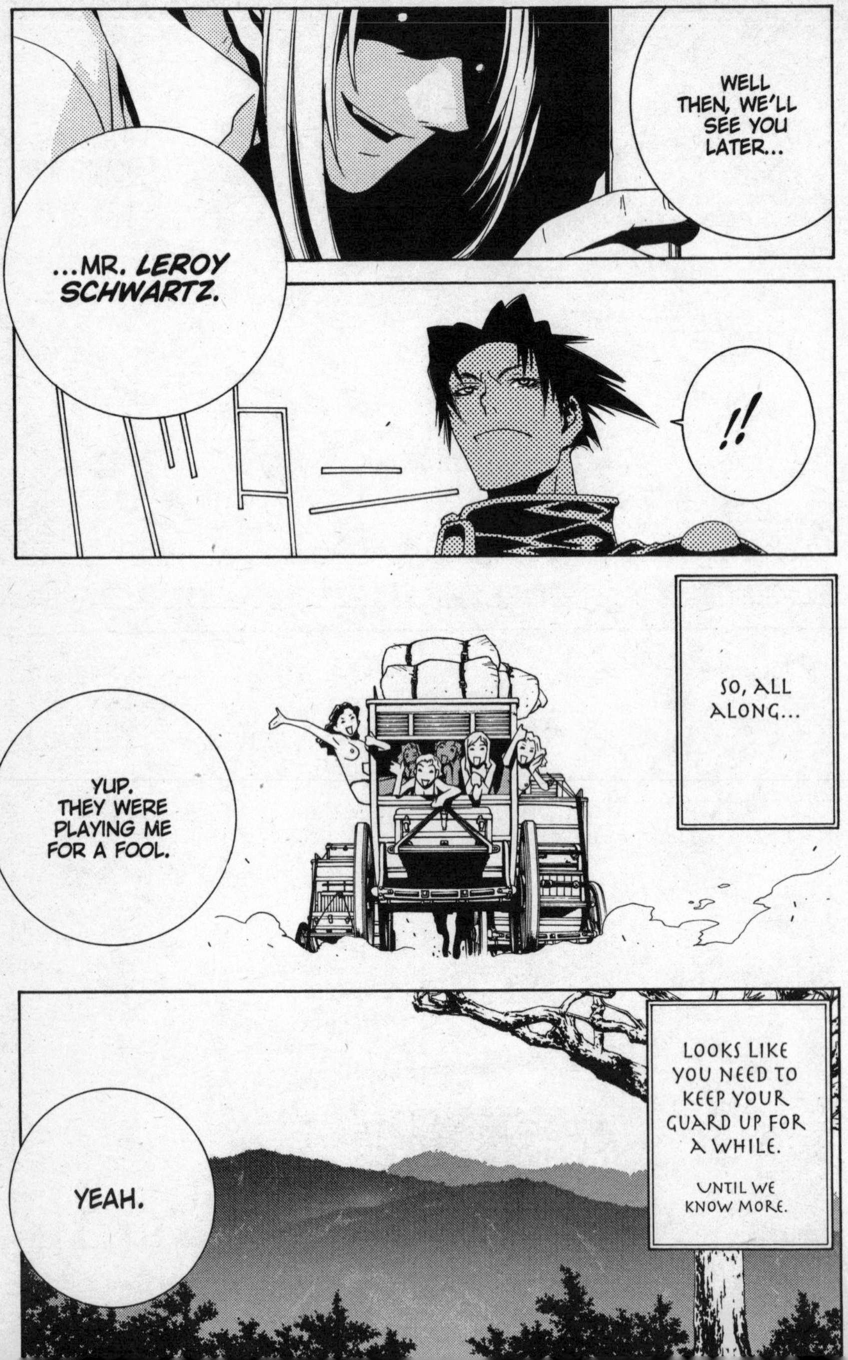
WELL THEN, WE'LL SEE YOU LATER...
...MR. LEROY SCHWARTZ.
!!
SO, ALL ALONG...
YUP. THEY WERE PLAYING ME FOR A FOOL.
LOOKS LIKE YOU NEED TO KEEP YOUR GUARD UP FOR A WHILE.
UNTIL WE KNOW MORE.
YEAH.

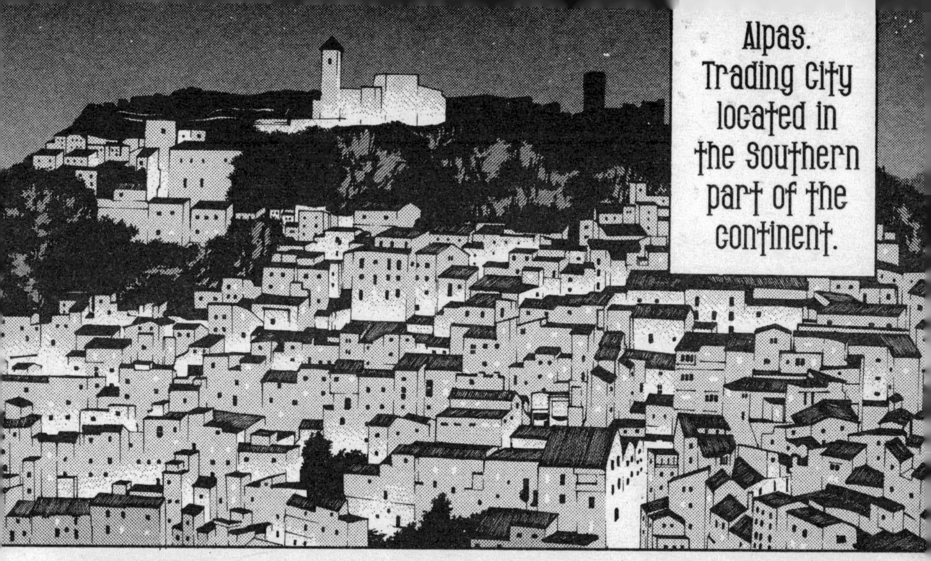
Alpas. Trading City located in the Southern part of the continent.

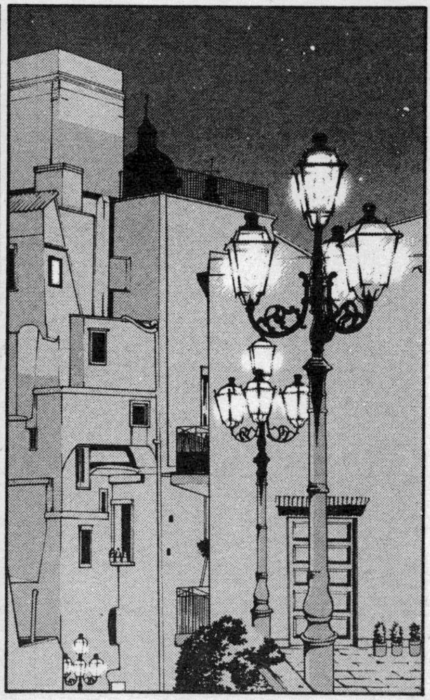

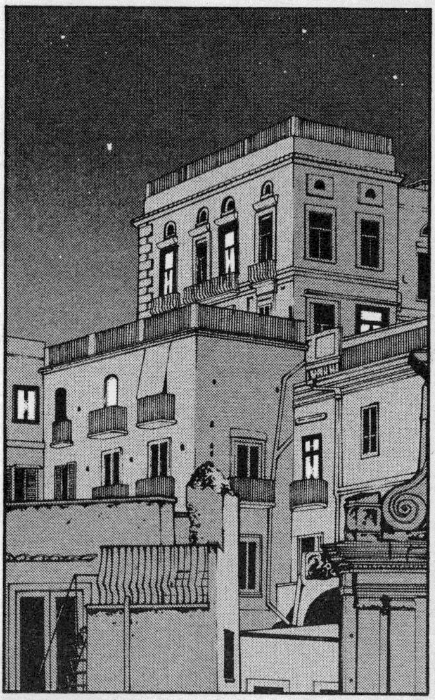

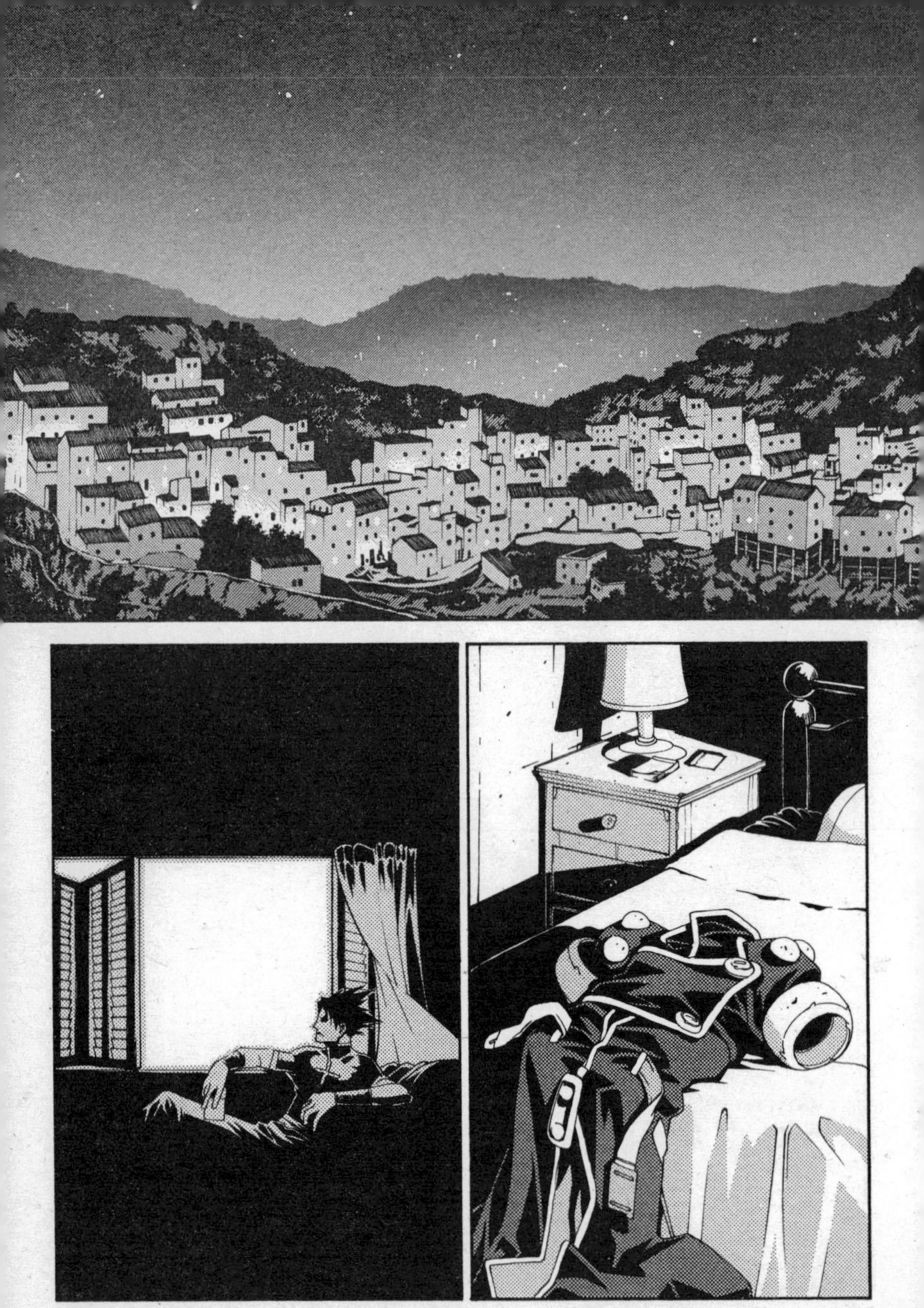

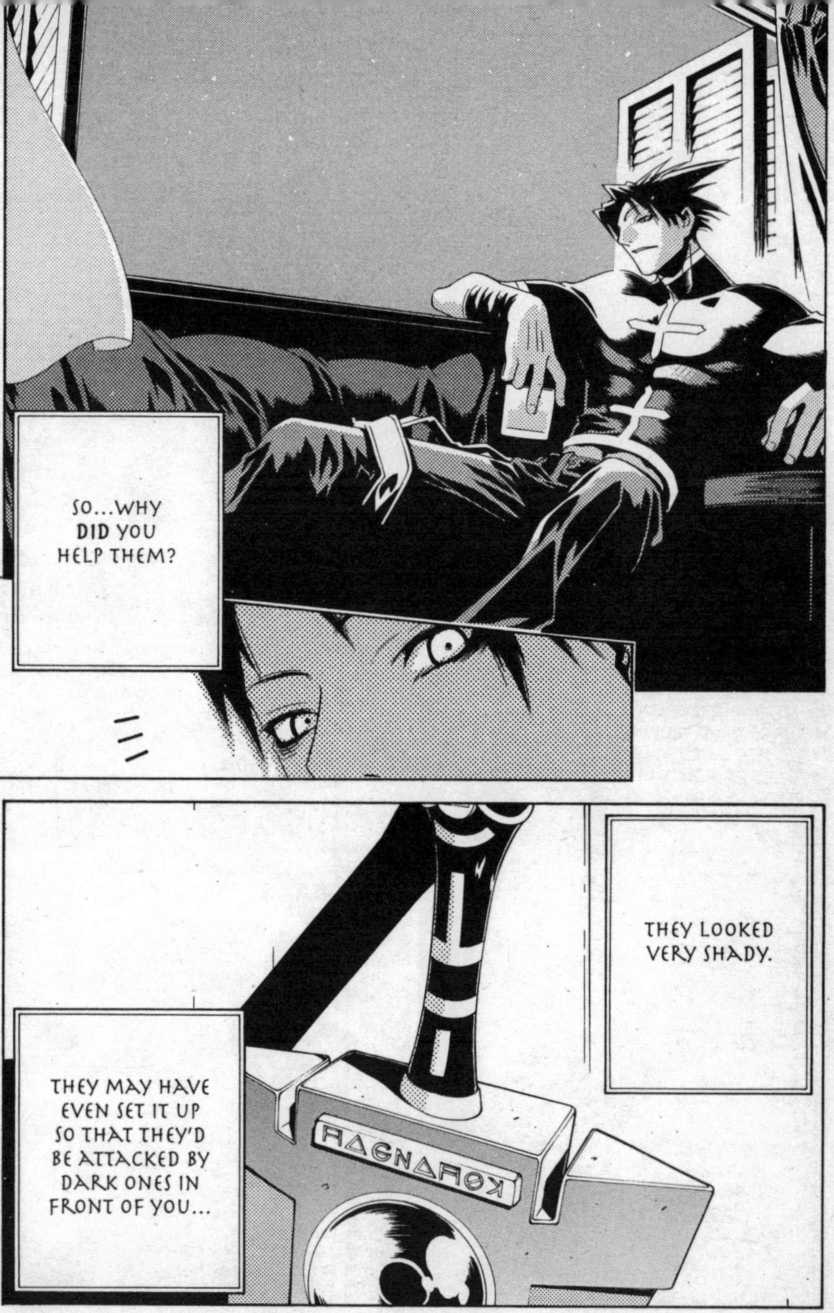
SO...WHY **DID** YOU HELP THEM?
THEY LOOKED VERY SHADY.
THEY MAY HAVE EVEN SET IT UP SO THAT THEY'D BE ATTACKED BY DARK ONES IN FRONT OF YOU...

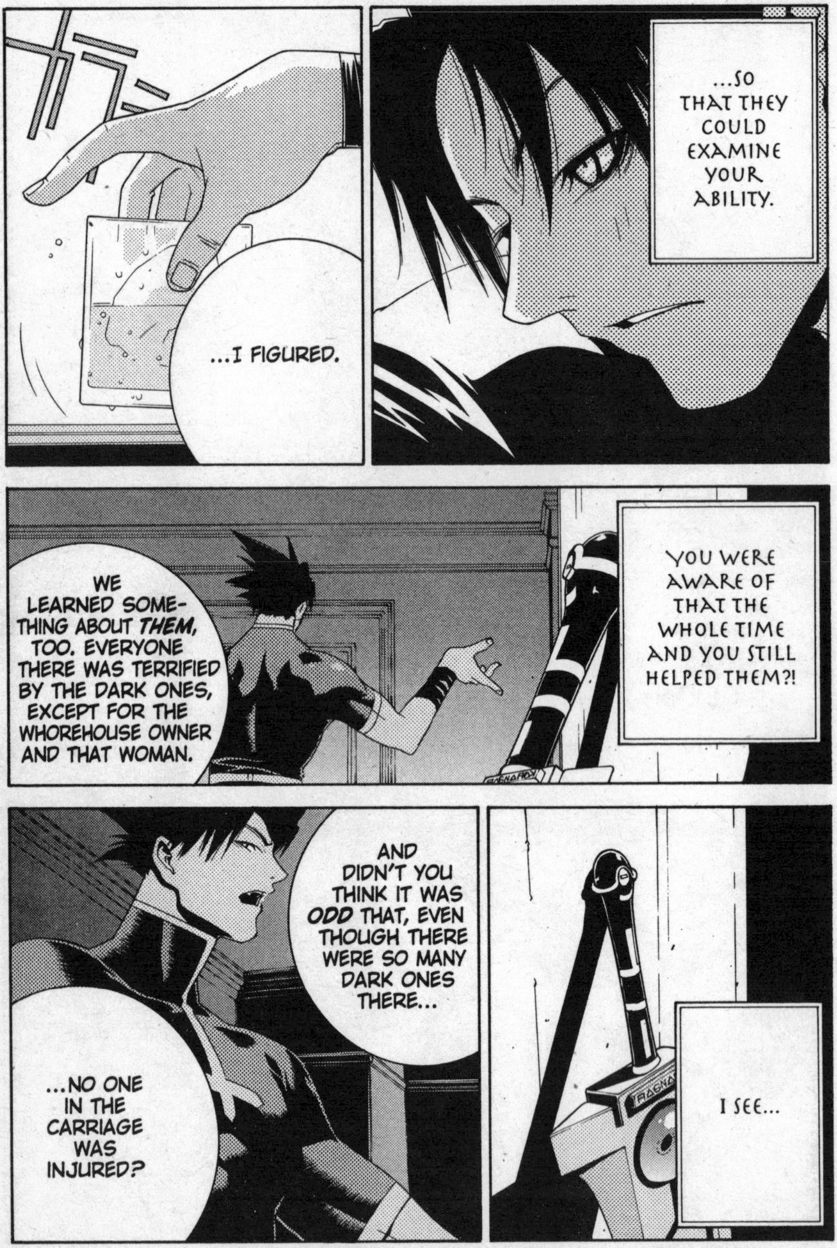
...SO THAT THEY COULD EXAMINE YOUR ABILITY.
...I FIGURED.
YOU WERE AWARE OF THAT THE WHOLE TIME AND YOU STILL HELPED THEM?!
WE LEARNED SOMETHING ABOUT *THEM*, TOO. EVERYONE THERE WAS TERRIFIED BY THE DARK ONES, EXCEPT FOR THE WHOREHOUSE OWNER AND THAT WOMAN.
I SEE...
AND DIDN'T YOU THINK IT WAS *ODD* THAT, EVEN THOUGH THERE WERE SO MANY DARK ONES THERE...
...NO ONE IN THE CARRIAGE WAS INJURED?

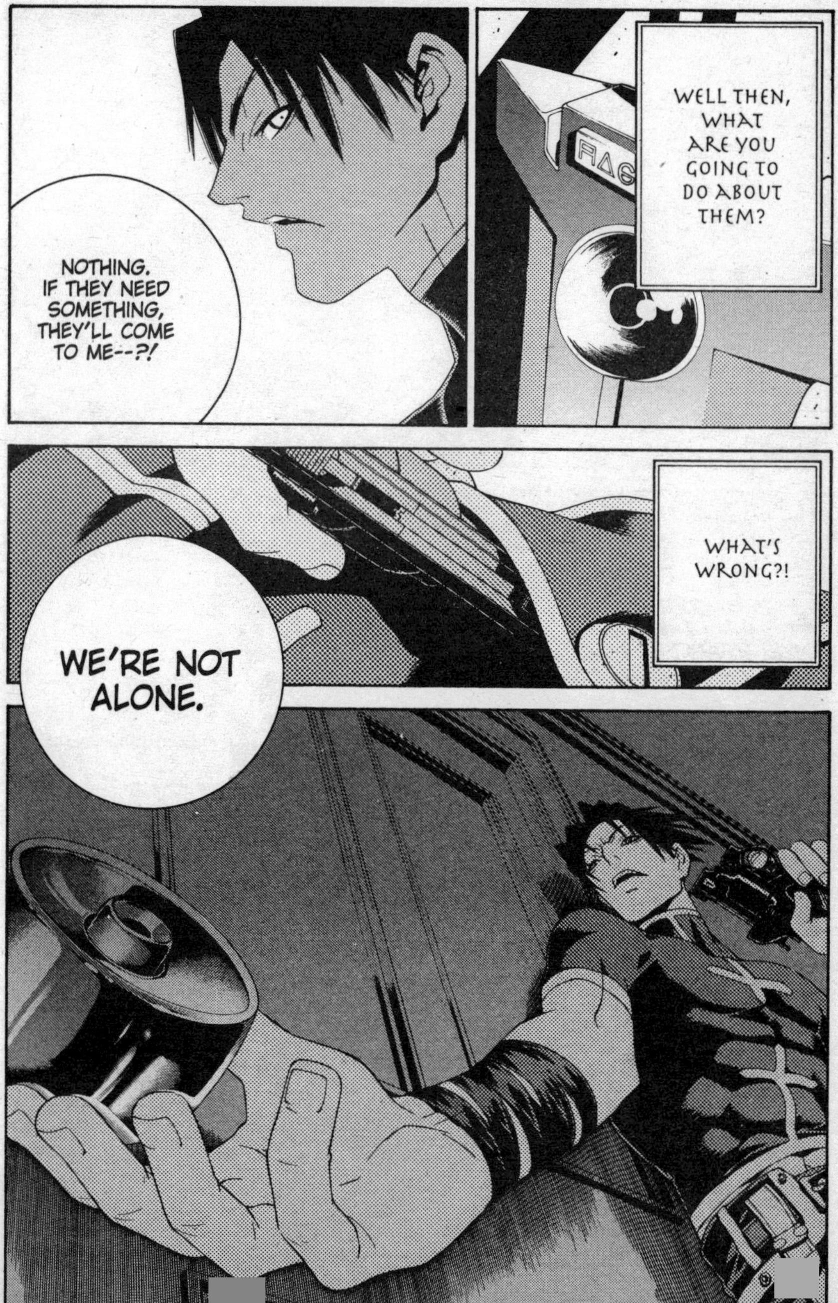
WELL THEN, WHAT ARE YOU GOING TO DO ABOUT THEM?
NOTHING. IF THEY NEED SOMETHING, THEY'LL COME TO ME--?!
WHAT'S WRONG?!
WE'RE NOT ALONE.

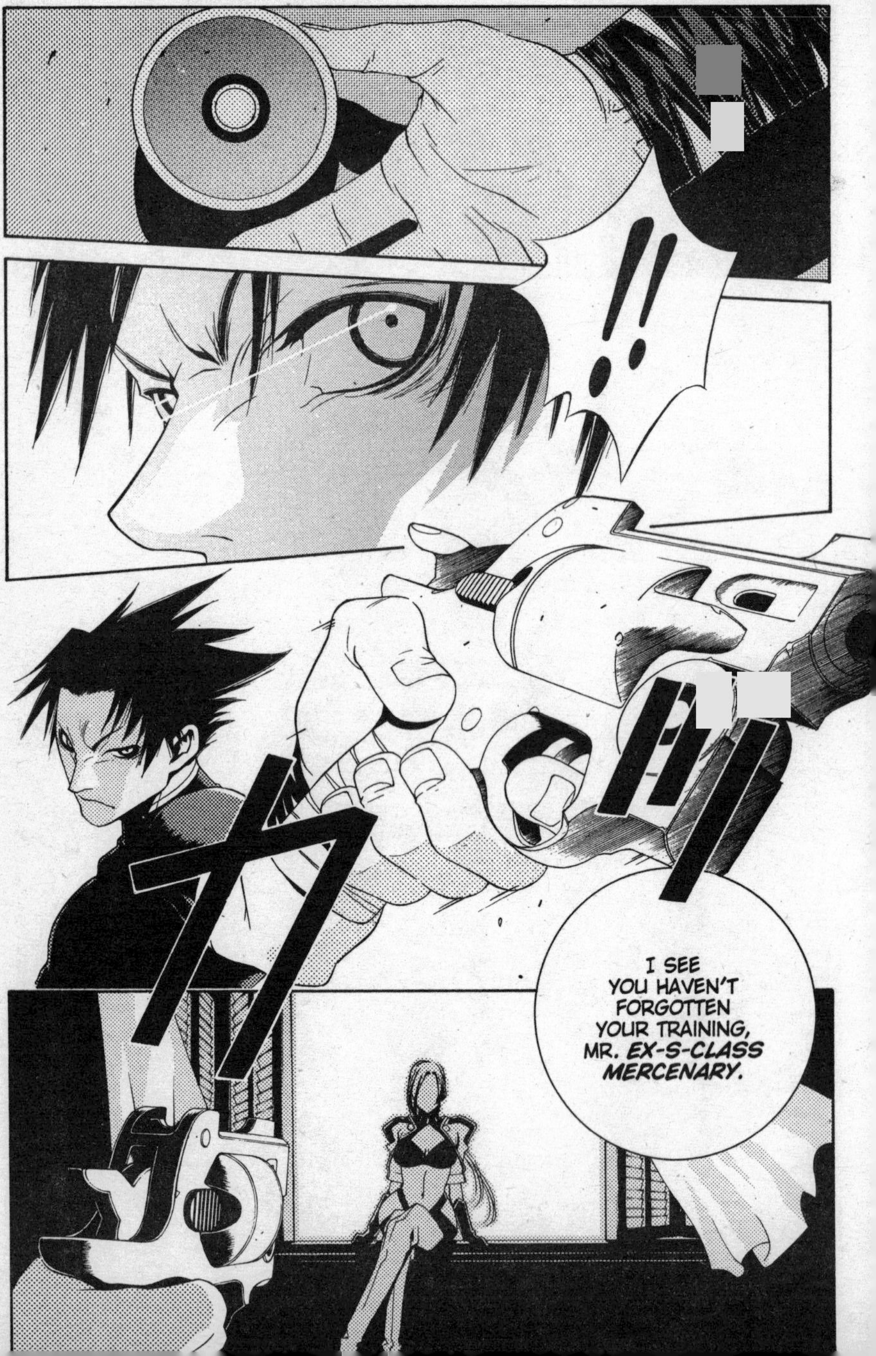
!!
I SEE YOU HAVEN'T FORGOTTEN YOUR TRAINING, MR. *EX-S-CLASS MERCENARY.*

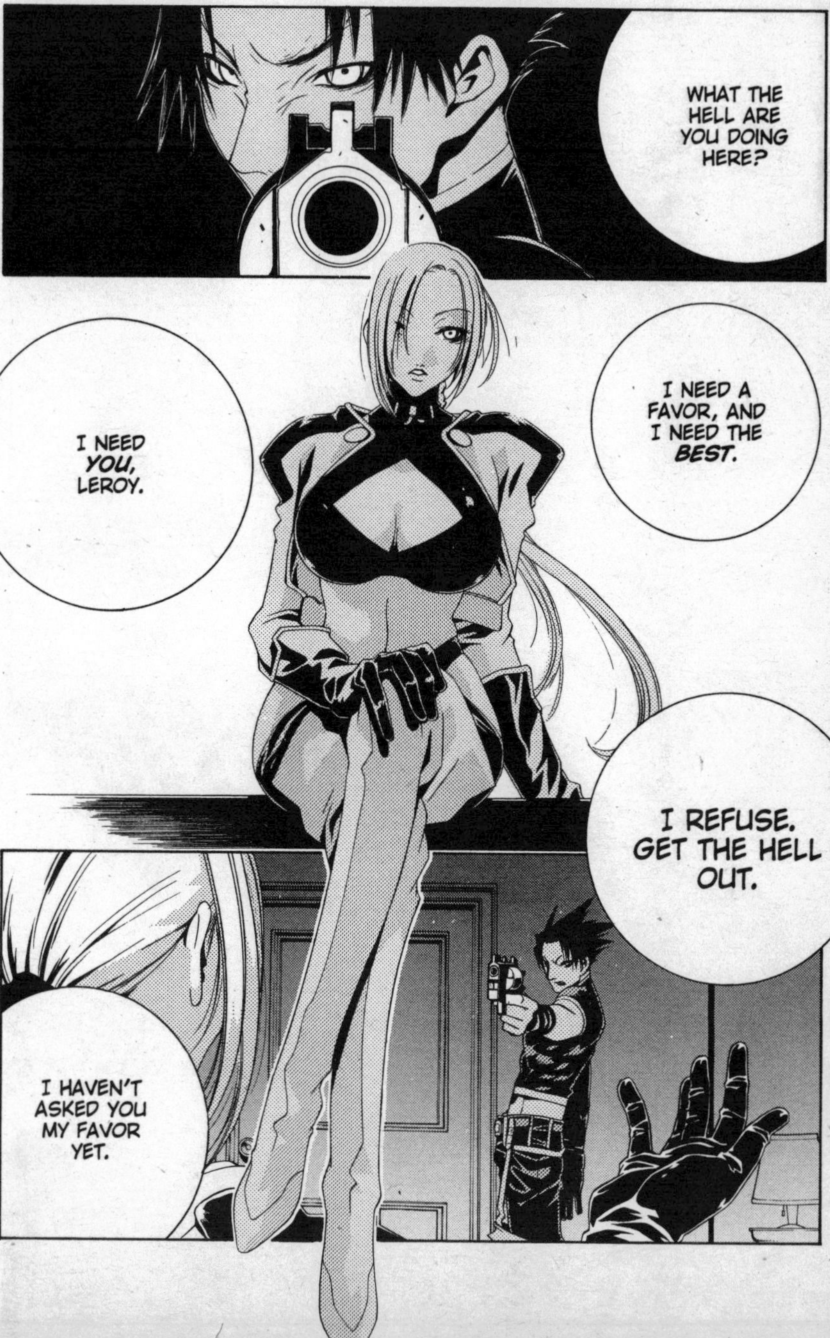
WHAT THE HELL ARE YOU DOING HERE?
I NEED A FAVOR, AND I NEED THE *BEST*.
I NEED *YOU*, LEROY.
I REFUSE. GET THE HELL OUT.
I HAVEN'T ASKED YOU MY FAVOR YET.

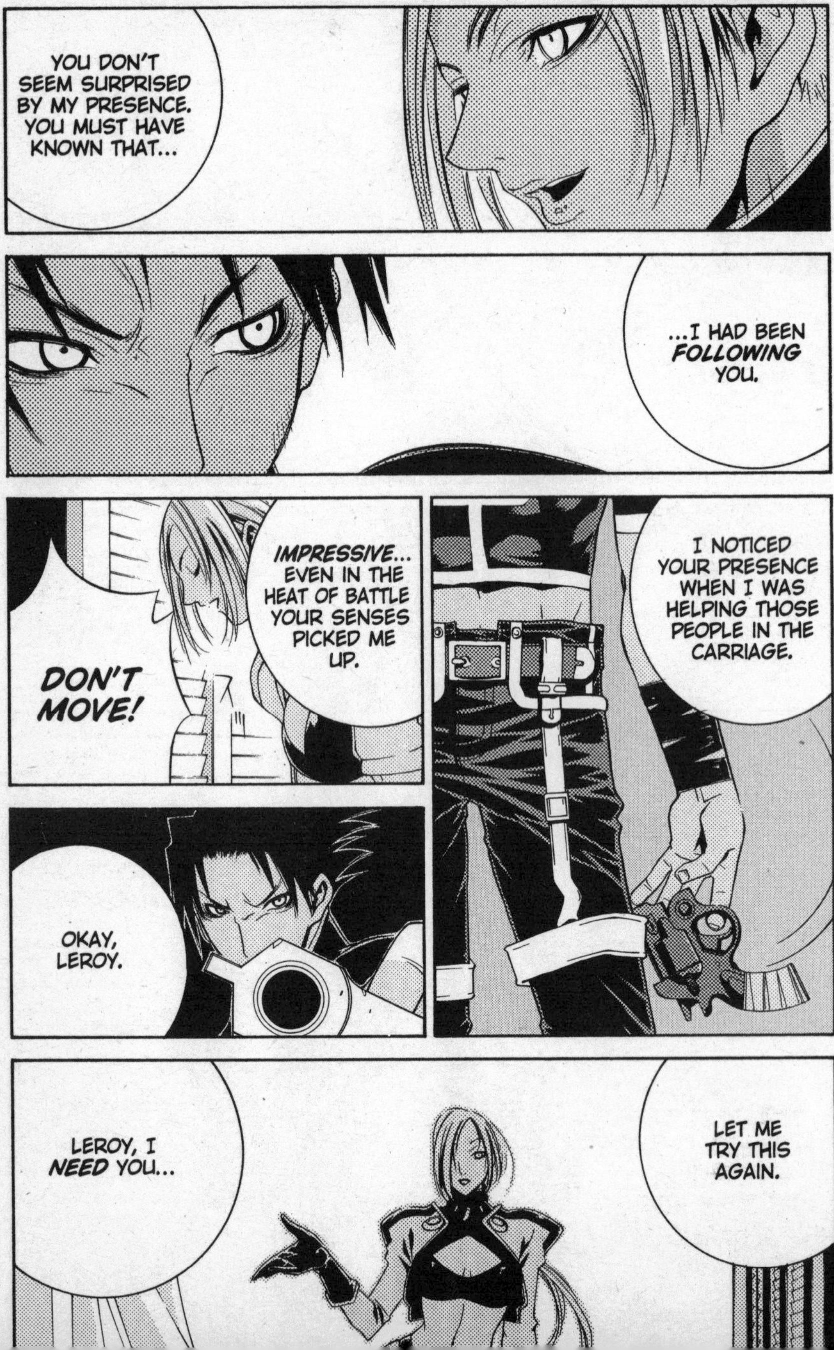
YOU DON'T SEEM SURPRISED BY MY PRESENCE. YOU MUST HAVE KNOWN THAT...
...I HAD BEEN *FOLLOWING* YOU.
I NOTICED YOUR PRESENCE WHEN I WAS HELPING THOSE PEOPLE IN THE CARRIAGE.
IMPRESSIVE... EVEN IN THE HEAT OF BATTLE YOUR SENSES PICKED ME UP.
DON'T MOVE!
OKAY, LEROY.
LET ME TRY THIS AGAIN.
LEROY, I *NEED* YOU...

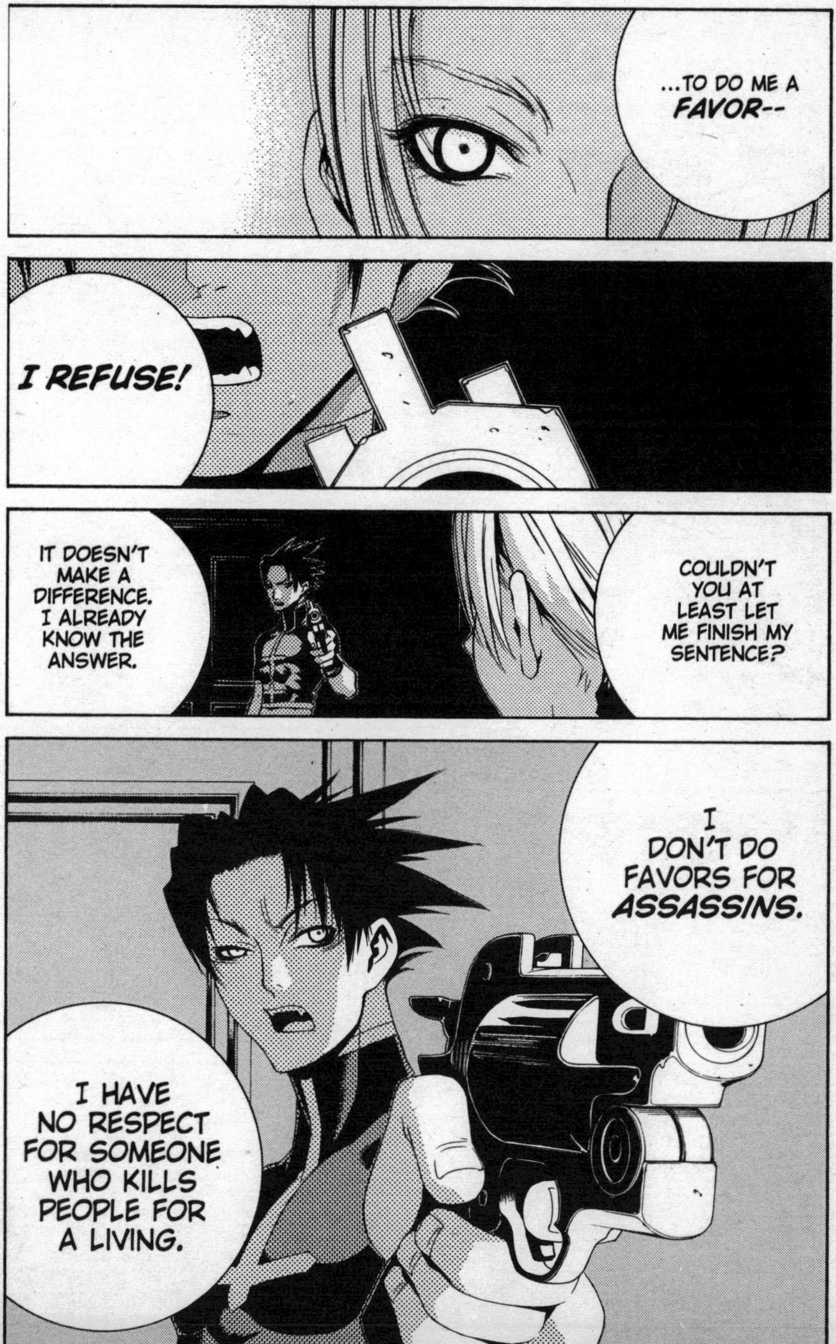
...TO DO ME A *FAVOR--*
I REFUSE!
COULDN'T YOU AT LEAST LET ME FINISH MY SENTENCE?
IT DOESN'T MAKE A DIFFERENCE. I ALREADY KNOW THE ANSWER.
I DON'T DO FAVORS FOR *ASSASSINS.*
I HAVE NO RESPECT FOR SOMEONE WHO KILLS PEOPLE FOR A LIVING.

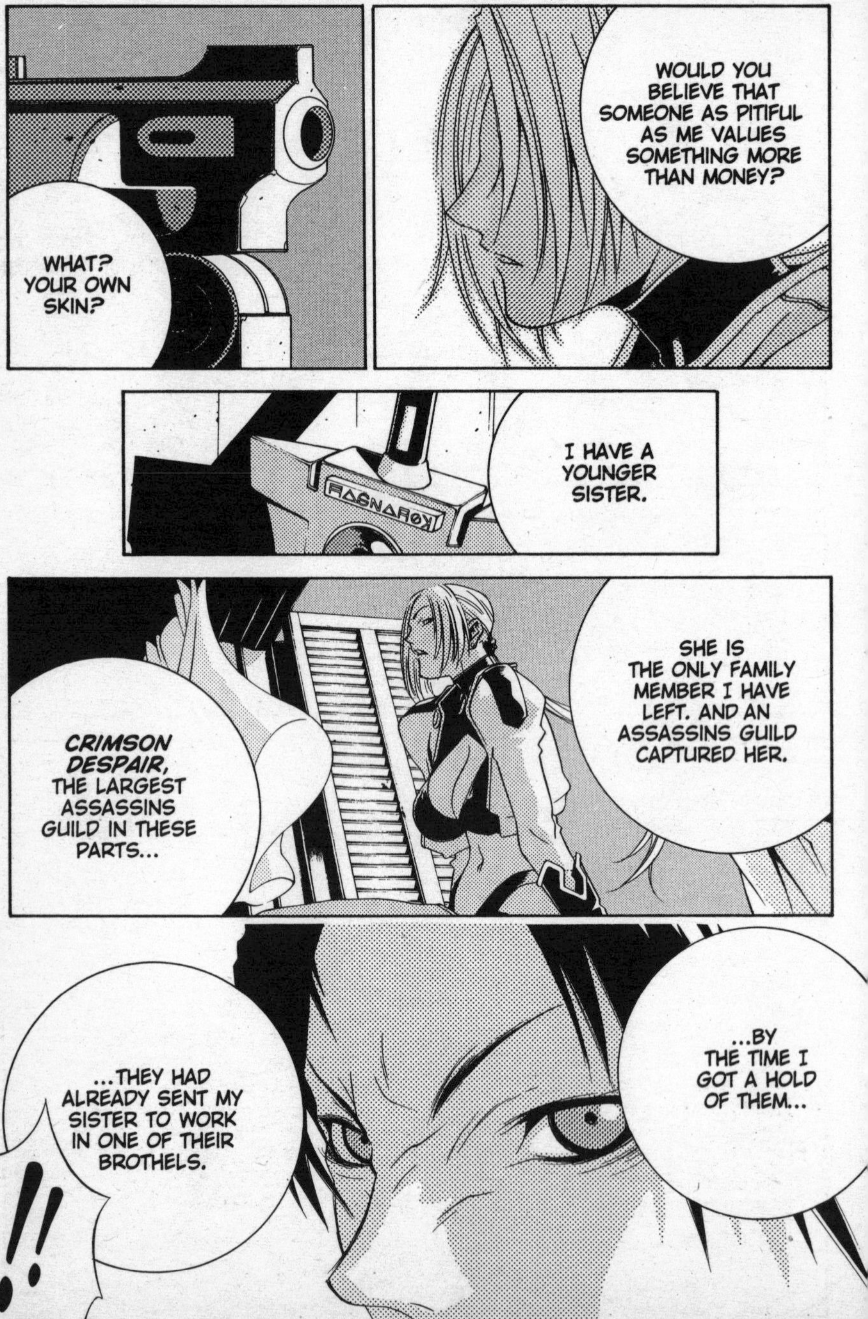
WOULD YOU BELIEVE THAT SOMEONE AS PITIFUL AS ME VALUES SOMETHING MORE THAN MONEY?
WHAT? YOUR OWN SKIN?
I HAVE A YOUNGER SISTER.
SHE IS THE ONLY FAMILY MEMBER I HAVE LEFT. AND AN ASSASSINS GUILD CAPTURED HER.
CRIMSON DESPAIR, THE LARGEST ASSASSINS GUILD IN THESE PARTS...
...BY THE TIME I GOT A HOLD OF THEM...
...THEY HAD ALREADY SENT MY SISTER TO WORK IN ONE OF THEIR BROTHELS.
!!

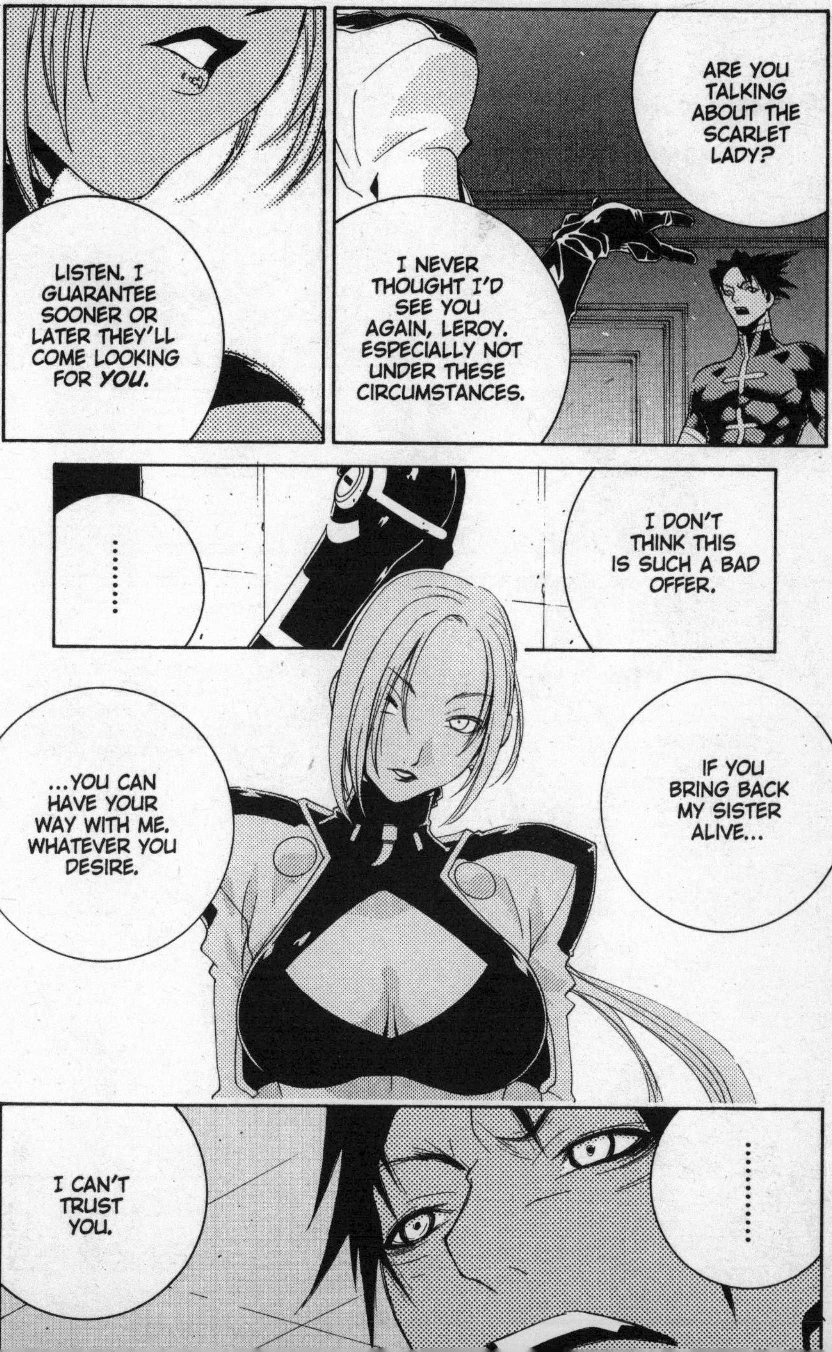
ARE YOU TALKING ABOUT THE SCARLET LADY?
I NEVER THOUGHT I'D SEE YOU AGAIN, LEROY. ESPECIALLY NOT UNDER THESE CIRCUMSTANCES.
LISTEN. I GUARANTEE SOONER OR LATER THEY'LL COME LOOKING FOR *YOU*.
I DON'T THINK THIS IS SUCH A BAD OFFER.
....
IF YOU BRING BACK MY SISTER ALIVE...
...YOU CAN HAVE YOUR WAY WITH ME. WHATEVER YOU DESIRE.
....
I CAN'T TRUST YOU.

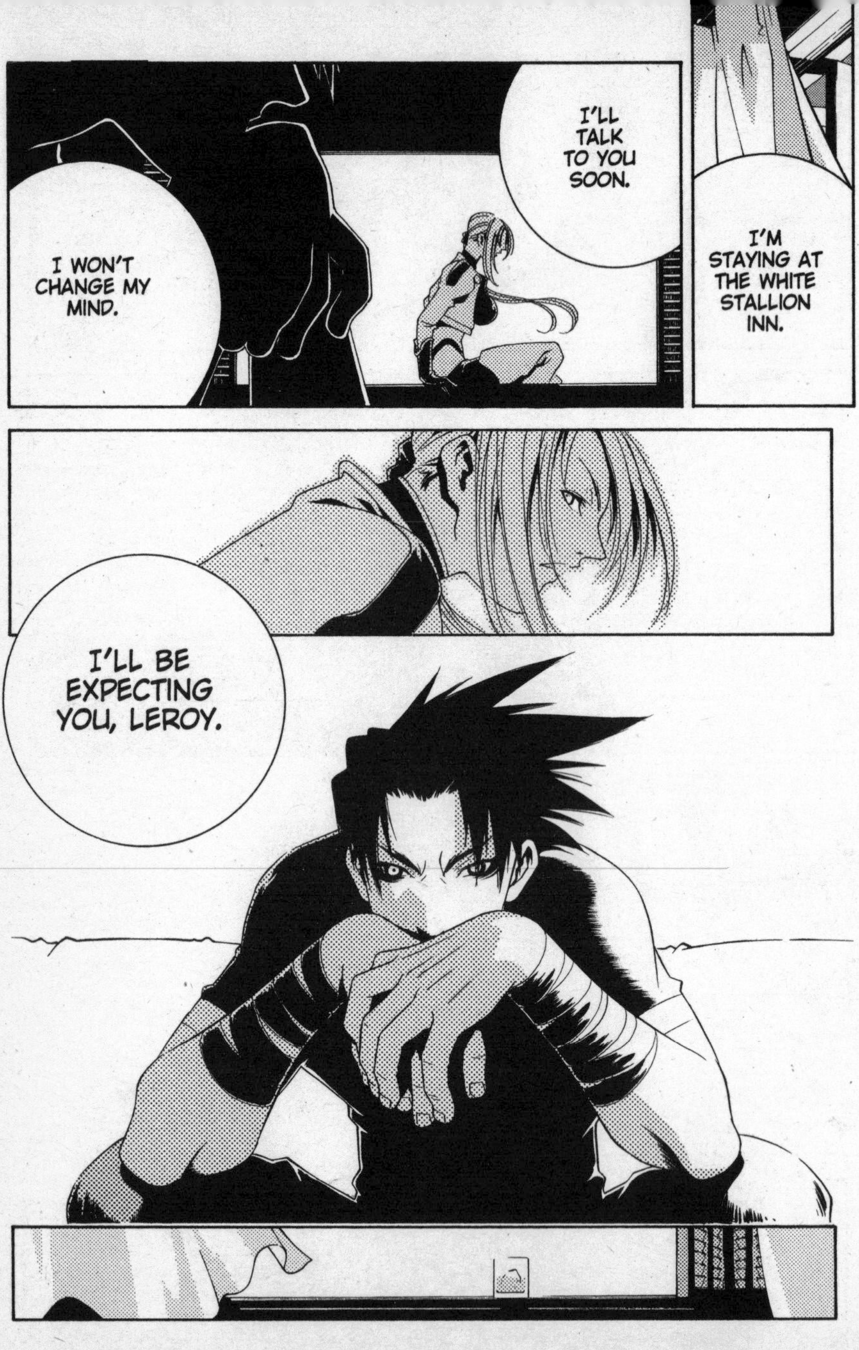
I'M STAYING AT THE WHITE STALLION INN.
I'LL TALK TO YOU SOON.
I WON'T CHANGE MY MIND.
I'LL BE EXPECTING YOU, LEROY.

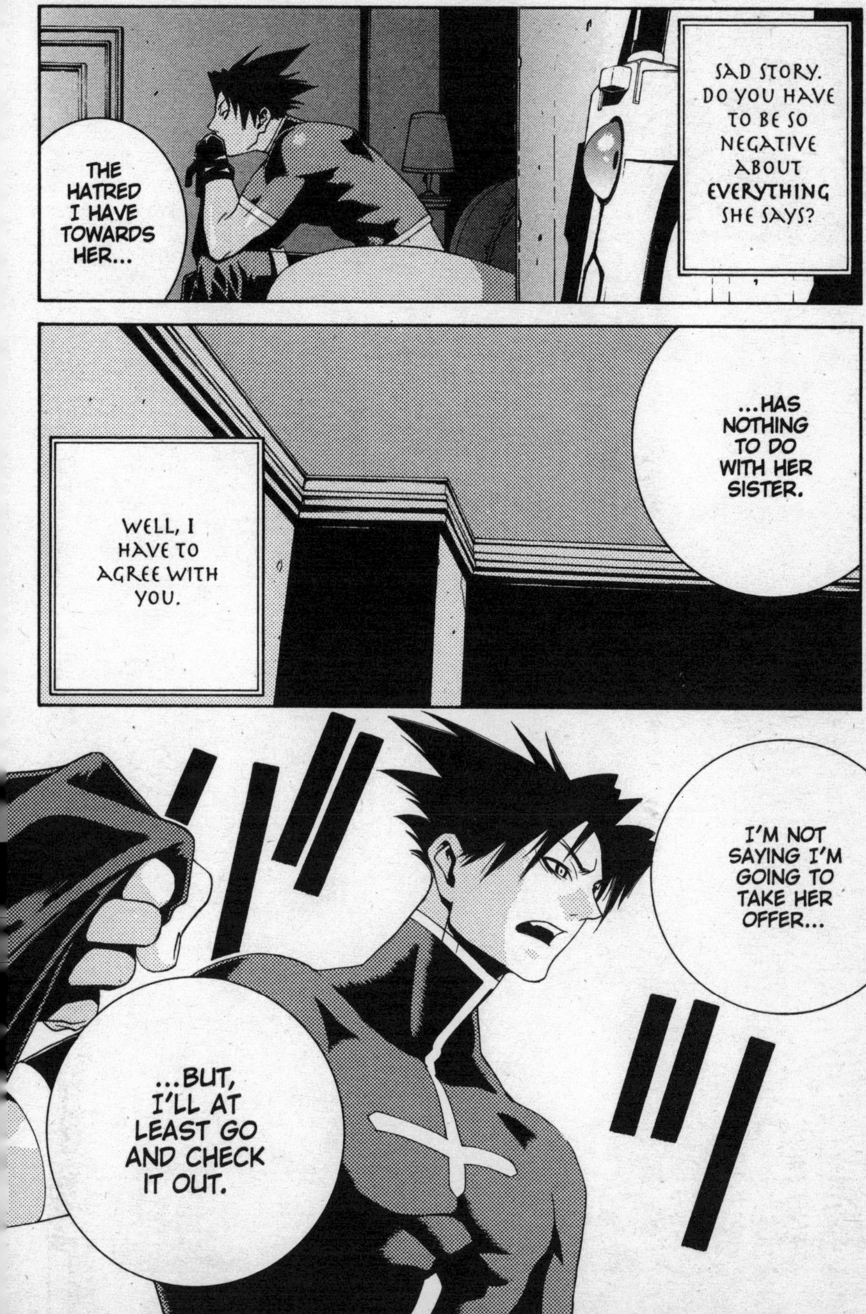
SAD STORY. DO YOU HAVE TO BE SO NEGATIVE ABOUT EVERYTHING SHE SAYS?
THE HATRED I HAVE TOWARDS HER...
...HAS NOTHING TO DO WITH HER SISTER.
WELL, I HAVE TO AGREE WITH YOU.
I'M NOT SAYING I'M GOING TO TAKE HER OFFER...
...BUT, I'LL AT LEAST GO AND CHECK IT OUT.

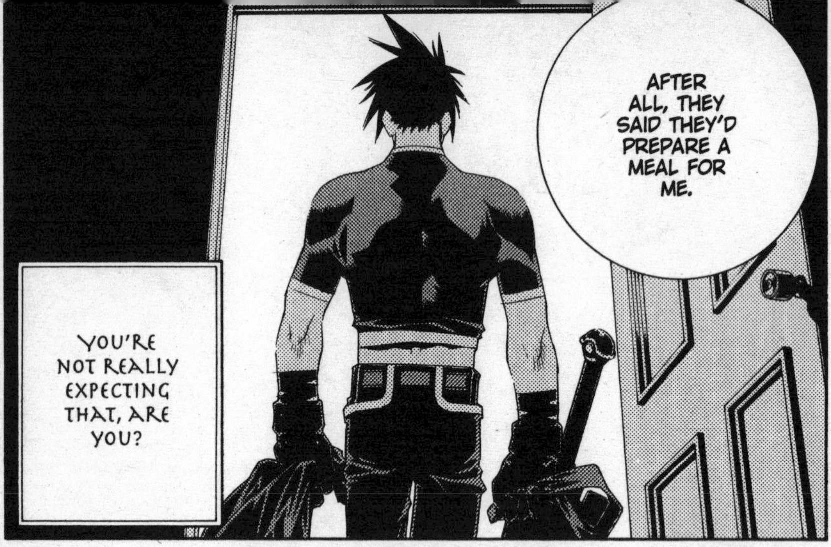
AFTER ALL, THEY SAID THEY'D PREPARE A MEAL FOR ME.
YOU'RE NOT REALLY EXPECTING THAT, ARE YOU?

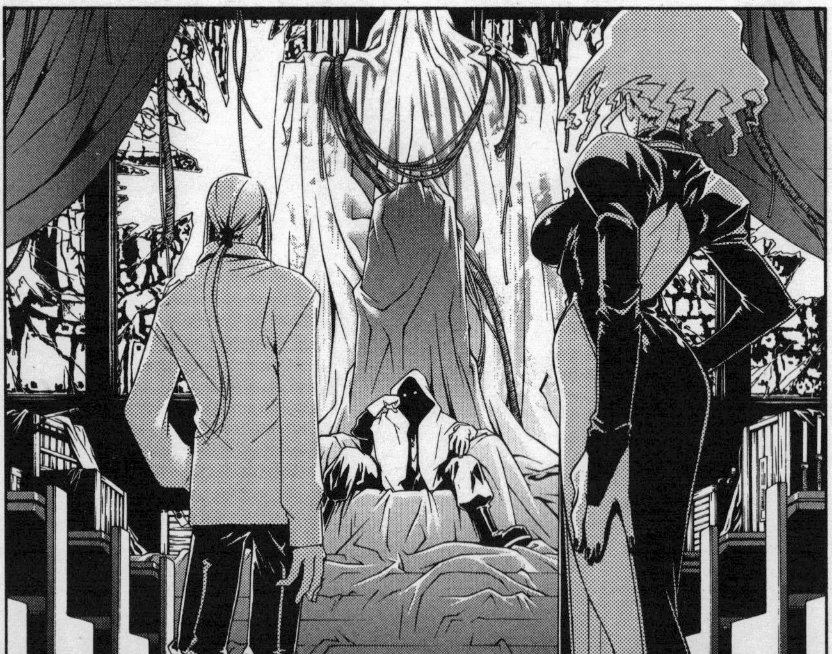

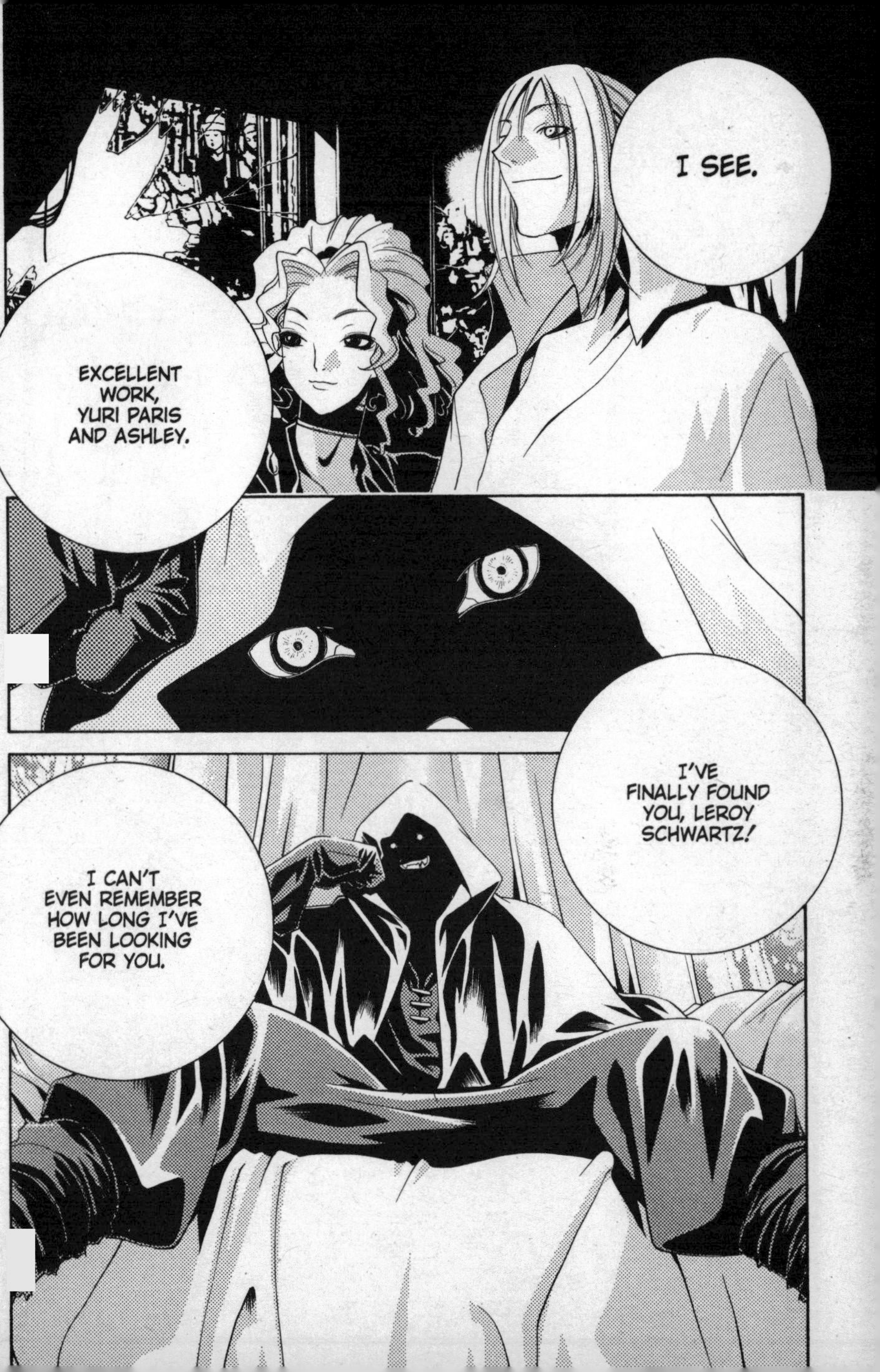
I SEE.
EXCELLENT WORK, YURI PARIS AND ASHLEY.
I'VE FINALLY FOUND YOU, LEROY SCHWARTZ!
I CAN'T EVEN REMEMBER HOW LONG I'VE BEEN LOOKING FOR YOU.

#2

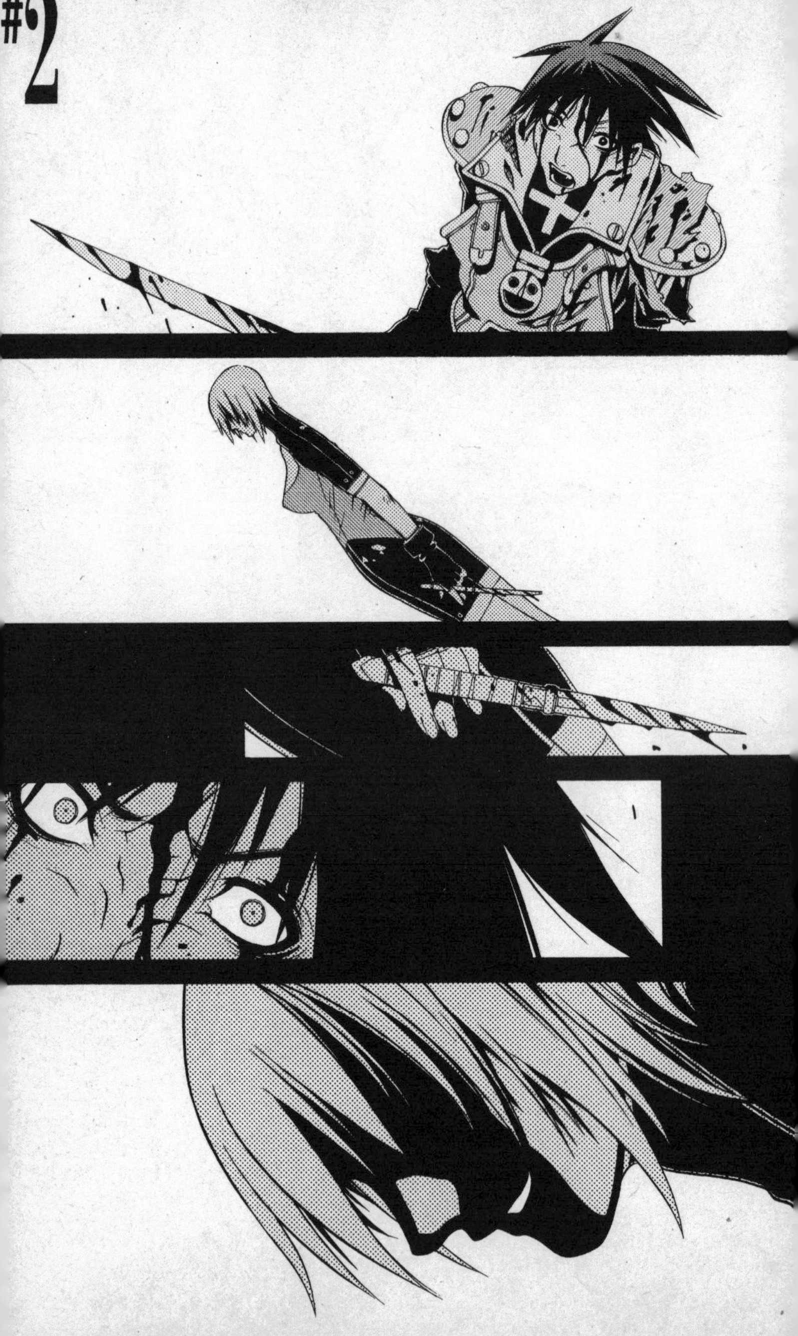

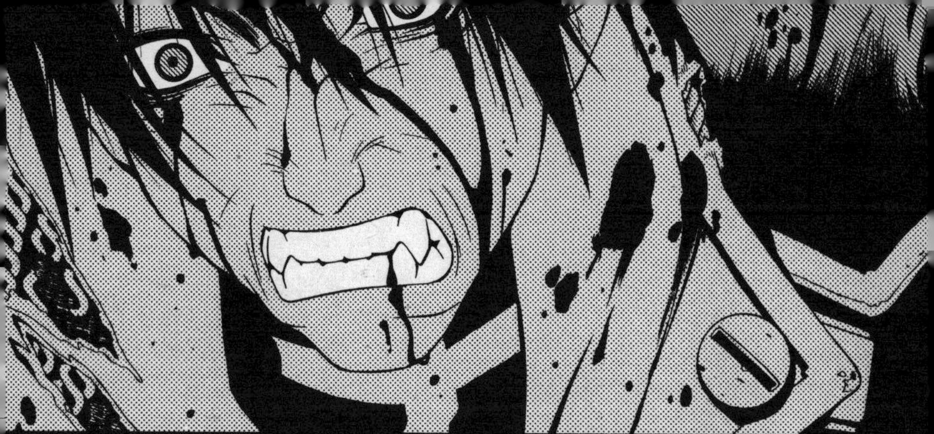

OF THE ONES

Chapter 2: The Bordello

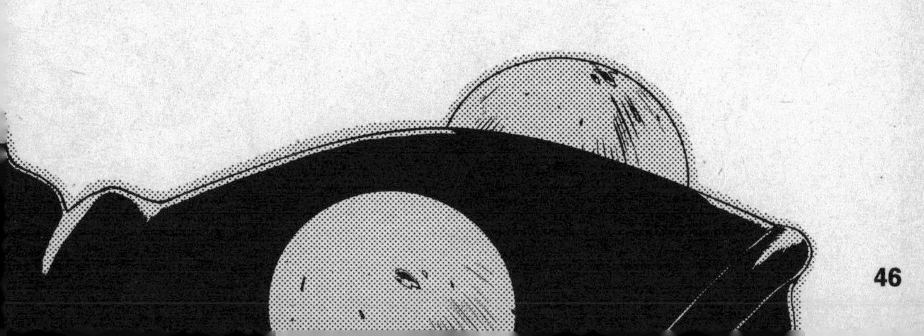

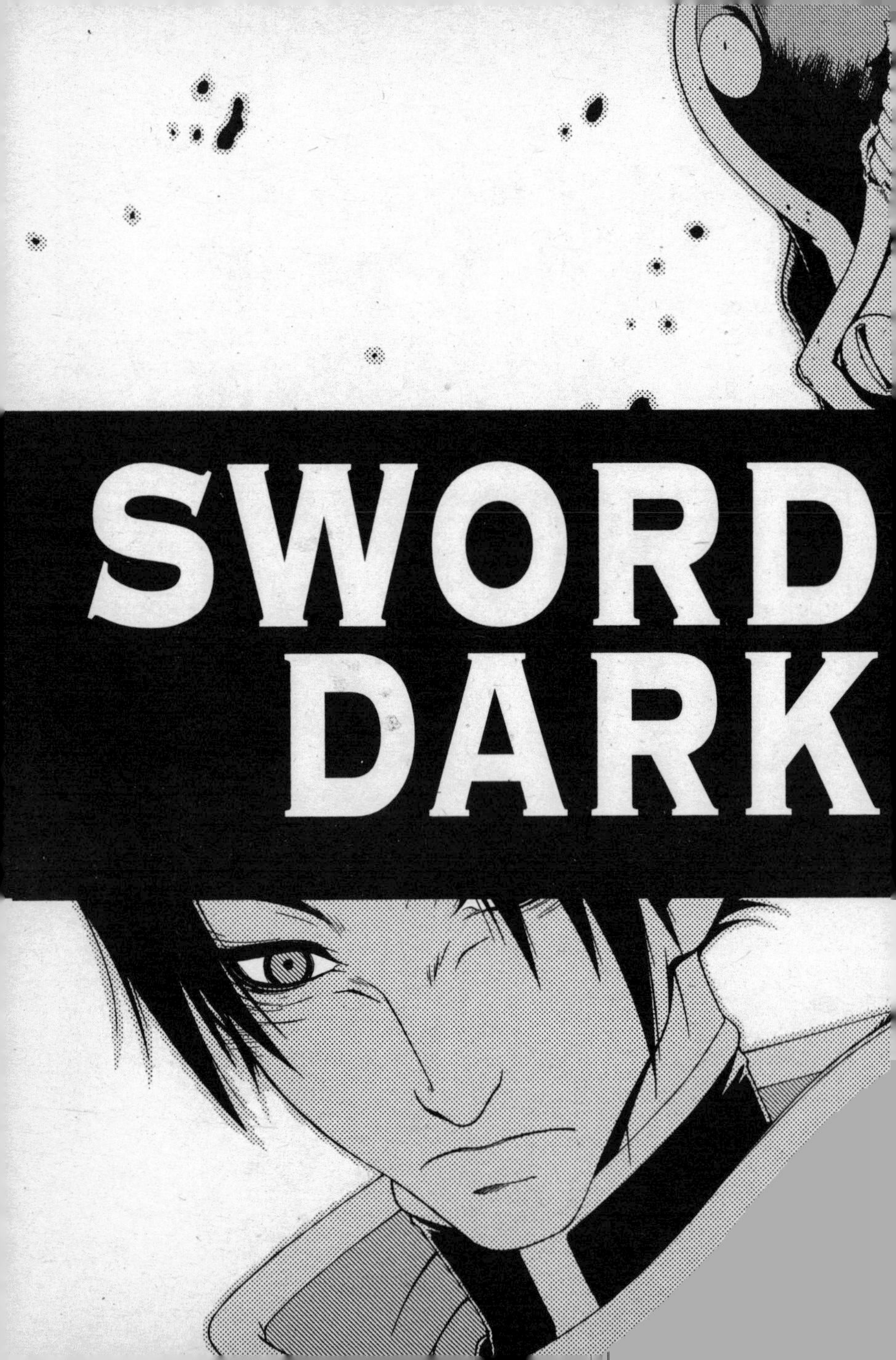
SWORD
DARK

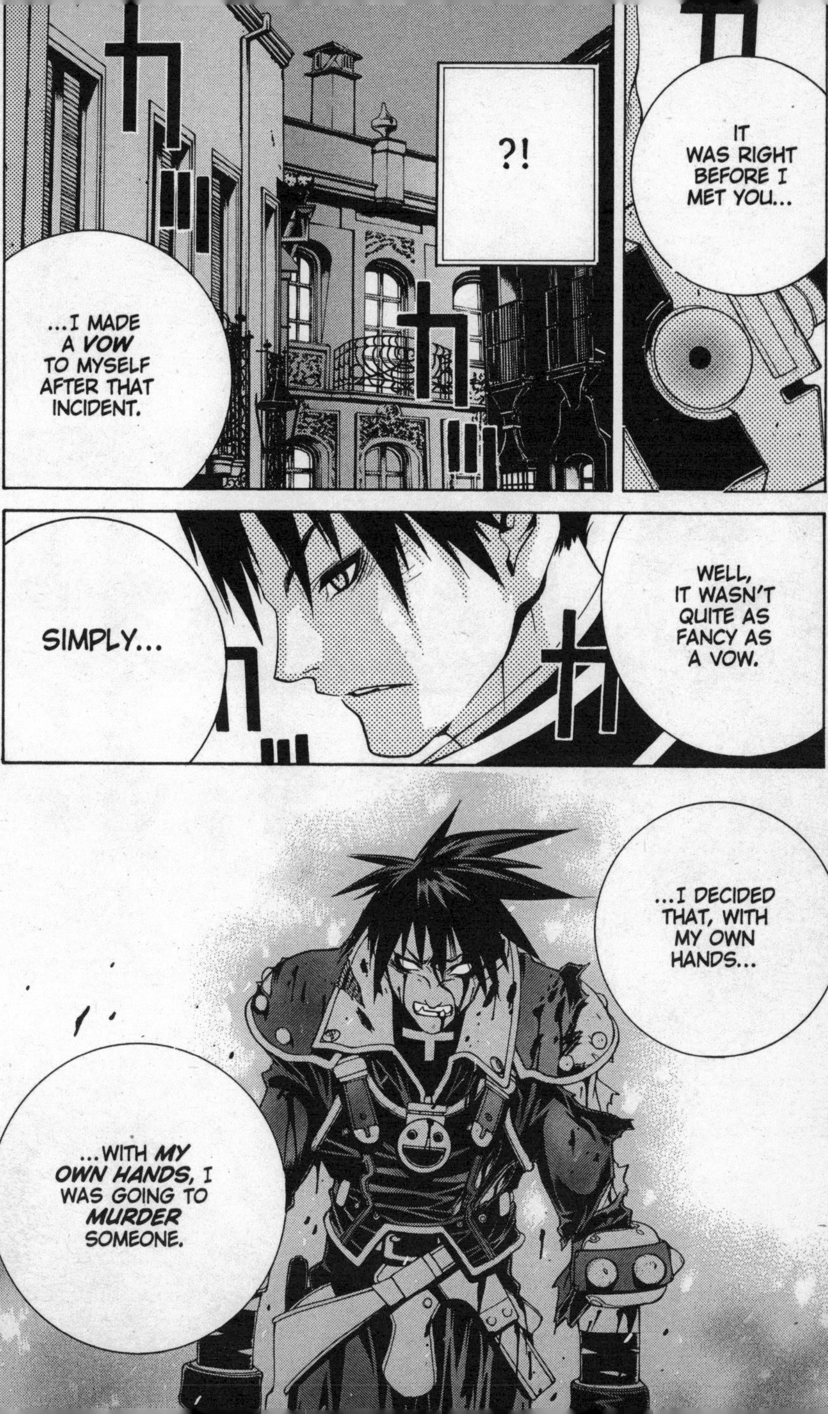
IT WAS RIGHT BEFORE I MET YOU...
?!
...I MADE A *VOW* TO MYSELF AFTER THAT INCIDENT.
WELL, IT WASN'T QUITE AS FANCY AS A VOW.
SIMPLY...
...I DECIDED THAT, WITH MY OWN HANDS...
...WITH *MY OWN HANDS,* I WAS GOING TO *MURDER* SOMEONE.

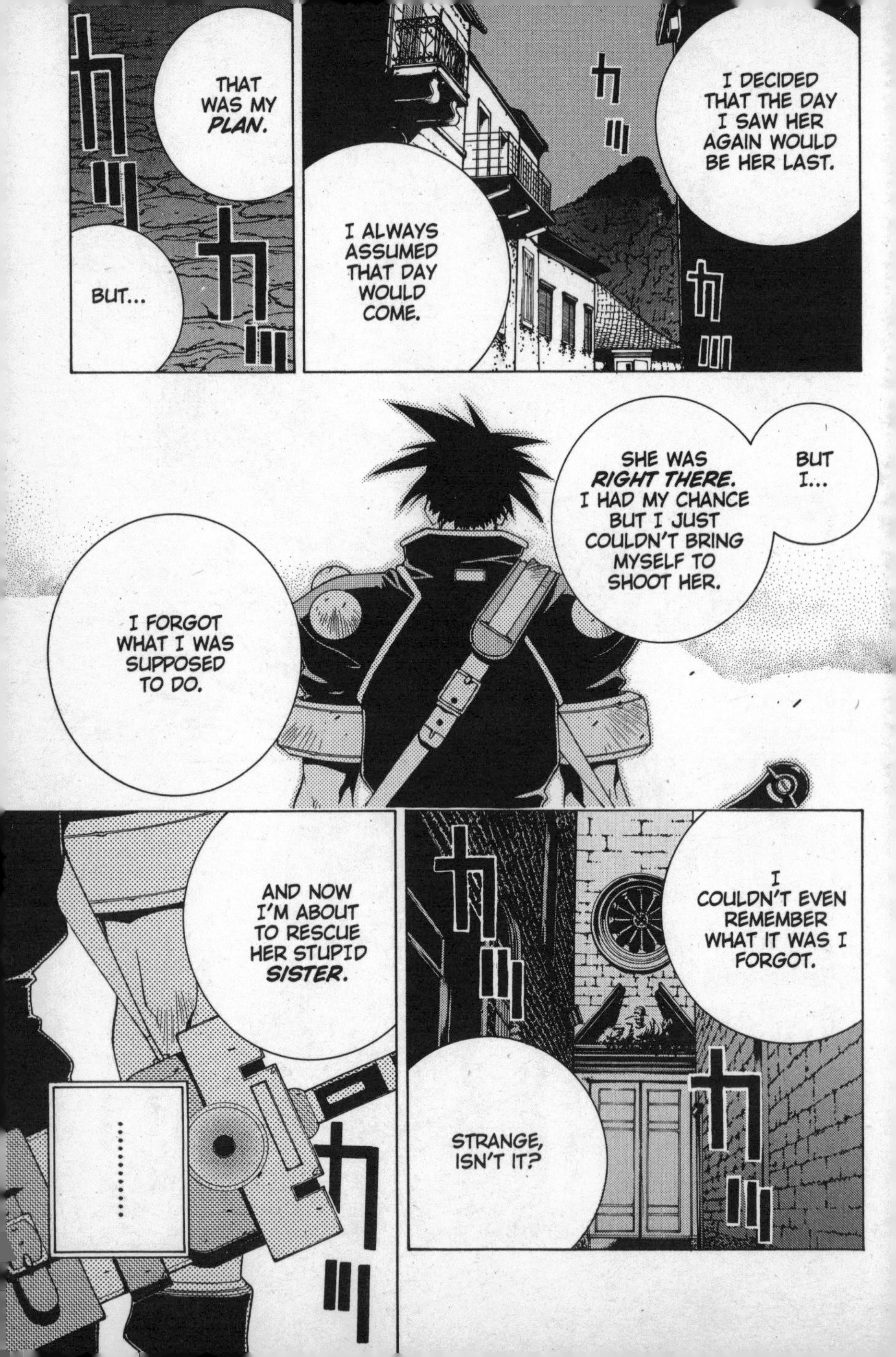
I DECIDED THAT THE DAY I SAW HER AGAIN WOULD BE HER LAST.
カッ
I ALWAYS ASSUMED THAT DAY WOULD COME.
THAT WAS MY *PLAN*.
カッ
BUT...
カッ
SHE WAS *RIGHT THERE*. I HAD MY CHANCE BUT I JUST COULDN'T BRING MYSELF TO SHOOT HER.
BUT I...
I FORGOT WHAT I WAS SUPPOSED TO DO.
I COULDN'T EVEN REMEMBER WHAT IT WAS I FORGOT.
カッ
カッ
STRANGE, ISN'T IT?
AND NOW I'M ABOUT TO RESCUE HER STUPID *SISTER*.
....
カッ

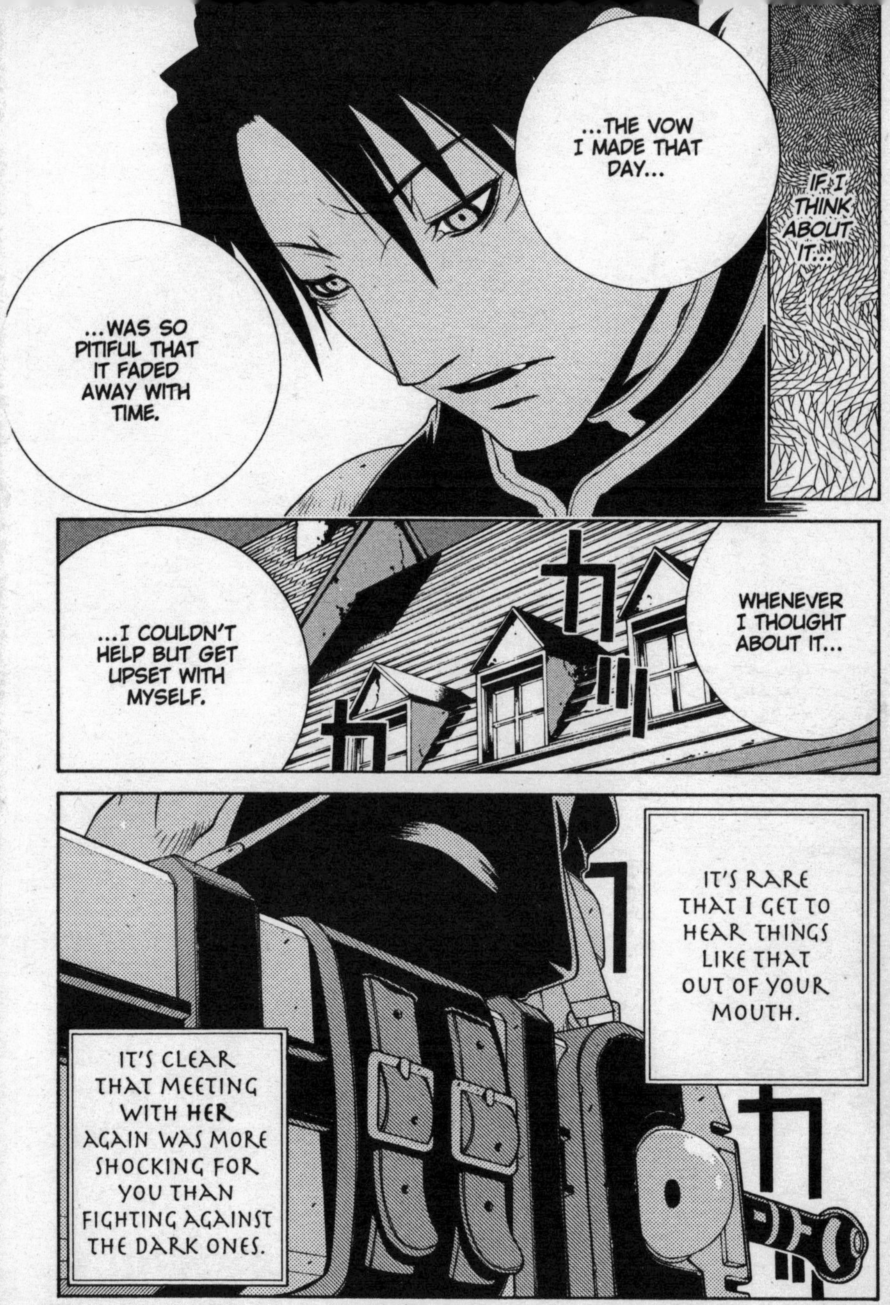
IF I THINK ABOUT IT...
...THE VOW I MADE THAT DAY...
...WAS SO PITIFUL THAT IT FADED AWAY WITH TIME.
WHENEVER I THOUGHT ABOUT IT...
...I COULDN'T HELP BUT GET UPSET WITH MYSELF.
IT'S RARE THAT I GET TO HEAR THINGS LIKE THAT OUT OF YOUR MOUTH.
IT'S CLEAR THAT MEETING WITH HER AGAIN WAS MORE SHOCKING FOR YOU THAN FIGHTING AGAINST THE DARK ONES.

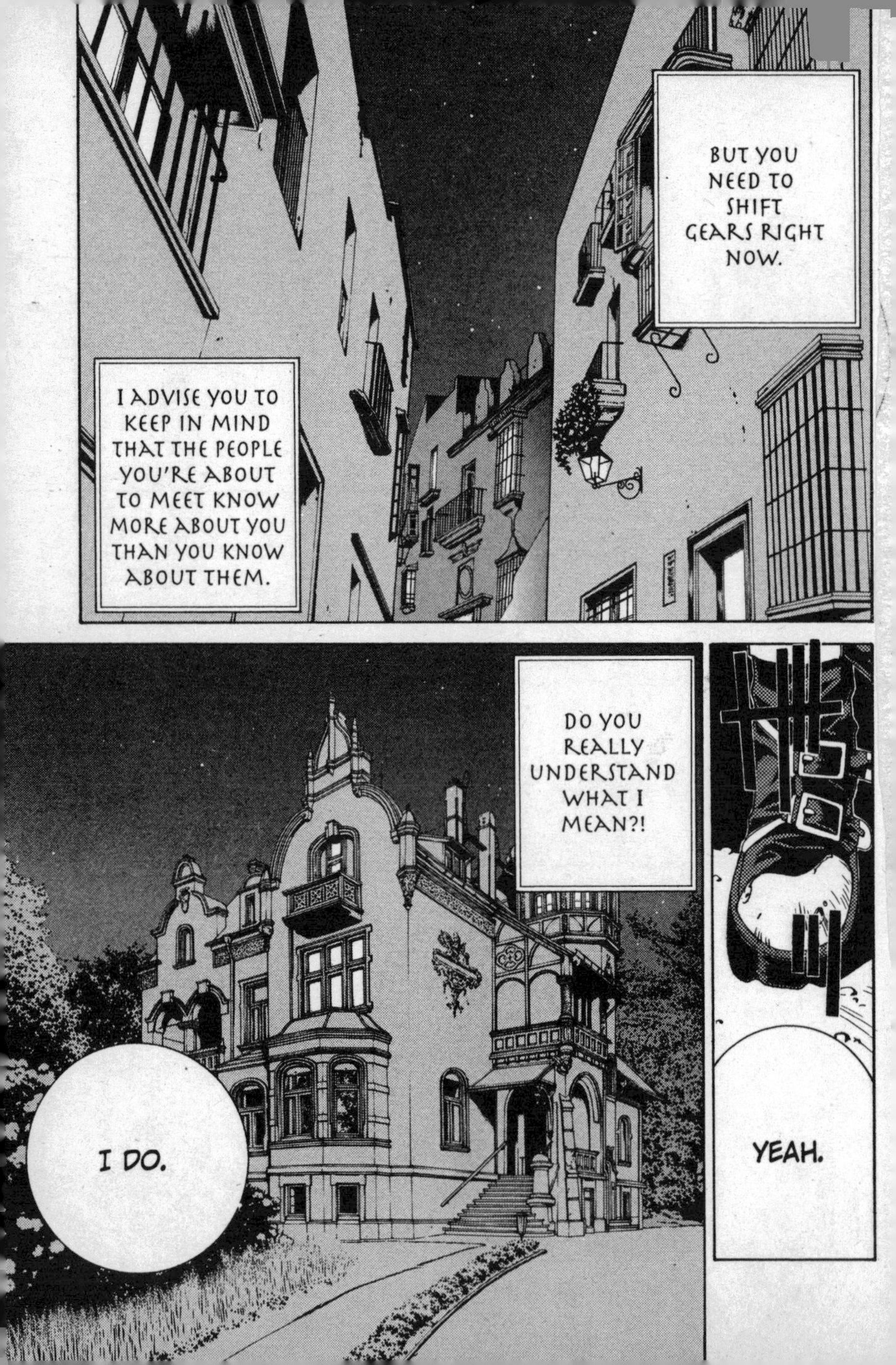
BUT YOU NEED TO SHIFT GEARS RIGHT NOW.
I ADVISE YOU TO KEEP IN MIND THAT THE PEOPLE YOU'RE ABOUT TO MEET KNOW MORE ABOUT YOU THAN YOU KNOW ABOUT THEM.
YEAH.
DO YOU REALLY UNDERSTAND WHAT I MEAN?!
I DO.

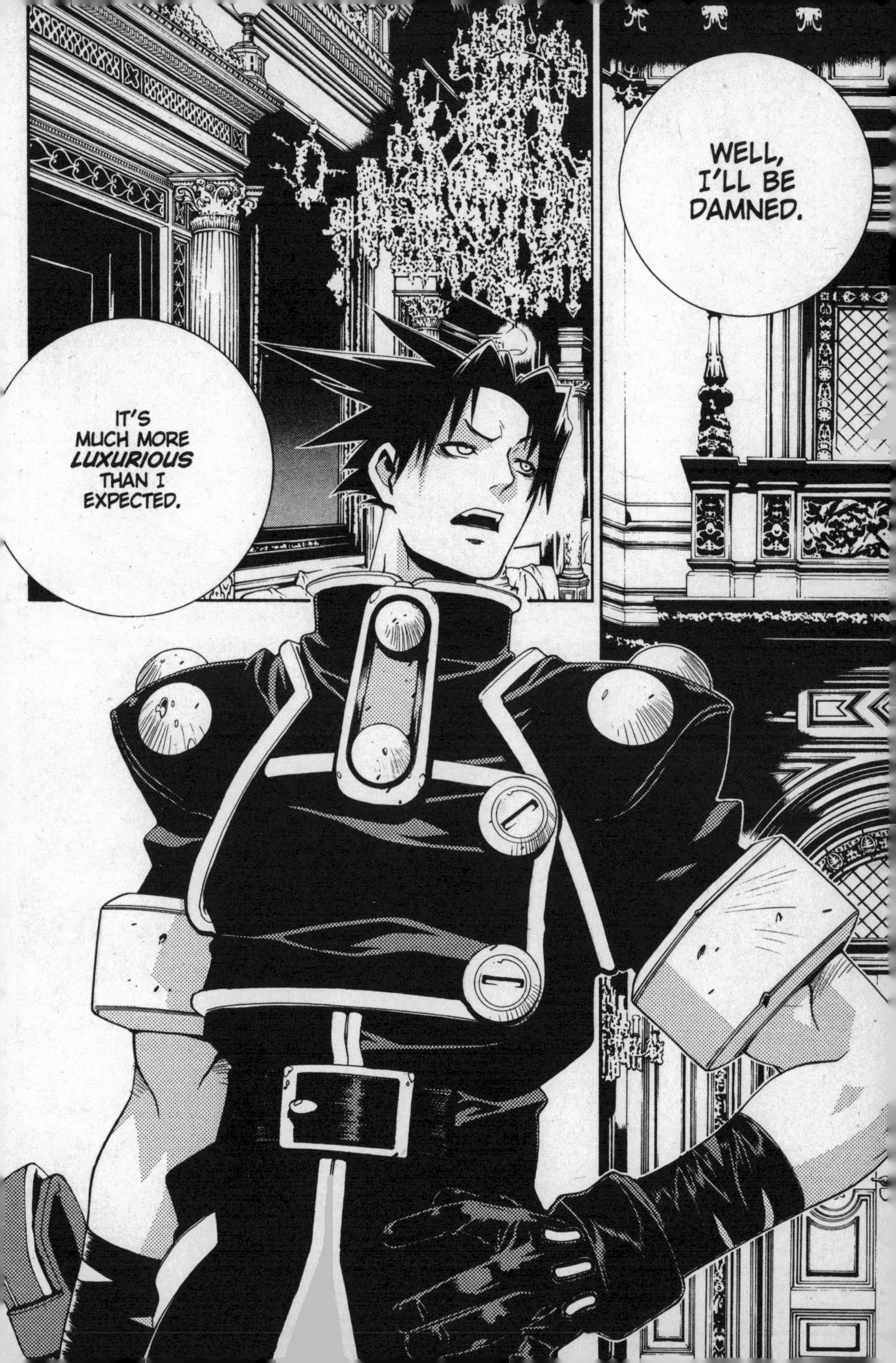
WELL, I'LL BE DAMNED.
IT'S MUCH MORE *LUXURIOUS* THAN I EXPECTED.

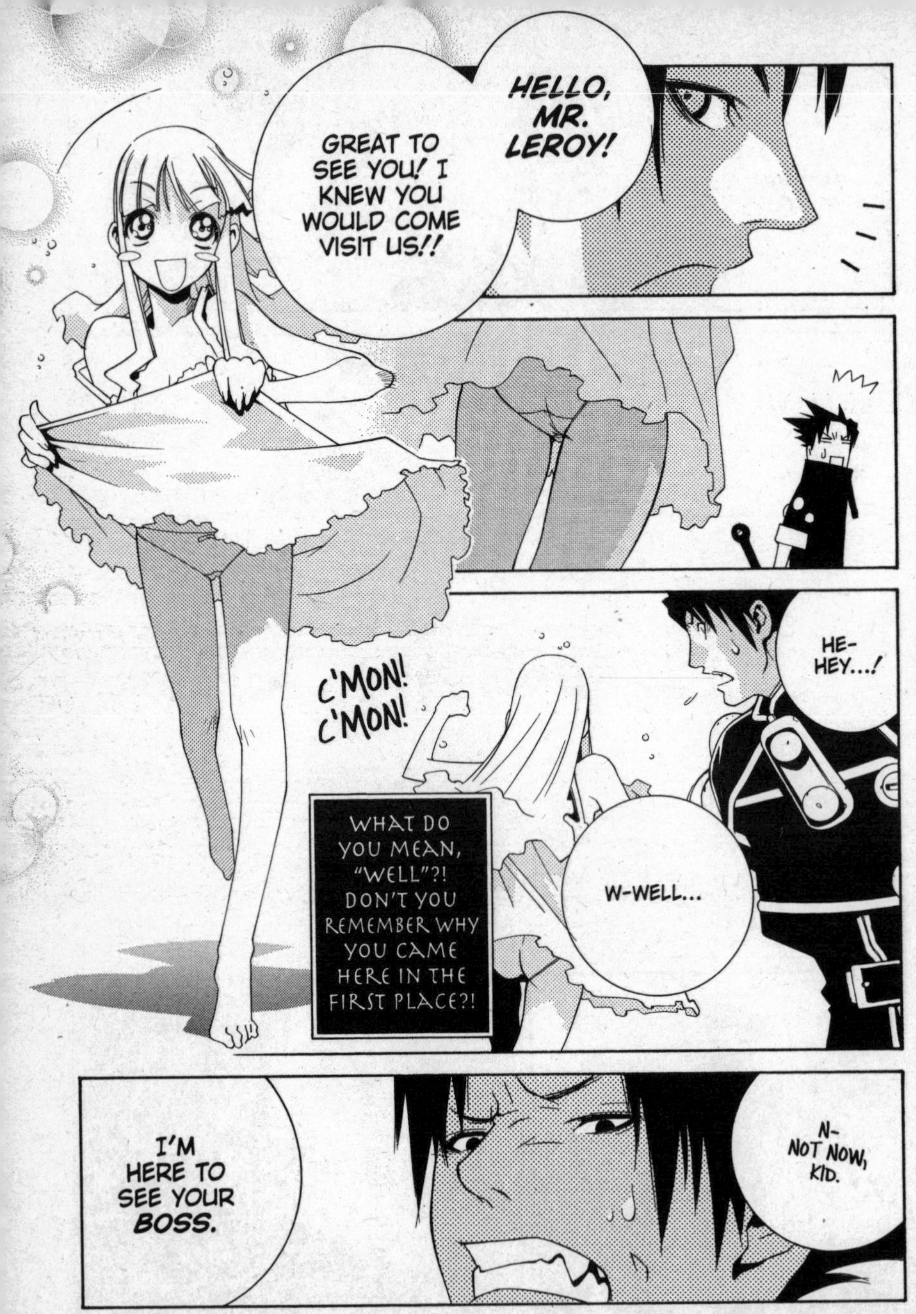
HELLO, MR. LEROY!
GREAT TO SEE YOU! I KNEW YOU WOULD COME VISIT US!!
HE- HEY...!
C'MON! C'MON!
W-WELL...
WHAT DO YOU MEAN, "WELL"?! DON'T YOU REMEMBER WHY YOU CAME HERE IN THE FIRST PLACE?!
N- NOT NOW, KID.
I'M HERE TO SEE YOUR BOSS.

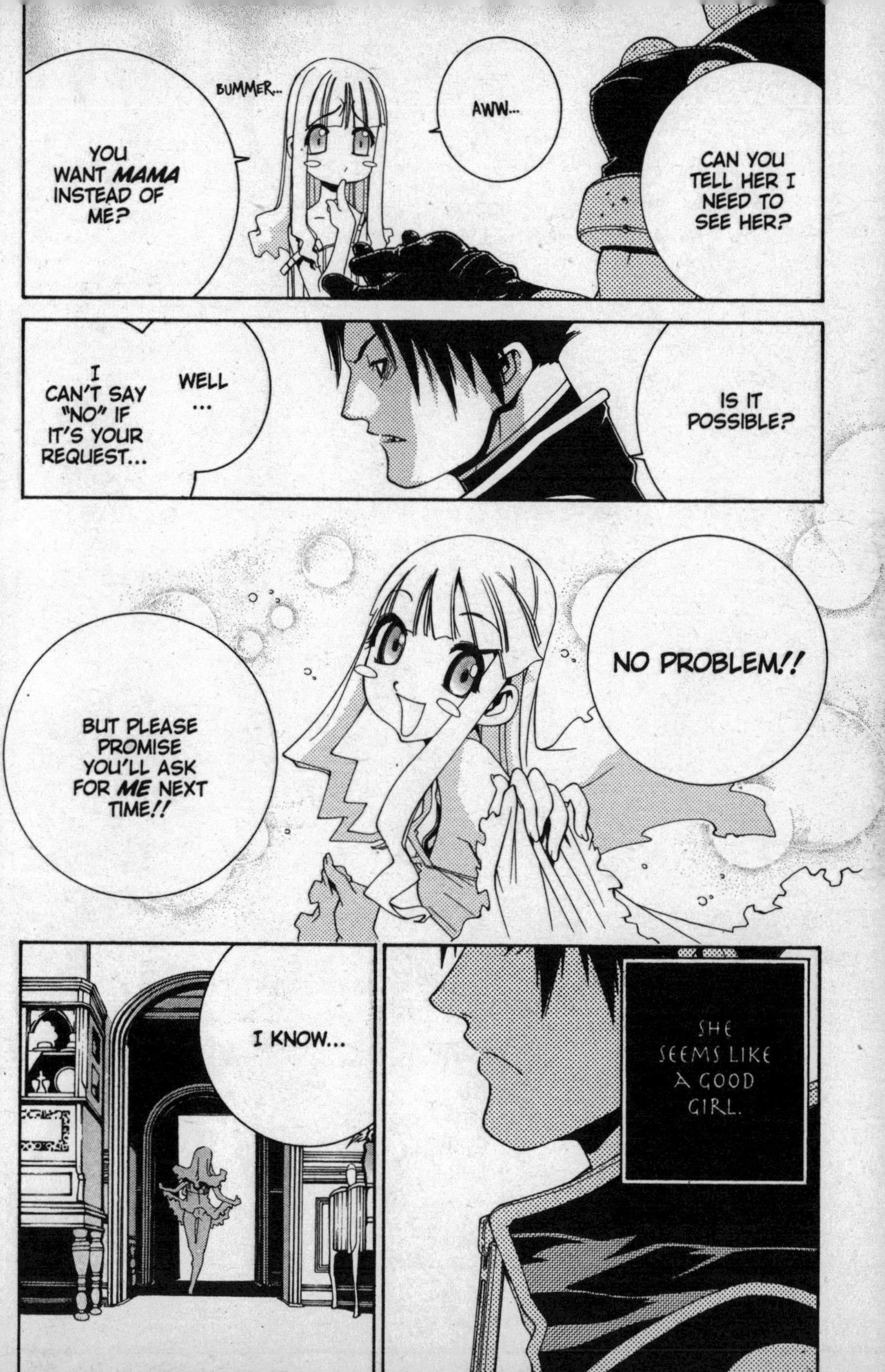
CAN YOU TELL HER I NEED TO SEE HER?
AWW...
BUMMER...
YOU WANT MAMA INSTEAD OF ME?
IS IT POSSIBLE?
WELL ...
I CAN'T SAY "NO" IF IT'S YOUR REQUEST...
NO PROBLEM!!
BUT PLEASE PROMISE YOU'LL ASK FOR ME NEXT TIME!!
SHE SEEMS LIKE A GOOD GIRL.
I KNOW...

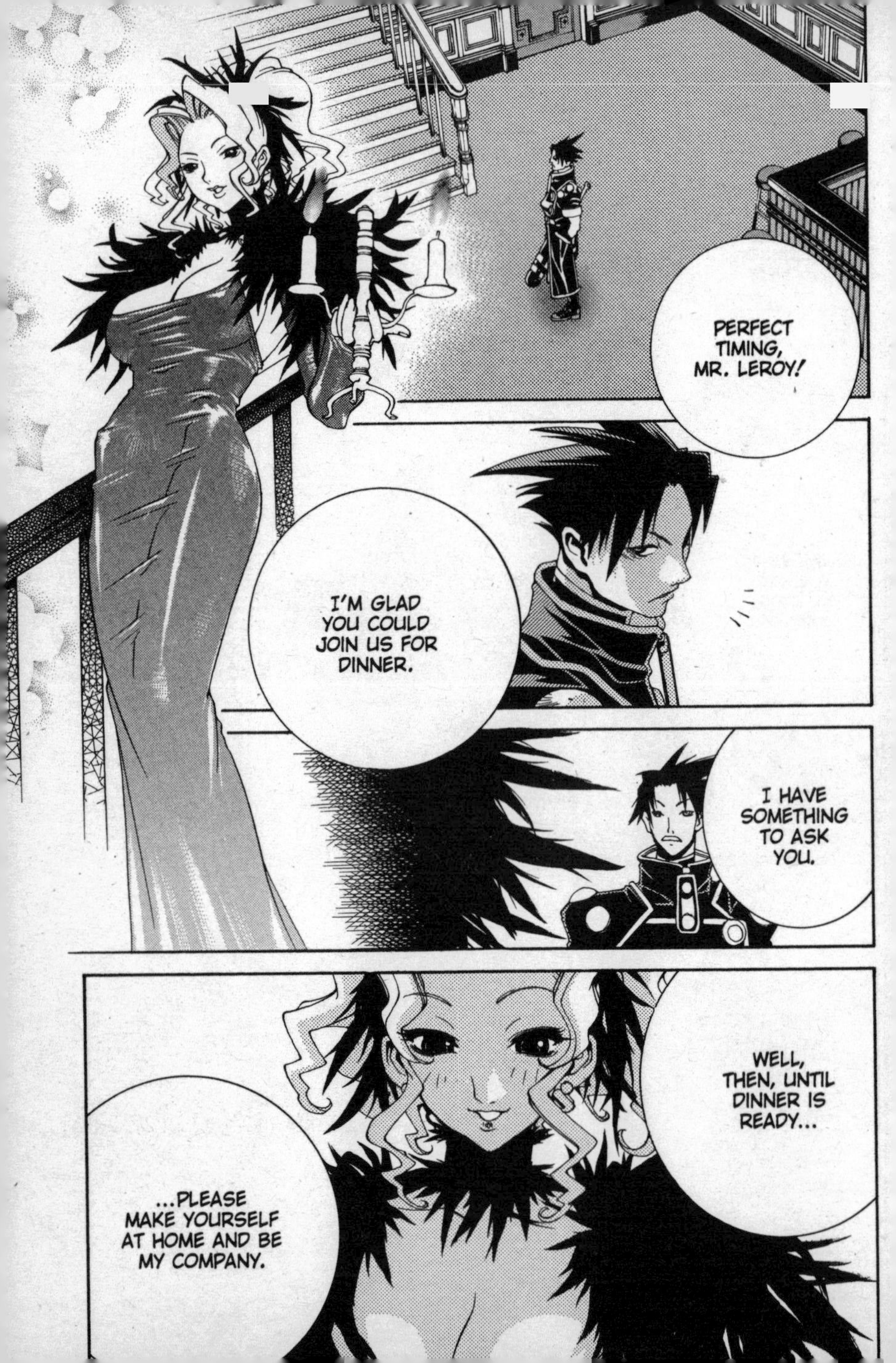
PERFECT TIMING, MR. LEROY!
I'M GLAD YOU COULD JOIN US FOR DINNER.
I HAVE SOMETHING TO ASK YOU.
WELL, THEN, UNTIL DINNER IS READY...
...PLEASE MAKE YOURSELF AT HOME AND BE MY COMPANY.

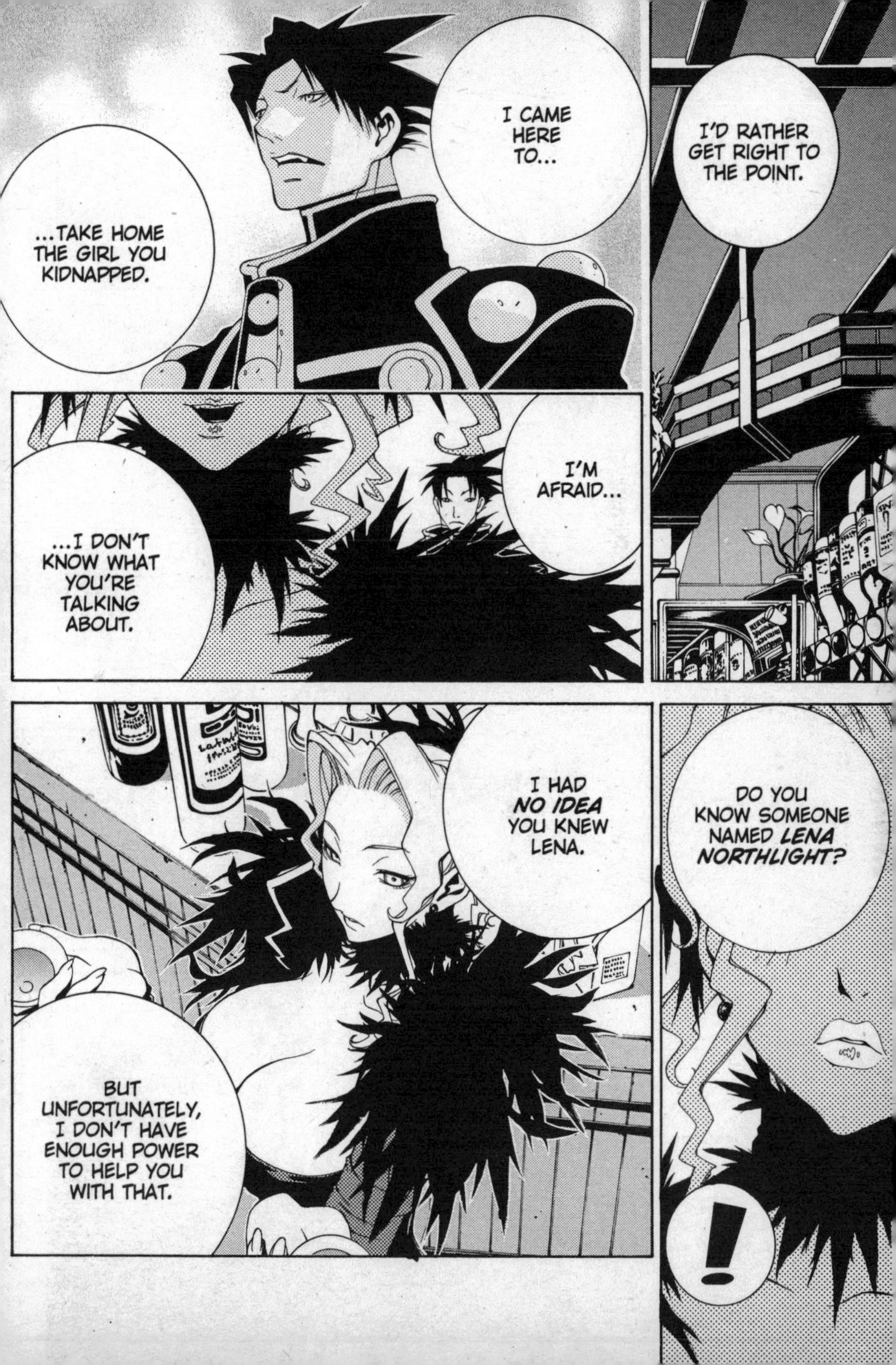
I'D RATHER GET RIGHT TO THE POINT.
I CAME HERE TO...
...TAKE HOME THE GIRL YOU KIDNAPPED.
I'M AFRAID...
...I DON'T KNOW WHAT YOU'RE TALKING ABOUT.
DO YOU KNOW SOMEONE NAMED *LENA NORTHLIGHT?*
!
I HAD *NO IDEA* YOU KNEW LENA.
BUT UNFORTUNATELY, I DON'T HAVE ENOUGH POWER TO HELP YOU WITH THAT.

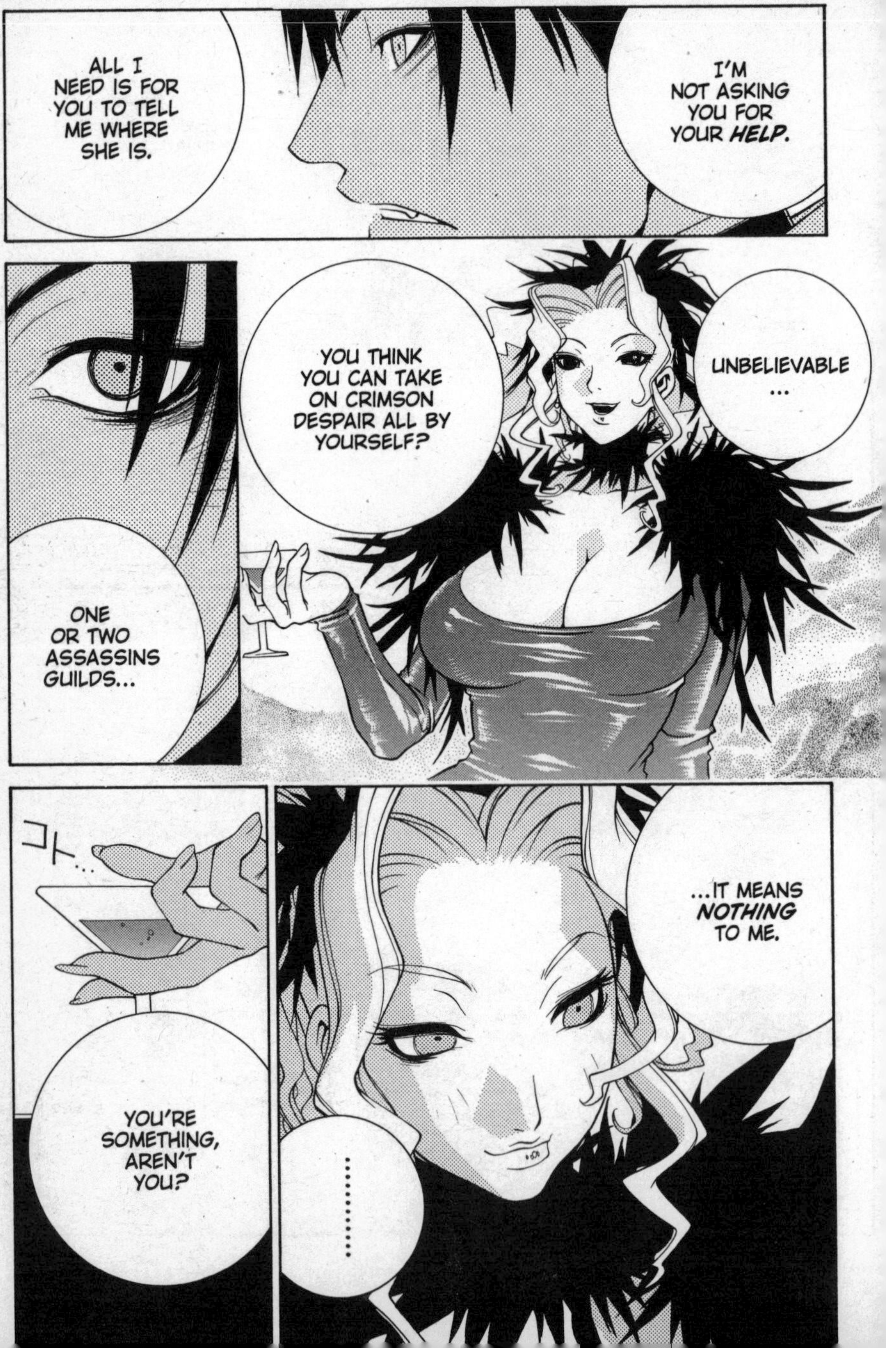

I'M NOT ASKING YOU FOR YOUR ***HELP.***
ALL I NEED IS FOR YOU TO TELL ME WHERE SHE IS.
UNBELIEVABLE...
YOU THINK YOU CAN TAKE ON CRIMSON DESPAIR ALL BY YOURSELF?
ONE OR TWO ASSASSINS GUILDS...
...IT MEANS ***NOTHING*** TO ME.
......
コト...
YOU'RE SOMETHING, AREN'T YOU?

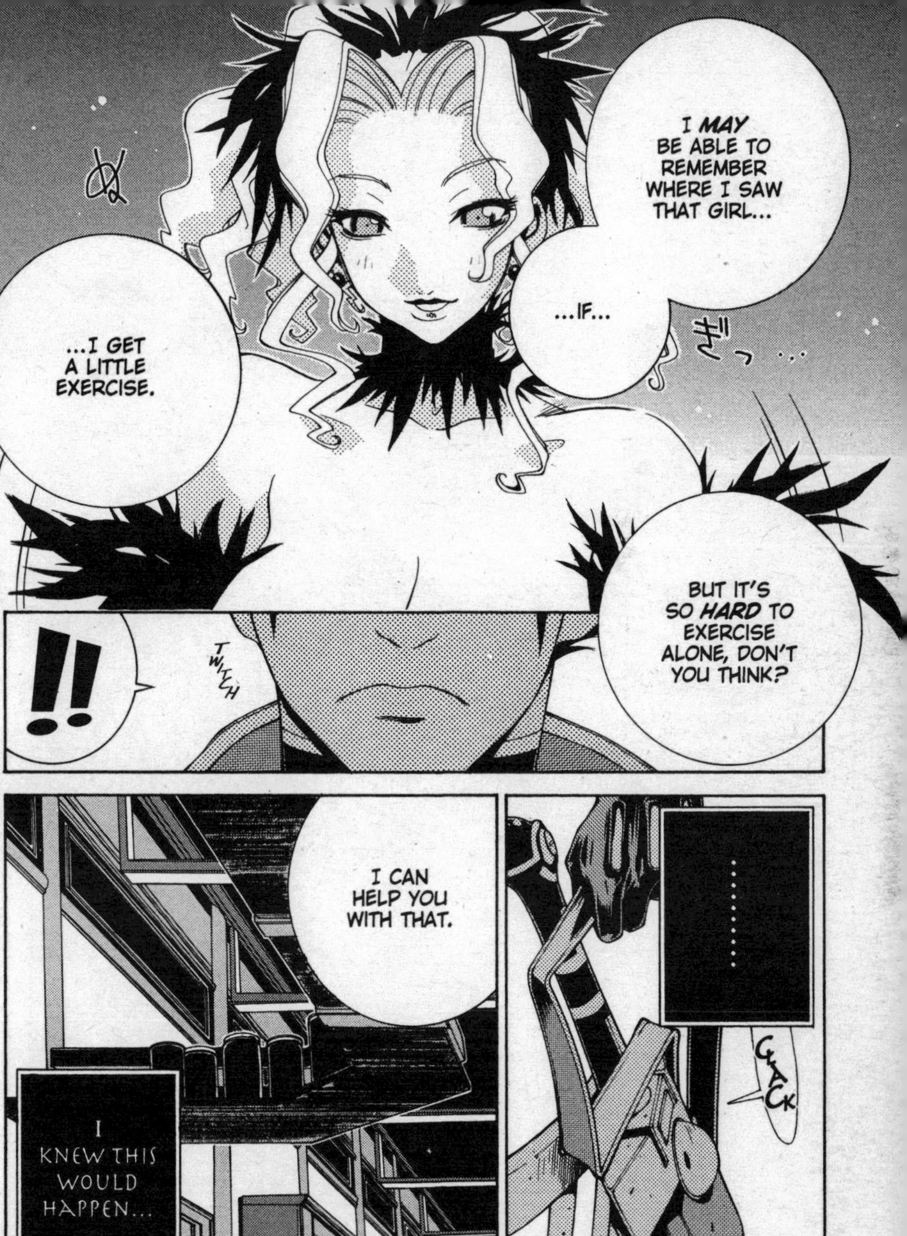
I *MAY* BE ABLE TO REMEMBER WHERE I SAW THAT GIRL...
...IF...
...I GET A LITTLE EXERCISE.
ぎっ...
BUT IT'S SO *HARD* TO EXERCISE ALONE, DON'T YOU THINK?
!!
TWITCH
....
CLACK
I CAN HELP YOU WITH THAT.
I KNEW THIS WOULD HAPPEN...

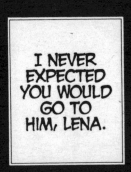

I NEVER
EXPECTED
YOU WOULD
GO TO
HIM, LENA.

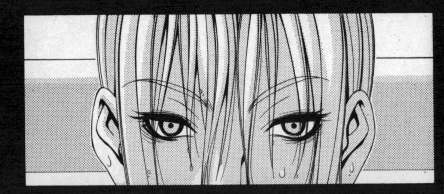

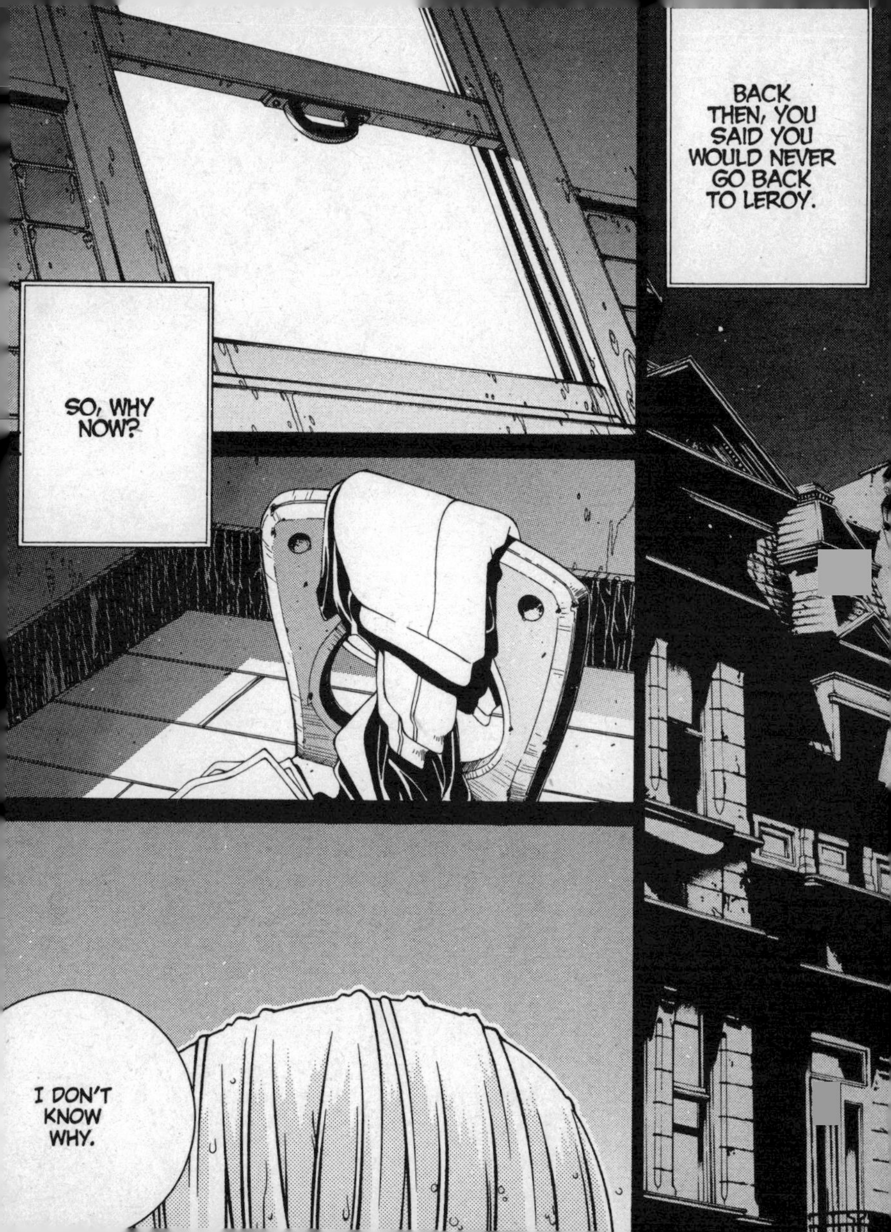
BACK THEN, YOU SAID YOU WOULD NEVER GO BACK TO LEROY.
SO, WHY NOW?
I DON'T KNOW WHY.

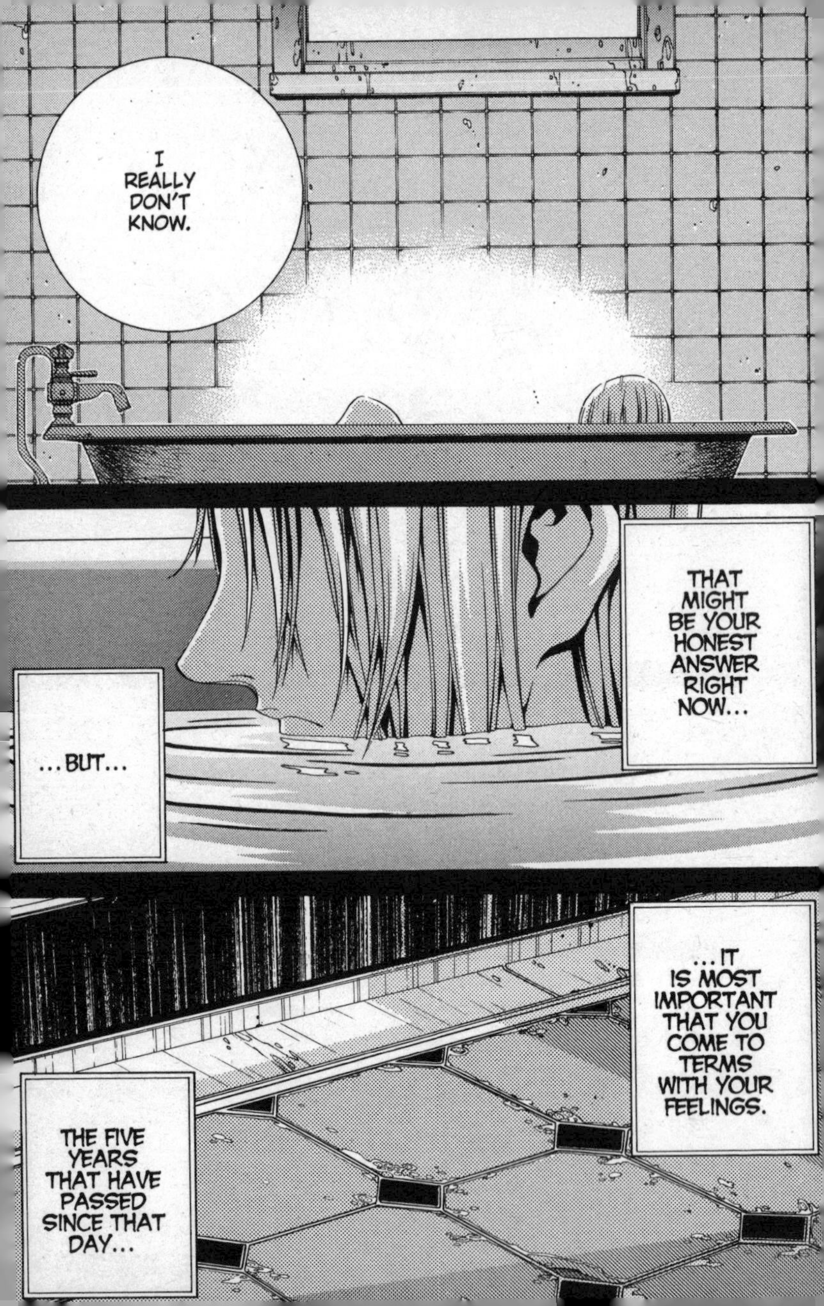
I REALLY DON'T KNOW.
THAT MIGHT BE YOUR HONEST ANSWER RIGHT NOW...
...BUT...
...IT IS MOST IMPORTANT THAT YOU COME TO TERMS WITH YOUR FEELINGS.
THE FIVE YEARS THAT HAVE PASSED SINCE THAT DAY...

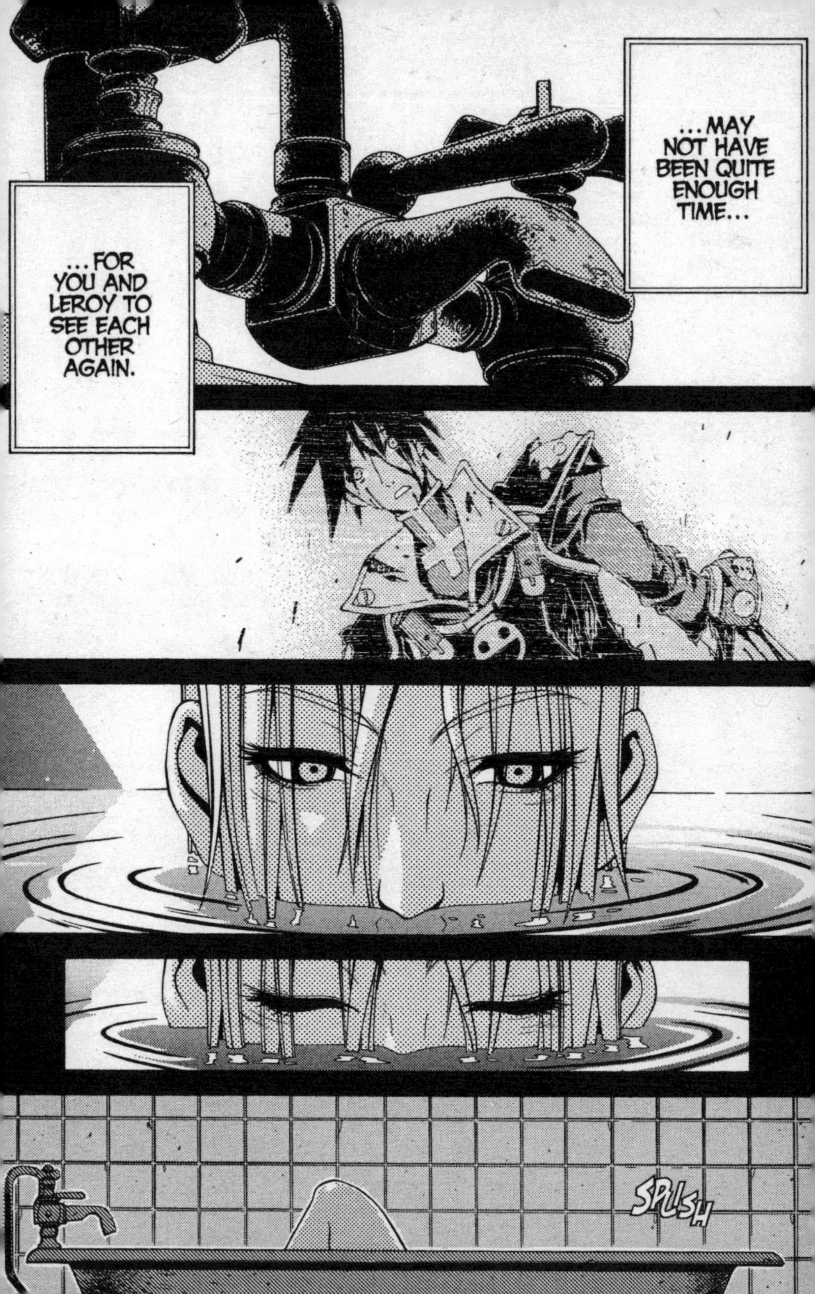
...MAY NOT HAVE BEEN QUITE ENOUGH TIME...
...FOR YOU AND LEROY TO SEE EACH OTHER AGAIN.
SPLISH

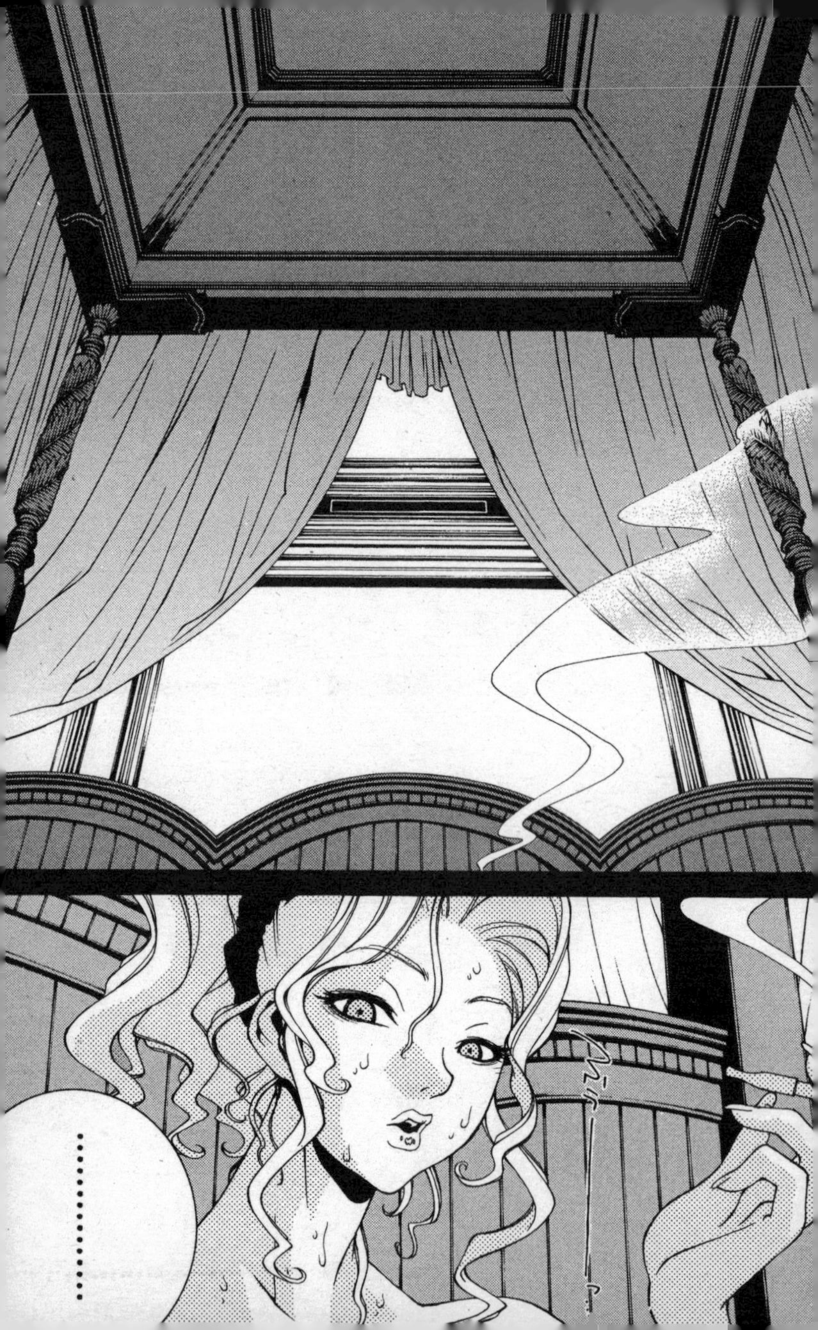
Ahh——h...
......

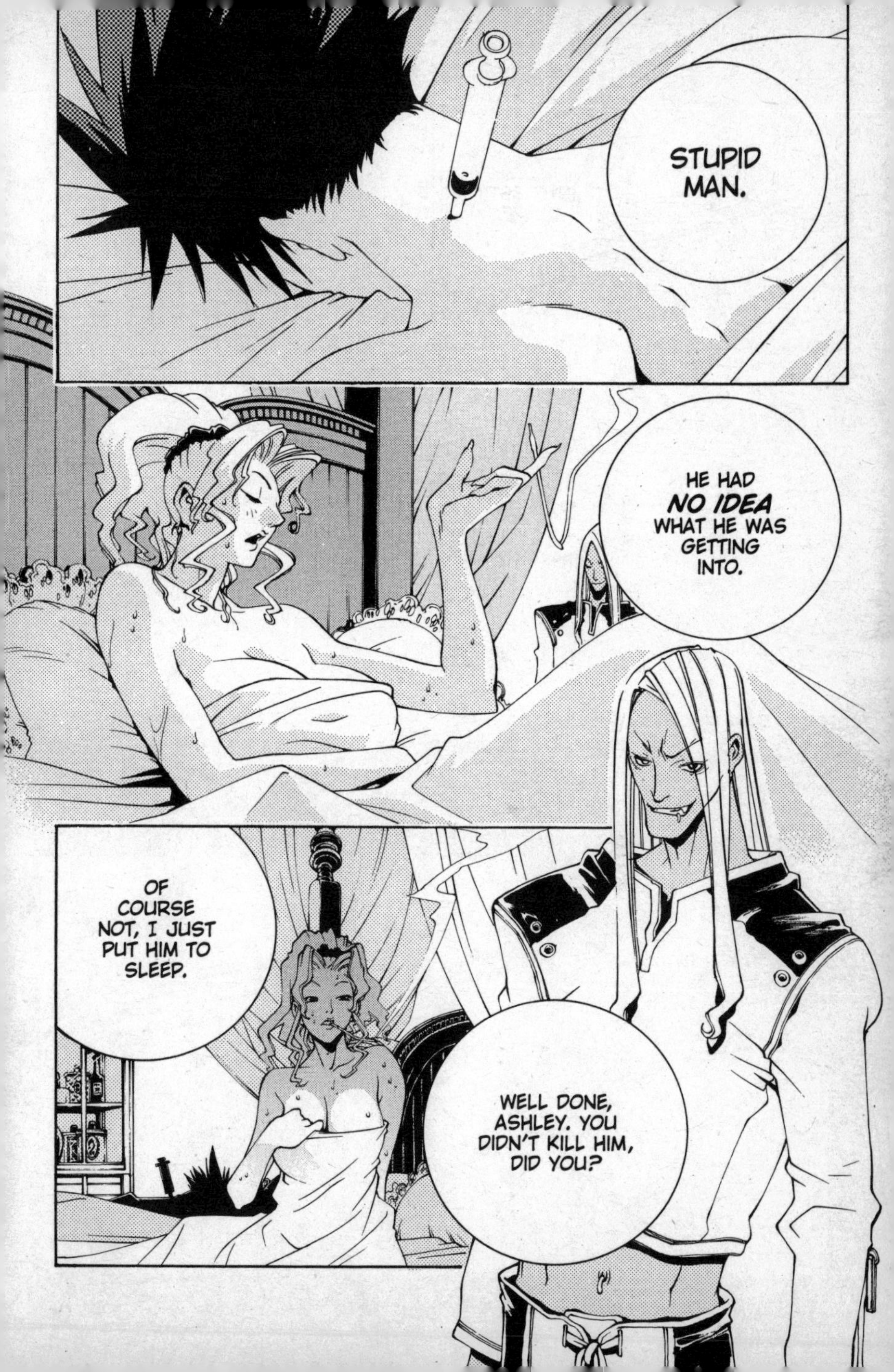
STUPID MAN.
HE HAD *NO IDEA* WHAT HE WAS GETTING INTO.
WELL DONE, ASHLEY. YOU DIDN'T KILL HIM, DID YOU?
OF COURSE NOT, I JUST PUT HIM TO SLEEP.

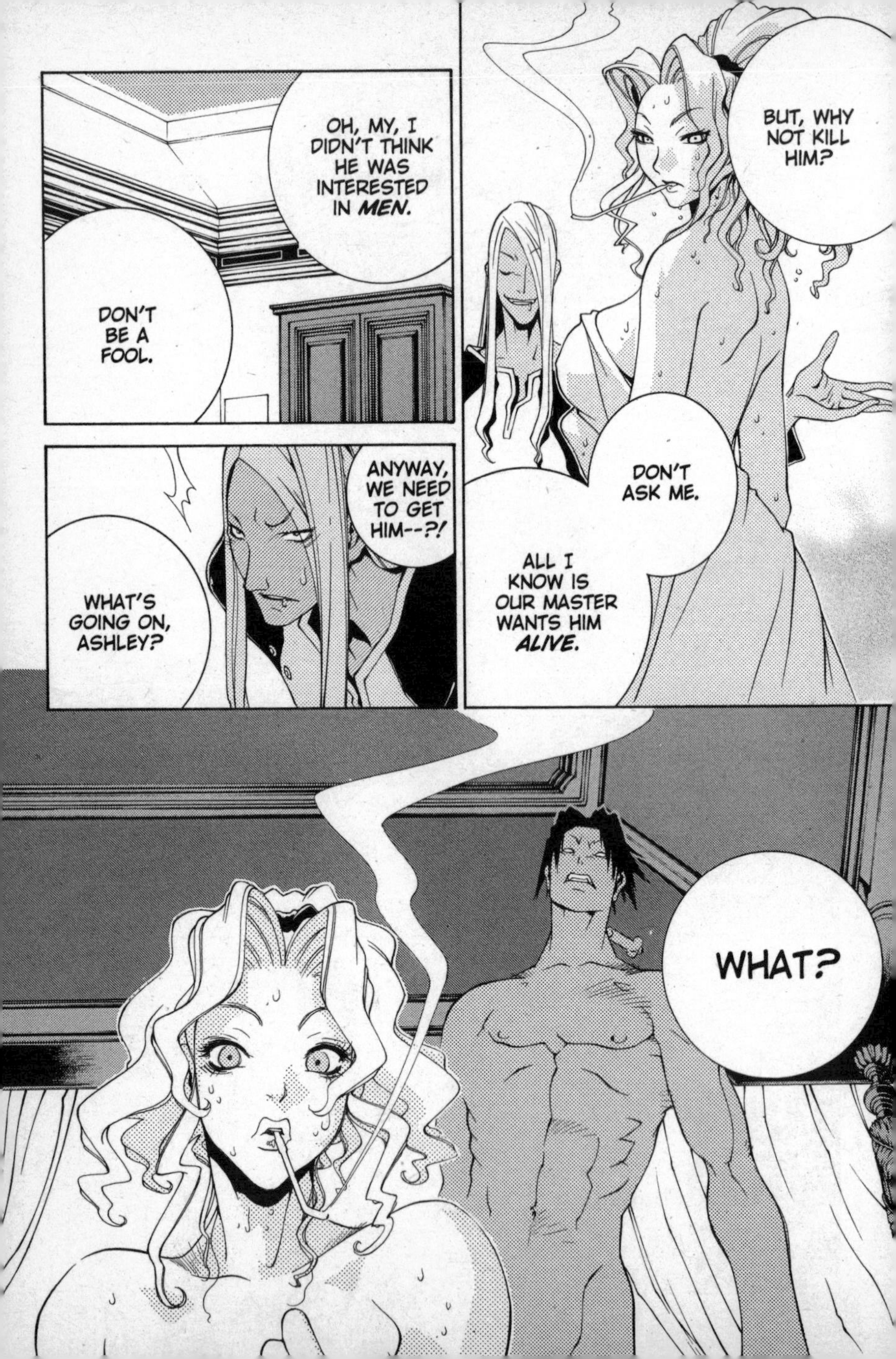
BUT, WHY NOT KILL HIM?
DON'T ASK ME.
ALL I KNOW IS OUR MASTER WANTS HIM *ALIVE*.
OH, MY, I DIDN'T THINK HE WAS INTERESTED IN *MEN*.
DON'T BE A FOOL.
ANYWAY, WE NEED TO GET HIM--?!
WHAT'S GOING ON, ASHLEY?
WHAT?

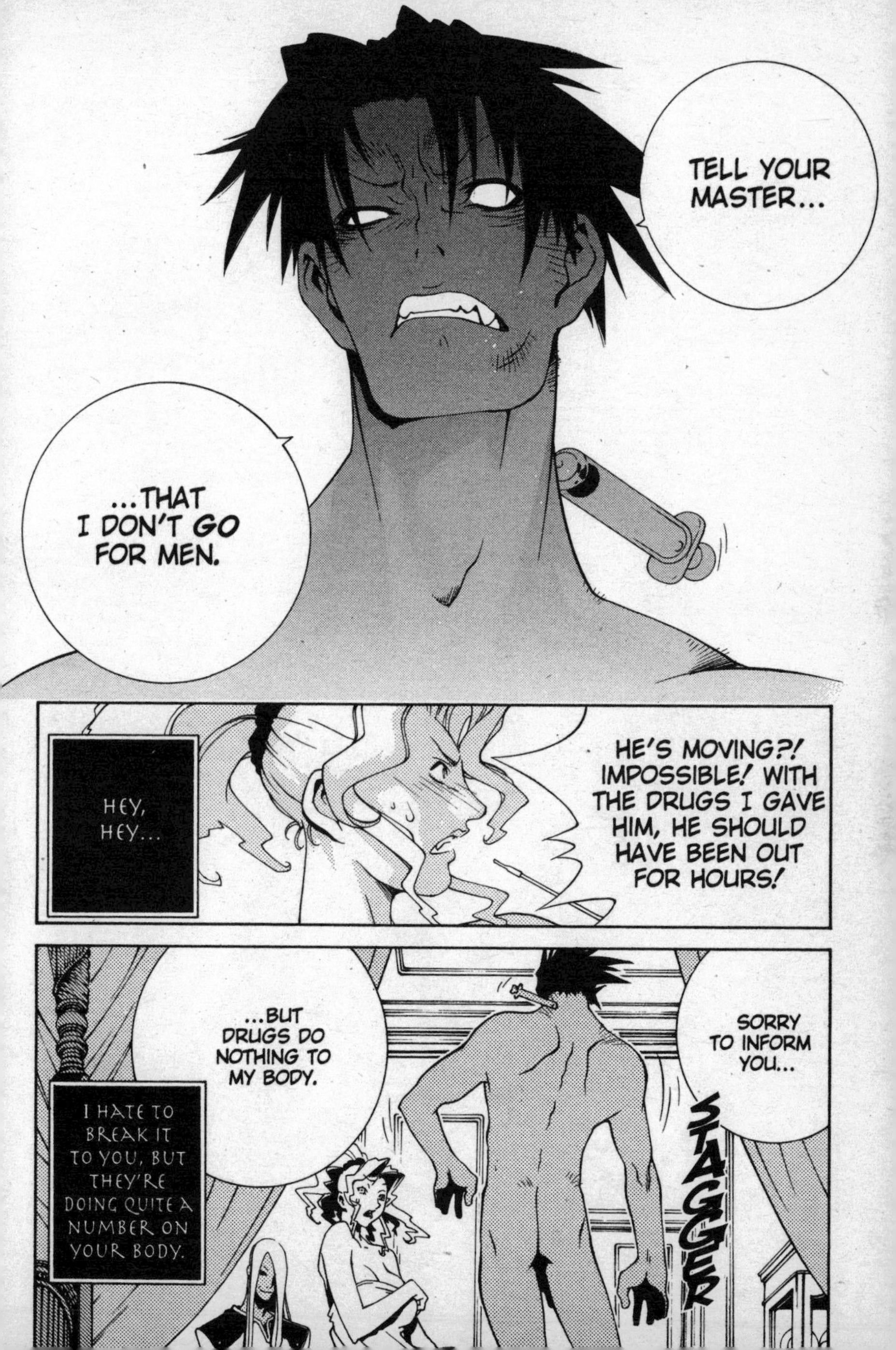
TELL YOUR MASTER...
...THAT I DON'T GO FOR MEN.
HE'S MOVING?! IMPOSSIBLE! WITH THE DRUGS I GAVE HIM, HE SHOULD HAVE BEEN OUT FOR HOURS!
HEY, HEY...
SORRY TO INFORM YOU...
...BUT DRUGS DO NOTHING TO MY BODY.
STAGGER
I HATE TO BREAK IT TO YOU, BUT THEY'RE DOING QUITE A NUMBER ON YOUR BODY.

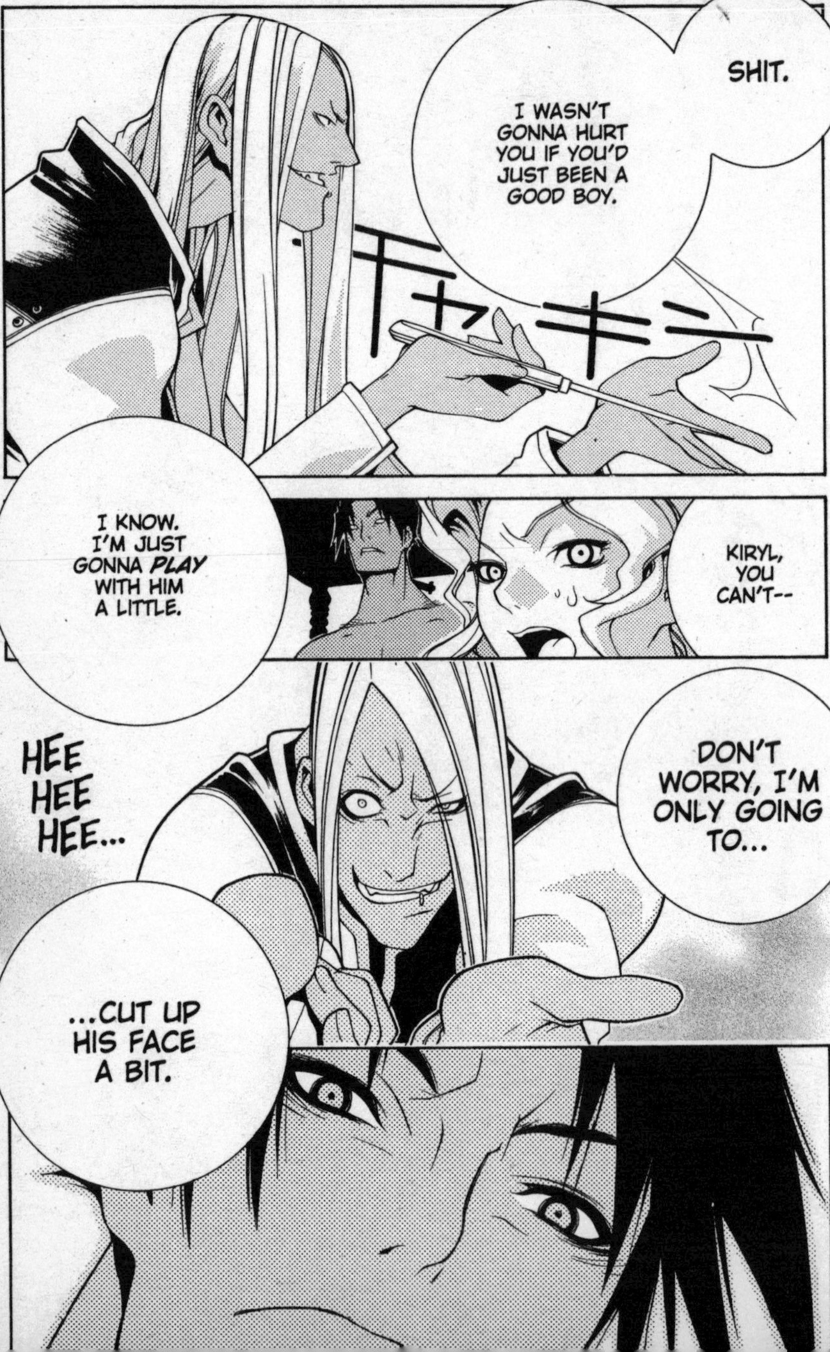
SHIT.
I WASN'T GONNA HURT YOU IF YOU'D JUST BEEN A GOOD BOY.
チャキン
KIRYL, YOU CAN'T--
I KNOW. I'M JUST GONNA *PLAY* WITH HIM A LITTLE.
DON'T WORRY, I'M ONLY GOING TO...
HEE HEE HEE...
...CUT UP HIS FACE A BIT.

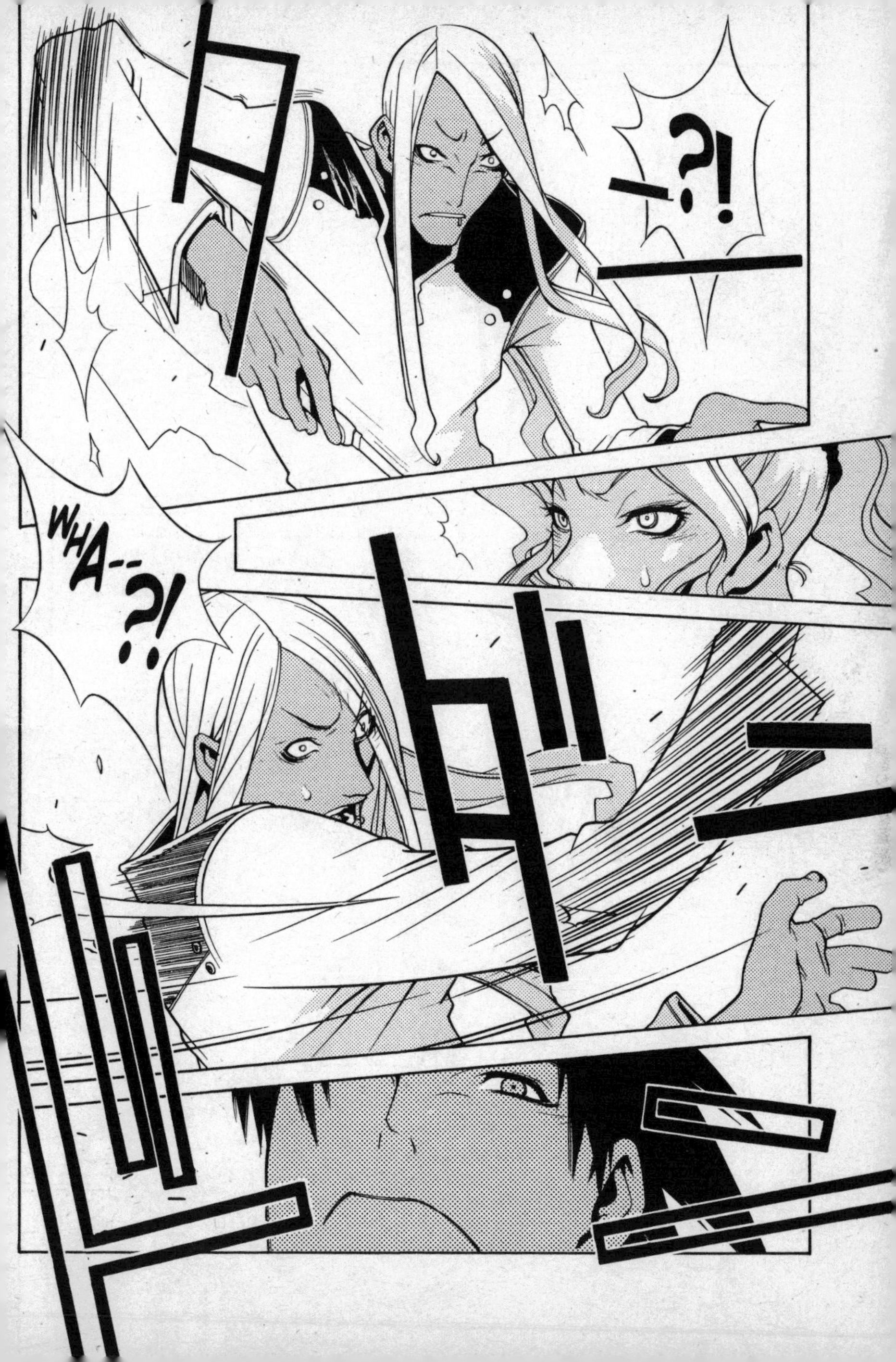
--?!
WHA--?!

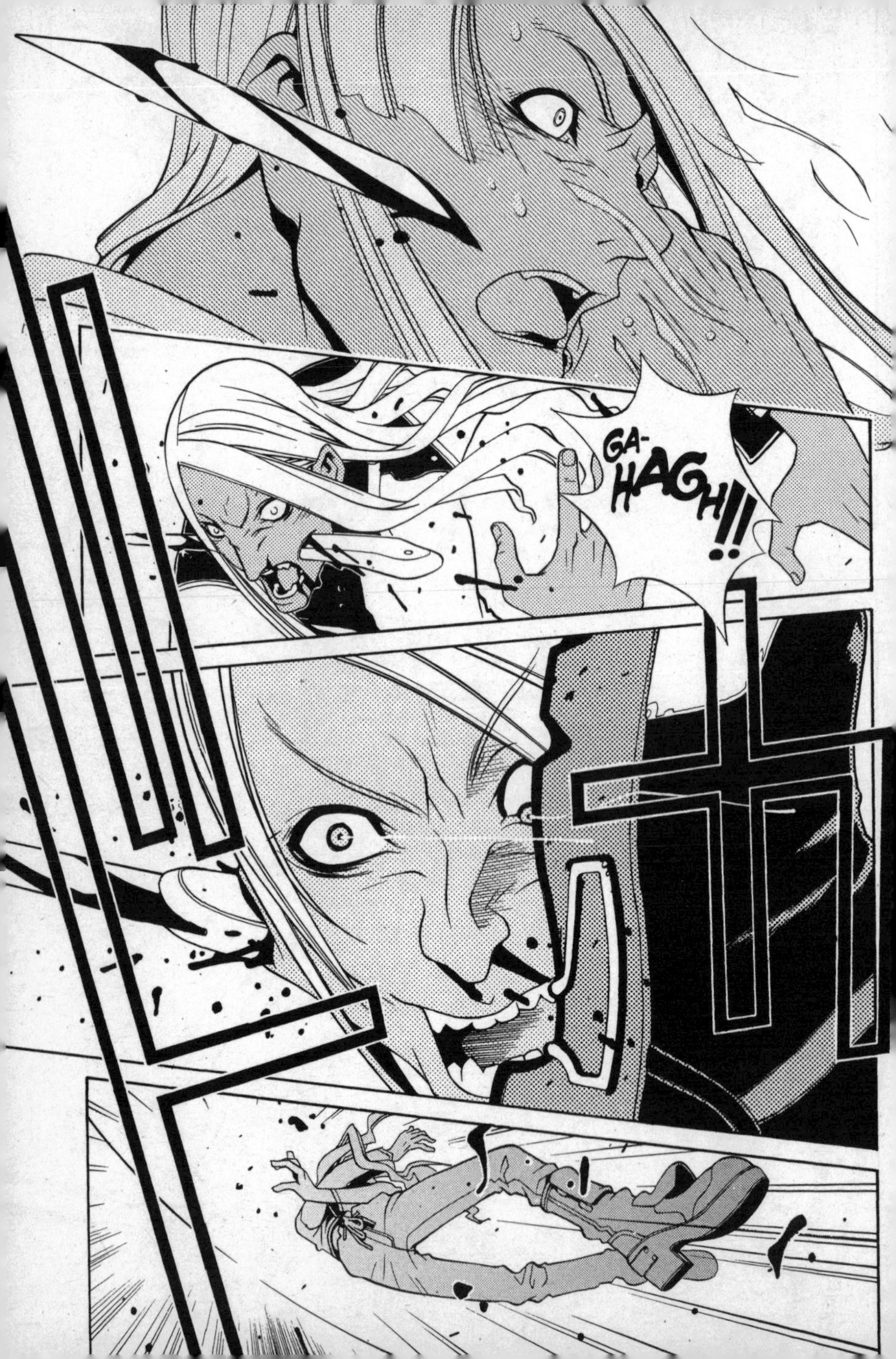
GA-HAGH!!

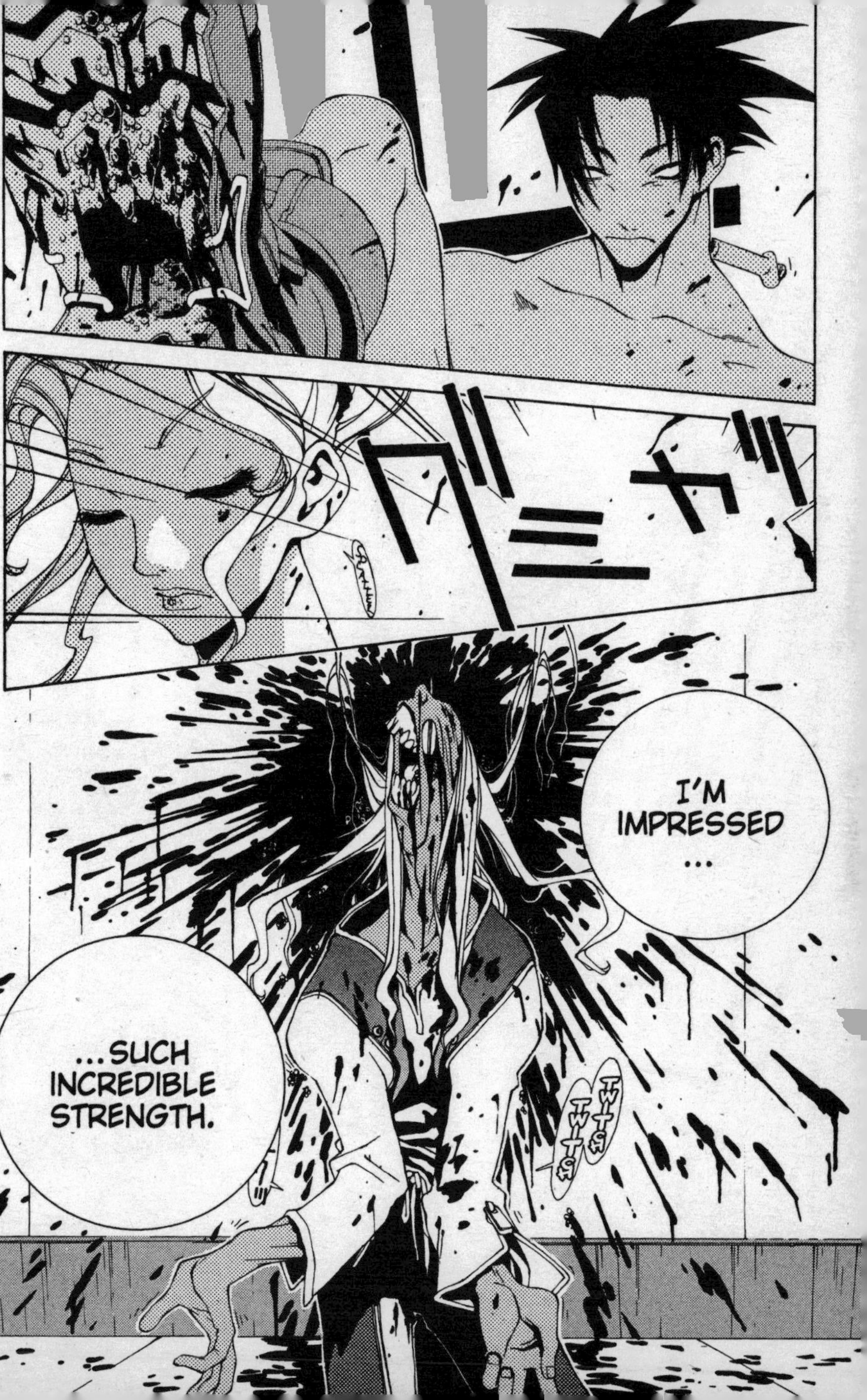

I'M IMPRESSED ...
TWITCH
TWITCH
...SUCH INCREDIBLE STRENGTH.

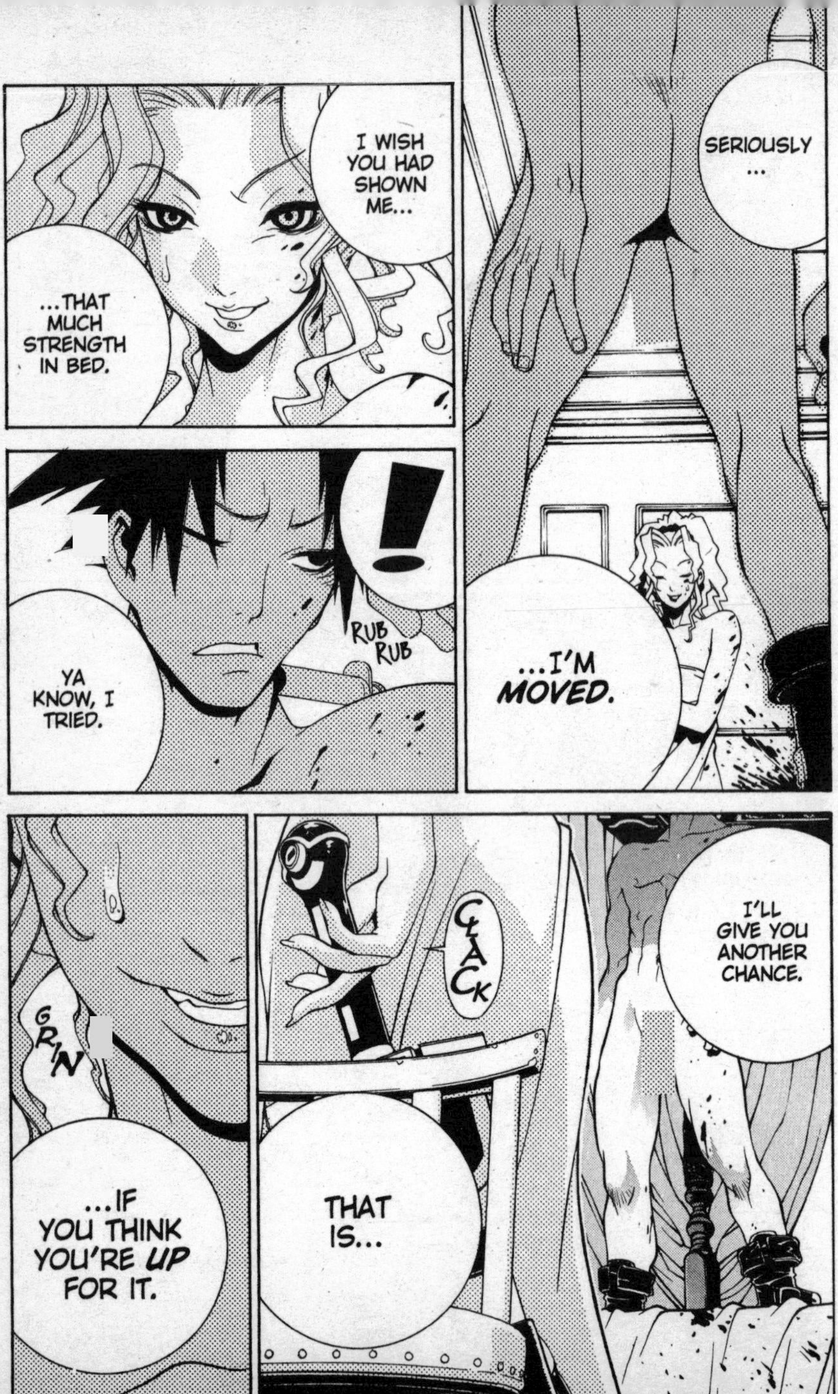
SERIOUSLY ...
...I'M *MOVED.*
I WISH YOU HAD SHOWN ME...
...THAT MUCH STRENGTH IN BED.
!
RUB RUB
YA KNOW, I TRIED.
I'LL GIVE YOU ANOTHER CHANCE.
CLACK
THAT IS...
GRIN
...IF YOU THINK YOU'RE *UP* FOR IT.

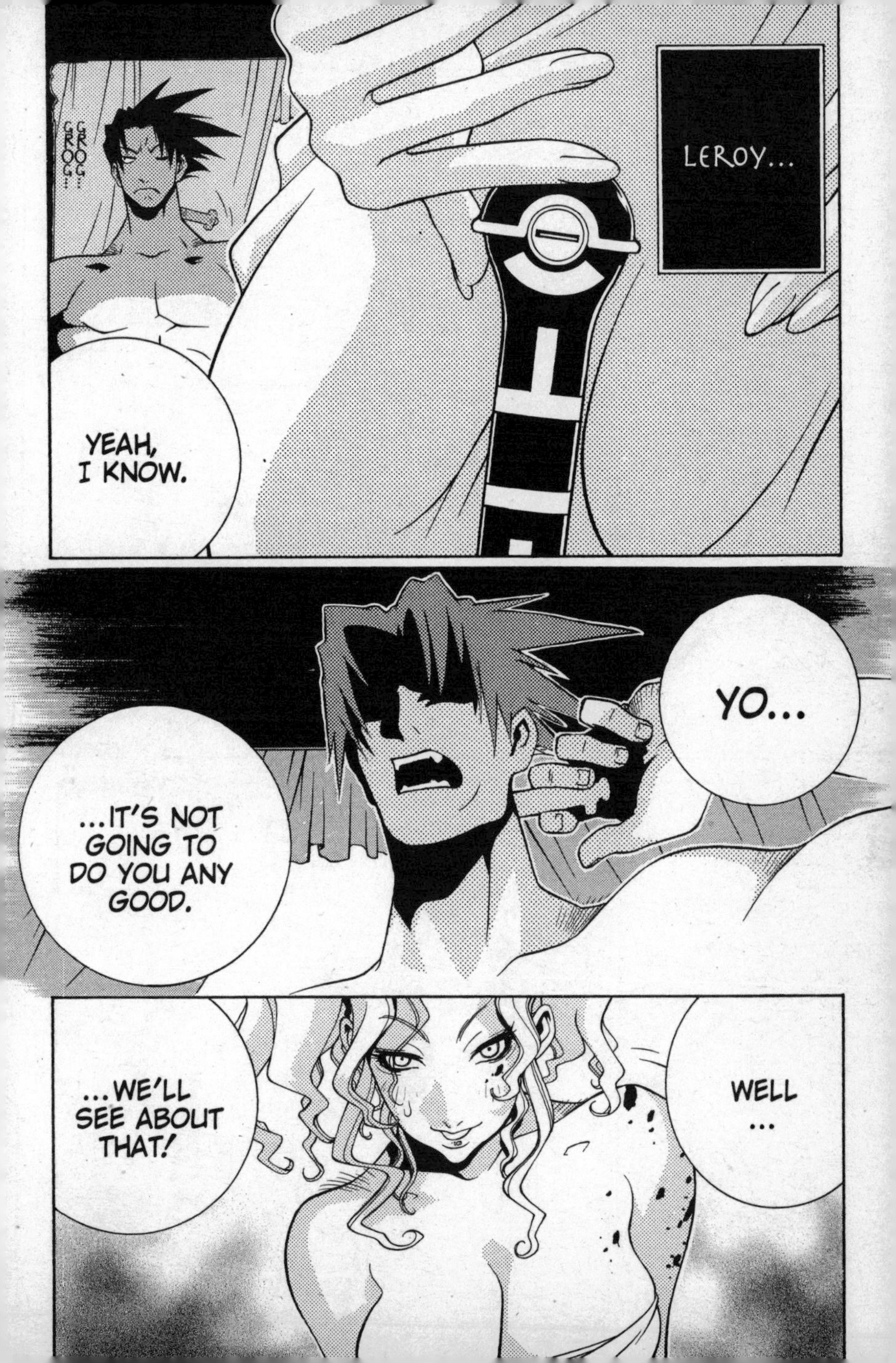
LEROY...
GROG... GROG...
YEAH, I KNOW.
YO...
...IT'S NOT GOING TO DO YOU ANY GOOD.
WELL ...
...WE'LL SEE ABOUT THAT!

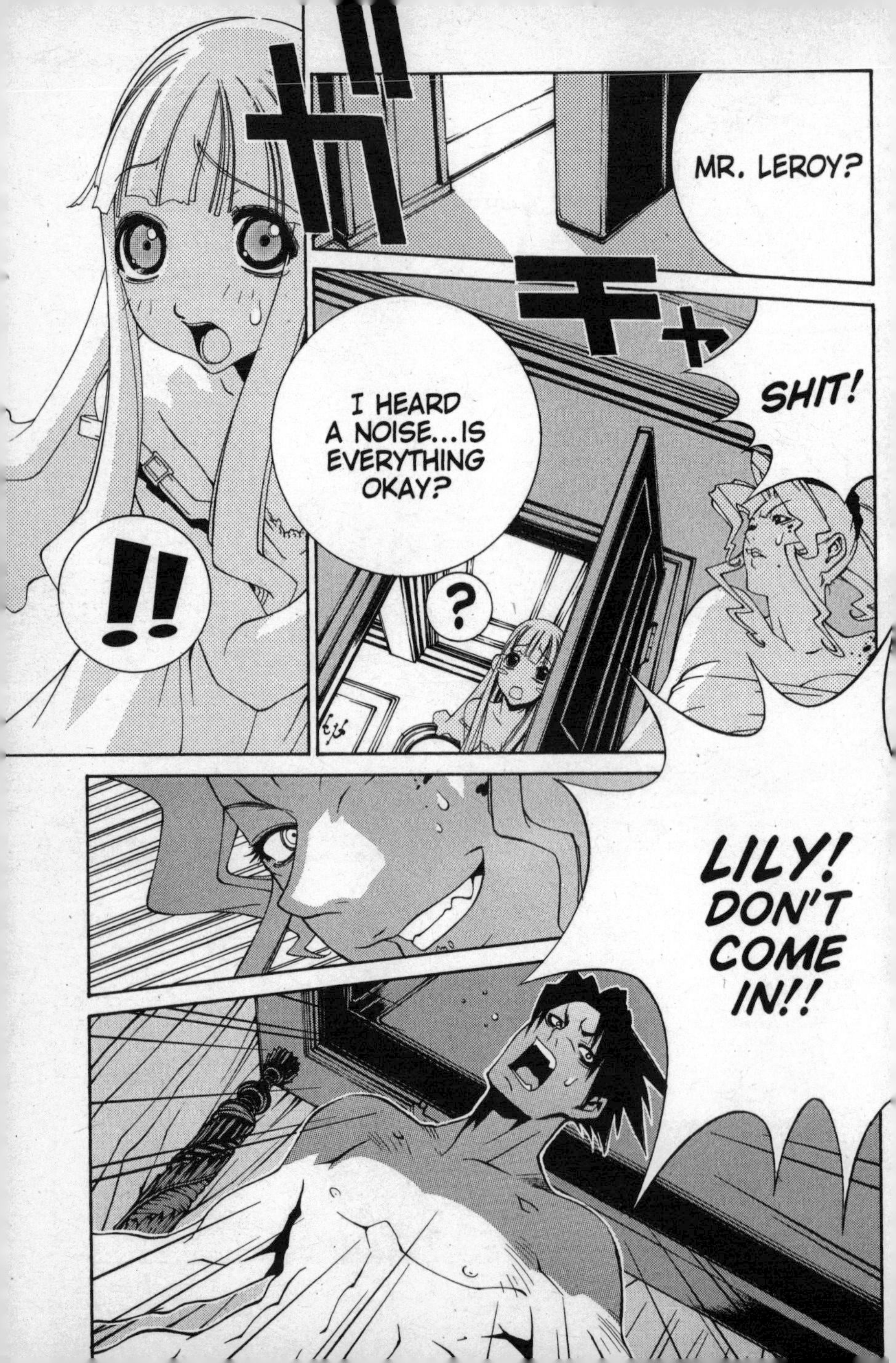
ガ
MR. LEROY?
チャ
SHIT!
I HEARD A NOISE...IS EVERYTHING OKAY?
?
!!
LILY! DON'T COME IN!!

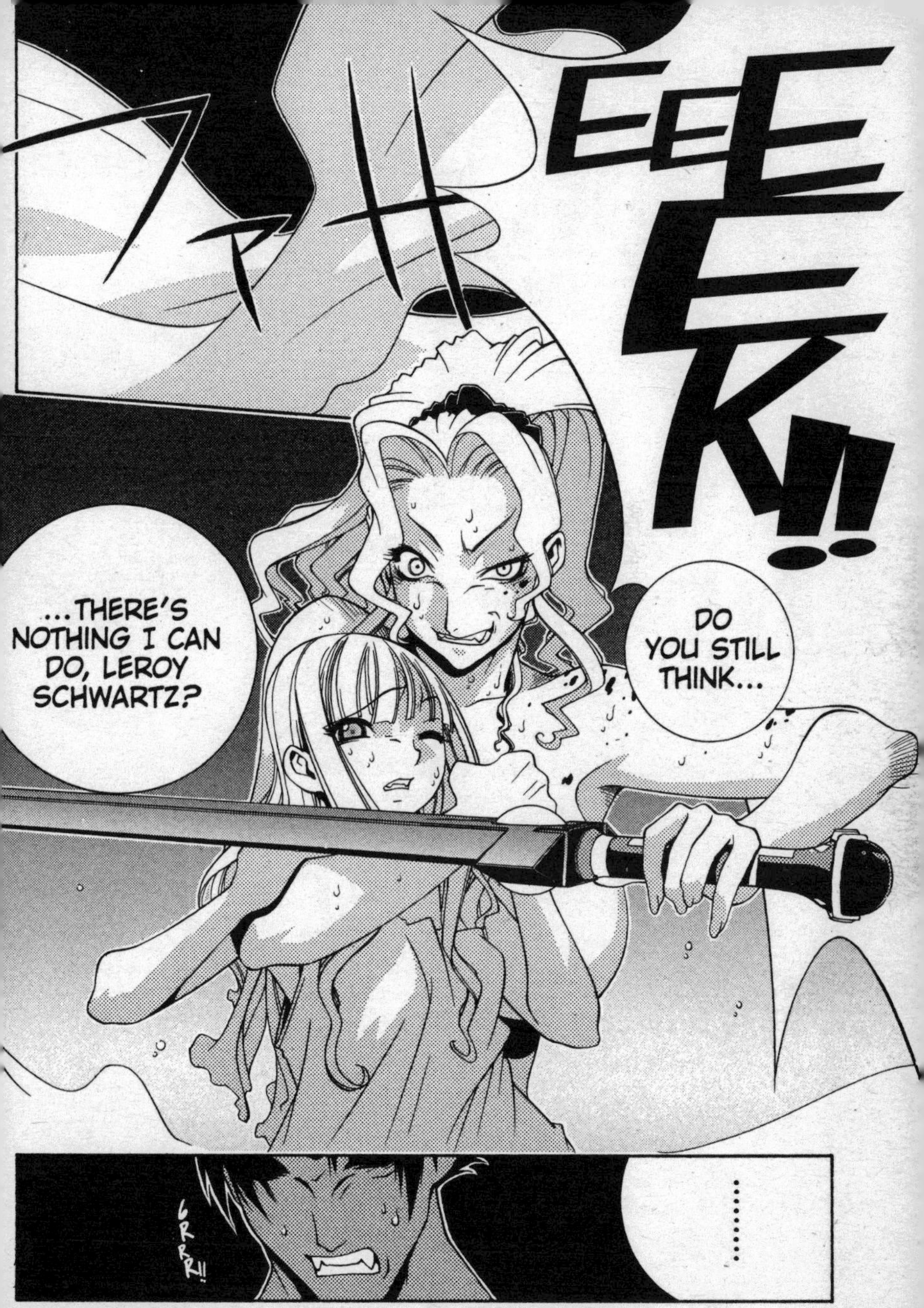
EEEEEK!!
DO YOU STILL THINK...
...THERE'S NOTHING I CAN DO, LEROY SCHWARTZ?
....
GRRR!!

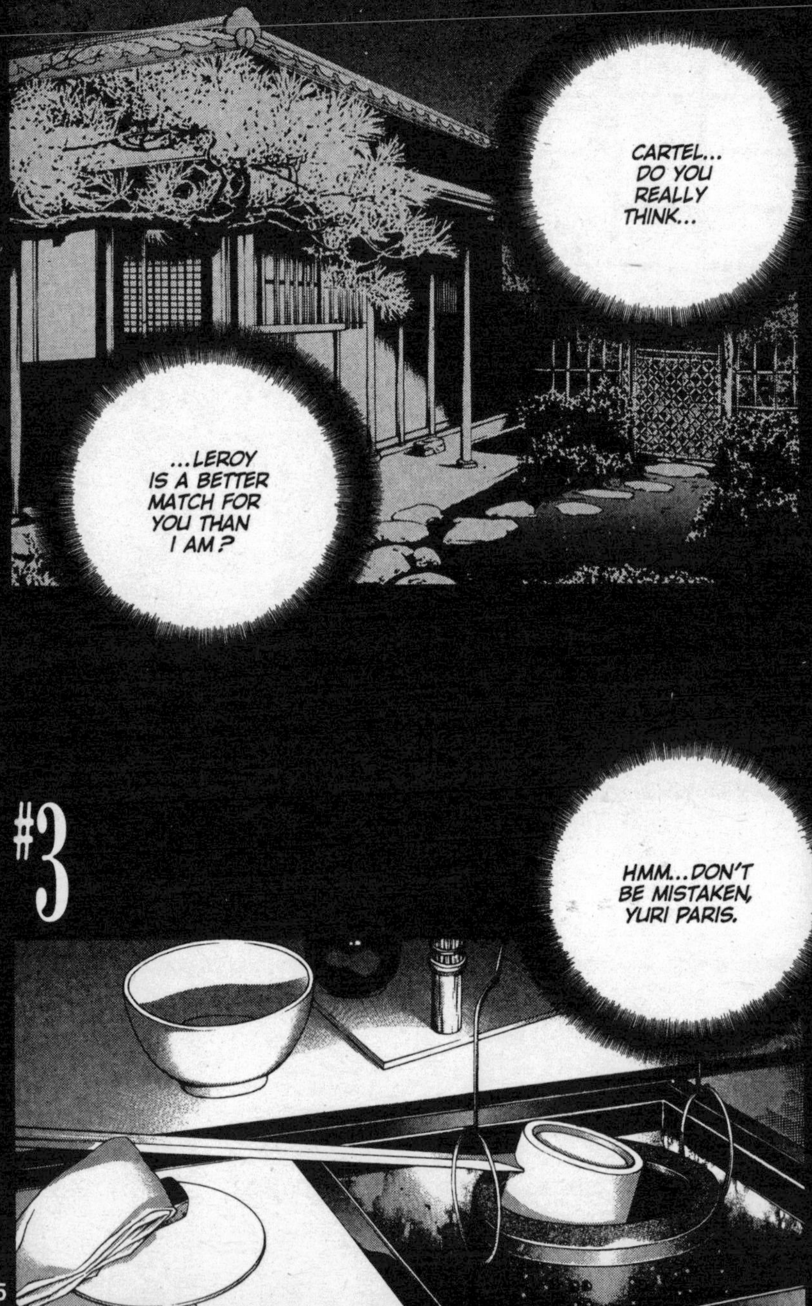
CARTEL... DO YOU REALLY THINK...
...LEROY IS A BETTER MATCH FOR YOU THAN I AM?
#3
HMM...DON'T BE MISTAKEN, YURI PARIS.

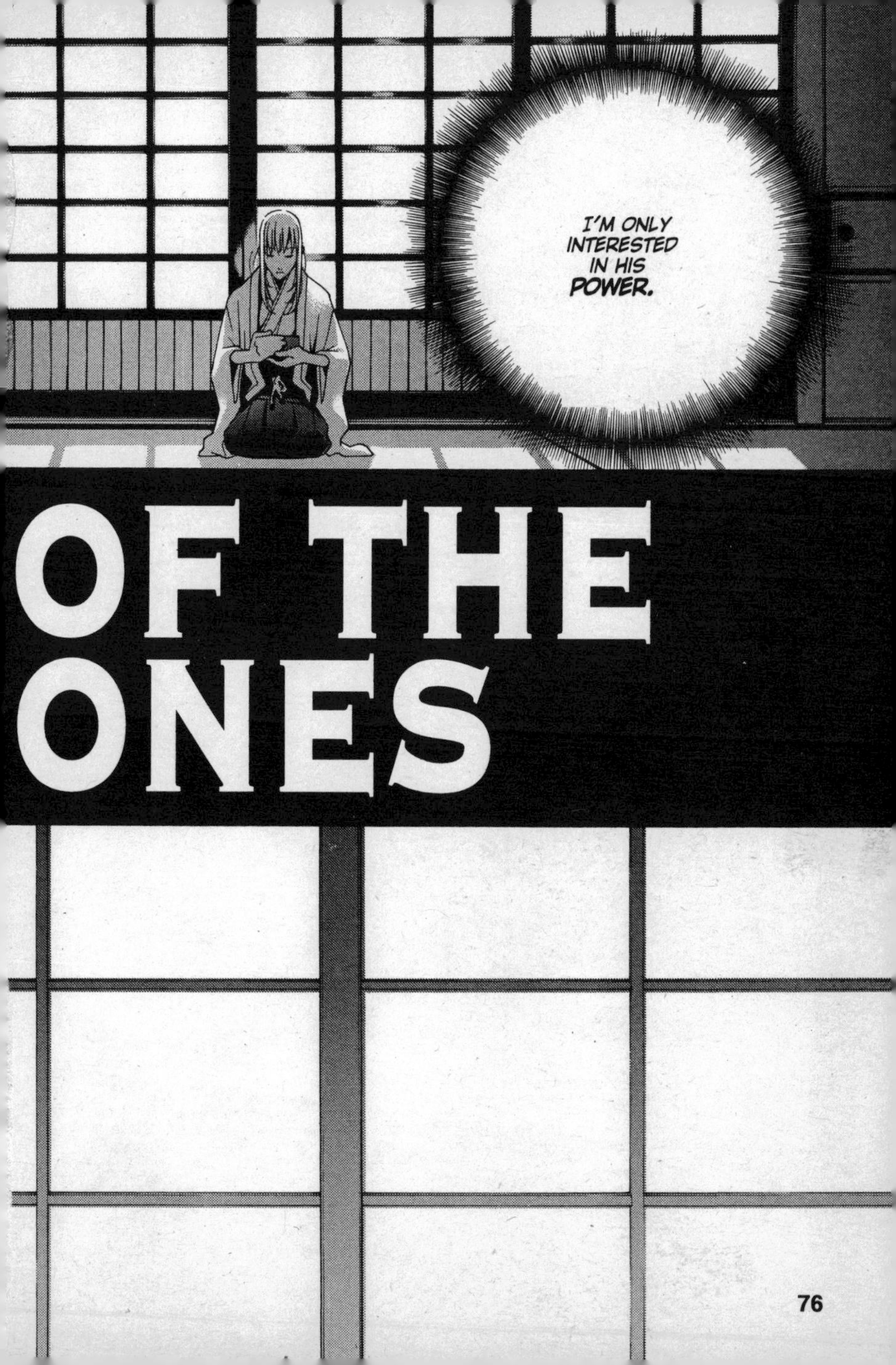
I'M ONLY INTERESTED IN HIS POWER.
OF THE ONES

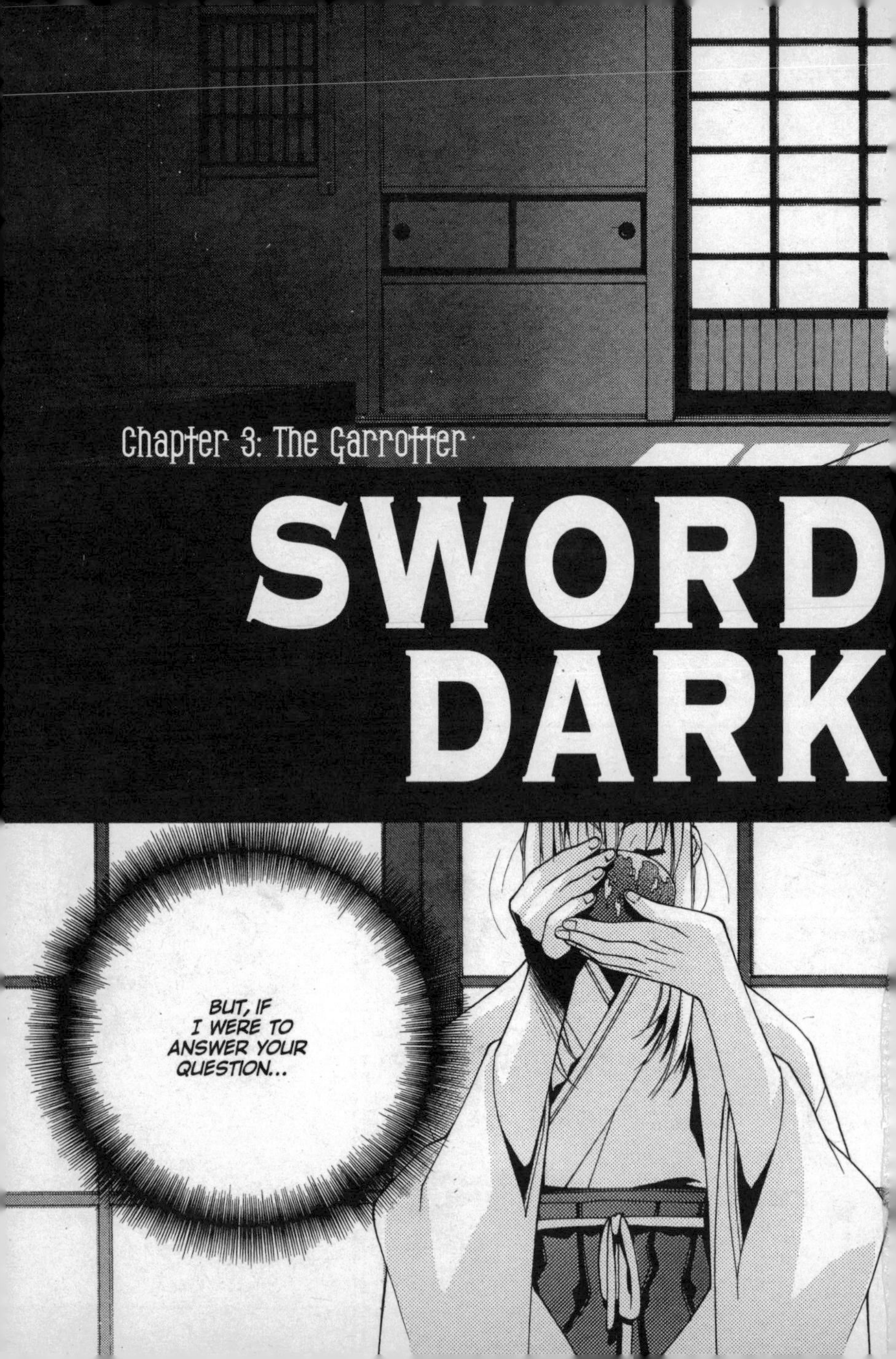
Chapter 3: The Garrotter
SWORD
DARK
BUT, IF I WERE TO ANSWER YOUR QUESTION...

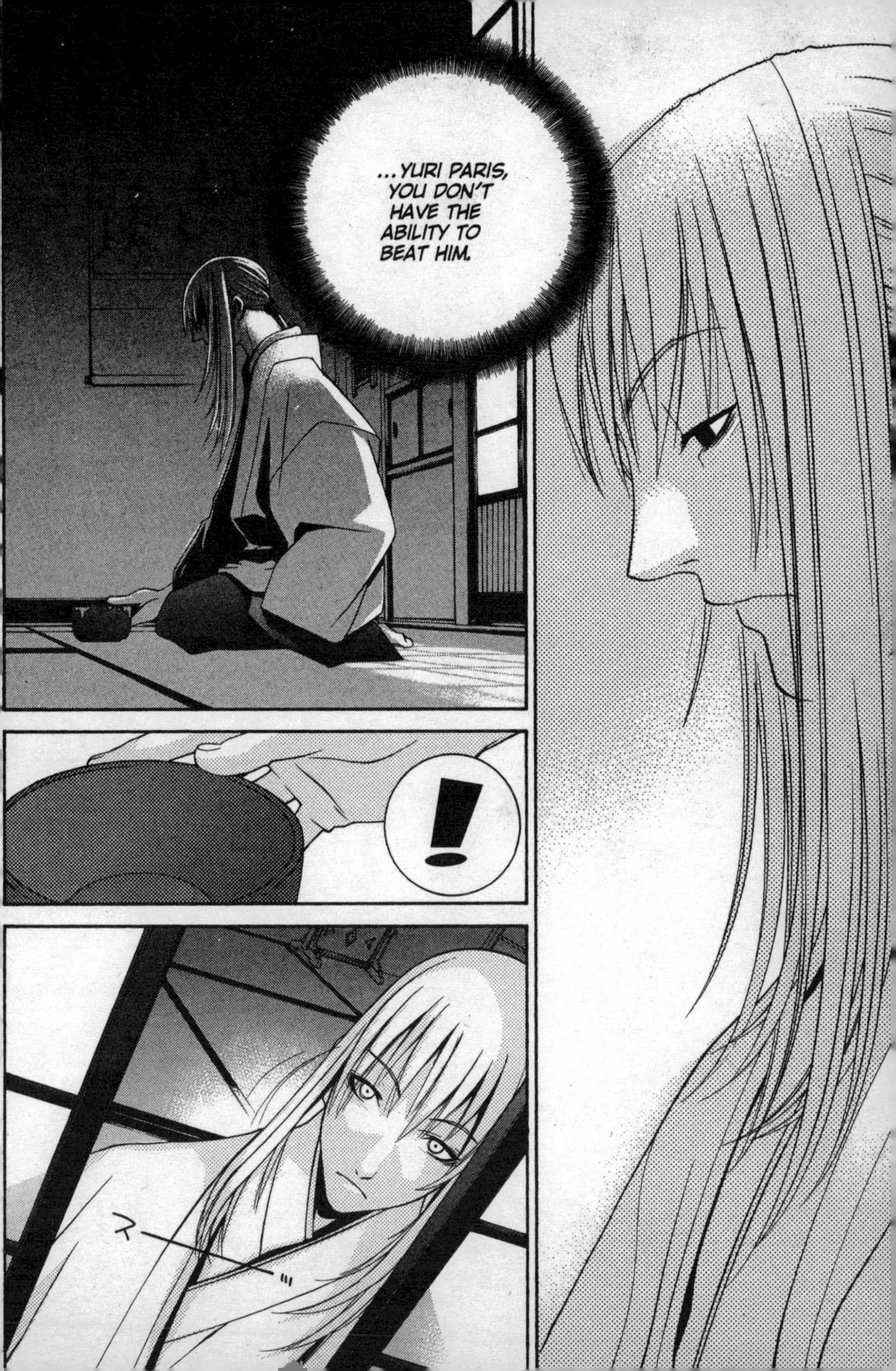
...YURI PARIS, YOU DON'T HAVE THE ABILITY TO BEAT HIM.
!
ス

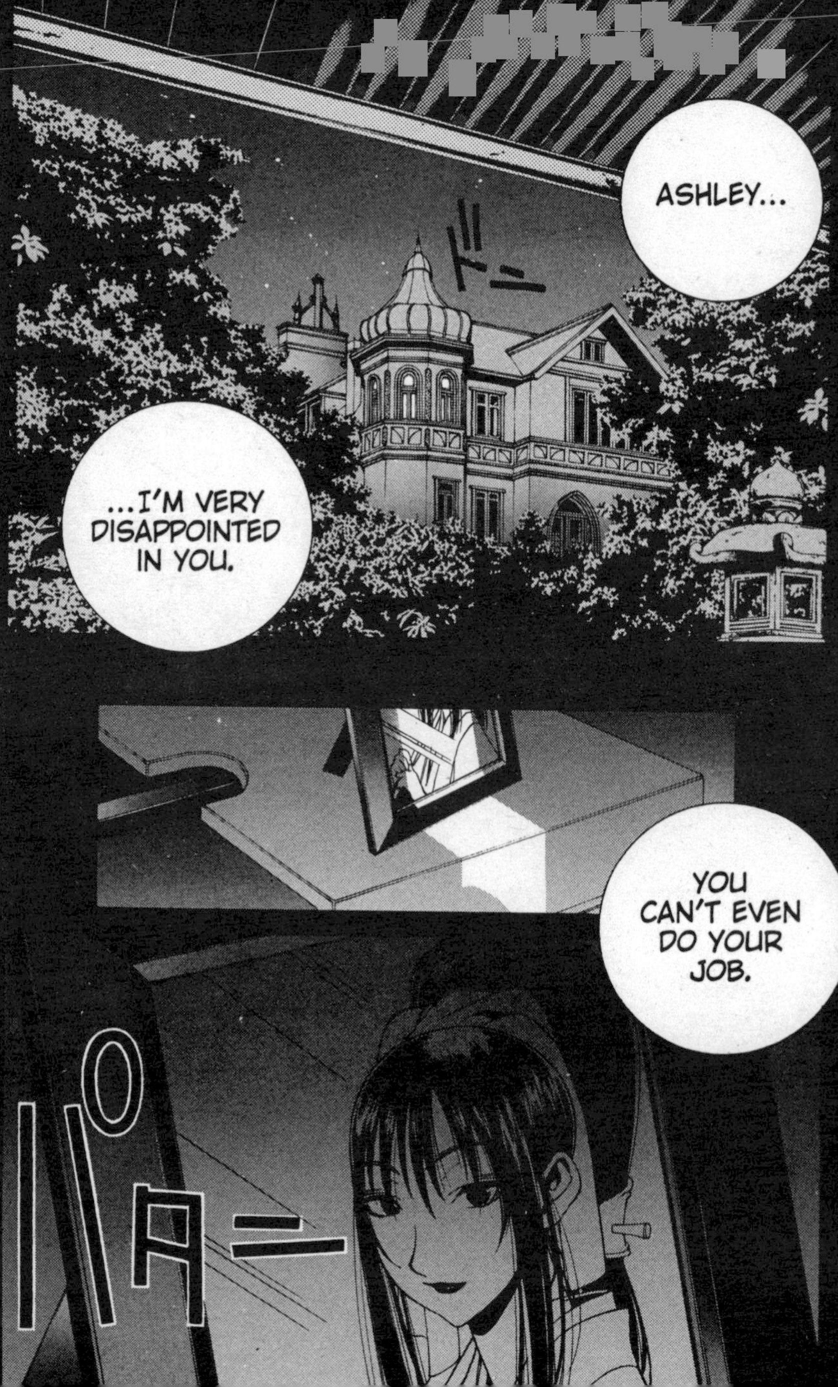
ASHLEY...
...I'M VERY DISAPPOINTED IN YOU.
YOU CAN'T EVEN DO YOUR JOB.

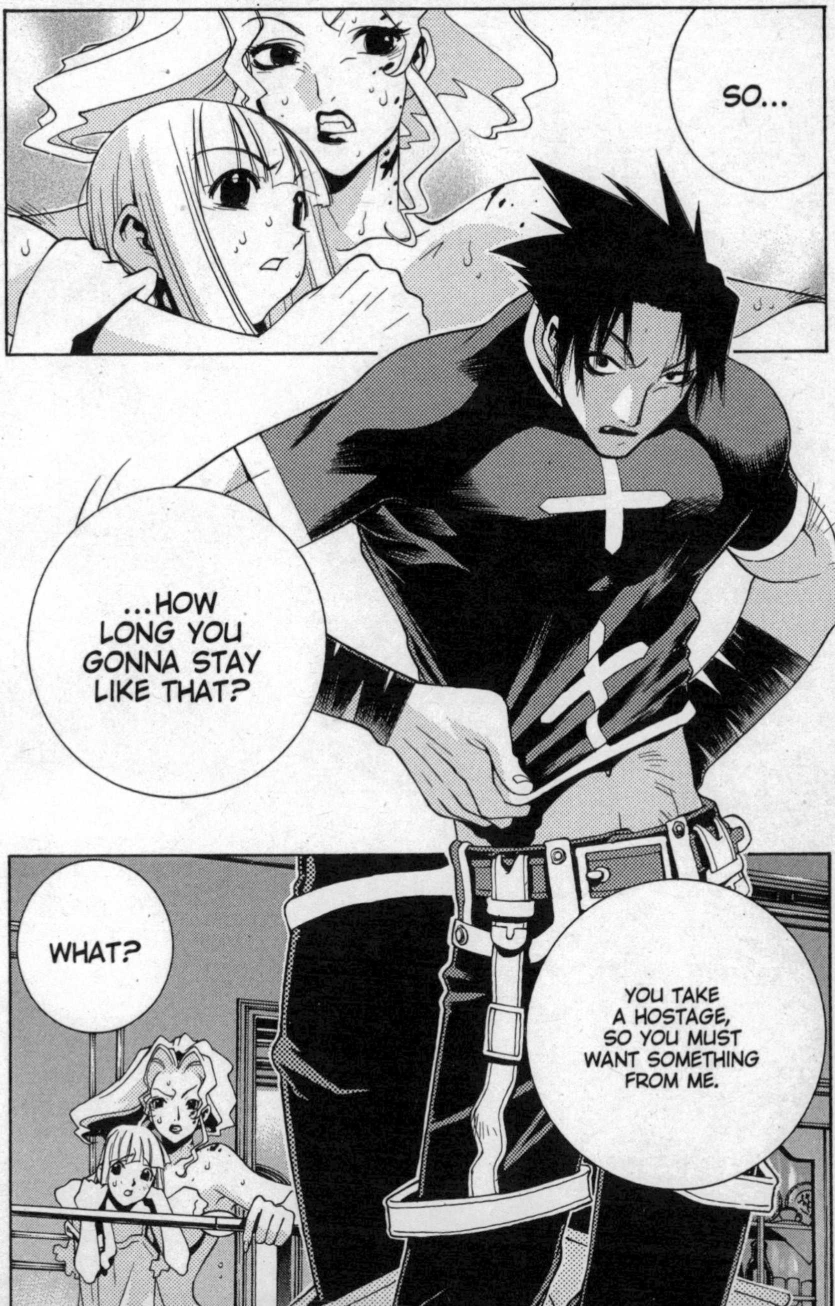
SO...
...HOW LONG YOU GONNA STAY LIKE THAT?
YOU TAKE A HOSTAGE, SO YOU MUST WANT SOMETHING FROM ME.
WHAT?

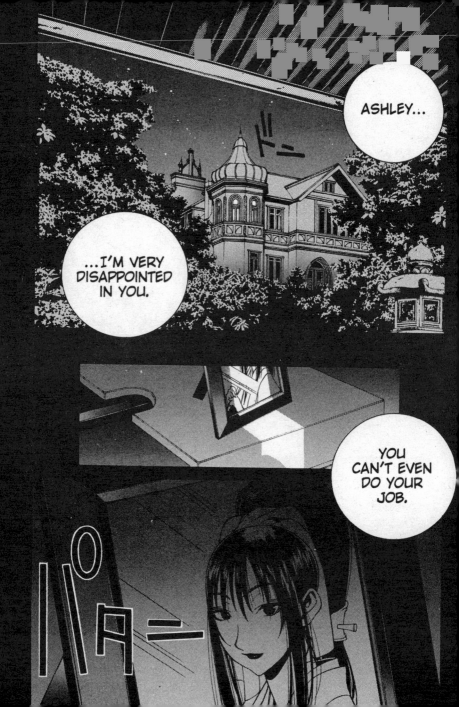

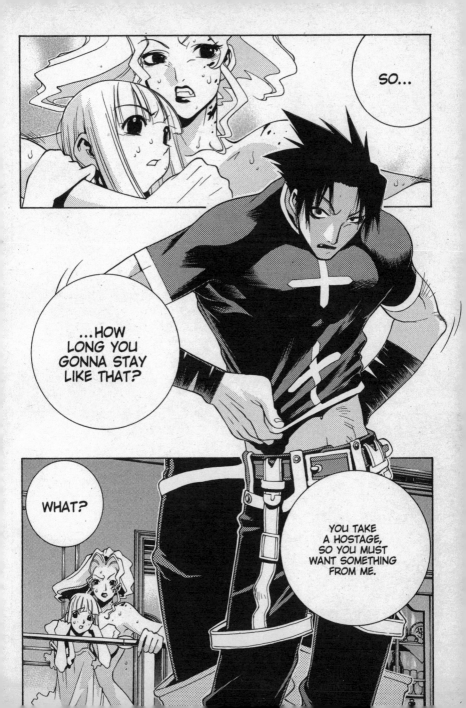

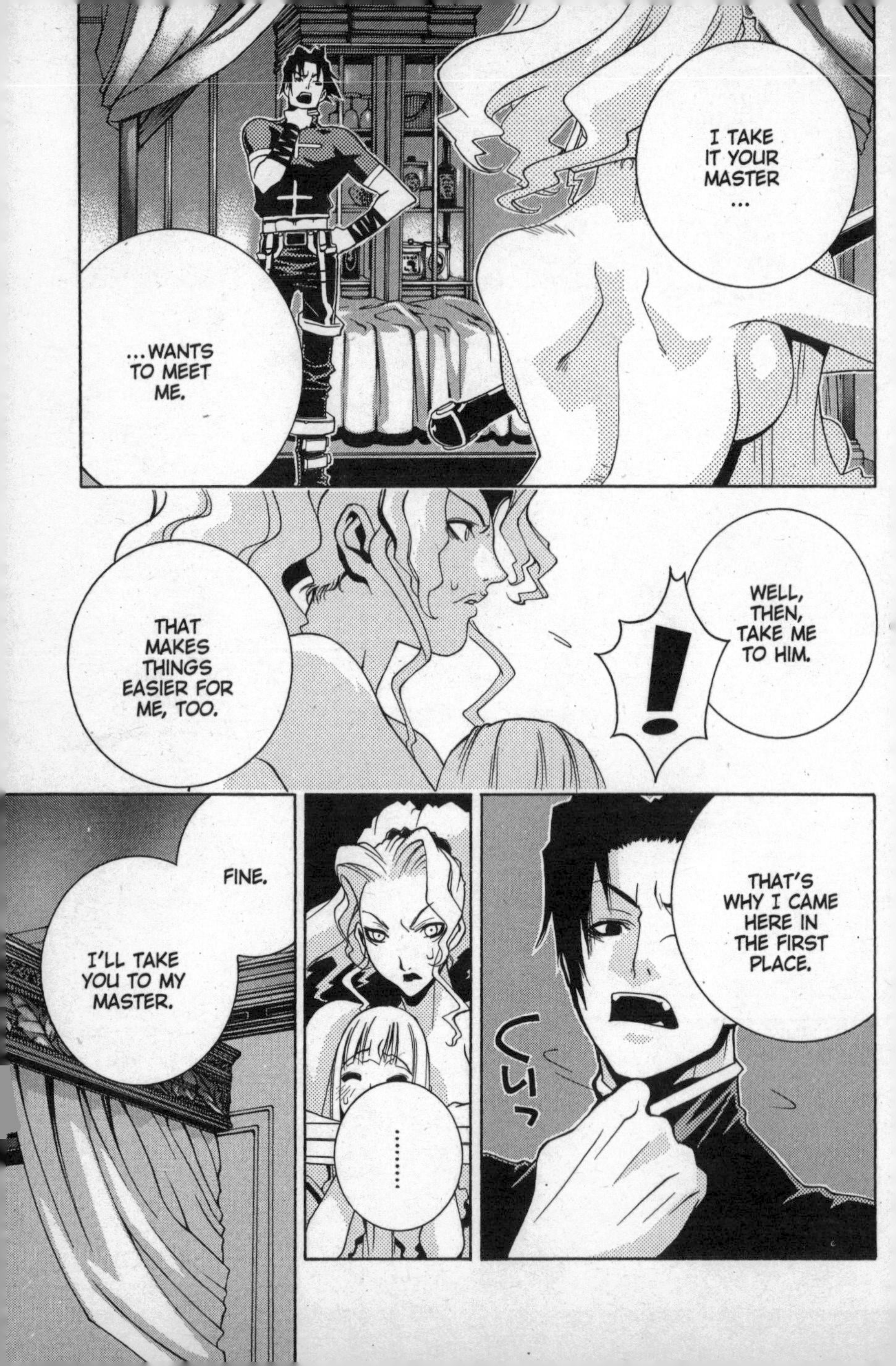
I TAKE IT YOUR MASTER ...
...WANTS TO MEET ME.
WELL, THEN, TAKE ME TO HIM.
!
THAT MAKES THINGS EASIER FOR ME, TOO.
THAT'S WHY I CAME HERE IN THE FIRST PLACE.
......
FINE.
I'LL TAKE YOU TO MY MASTER.

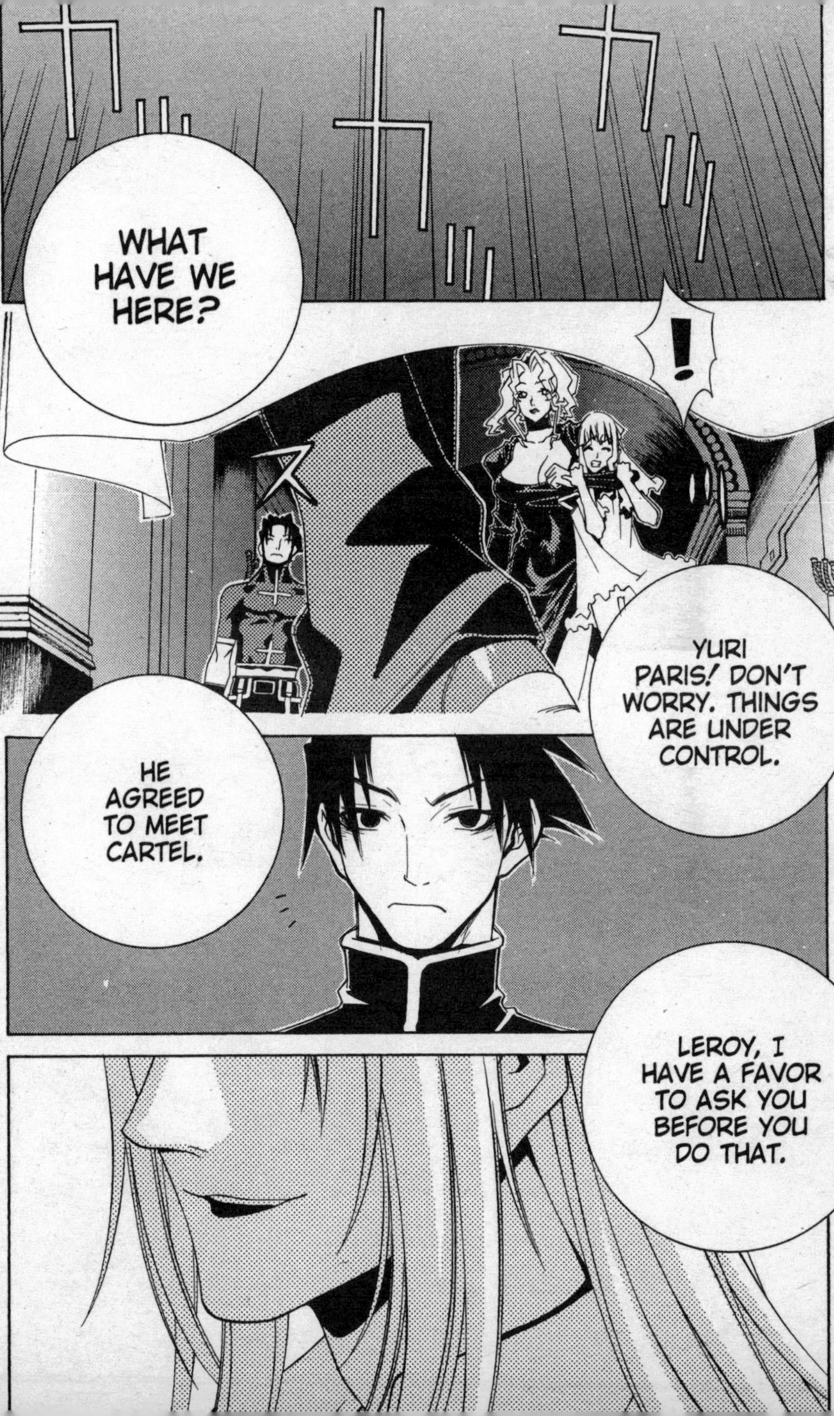
WHAT HAVE WE HERE?
!
YURI PARIS! DON'T WORRY. THINGS ARE UNDER CONTROL.
HE AGREED TO MEET CARTEL.
LEROY, I HAVE A FAVOR TO ASK YOU BEFORE YOU DO THAT.

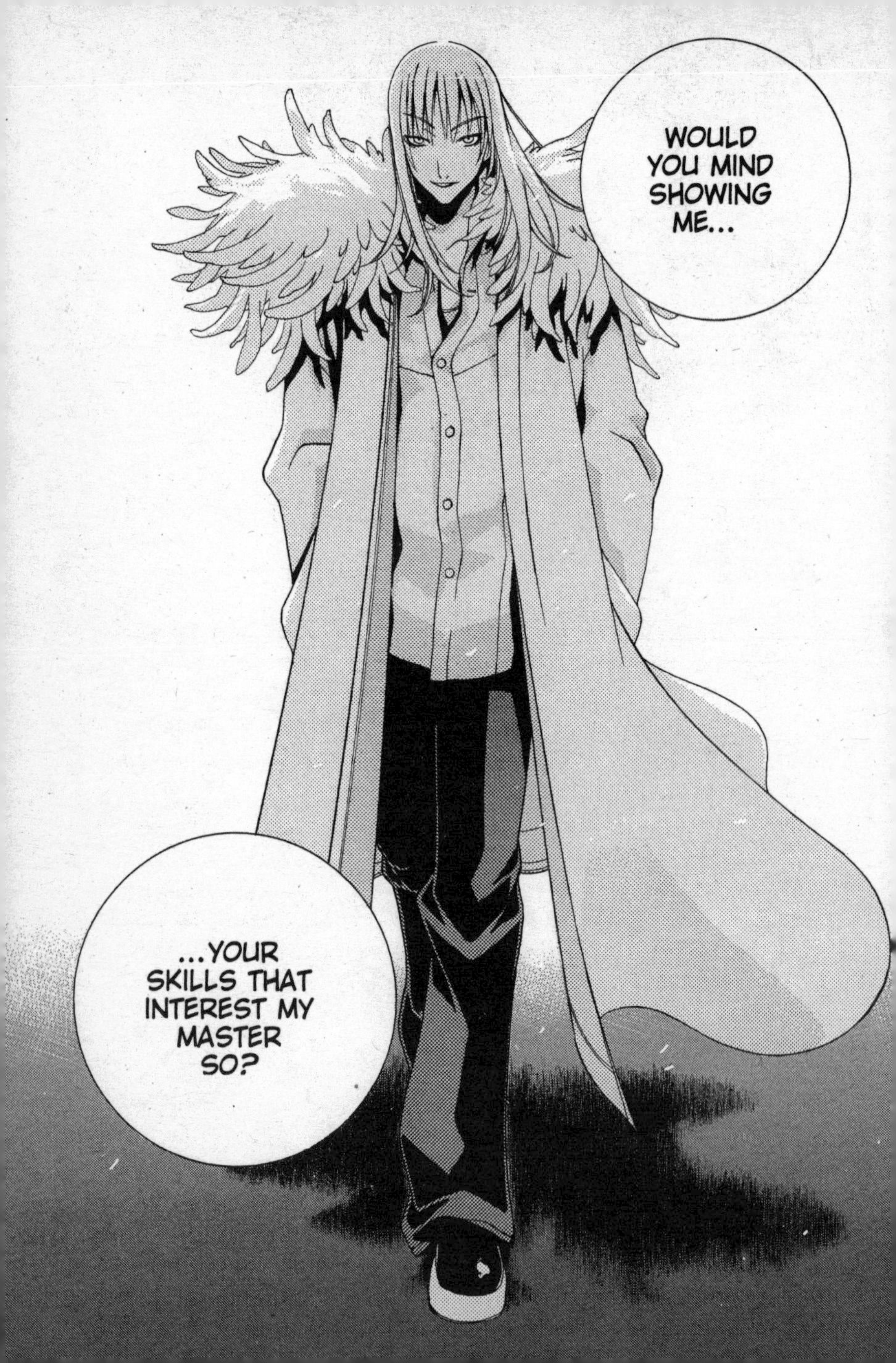
WOULD YOU MIND SHOWING ME...
...YOUR SKILLS THAT INTEREST MY MASTER SO?

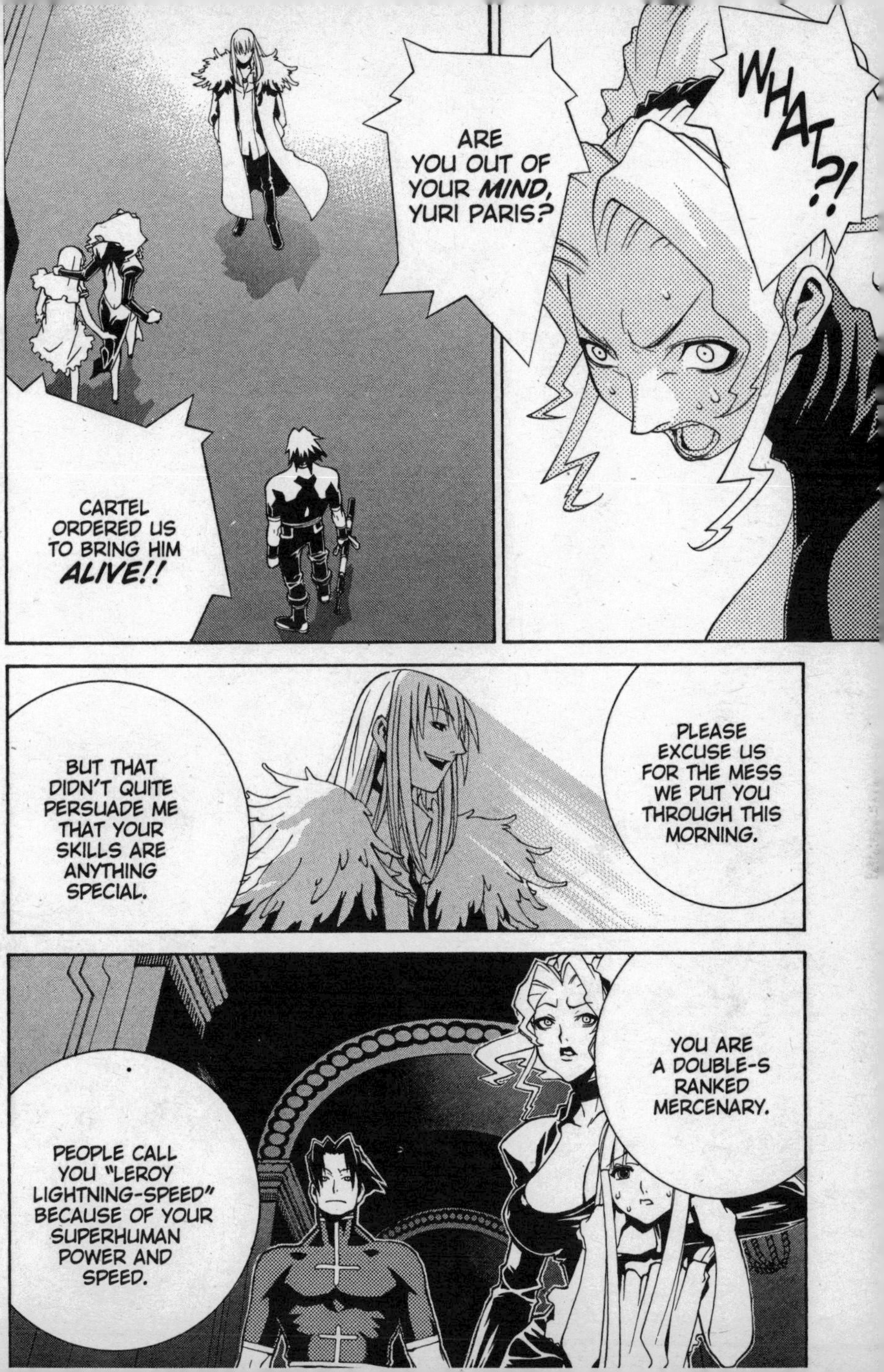
WHAT?!
ARE YOU OUT OF YOUR MIND, YURI PARIS?
CARTEL ORDERED US TO BRING HIM ALIVE!!
PLEASE EXCUSE US FOR THE MESS WE PUT YOU THROUGH THIS MORNING.
BUT THAT DIDN'T QUITE PERSUADE ME THAT YOUR SKILLS ARE ANYTHING SPECIAL.
YOU ARE A DOUBLE-S RANKED MERCENARY.
PEOPLE CALL YOU "LEROY LIGHTNING-SPEED" BECAUSE OF YOUR SUPERHUMAN POWER AND SPEED.

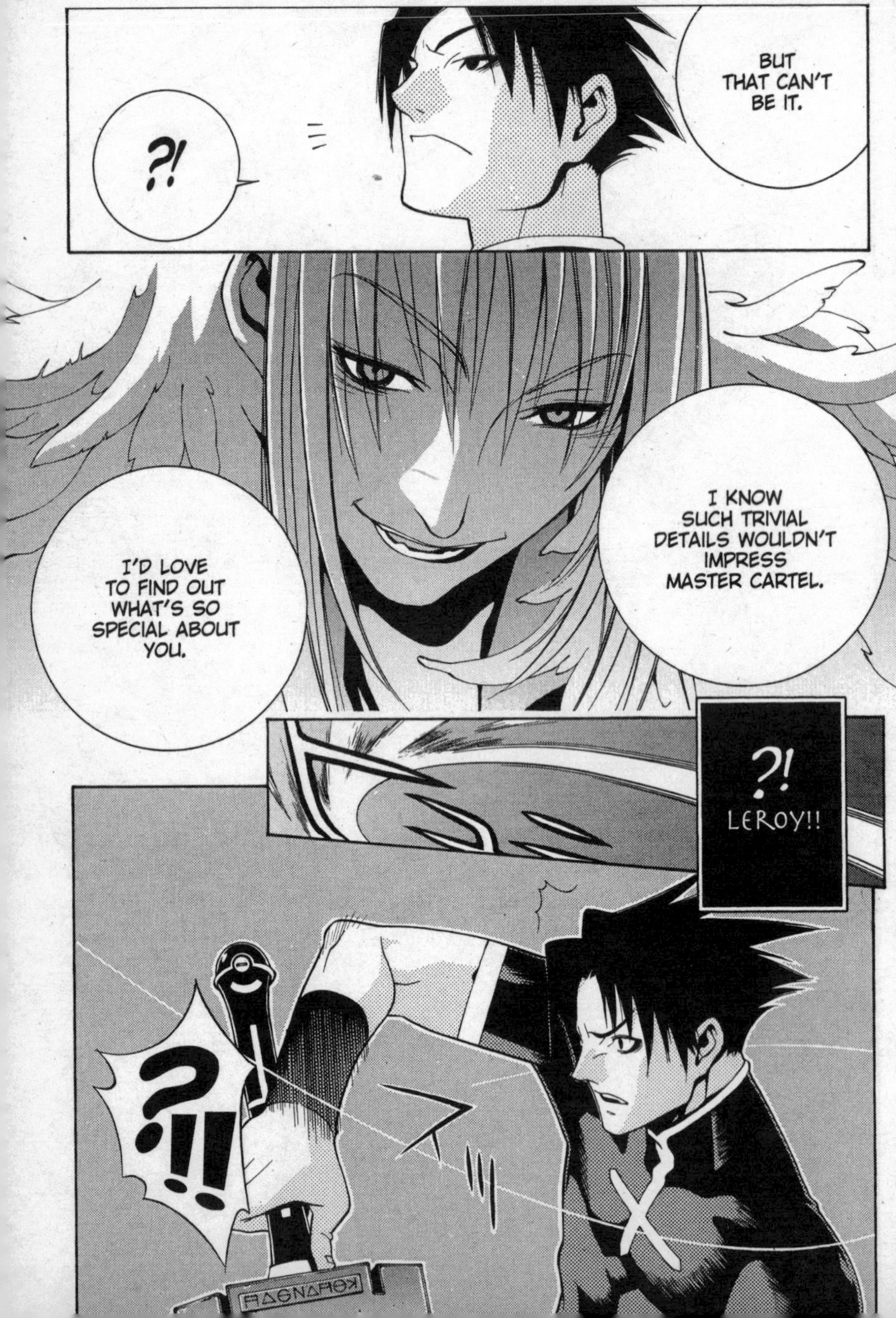
BUT THAT CAN'T BE IT.
?!
I KNOW SUCH TRIVIAL DETAILS WOULDN'T IMPRESS MASTER CARTEL.
I'D LOVE TO FIND OUT WHAT'S SO SPECIAL ABOUT YOU.
?! LEROY!!
?!!

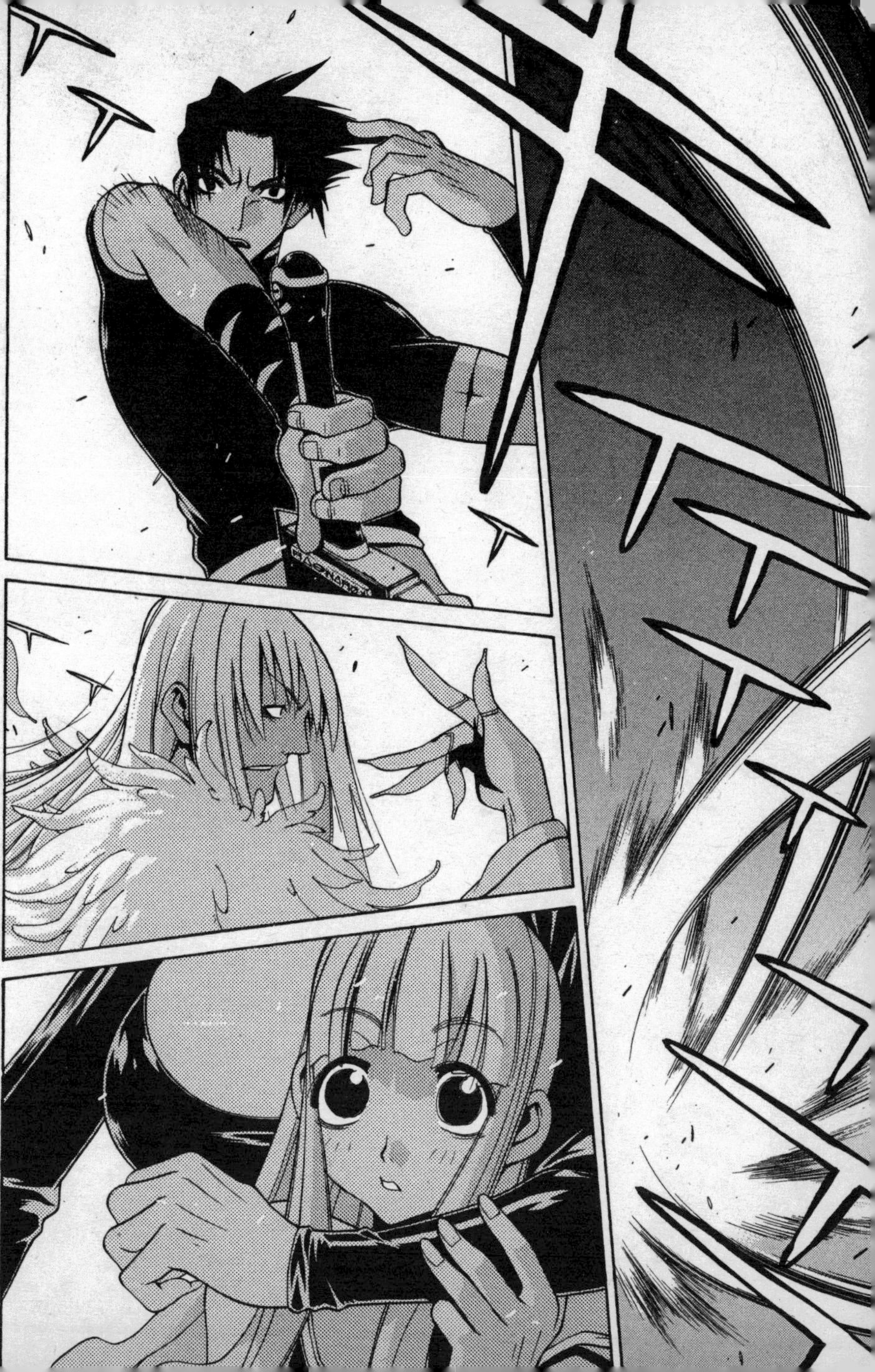

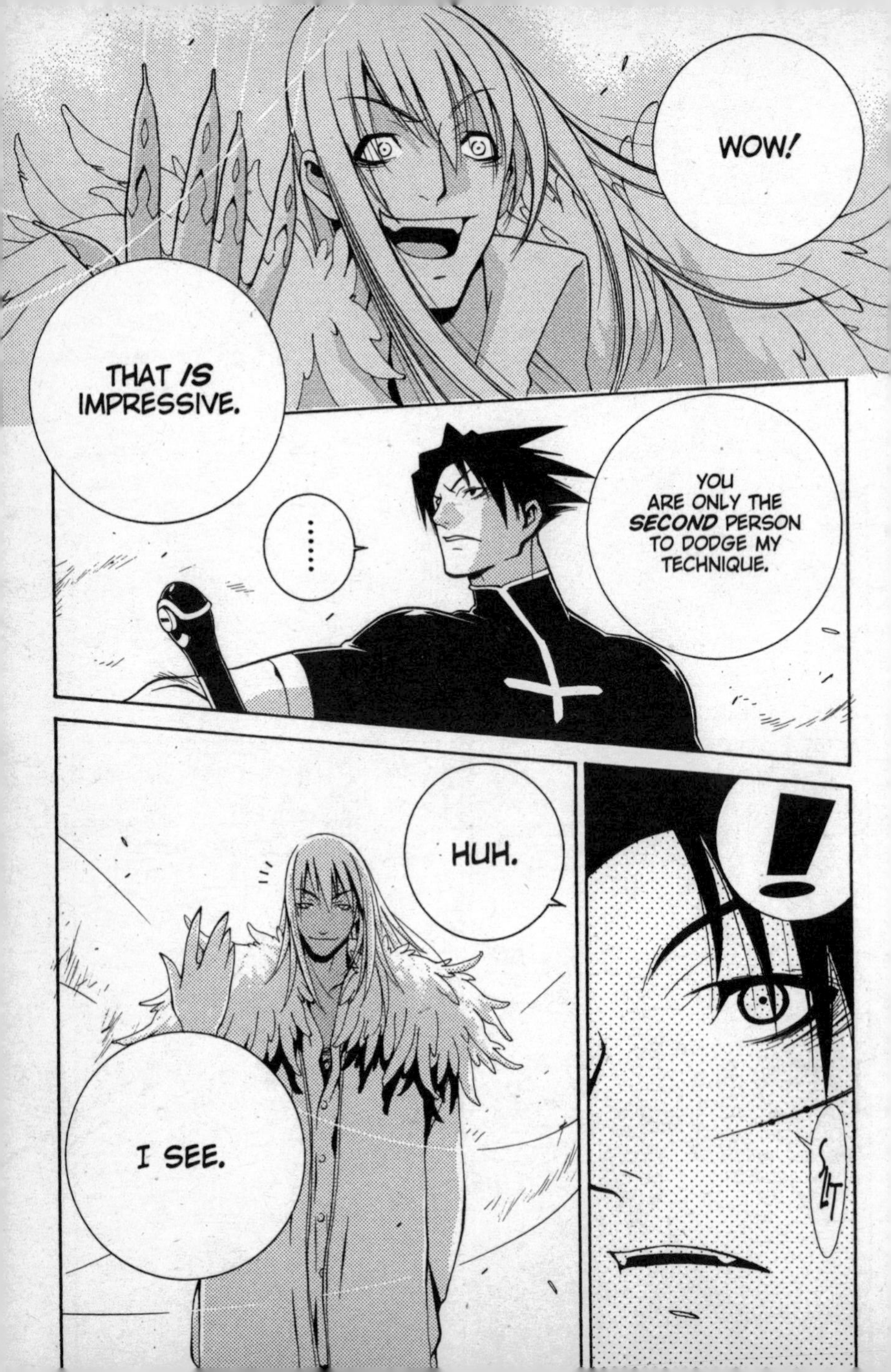
WOW!
THAT *IS* IMPRESSIVE.
YOU ARE ONLY THE *SECOND* PERSON TO DODGE MY TECHNIQUE.
.....
!
SLIT
HUH.
I SEE.

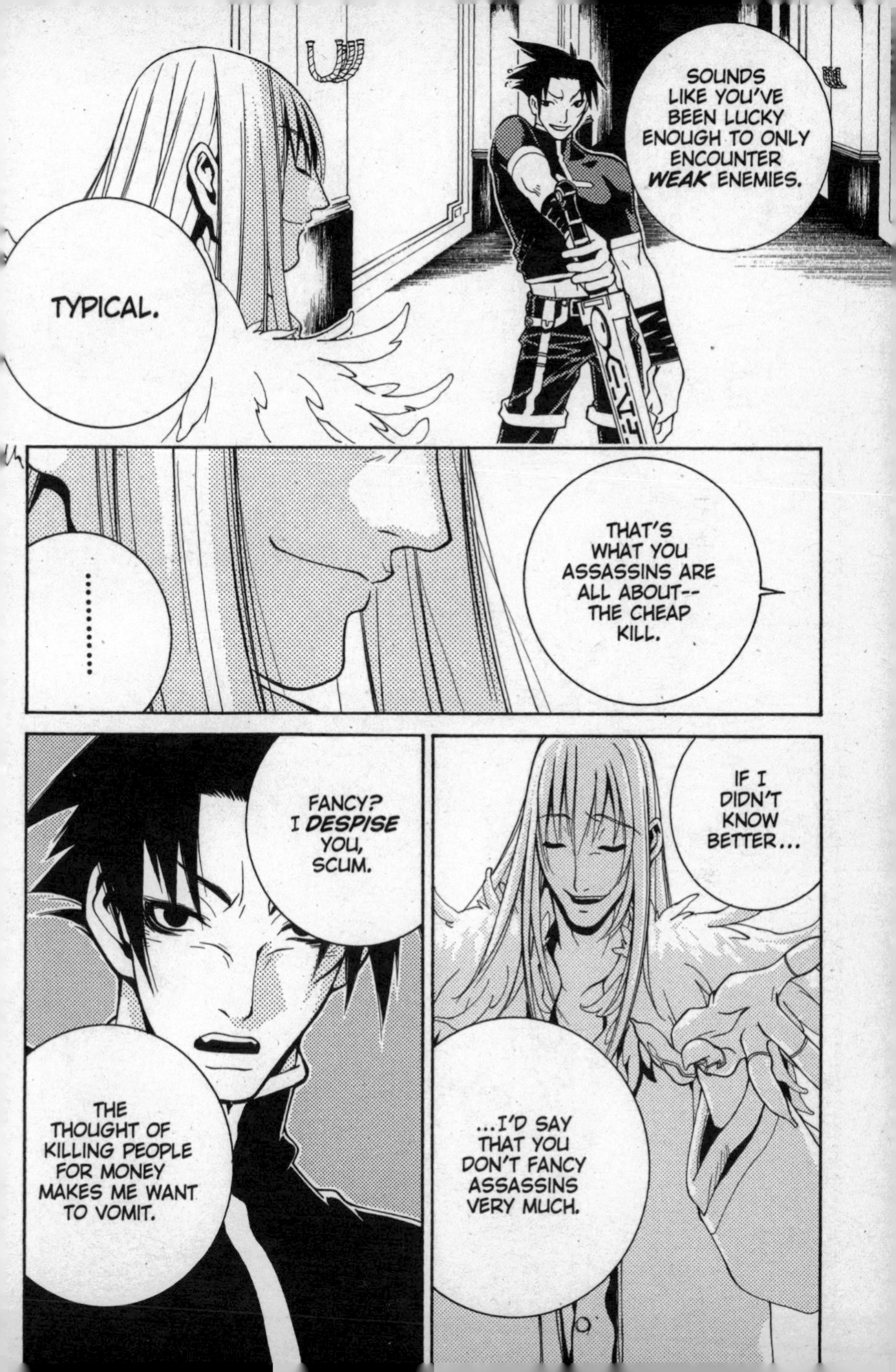
SOUNDS LIKE YOU'VE BEEN LUCKY ENOUGH TO ONLY ENCOUNTER WEAK ENEMIES.
TYPICAL.
THAT'S WHAT YOU ASSASSINS ARE ALL ABOUT-- THE CHEAP KILL.
....
IF I DIDN'T KNOW BETTER...
...I'D SAY THAT YOU DON'T FANCY ASSASSINS VERY MUCH.
FANCY? I DESPISE YOU, SCUM.
THE THOUGHT OF KILLING PEOPLE FOR MONEY MAKES ME WANT TO VOMIT.

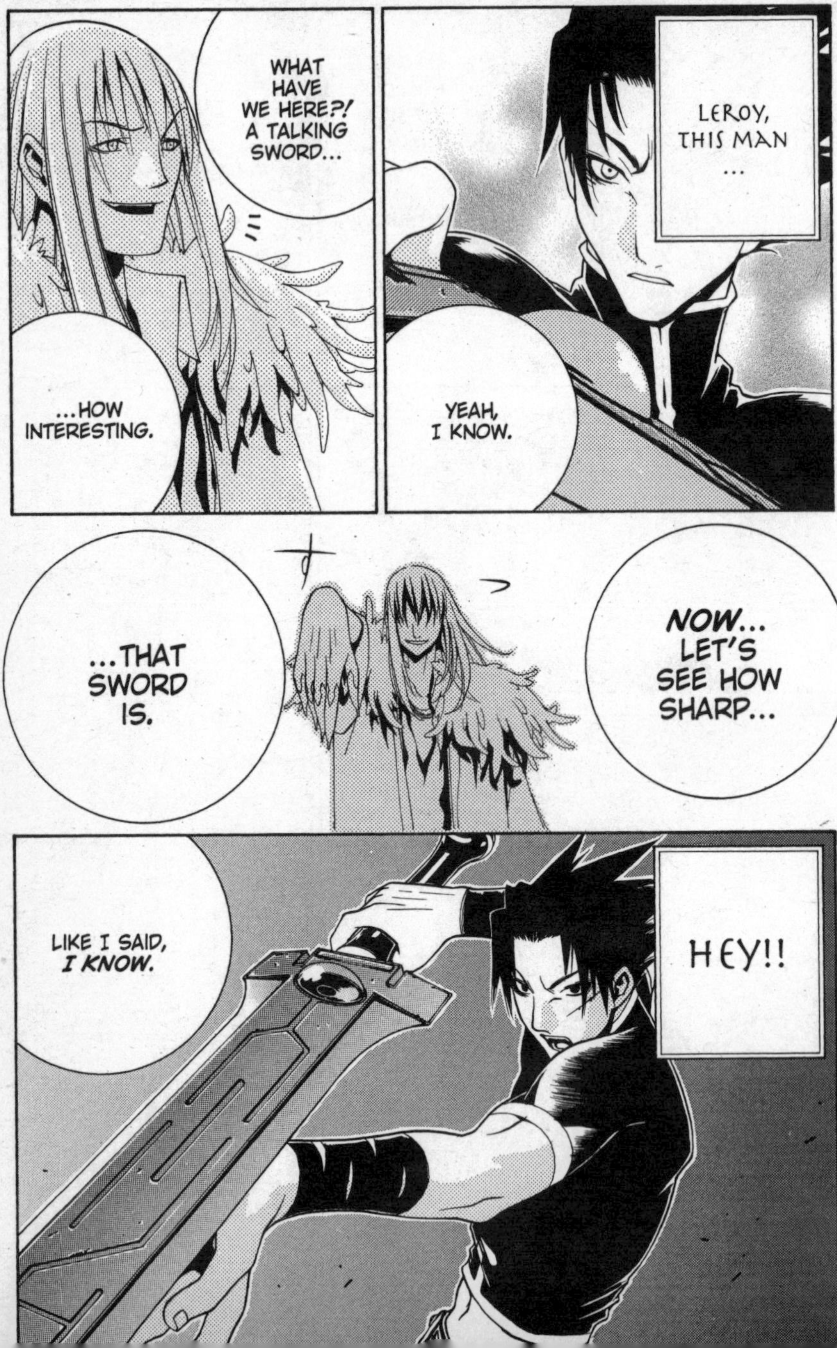
LEROY, THIS MAN ...
YEAH, I KNOW.
WHAT HAVE WE HERE?! A TALKING SWORD...
...HOW INTERESTING.
NOW... LET'S SEE HOW SHARP...
...THAT SWORD IS.
HEY!!
LIKE I SAID, I KNOW.

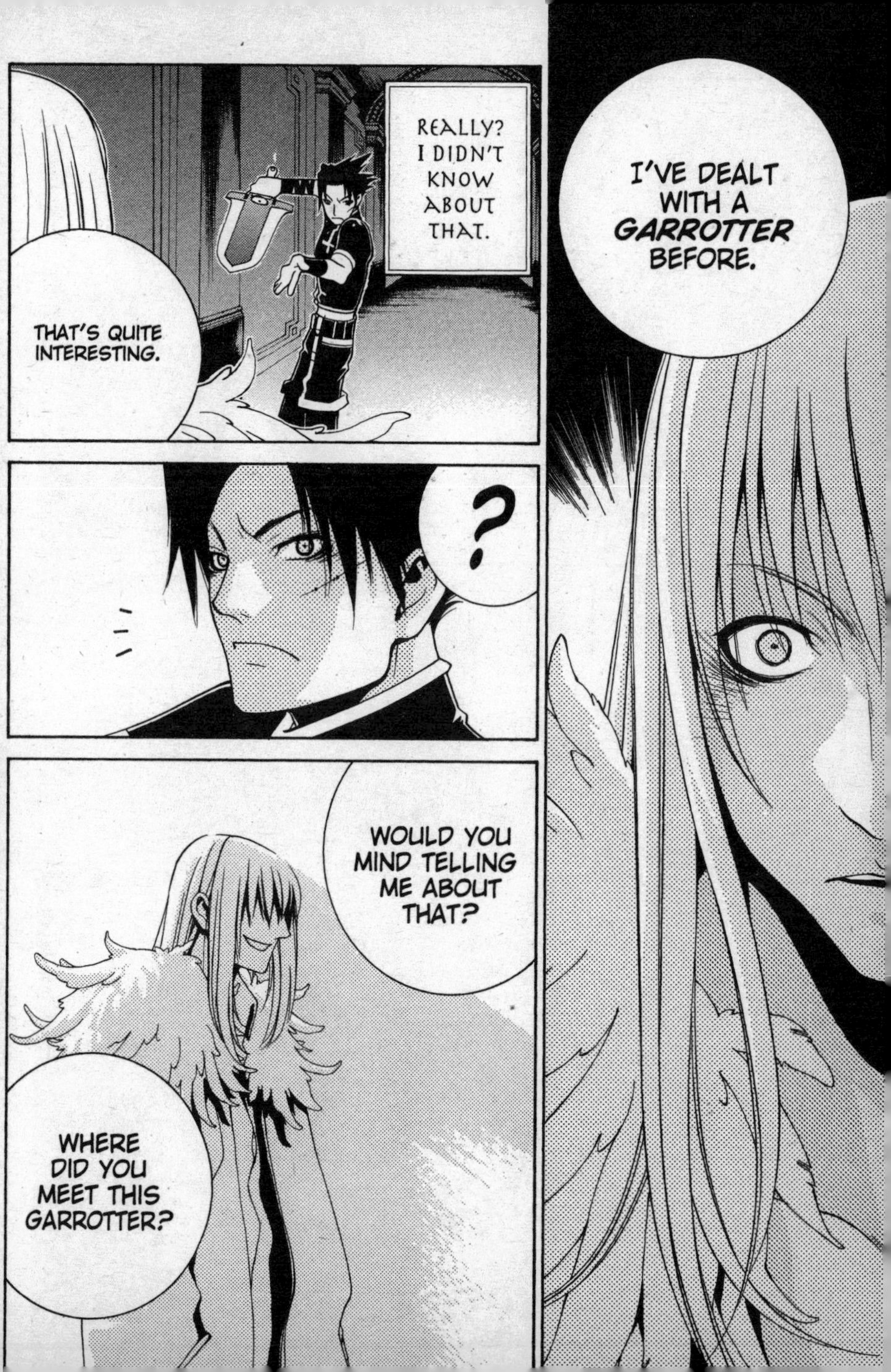
I'VE DEALT WITH A GARROTTER BEFORE.
REALLY? I DIDN'T KNOW ABOUT THAT.
THAT'S QUITE INTERESTING.
?
WOULD YOU MIND TELLING ME ABOUT THAT?
WHERE DID YOU MEET THIS GARROTTER?

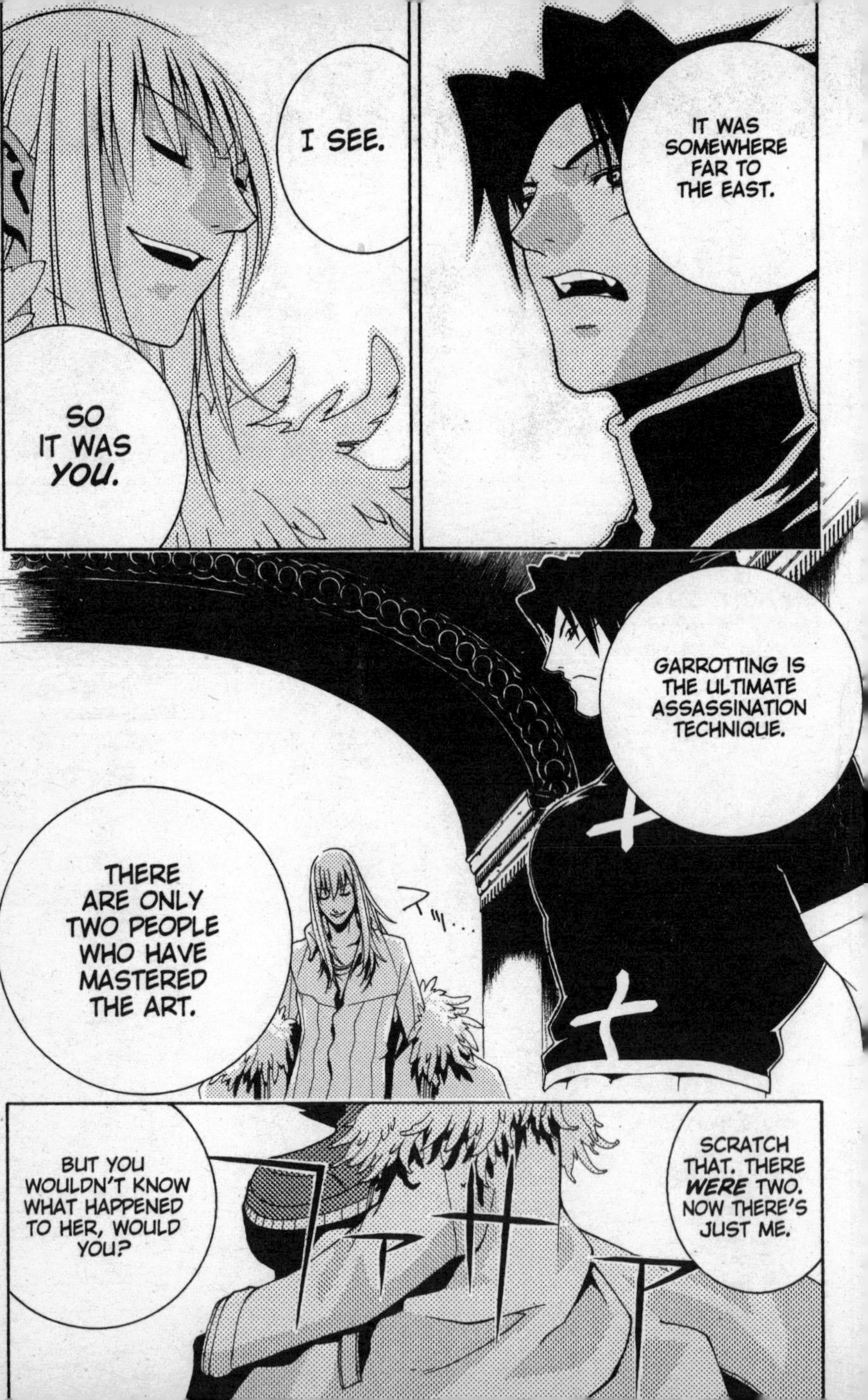
IT WAS SOMEWHERE FAR TO THE EAST.
I SEE.
SO IT WAS *YOU.*
GARROTTING IS THE ULTIMATE ASSASSINATION TECHNIQUE.
THERE ARE ONLY TWO PEOPLE WHO HAVE MASTERED THE ART.
スッ…
SCRATCH THAT. THERE *WERE* TWO. NOW THERE'S JUST ME.
BUT YOU WOULDN'T KNOW WHAT HAPPENED TO HER, WOULD YOU?

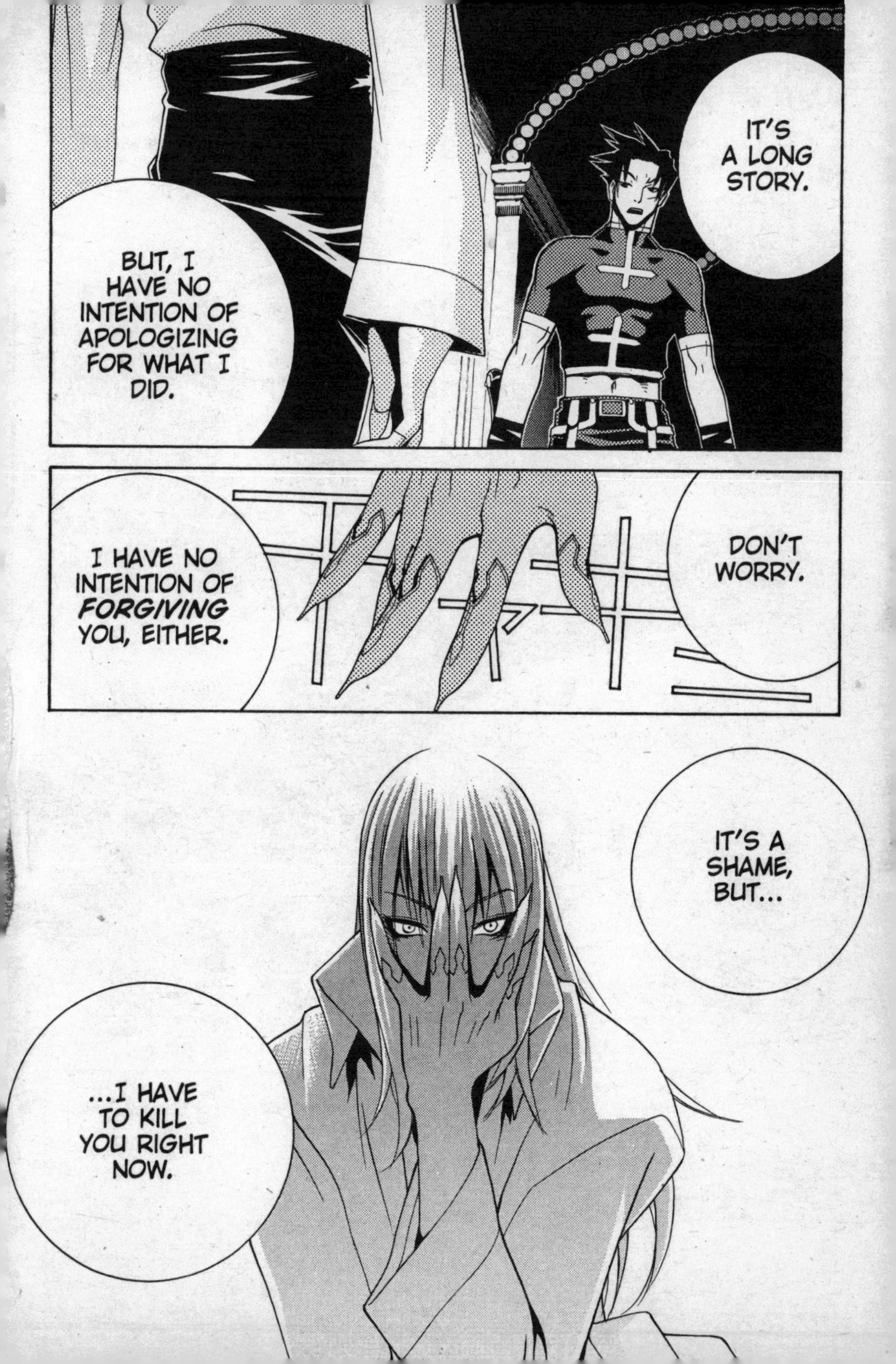
IT'S A LONG STORY.
BUT, I HAVE NO INTENTION OF APOLOGIZING FOR WHAT I DID.
DON'T WORRY.
I HAVE NO INTENTION OF *FORGIVING* YOU, EITHER.
IT'S A SHAME, BUT...
...I HAVE TO KILL YOU RIGHT NOW.

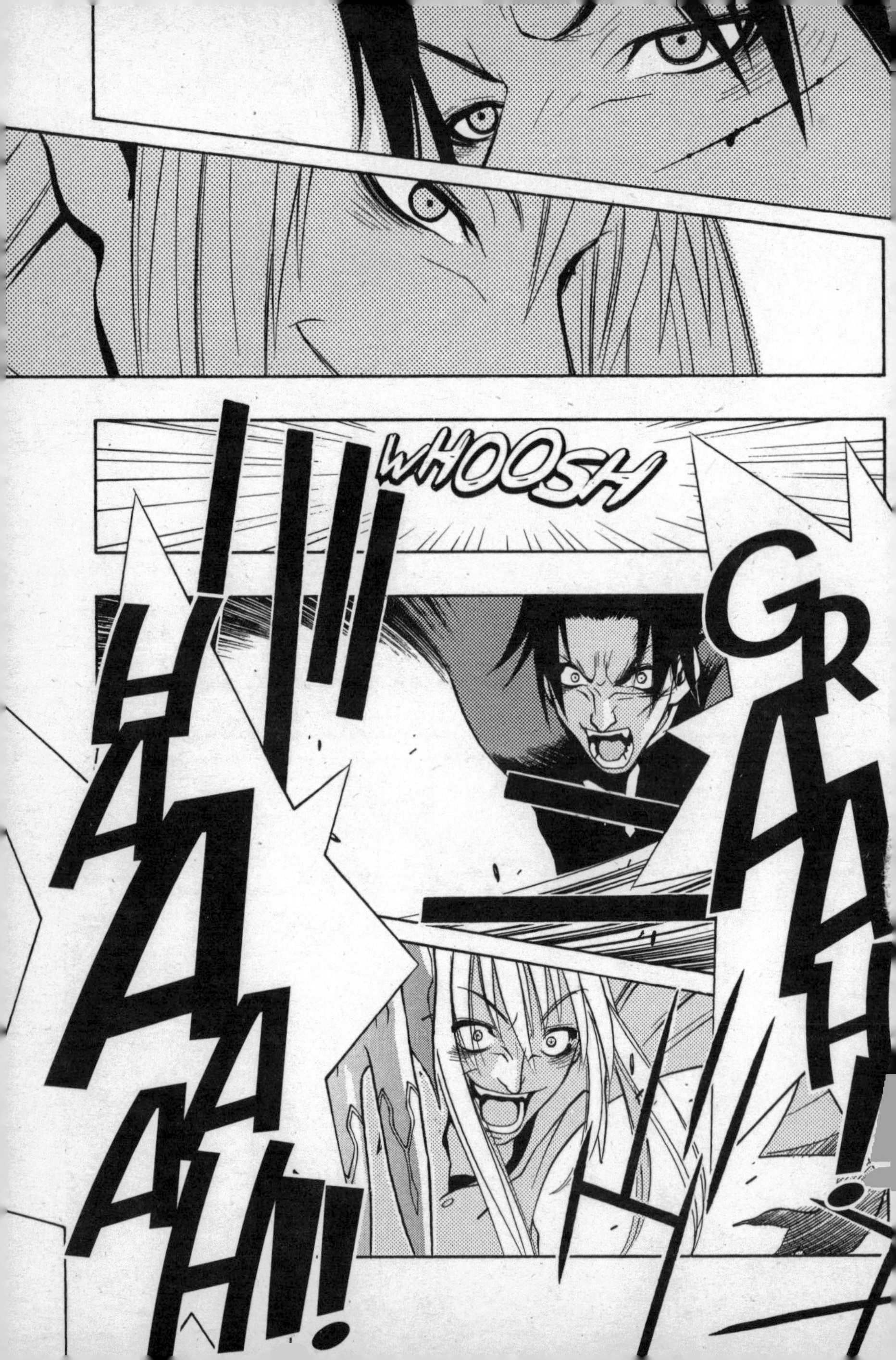
WHOOSH
GRAAAH!
HAAAAH!

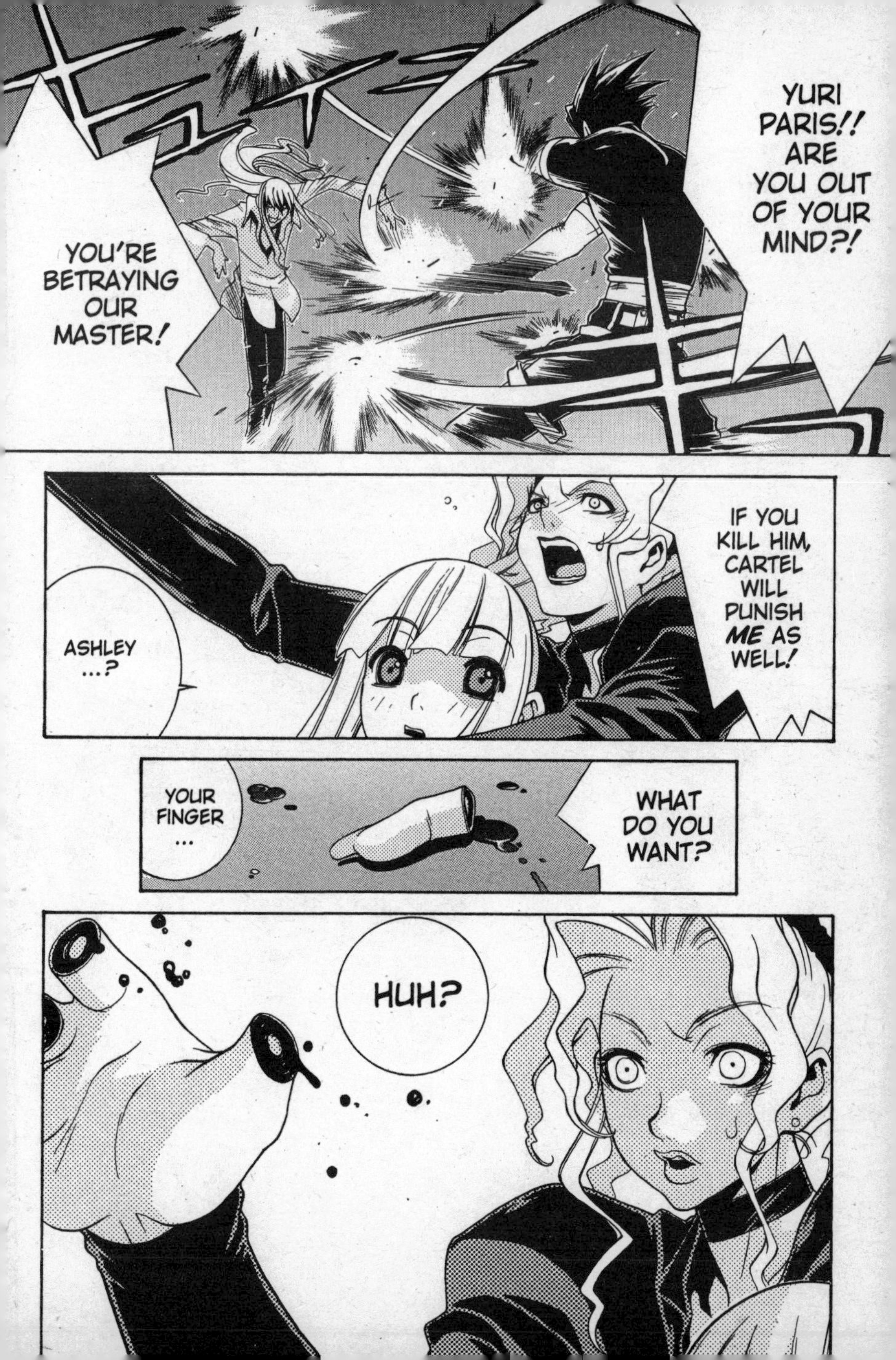
YURI PARIS!! ARE YOU OUT OF YOUR MIND?!
YOU'RE BETRAYING OUR MASTER!
IF YOU KILL HIM, CARTEL WILL PUNISH *ME* AS WELL!
ASHLEY ...?
WHAT DO YOU WANT?
YOUR FINGER ...
HUH?

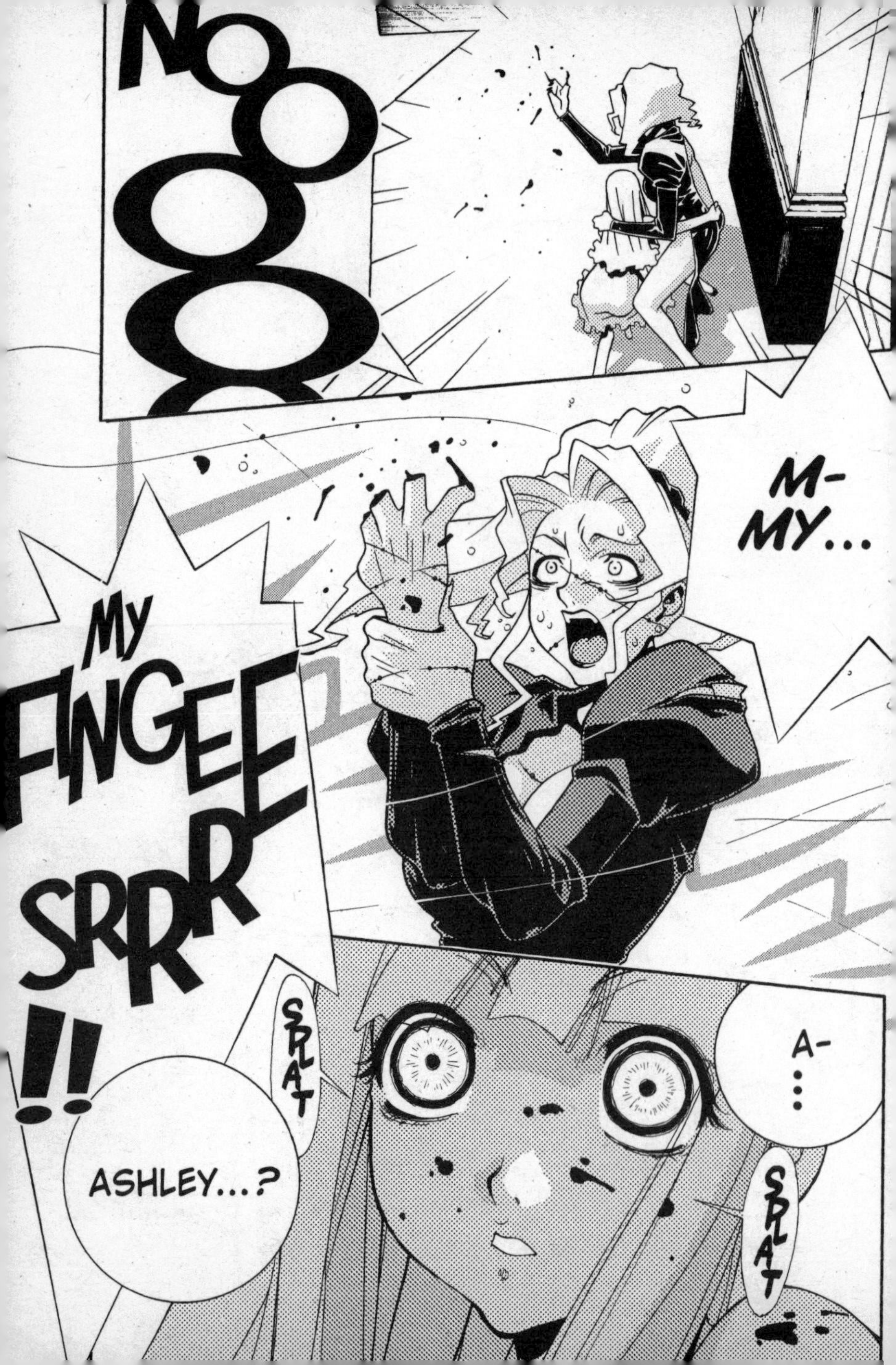
NOOOOO
M- MY...
My FINGEEERSRRR!!
A-...
SPLAT
SPLAT
ASHLEY...?

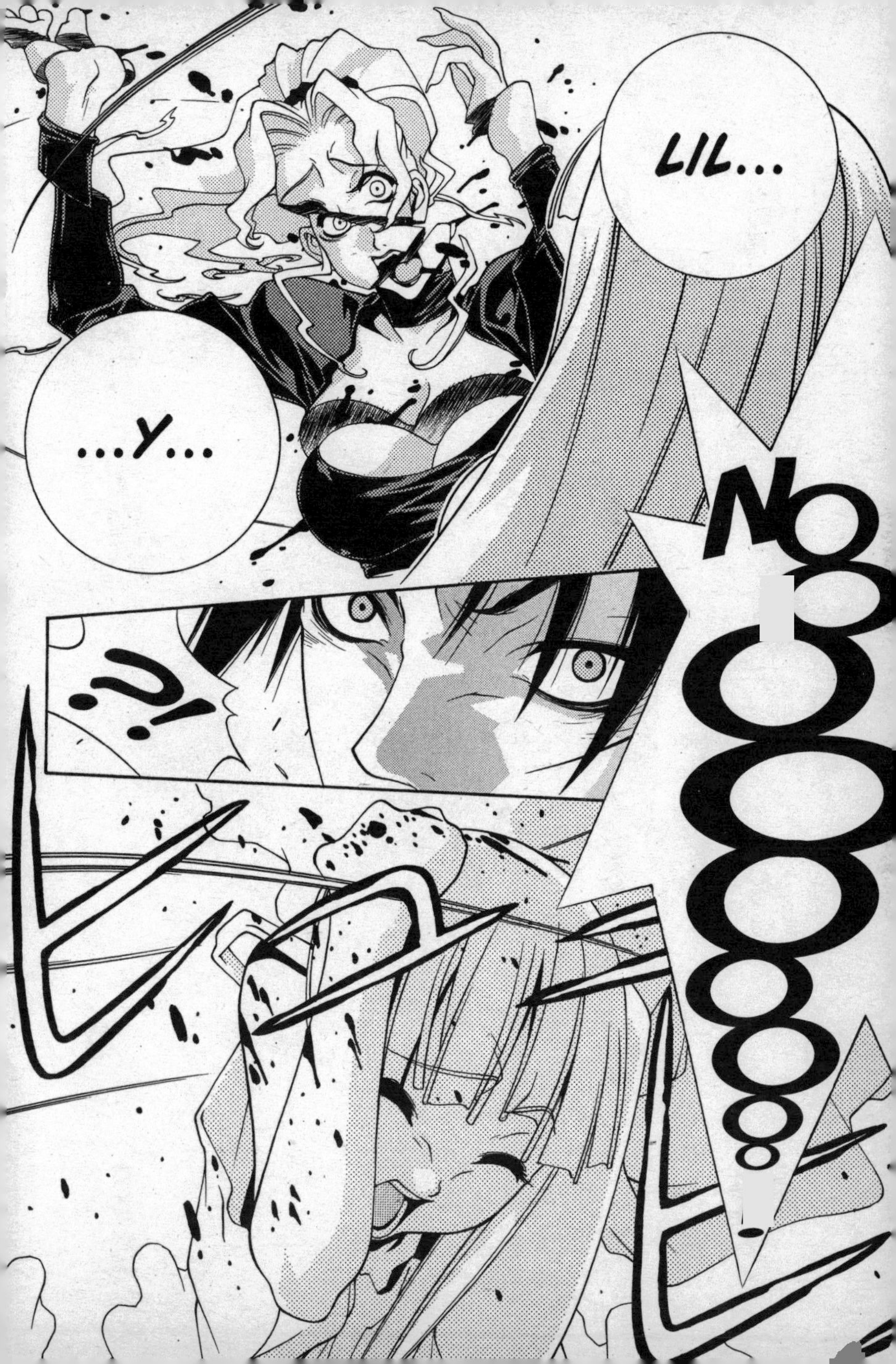
LIL...
...Y...
NOOOOOOOO!
?!

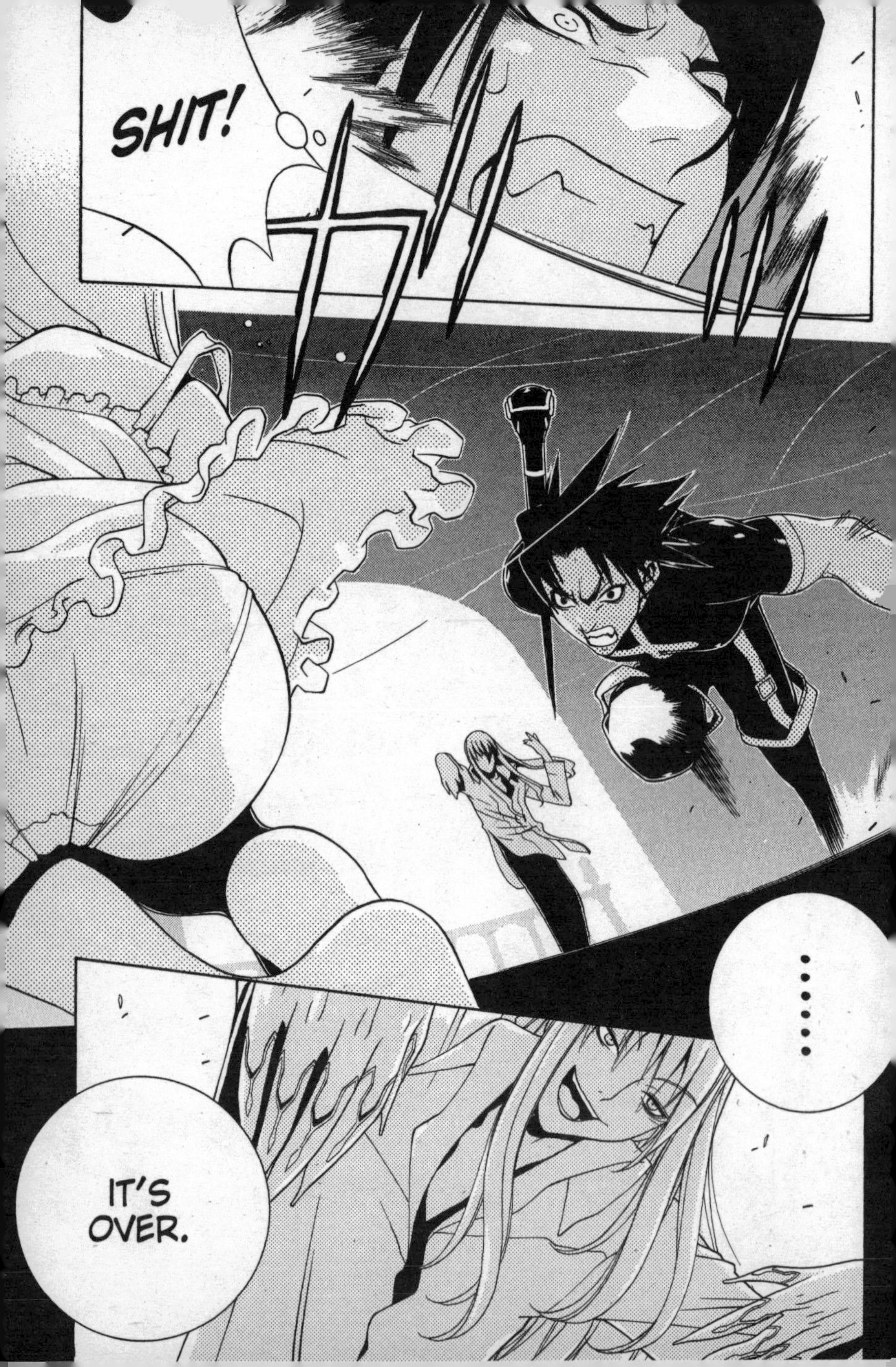
SHIT!
......
IT'S OVER.

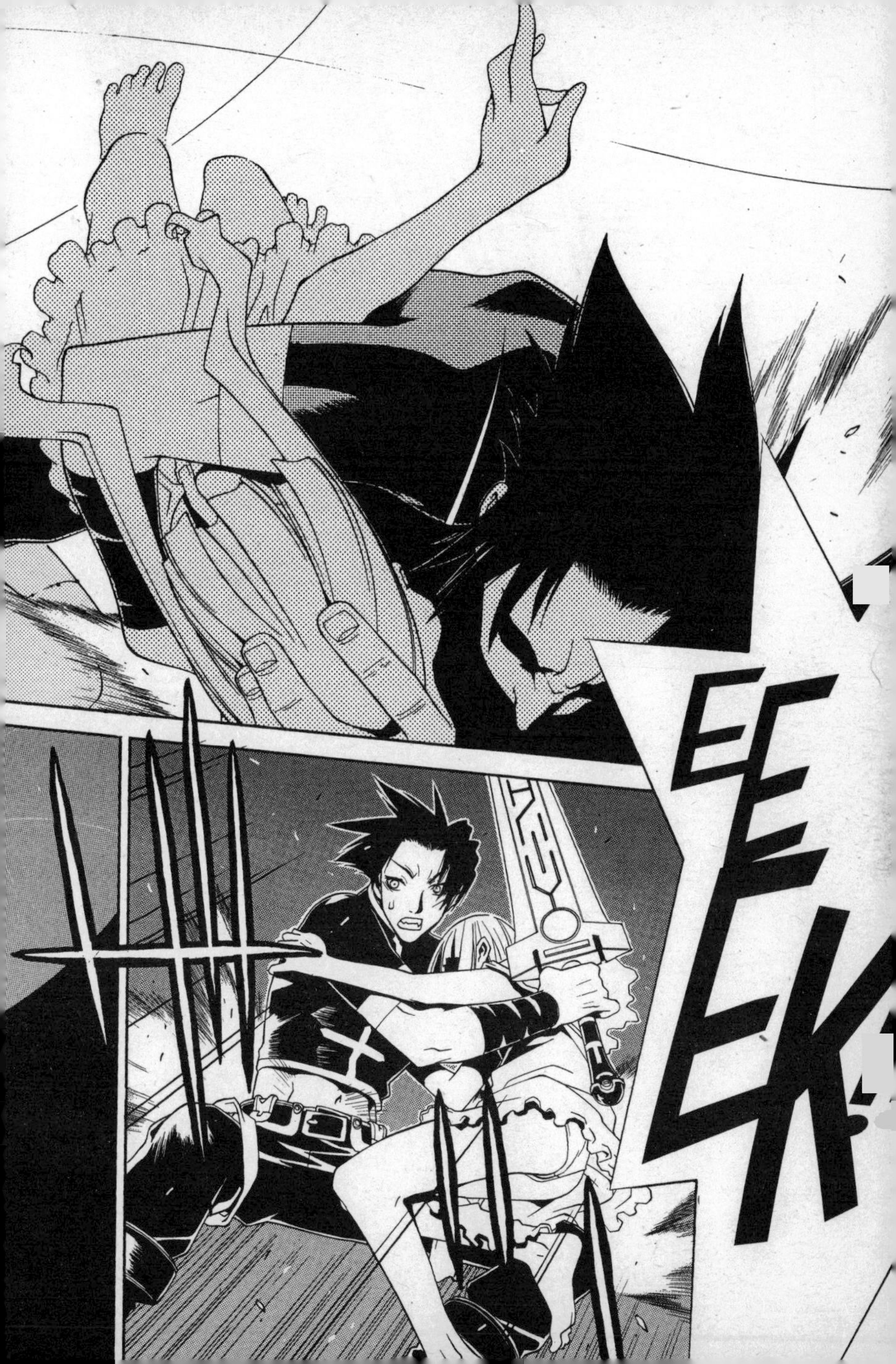
EEEEK!

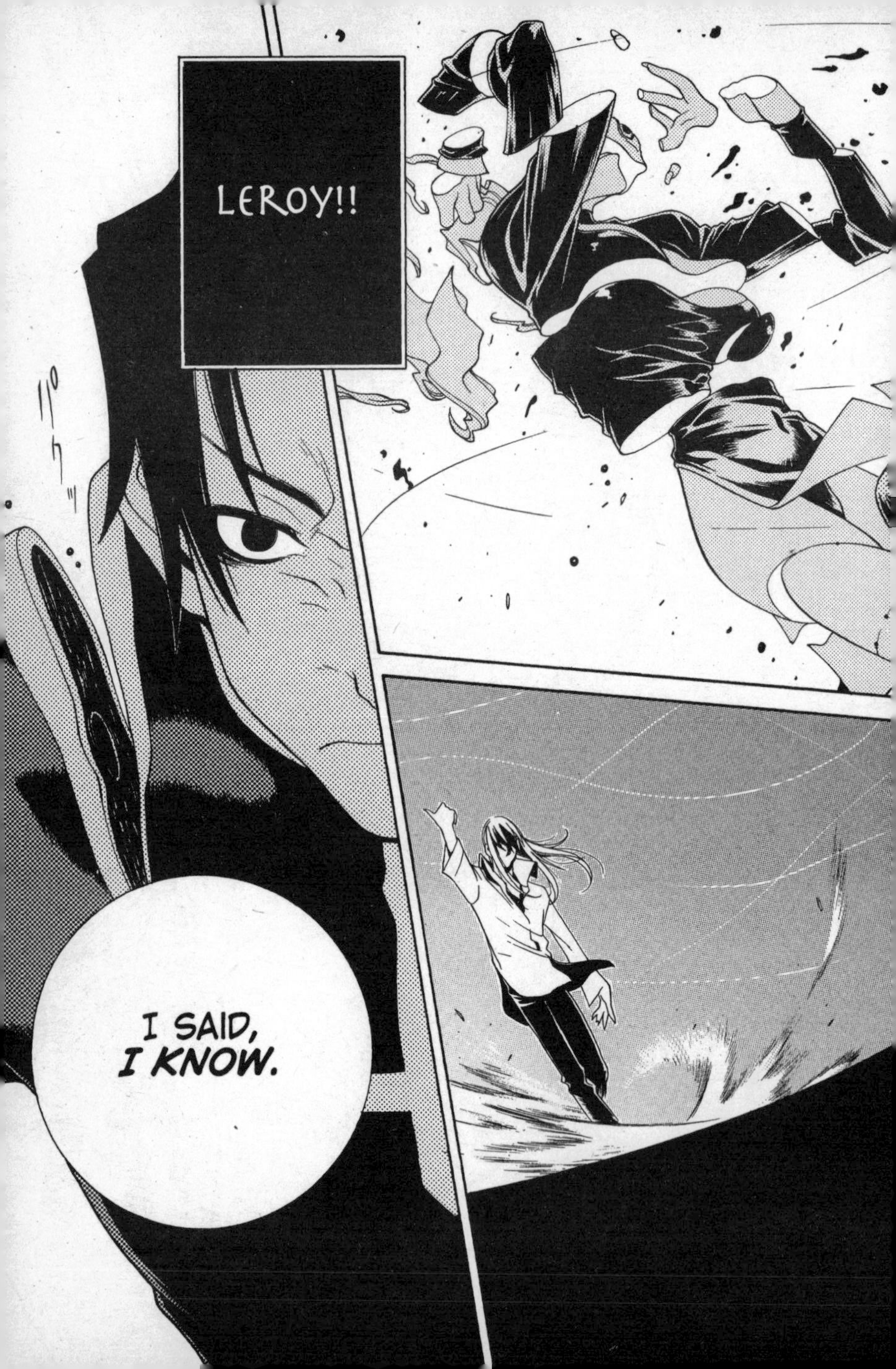
LEROY!!
I SAID, I KNOW.

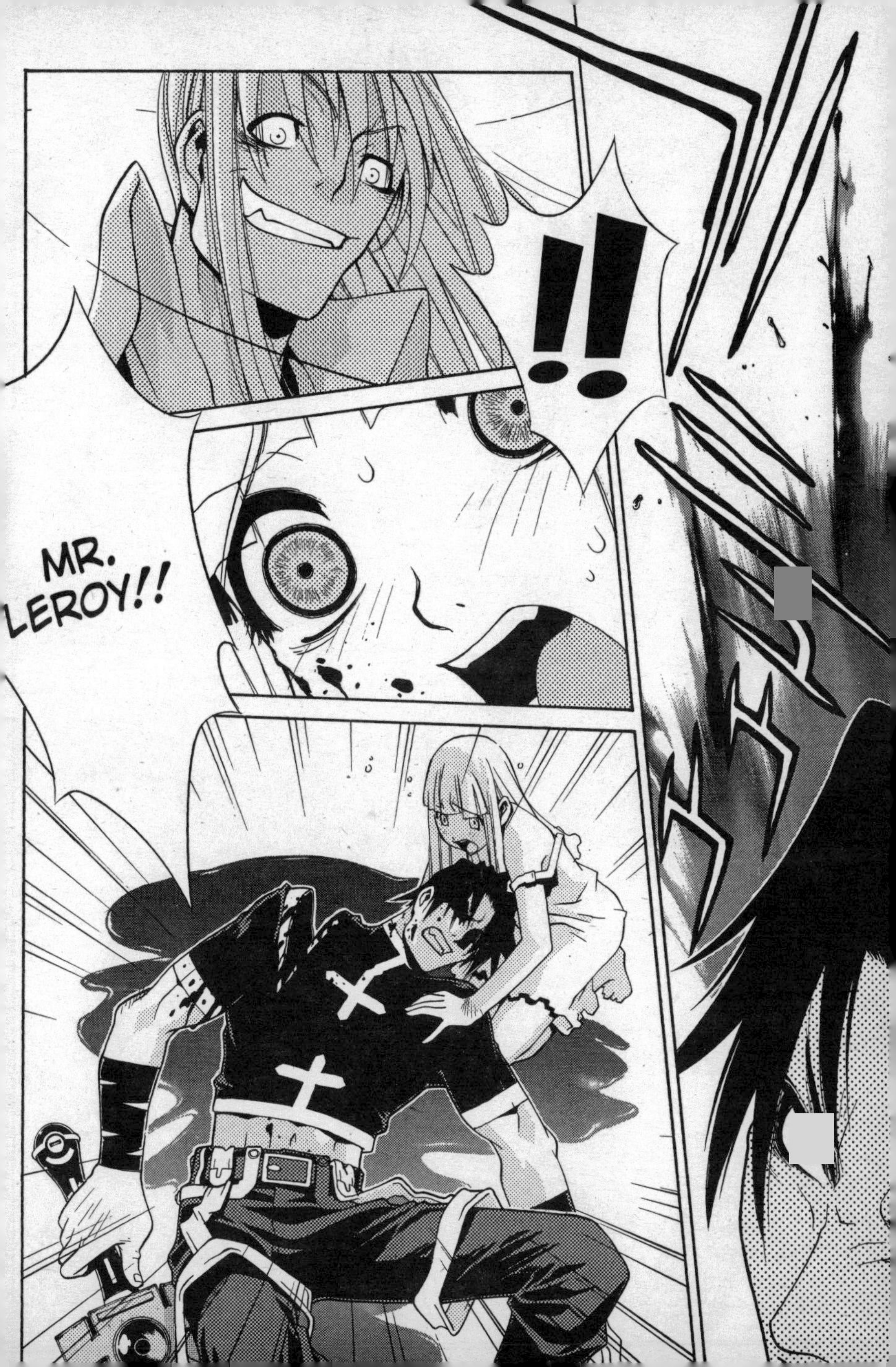
!!
MR. LEROY!!

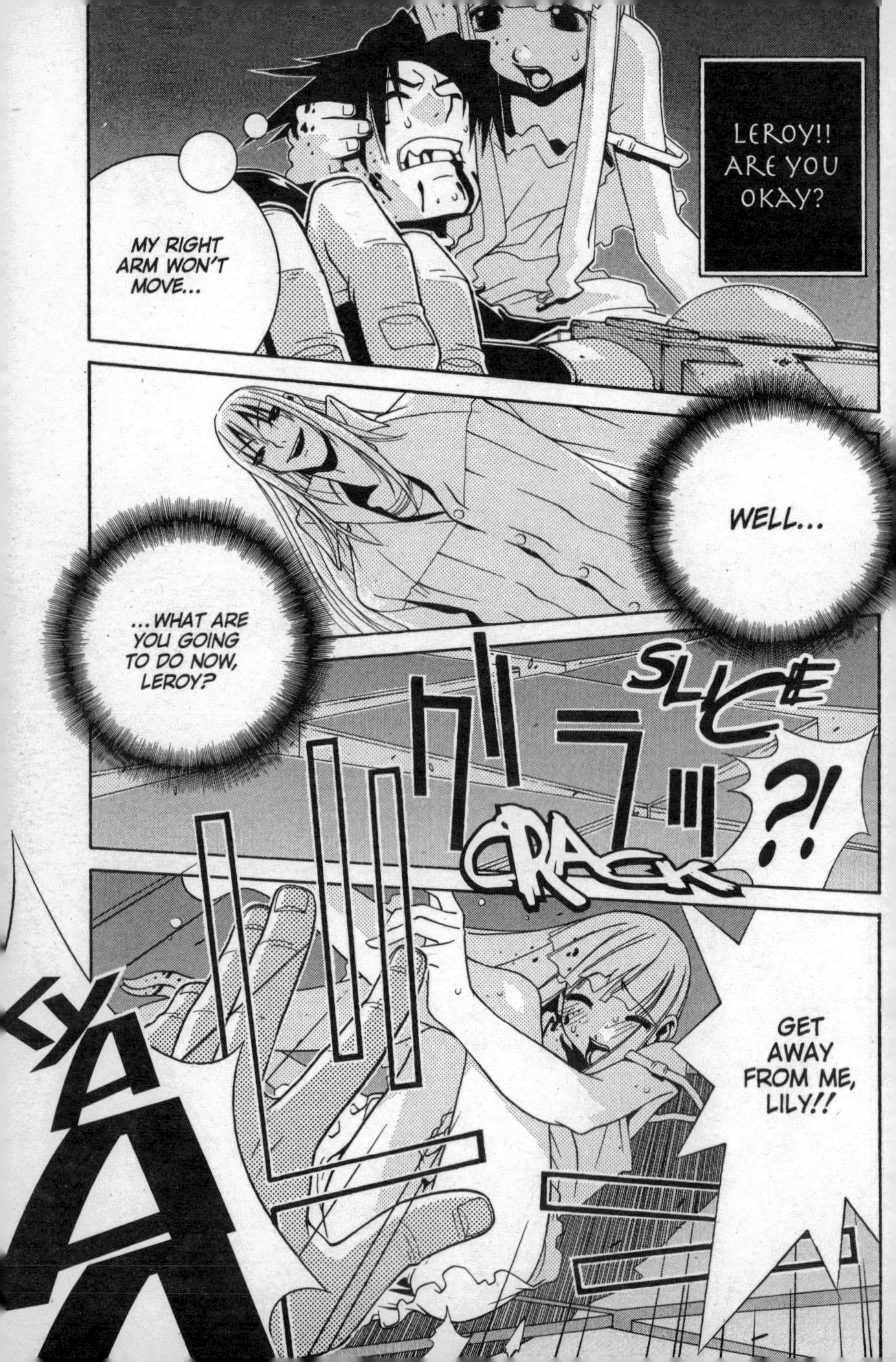
LEROY!! ARE YOU OKAY?
MY RIGHT ARM WON'T MOVE...
WELL...
...WHAT ARE YOU GOING TO DO NOW, LEROY?
SLICE
CRACK
?!
GET AWAY FROM ME, LILY!!

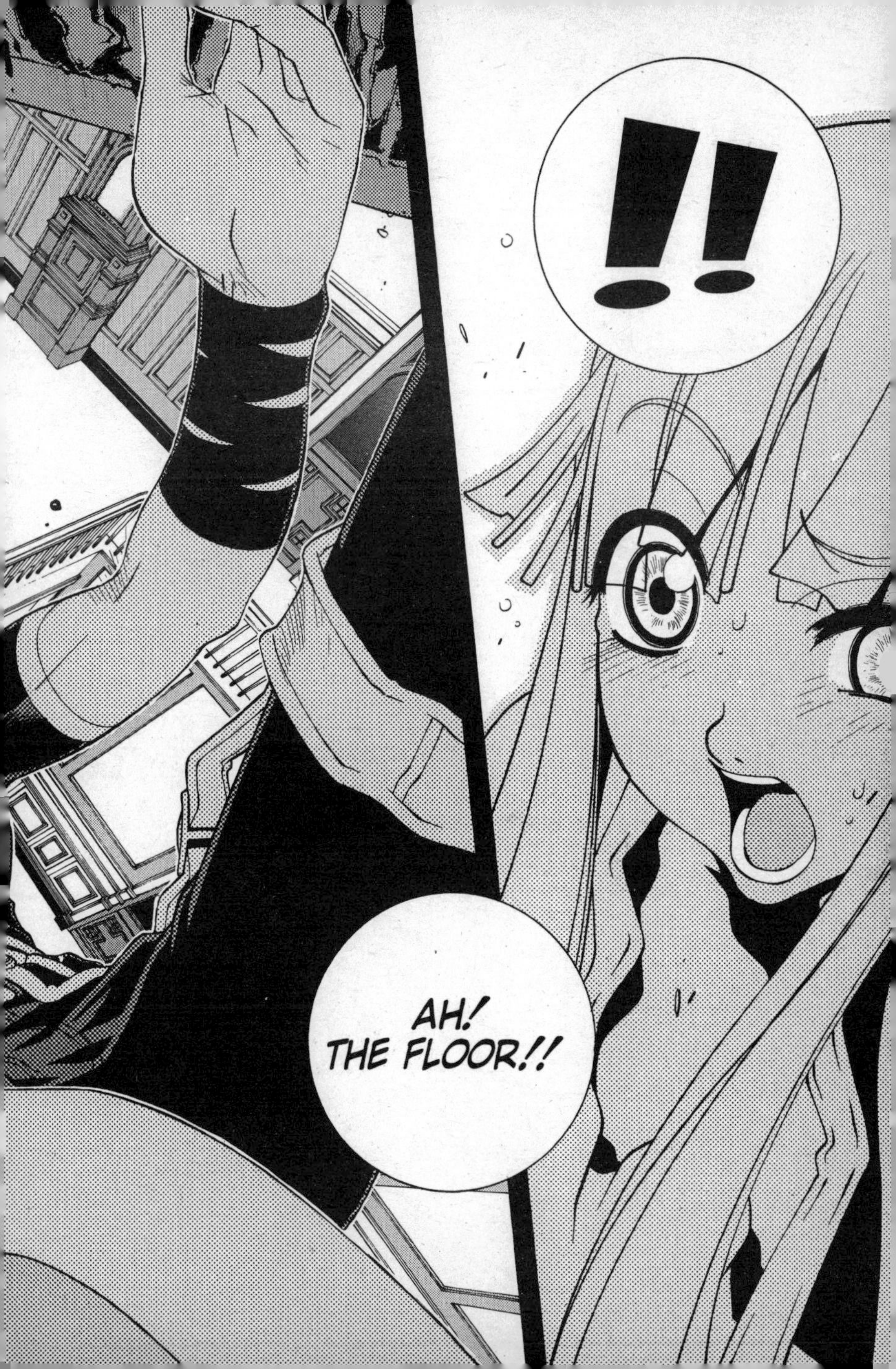
!!
AH! THE FLOOR!!

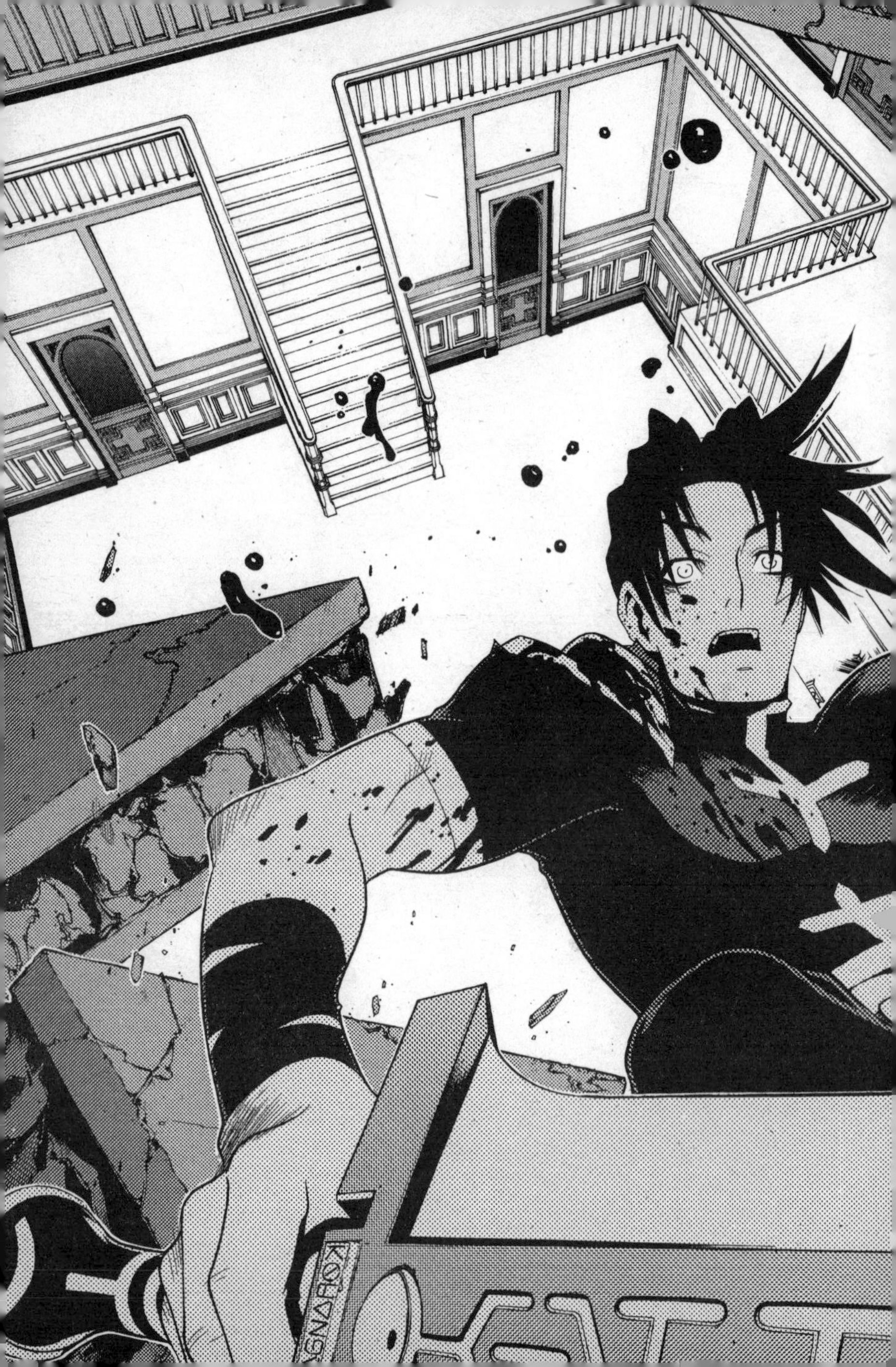

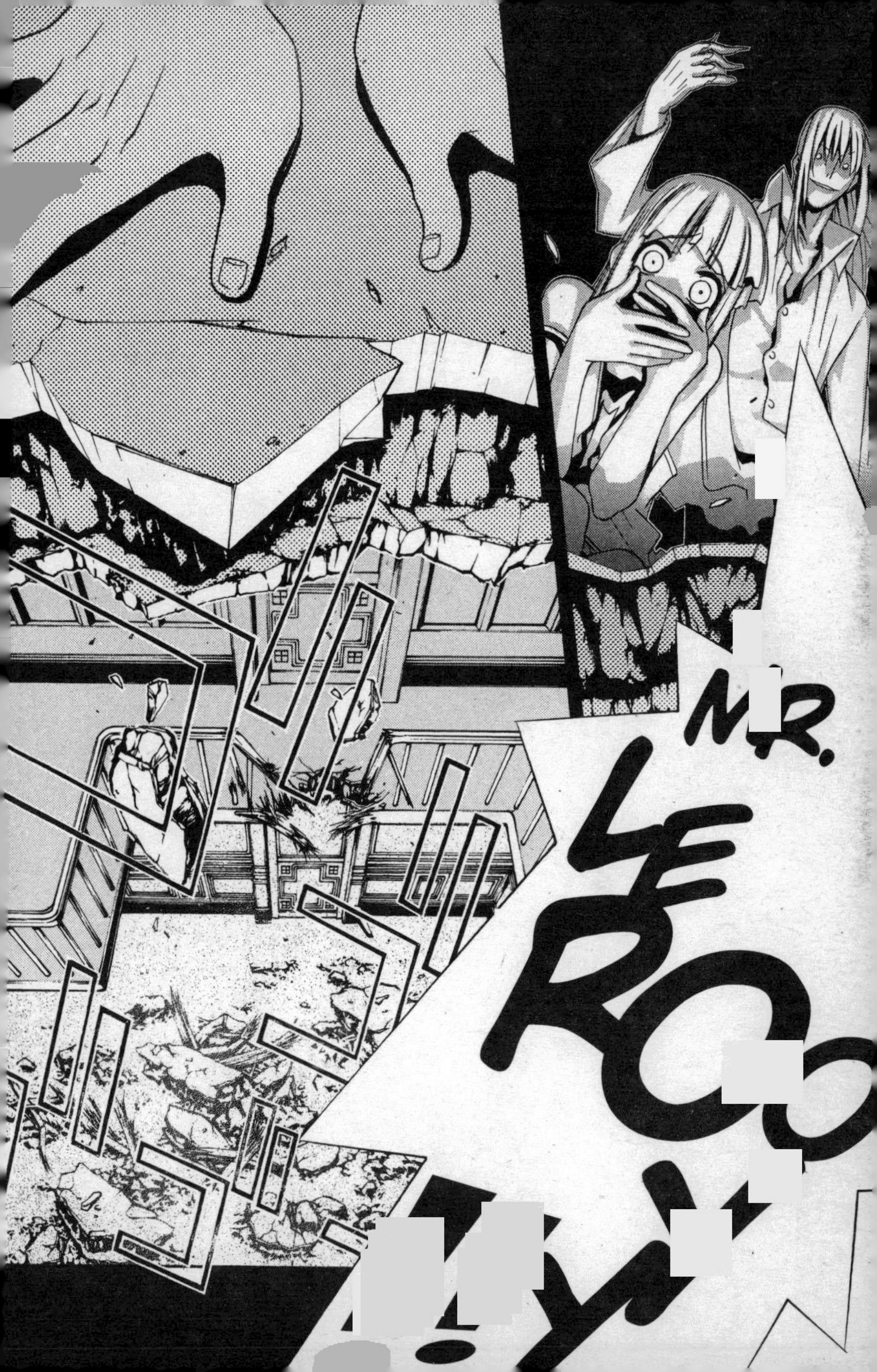
MR. LEROOY!

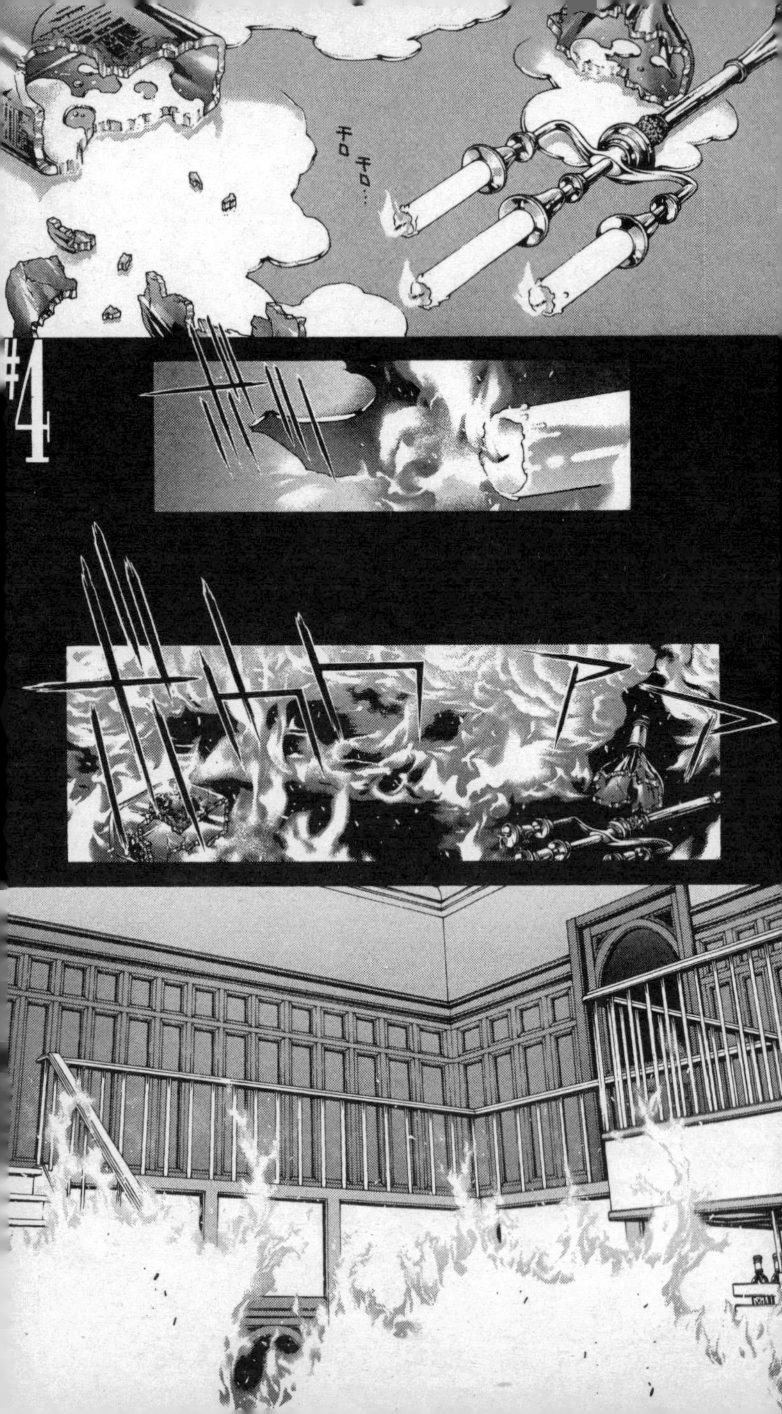
チロ チロ…
#4

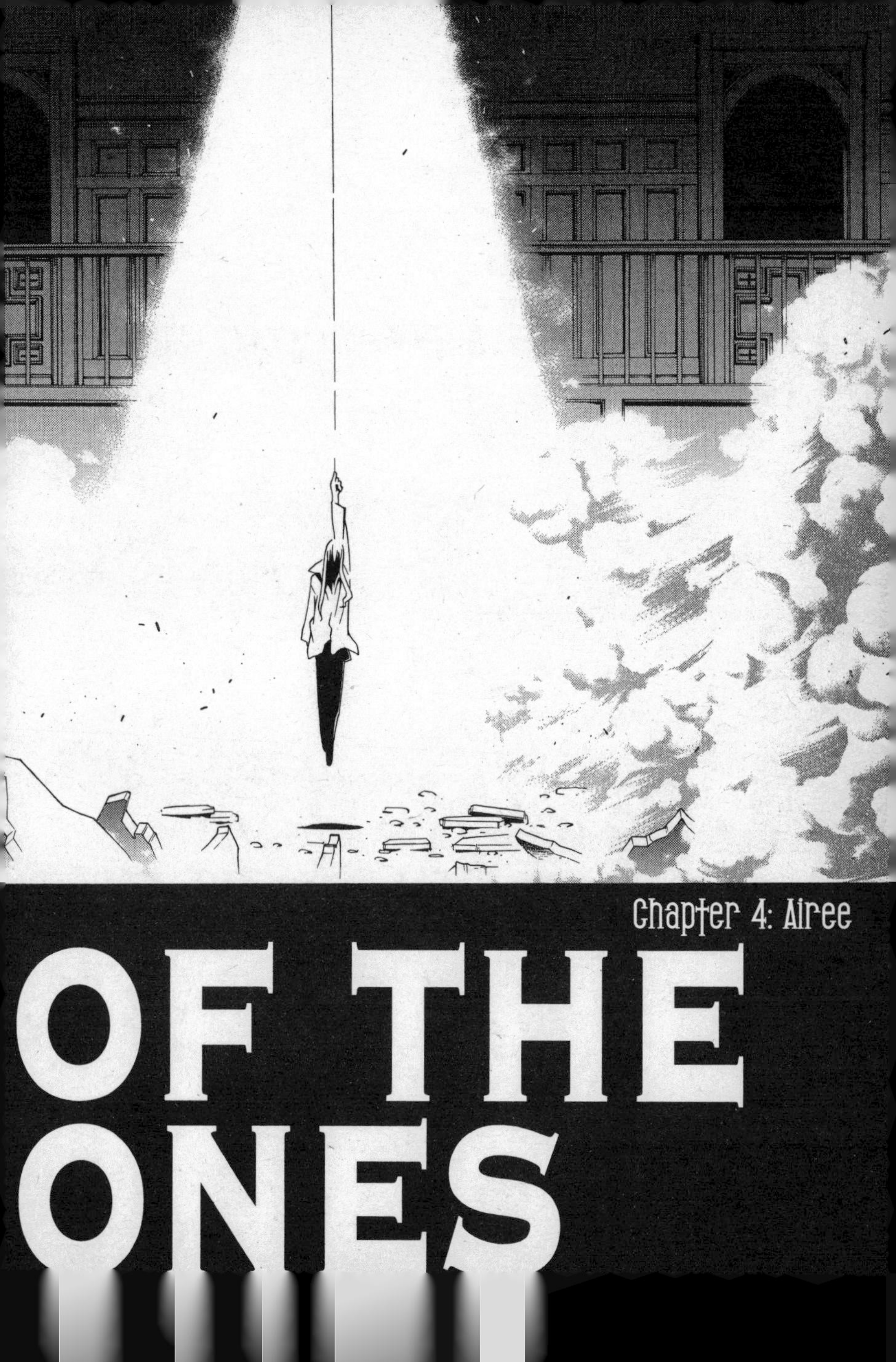

Chapter 4: Airee

OF THE ONES

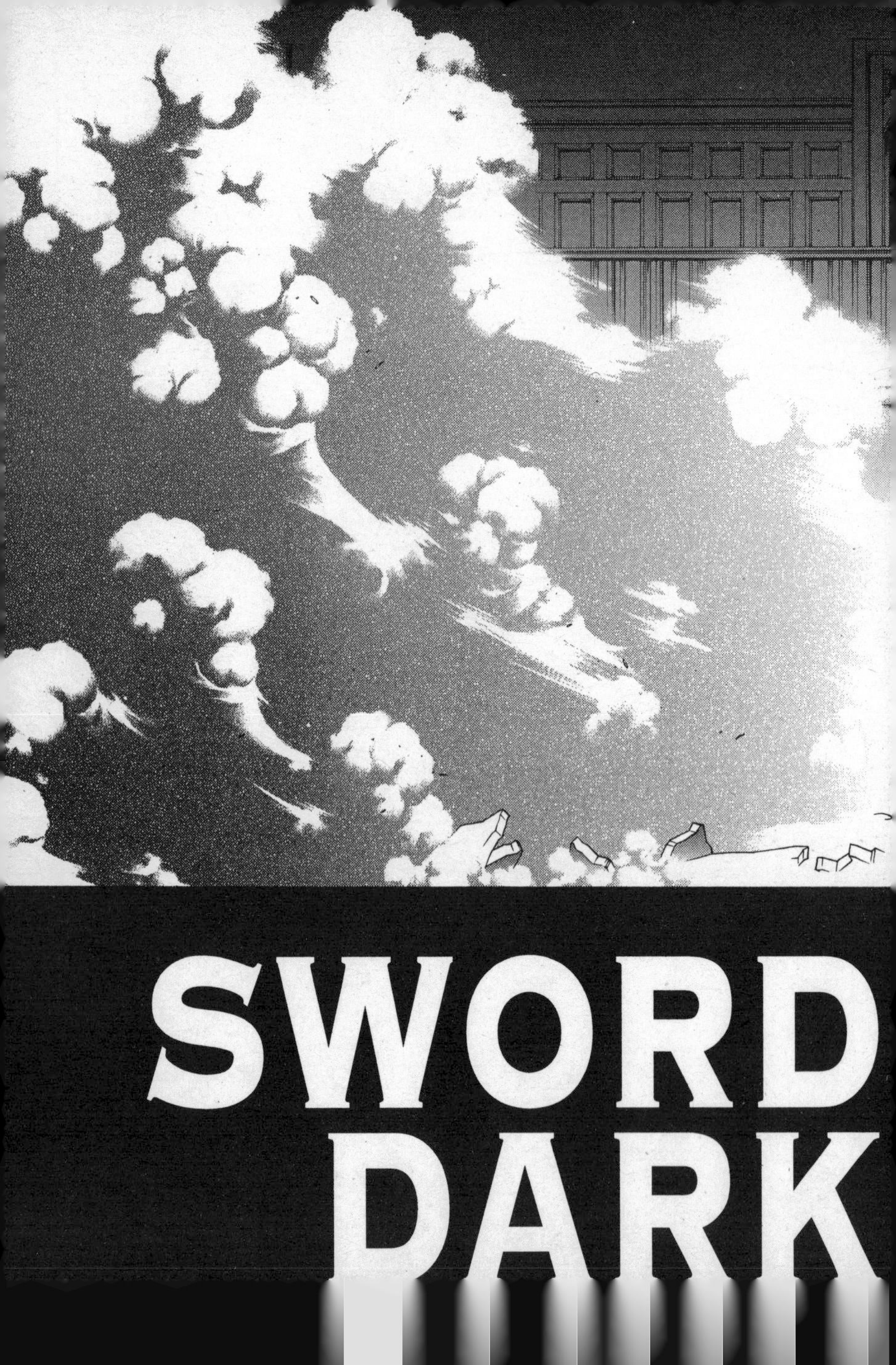
SWORD
DARK

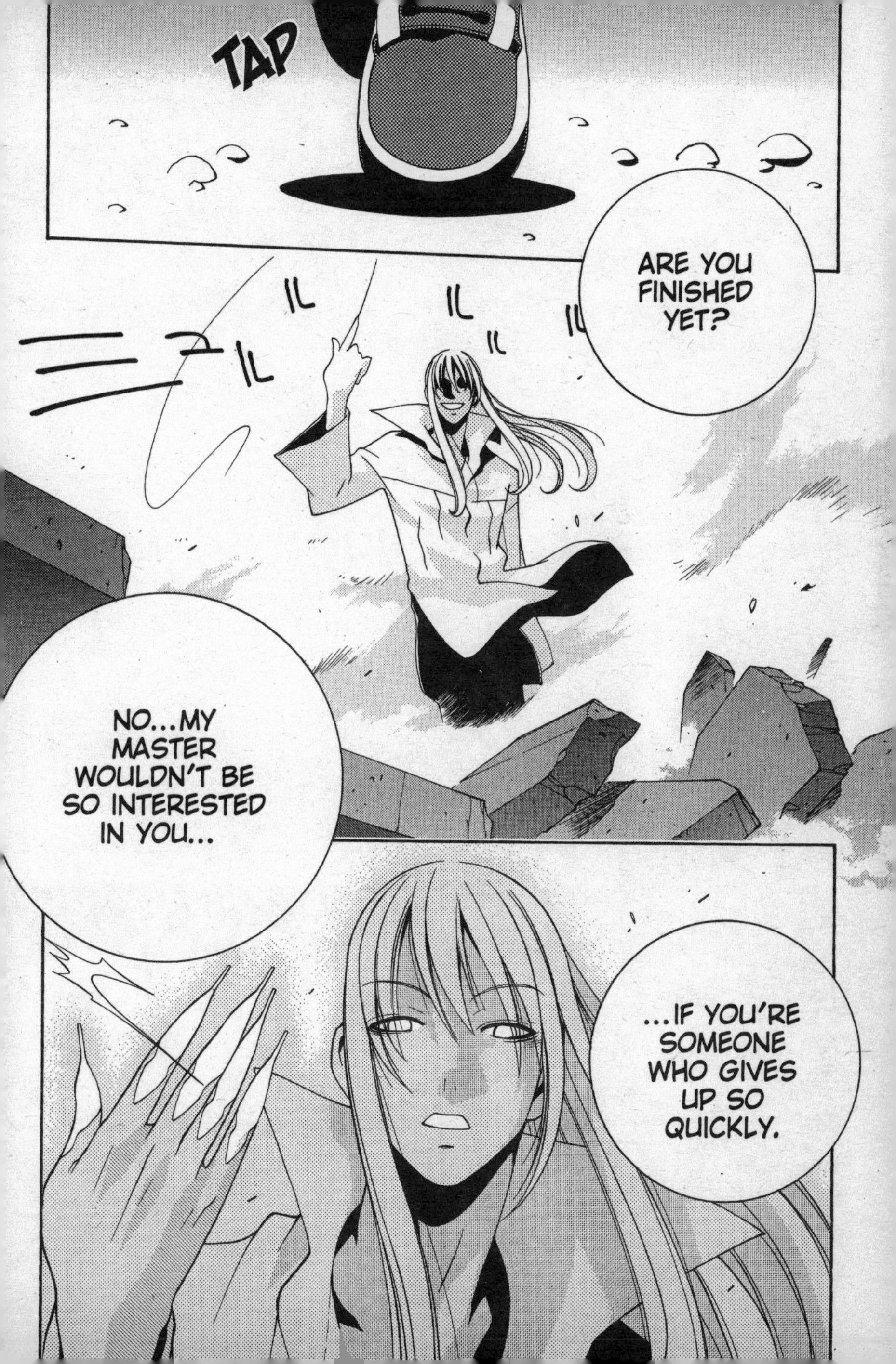
TAP
ARE YOU FINISHED YET?
NO...MY MASTER WOULDN'T BE SO INTERESTED IN YOU...
...IF YOU'RE SOMEONE WHO GIVES UP SO QUICKLY.

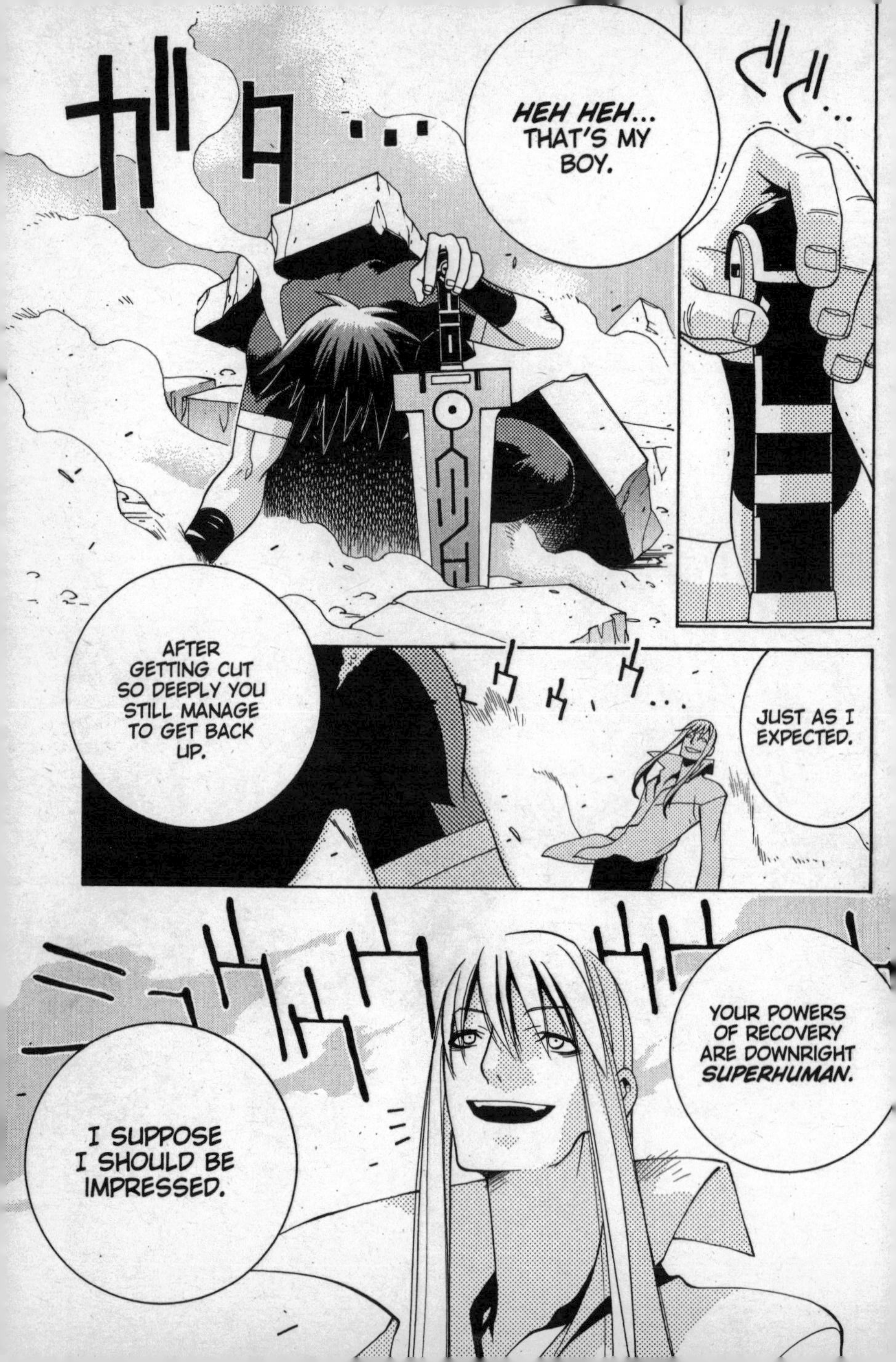
ガタ...
HEH HEH... THAT'S MY BOY.
JUST AS I EXPECTED.
AFTER GETTING CUT SO DEEPLY YOU STILL MANAGE TO GET BACK UP.
YOUR POWERS OF RECOVERY ARE DOWNRIGHT SUPERHUMAN.
I SUPPOSE I SHOULD BE IMPRESSED.

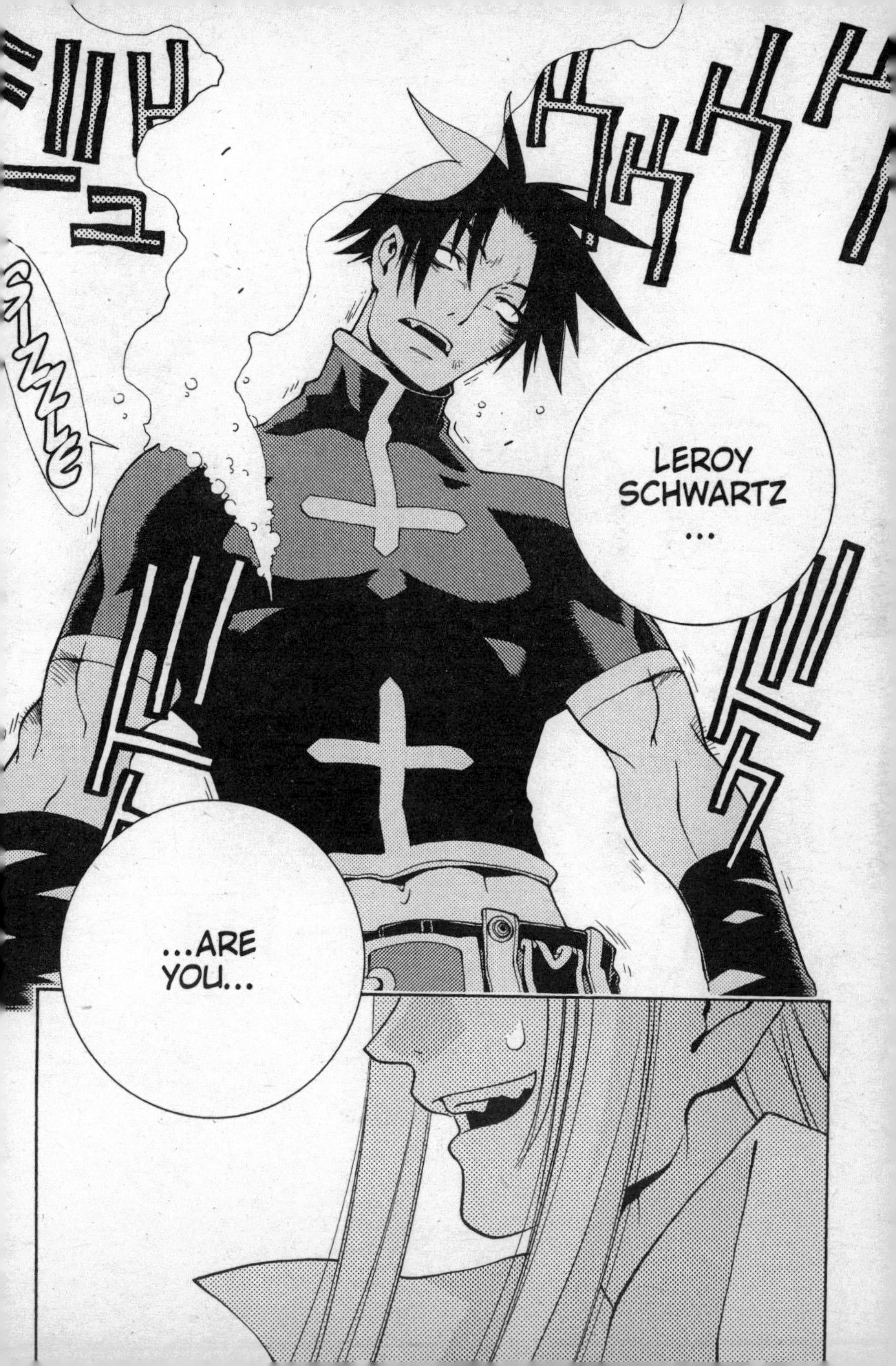
LEROY SCHWARTZ ...
SIZZLE
...ARE YOU...

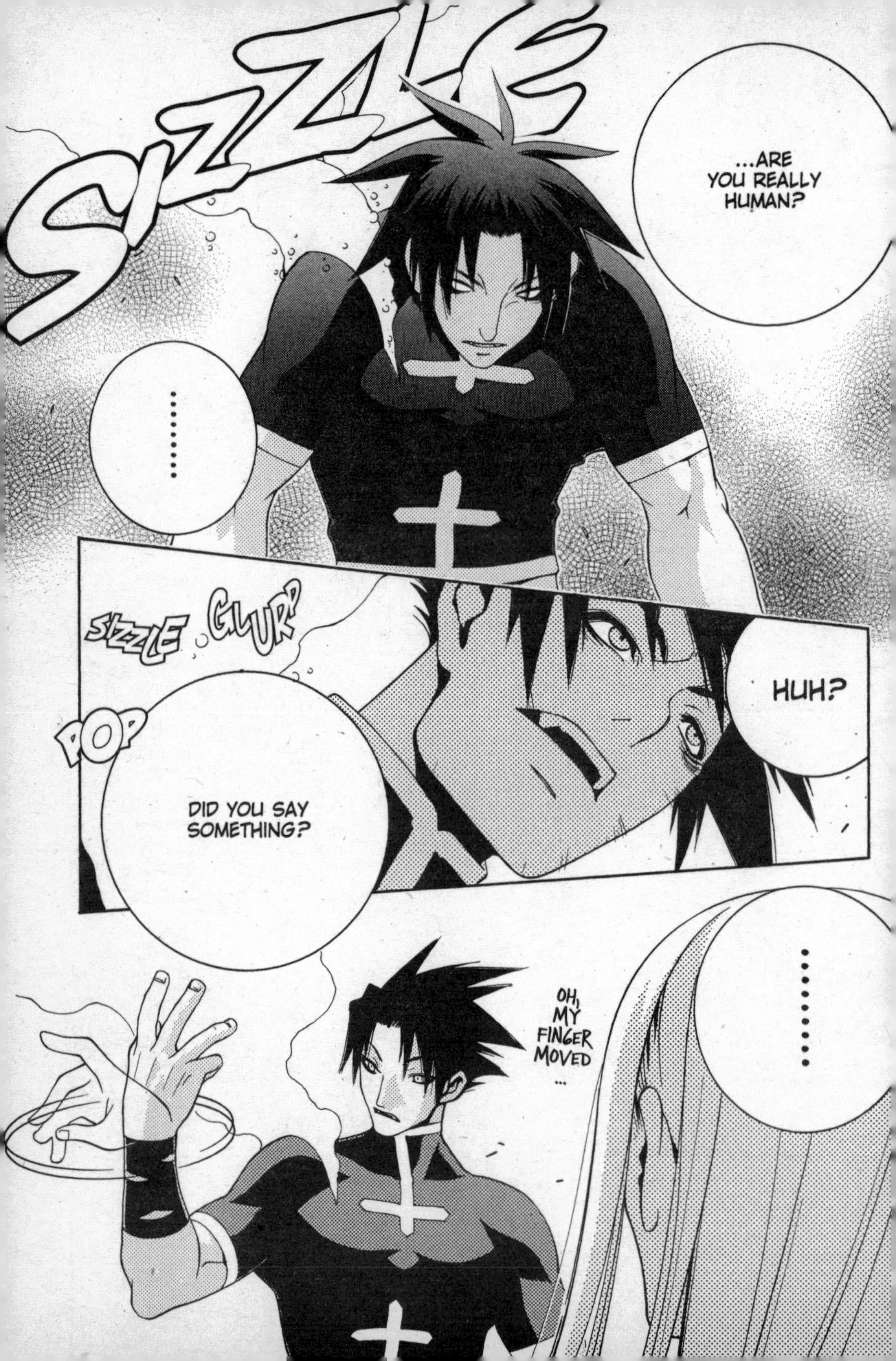

...ARE YOU REALLY HUMAN?
SIZZLE
......
HUH?
SIZZLE
GLURP
POP
DID YOU SAY SOMETHING?
....
OH, MY FINGER MOVED ...

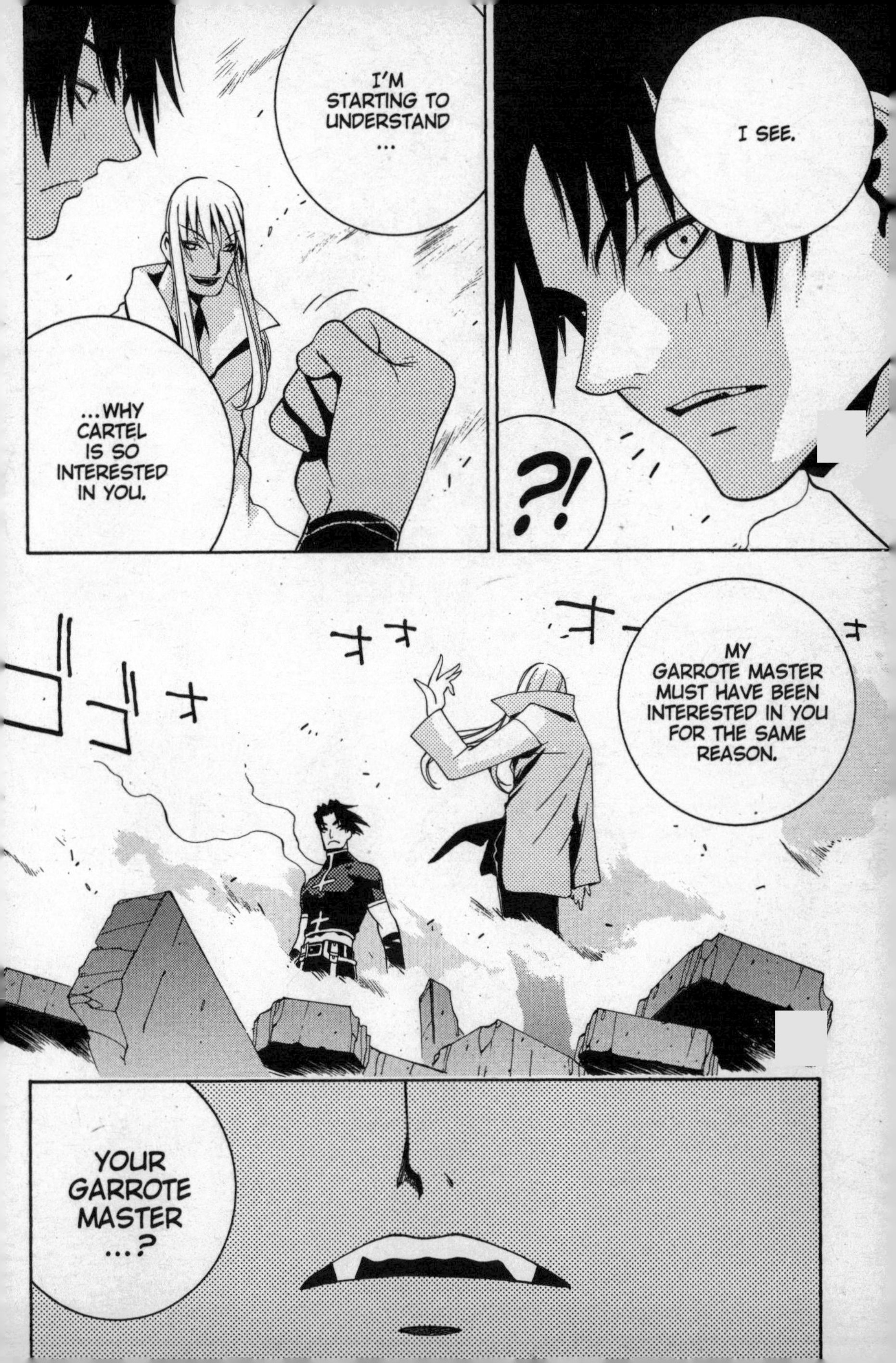
I SEE.
?!
I'M STARTING TO UNDERSTAND ...
...WHY CARTEL IS SO INTERESTED IN YOU.
MY GARROTE MASTER MUST HAVE BEEN INTERESTED IN YOU FOR THE SAME REASON.
YOUR GARROTE MASTER ...?

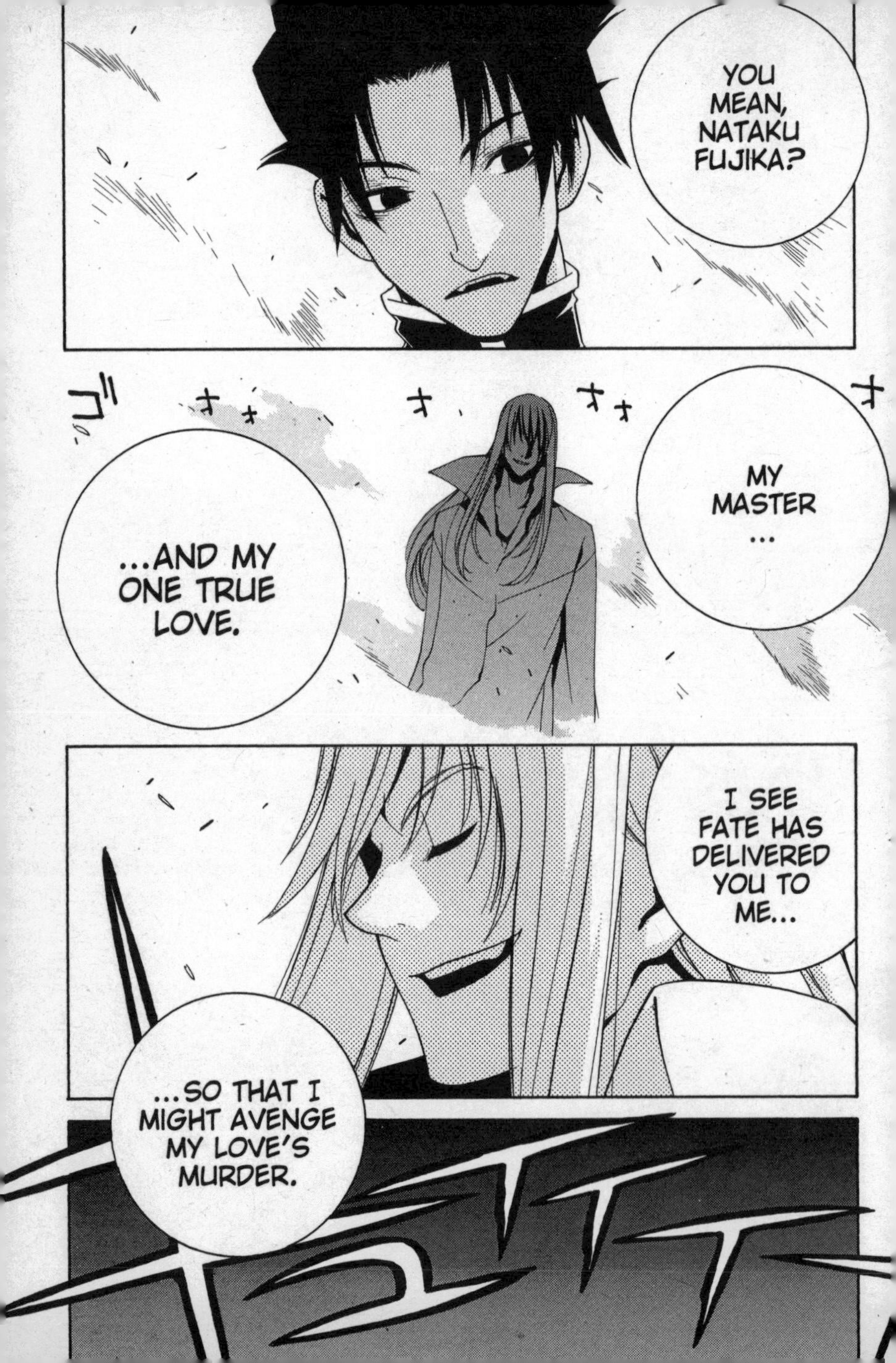
YOU MEAN, NATAKU FUJIKA?
MY MASTER...
...AND MY ONE TRUE LOVE.
I SEE FATE HAS DELIVERED YOU TO ME...
...SO THAT I MIGHT AVENGE MY LOVE'S MURDER.

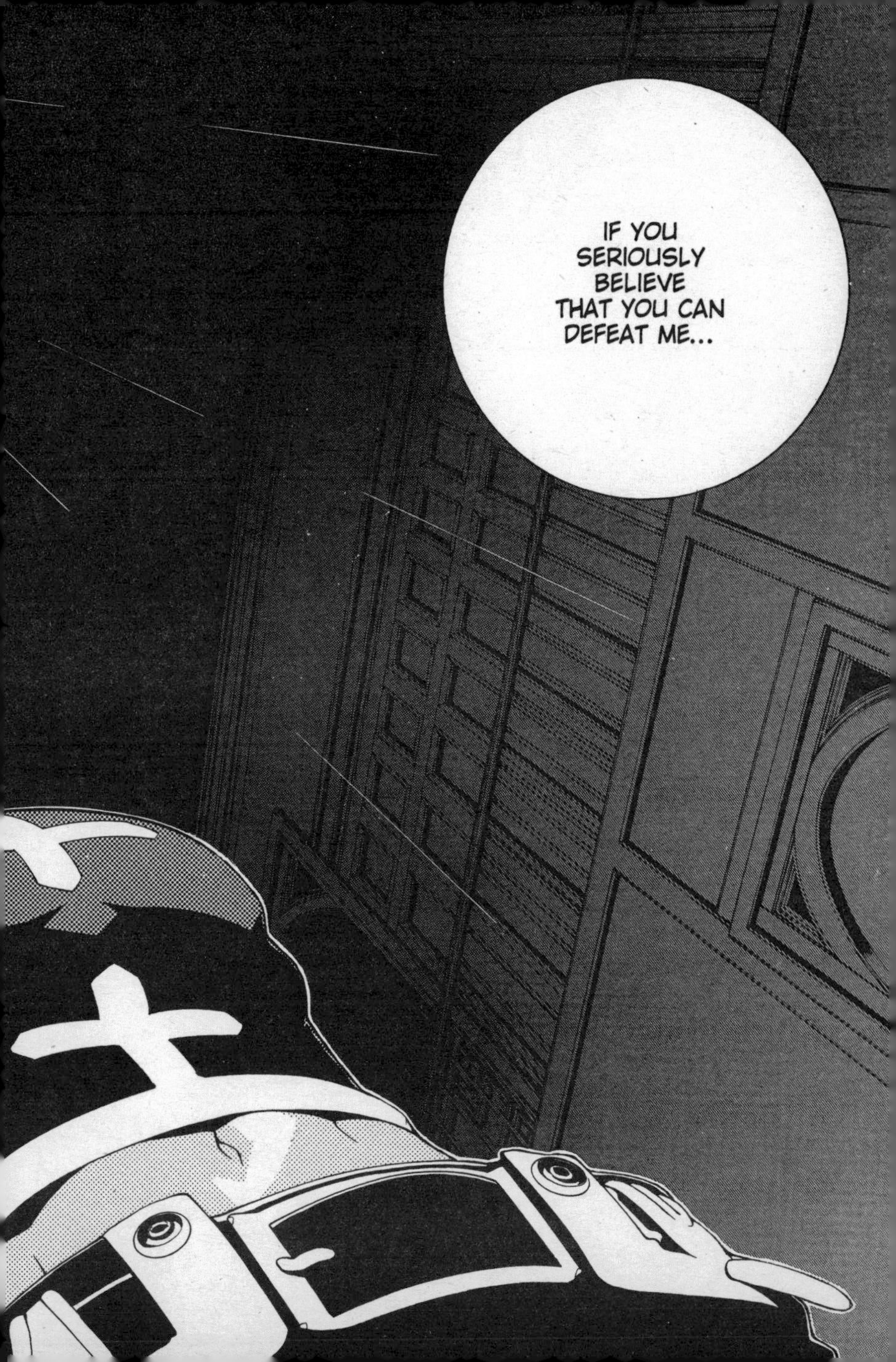
IF YOU SERIOUSLY BELIEVE THAT YOU CAN DEFEAT ME...

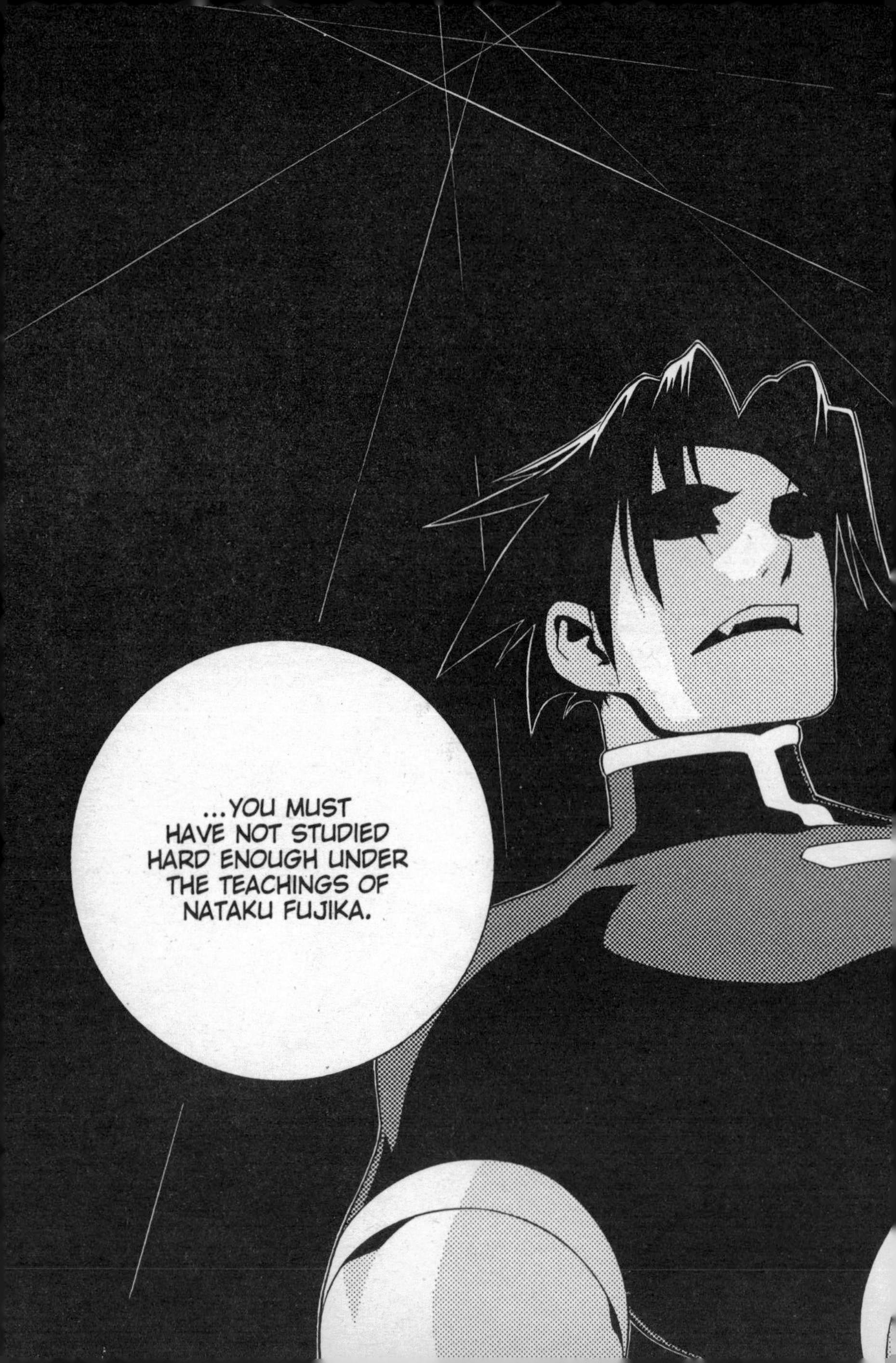
...YOU MUST HAVE NOT STUDIED HARD ENOUGH UNDER THE TEACHINGS OF NATAKU FUJIKA.

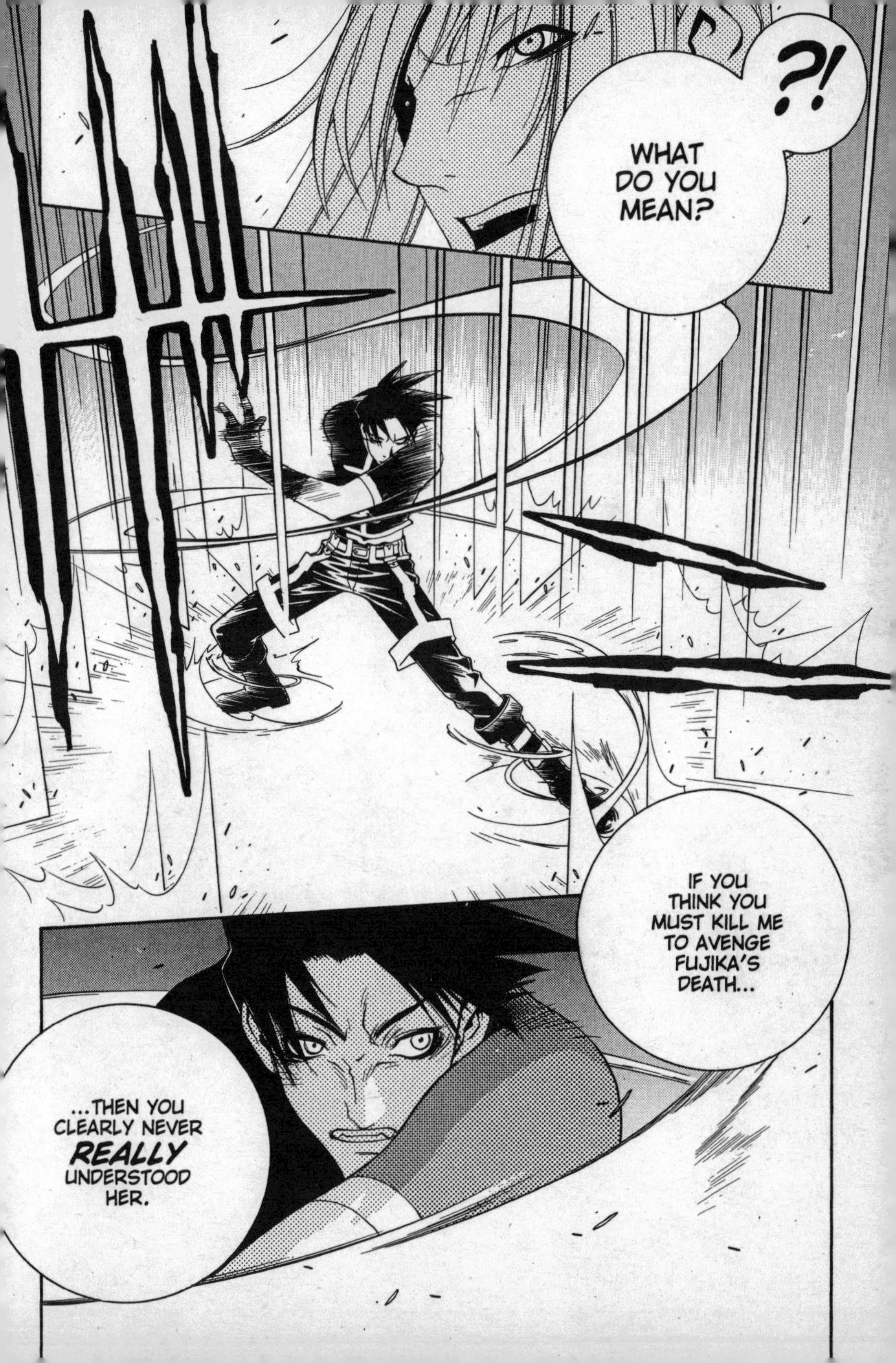
?!
WHAT DO YOU MEAN?
IF YOU THINK YOU MUST KILL ME TO AVENGE FUJIKA'S DEATH...
...THEN YOU CLEARLY NEVER **REALLY** UNDERSTOOD HER.

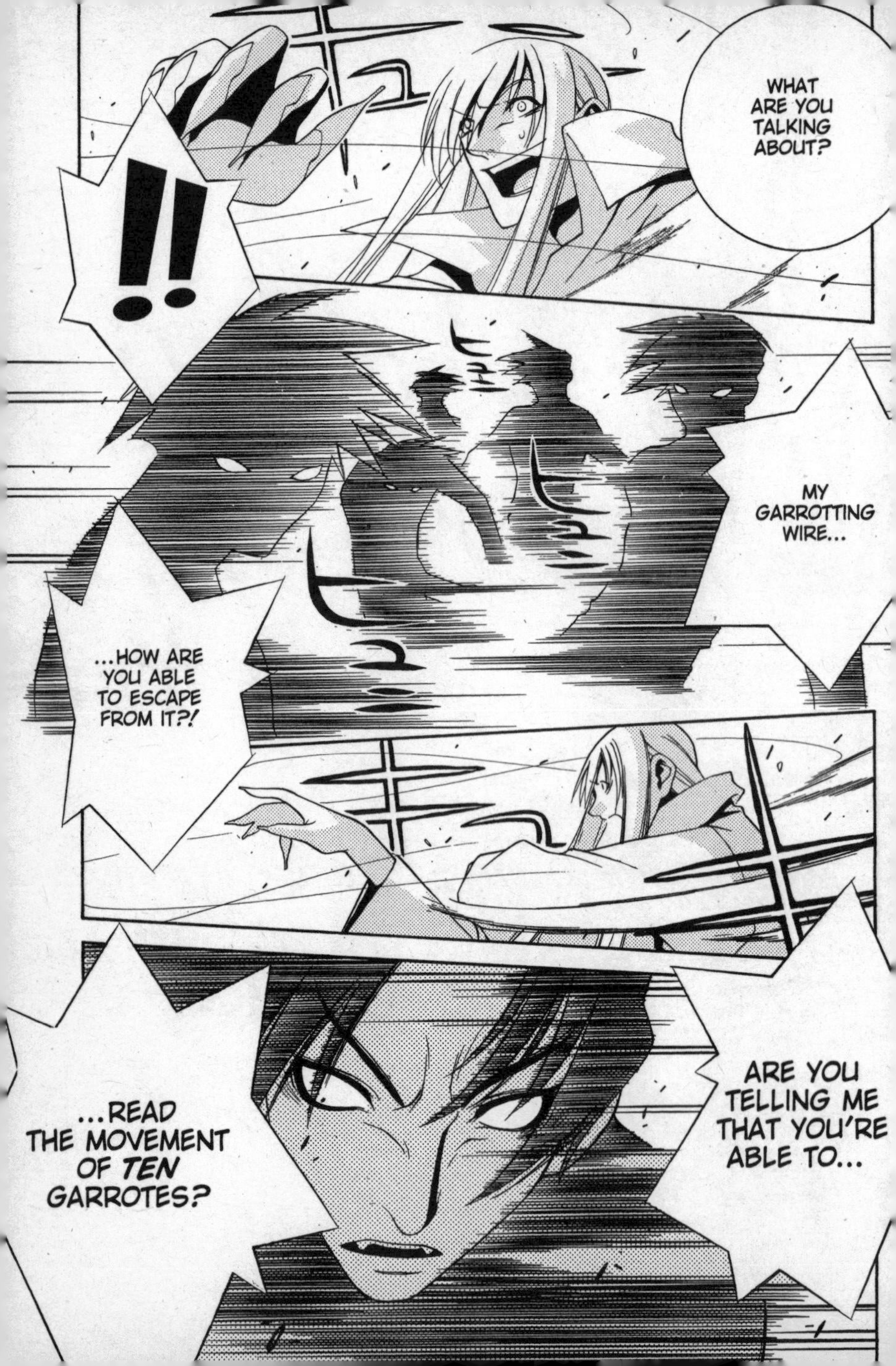
WHAT ARE YOU TALKING ABOUT?
!!
MY GARROTTING WIRE...
...HOW ARE YOU ABLE TO ESCAPE FROM IT?!
ARE YOU TELLING ME THAT YOU'RE ABLE TO...
...READ THE MOVEMENT OF *TEN* GARROTES?

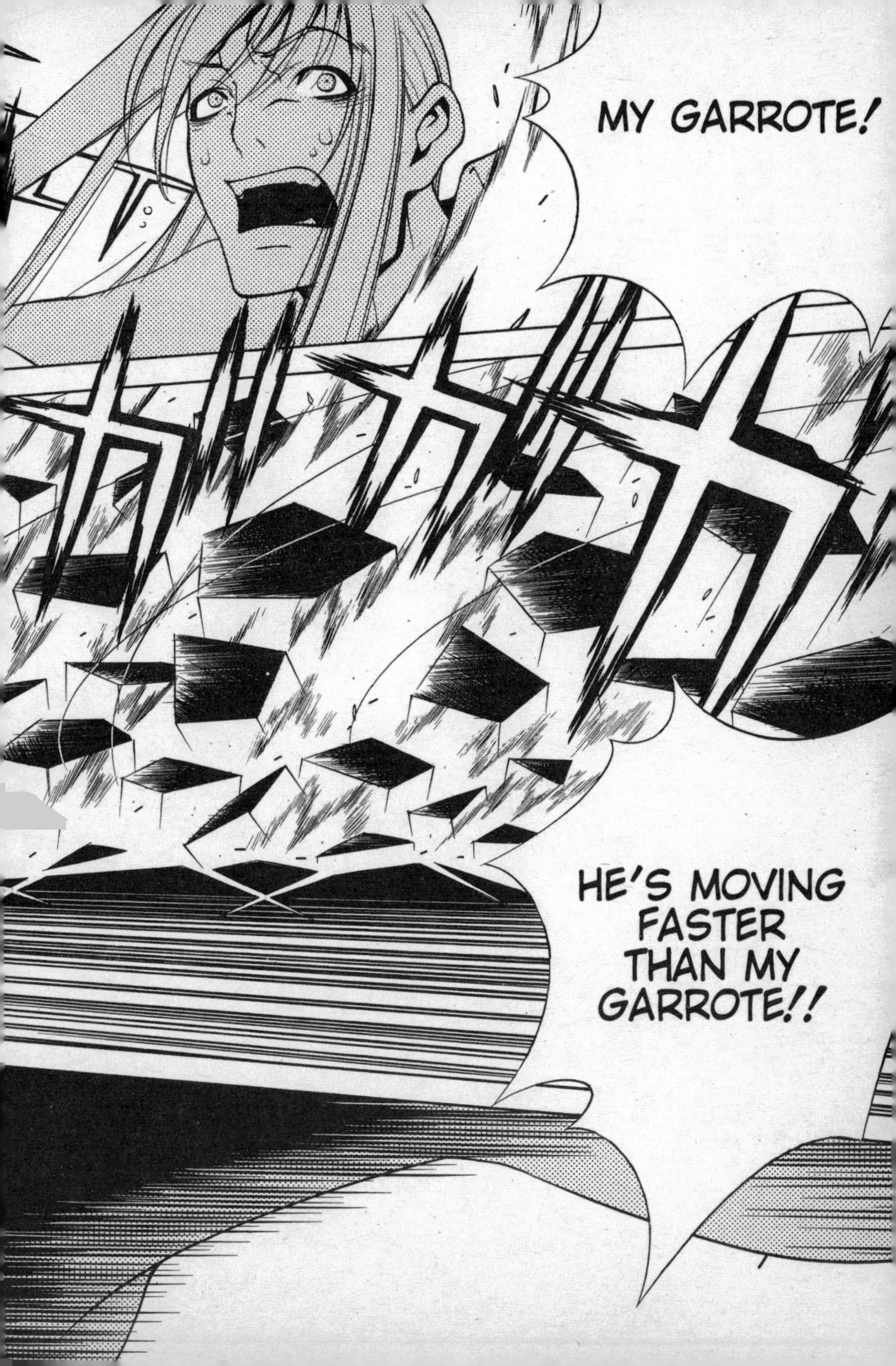
MY GARROTE!
HE'S MOVING FASTER THAN MY GARROTE!!

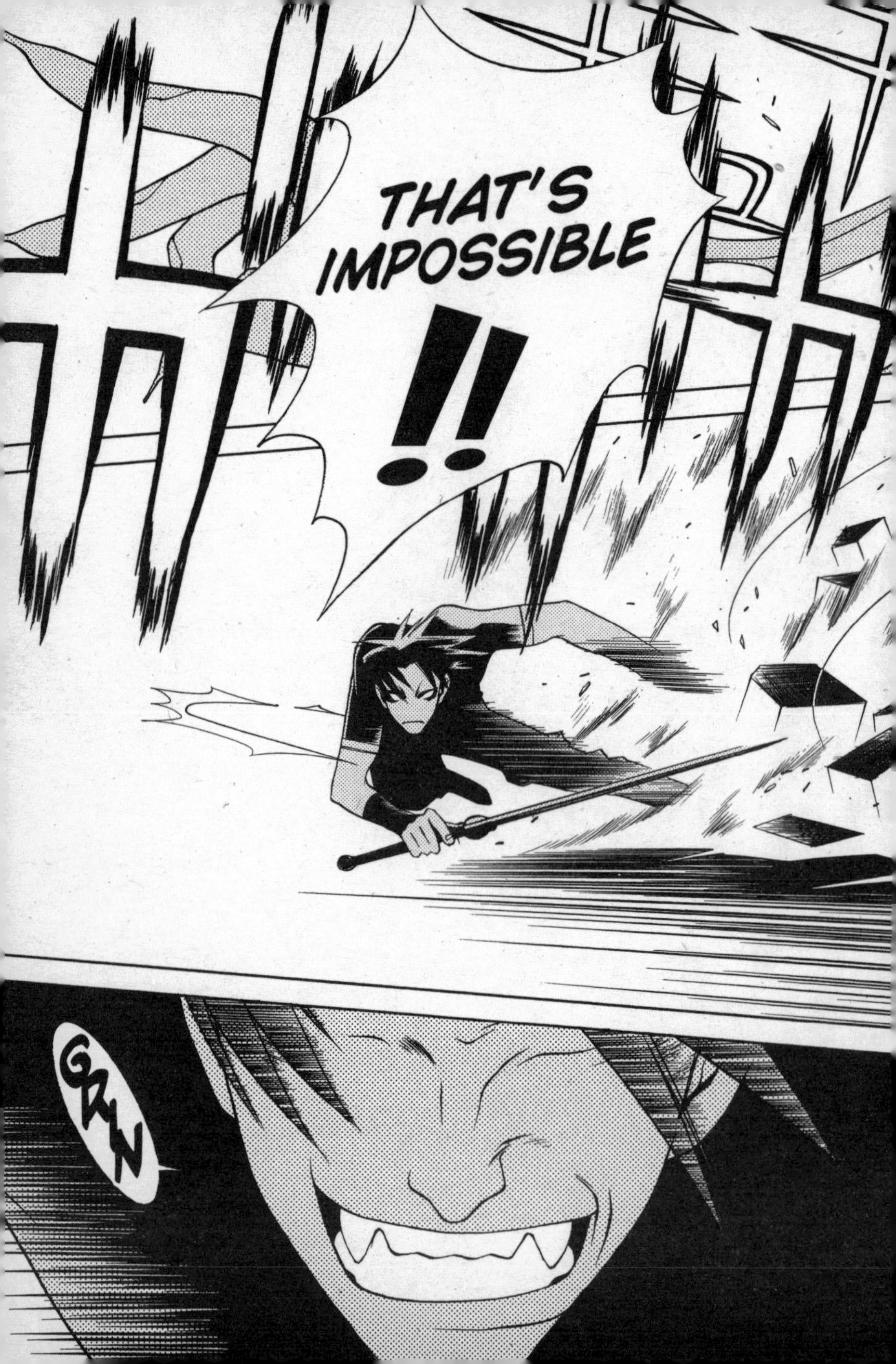
THAT'S IMPOSSIBLE!!
GRIN

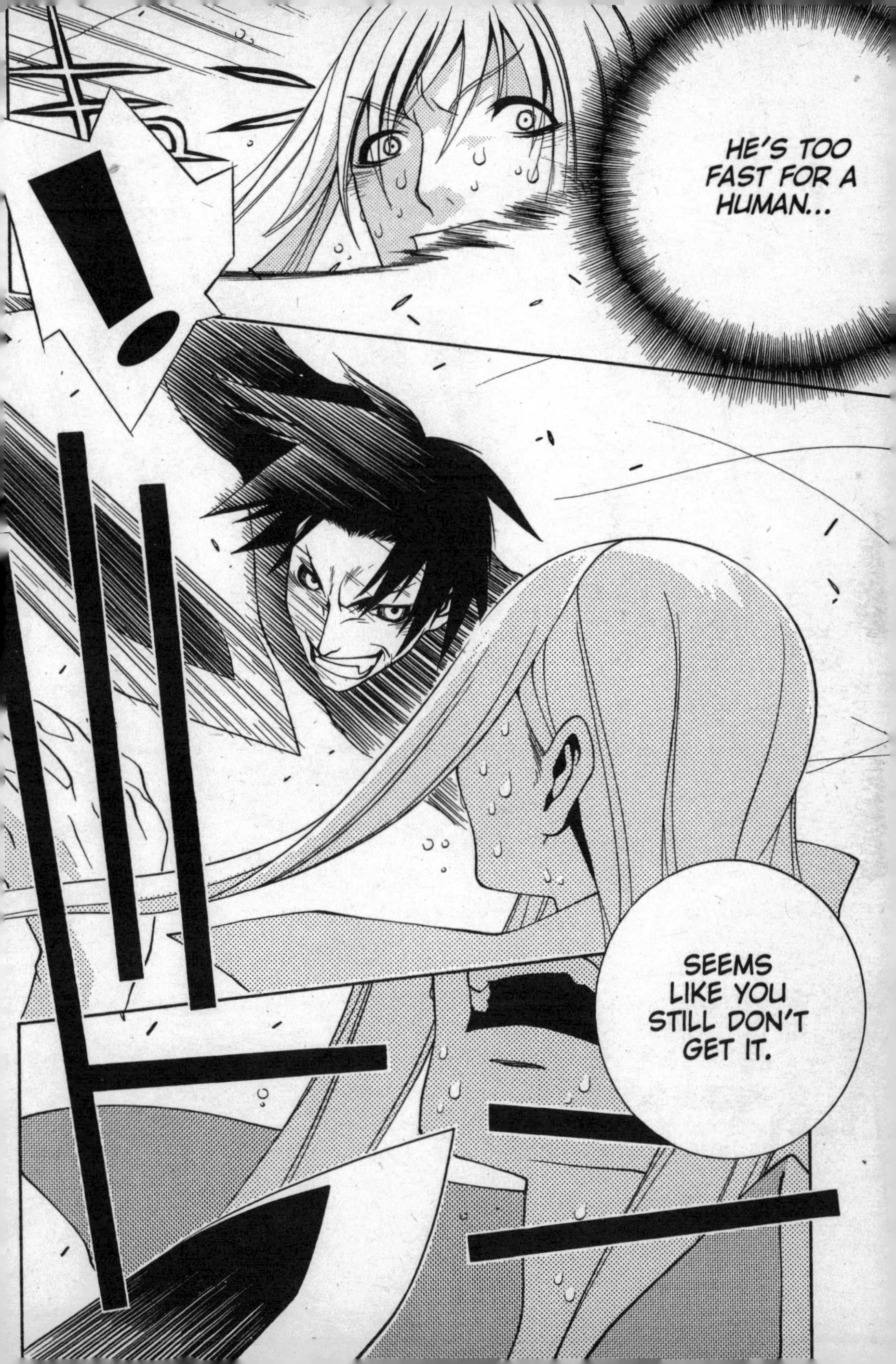
HE'S TOO FAST FOR A HUMAN...
!
SEEMS LIKE YOU STILL DON'T GET IT.

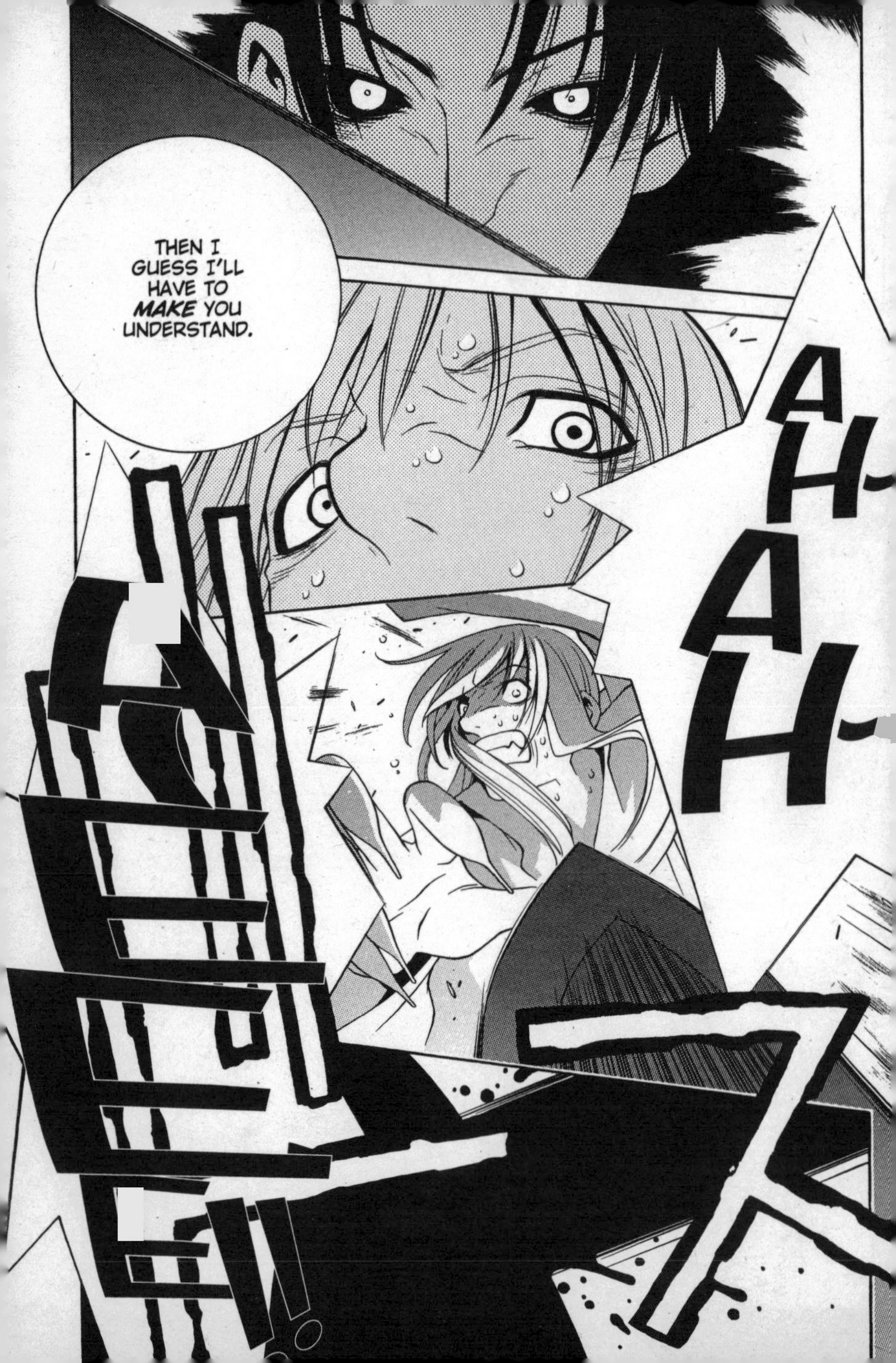
THEN I GUESS I'LL HAVE TO ***MAKE*** YOU UNDERSTAND.
AH-AH-AH-

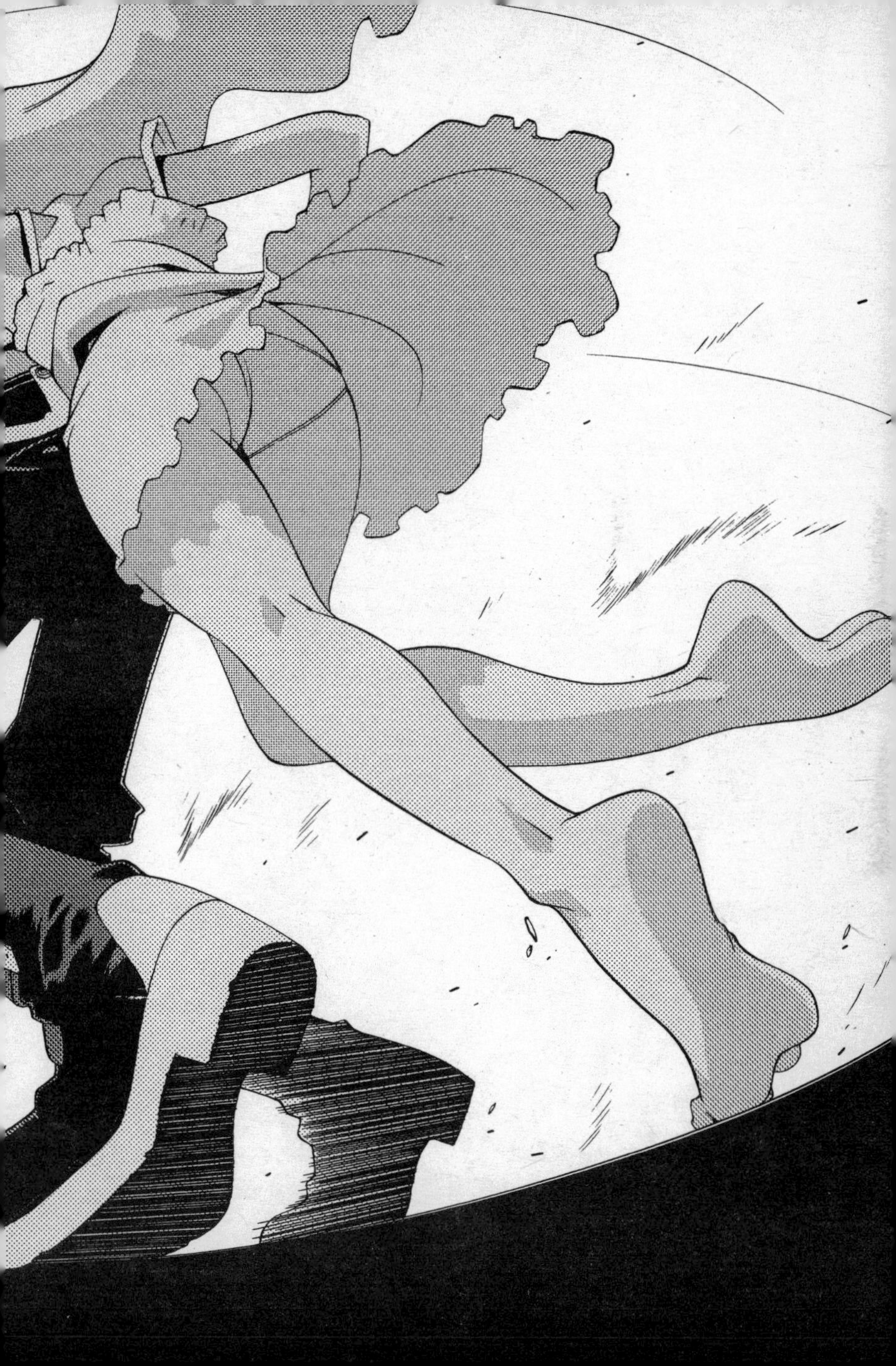

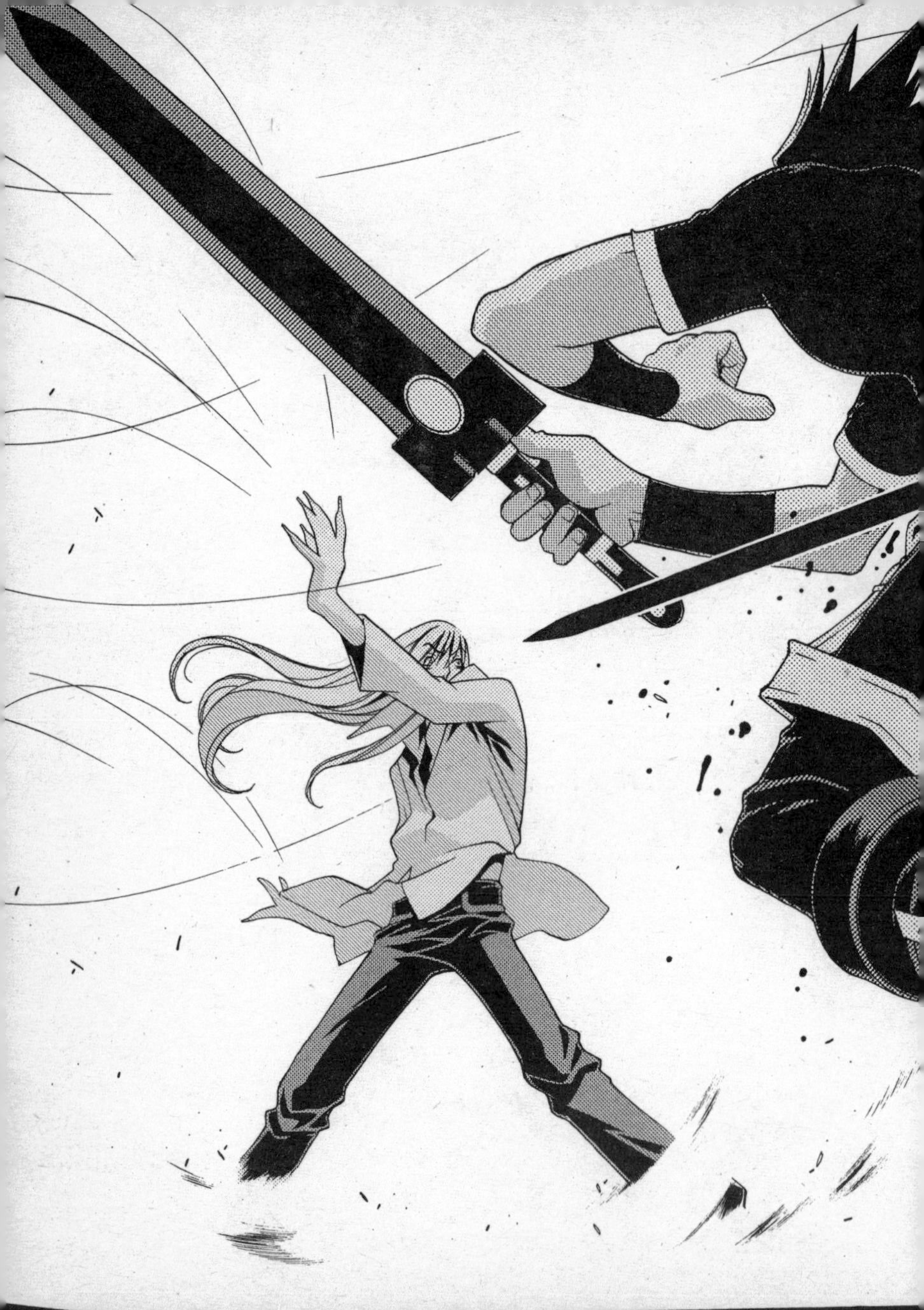

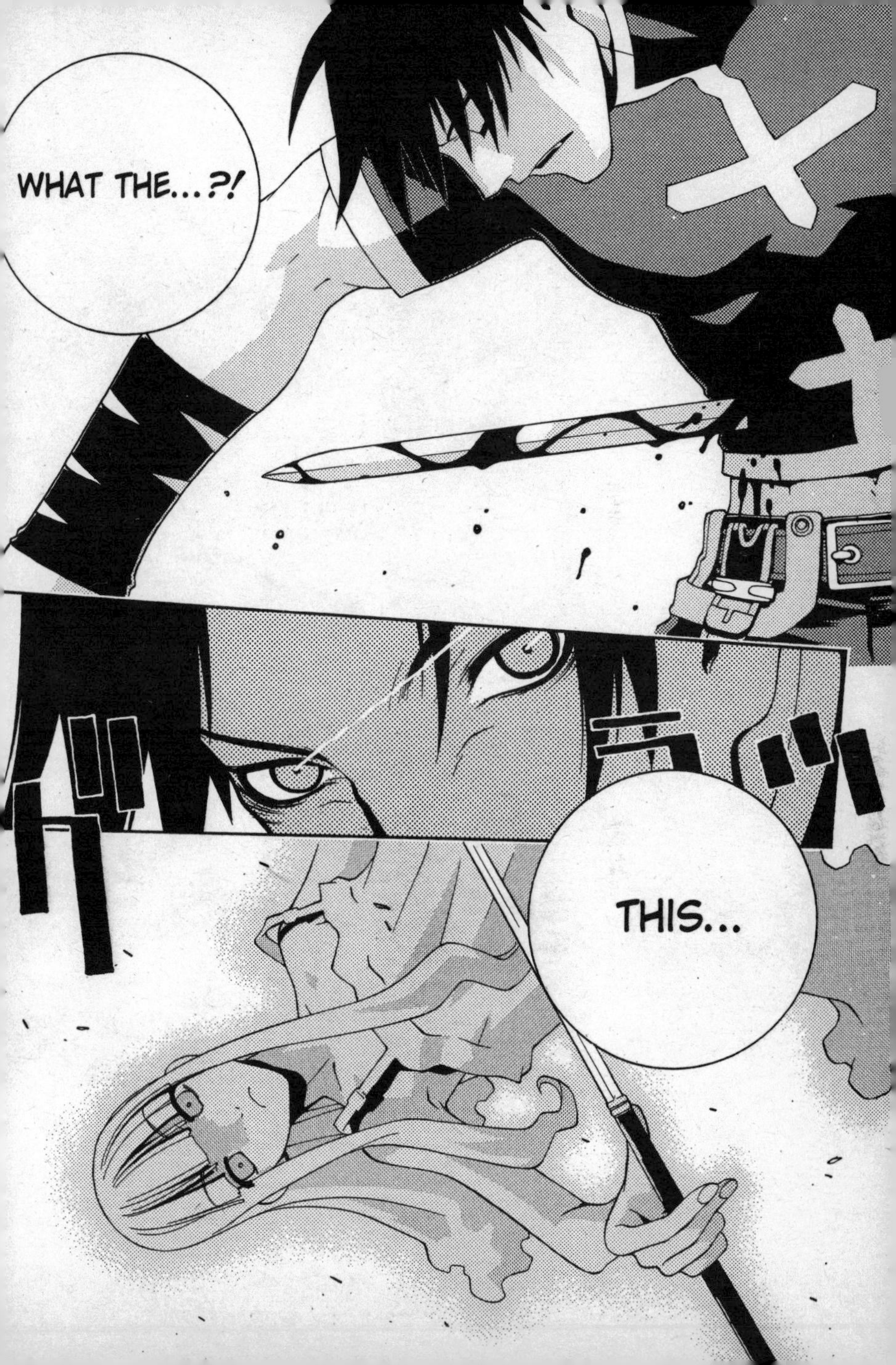
WHAT THE...?!
THIS...

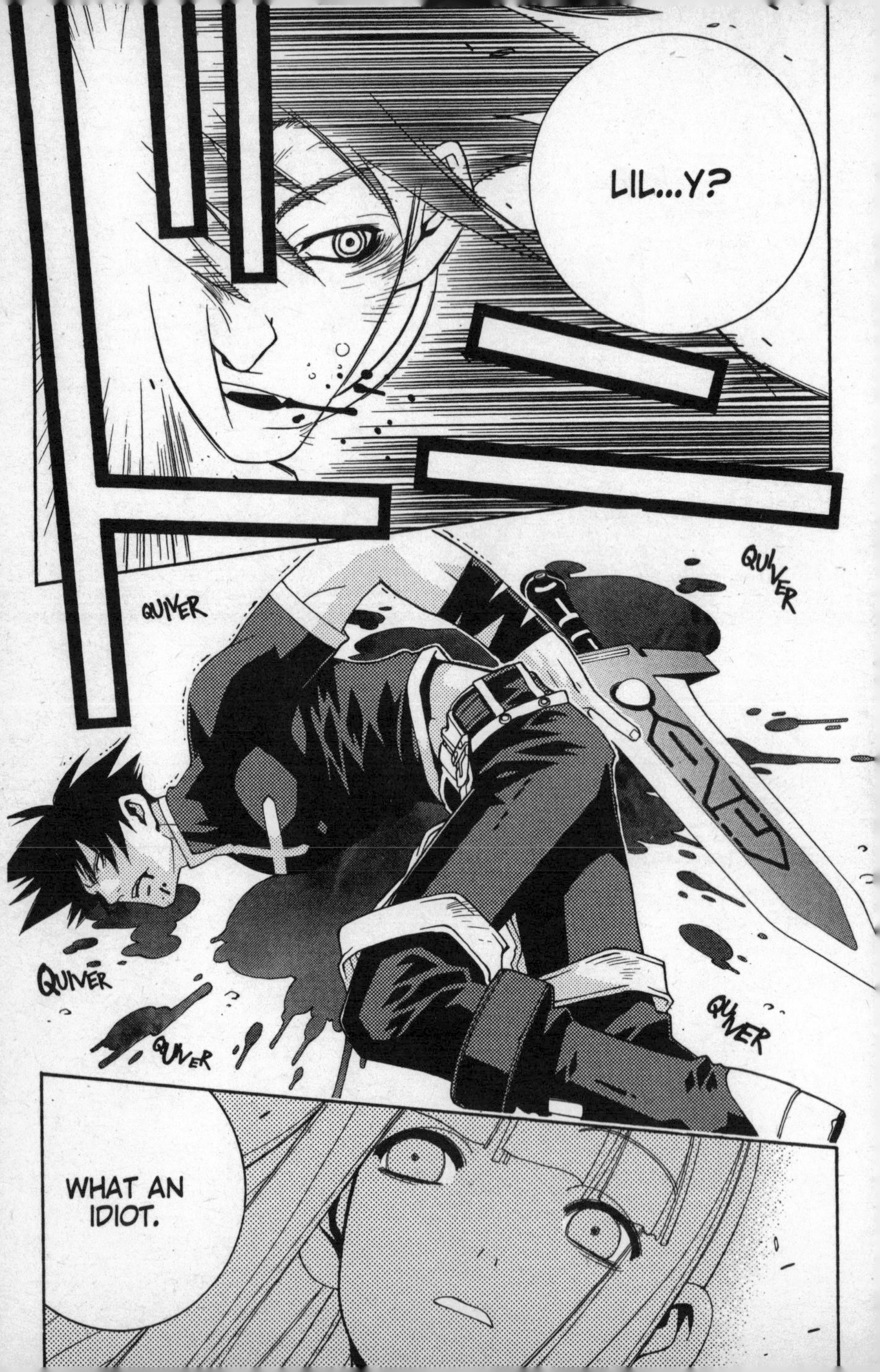
LIL...Y?
QUIVER
QUIVER
QUIVER
QUIVER
QUIVER
WHAT AN IDIOT.

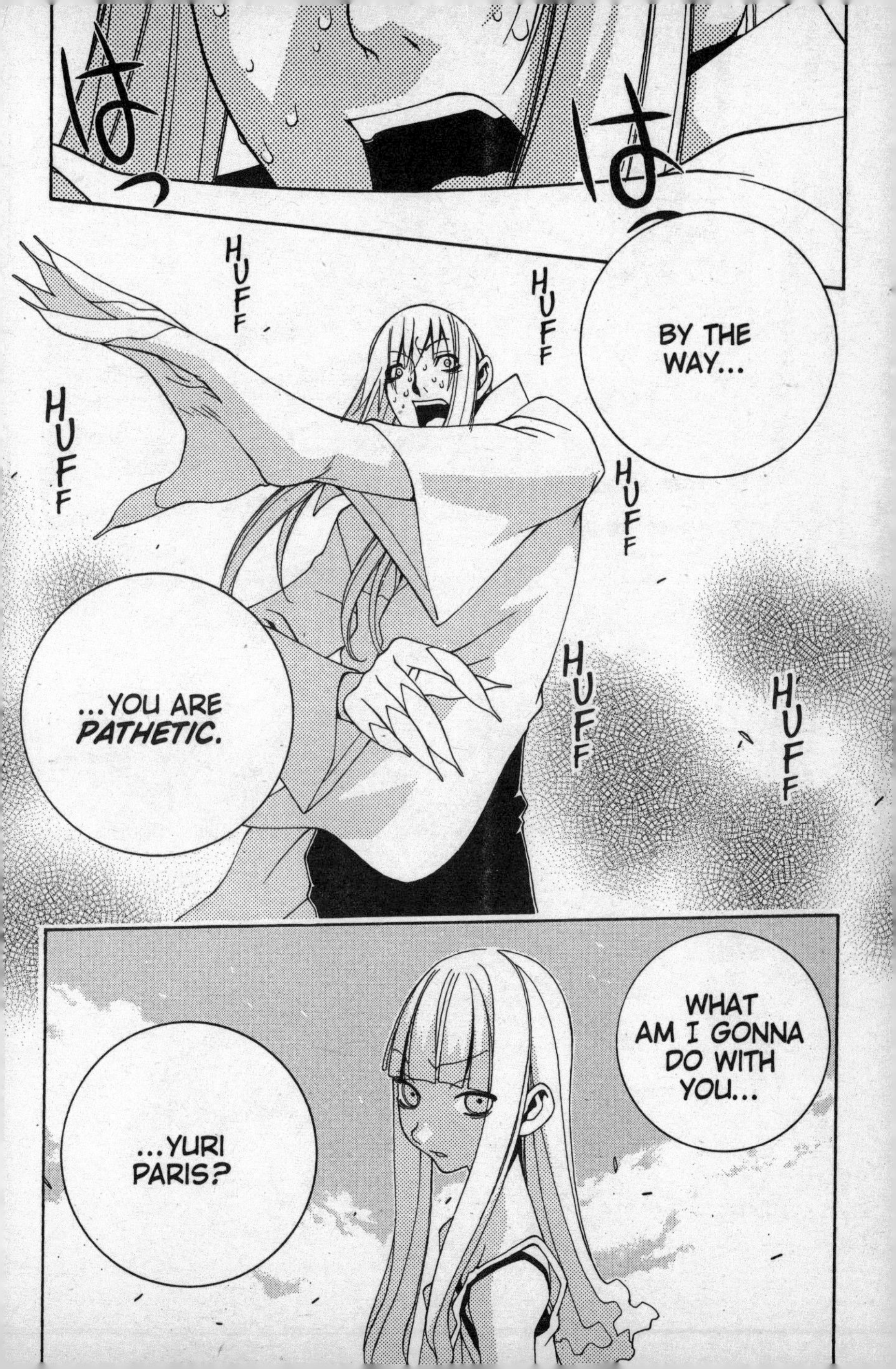

は
はっ
HUFF
HUFF
BY THE WAY...
HUFF
HUFF
HUFF
HUFF
...YOU ARE *PATHETIC.*
WHAT AM I GONNA DO WITH YOU...
...YURI PARIS?

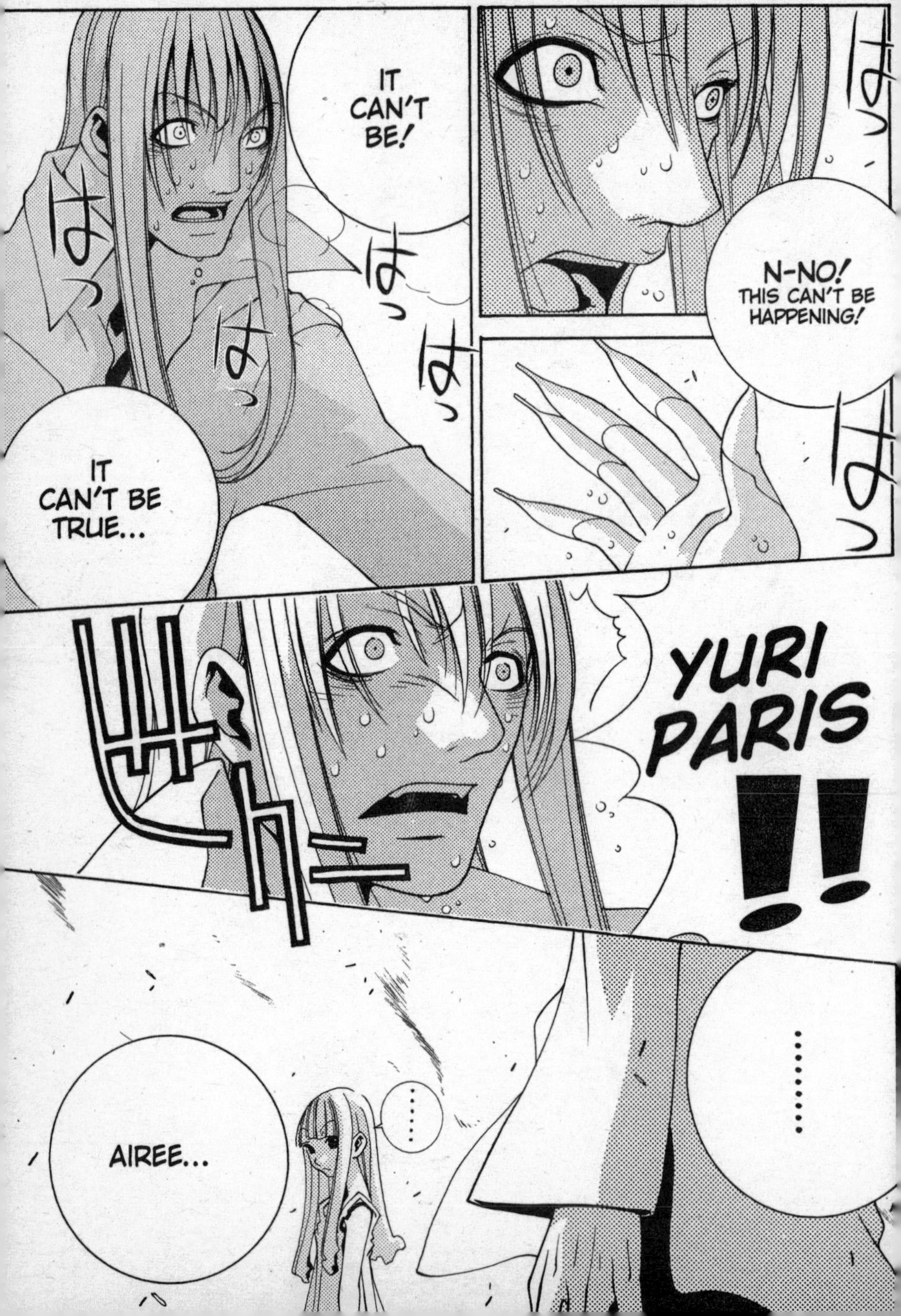

はっ
N-NO! THIS CAN'T BE HAPPENING!
はっ
IT CAN'T BE!
はっ
はっ
はっ
はっ
IT CAN'T BE TRUE...
YURI PARIS!!
....
.....
AIREE...

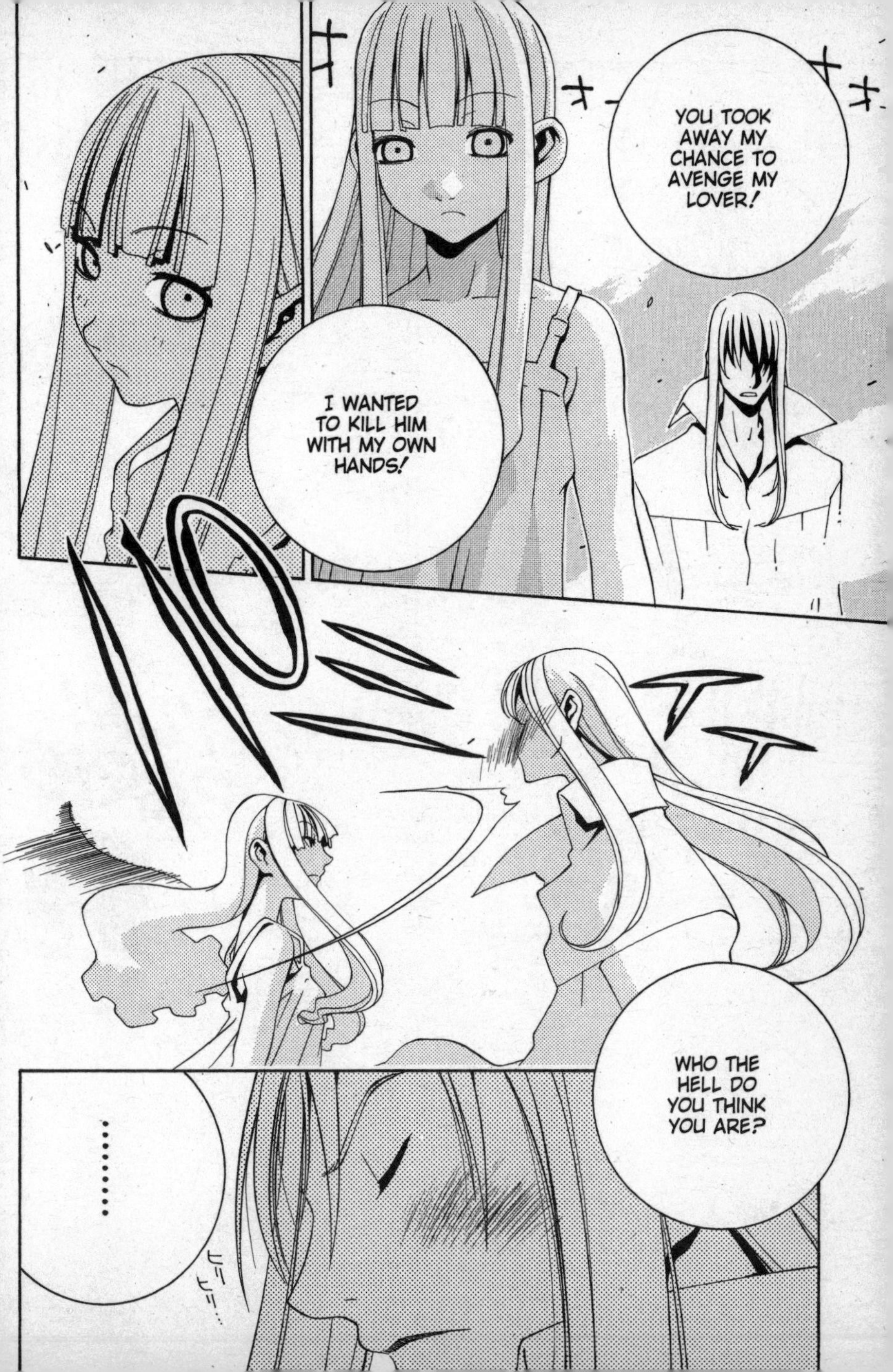
YOU TOOK AWAY MY CHANCE TO AVENGE MY LOVER!
I WANTED TO KILL HIM WITH MY OWN HANDS!
WHO THE HELL DO YOU THINK YOU ARE?
....

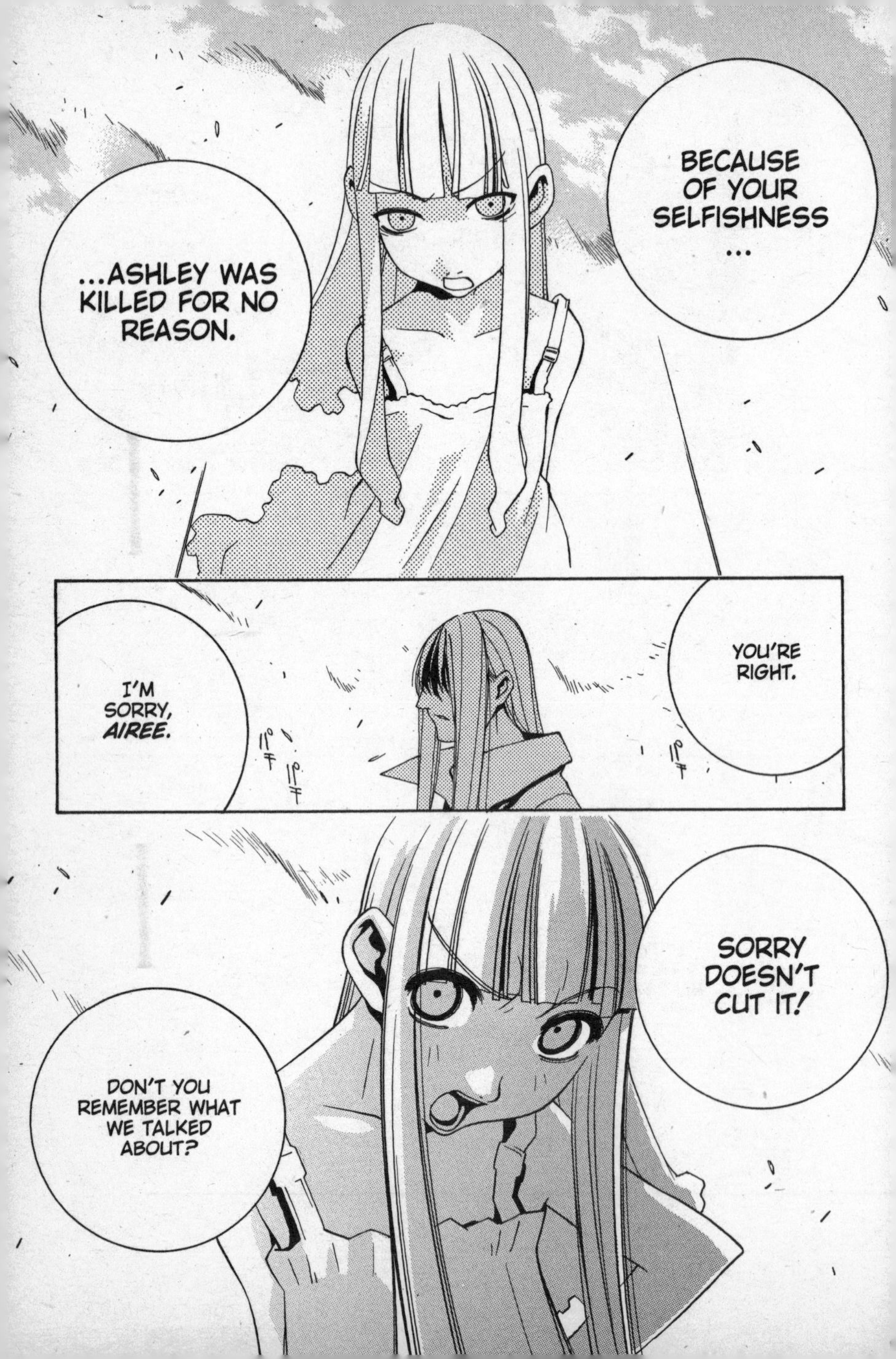
BECAUSE OF YOUR SELFISHNESS ...
...ASHLEY WAS KILLED FOR NO REASON.
YOU'RE RIGHT.
I'M SORRY, *AIREE*.
SORRY DOESN'T CUT IT!
DON'T YOU REMEMBER WHAT WE TALKED ABOUT?

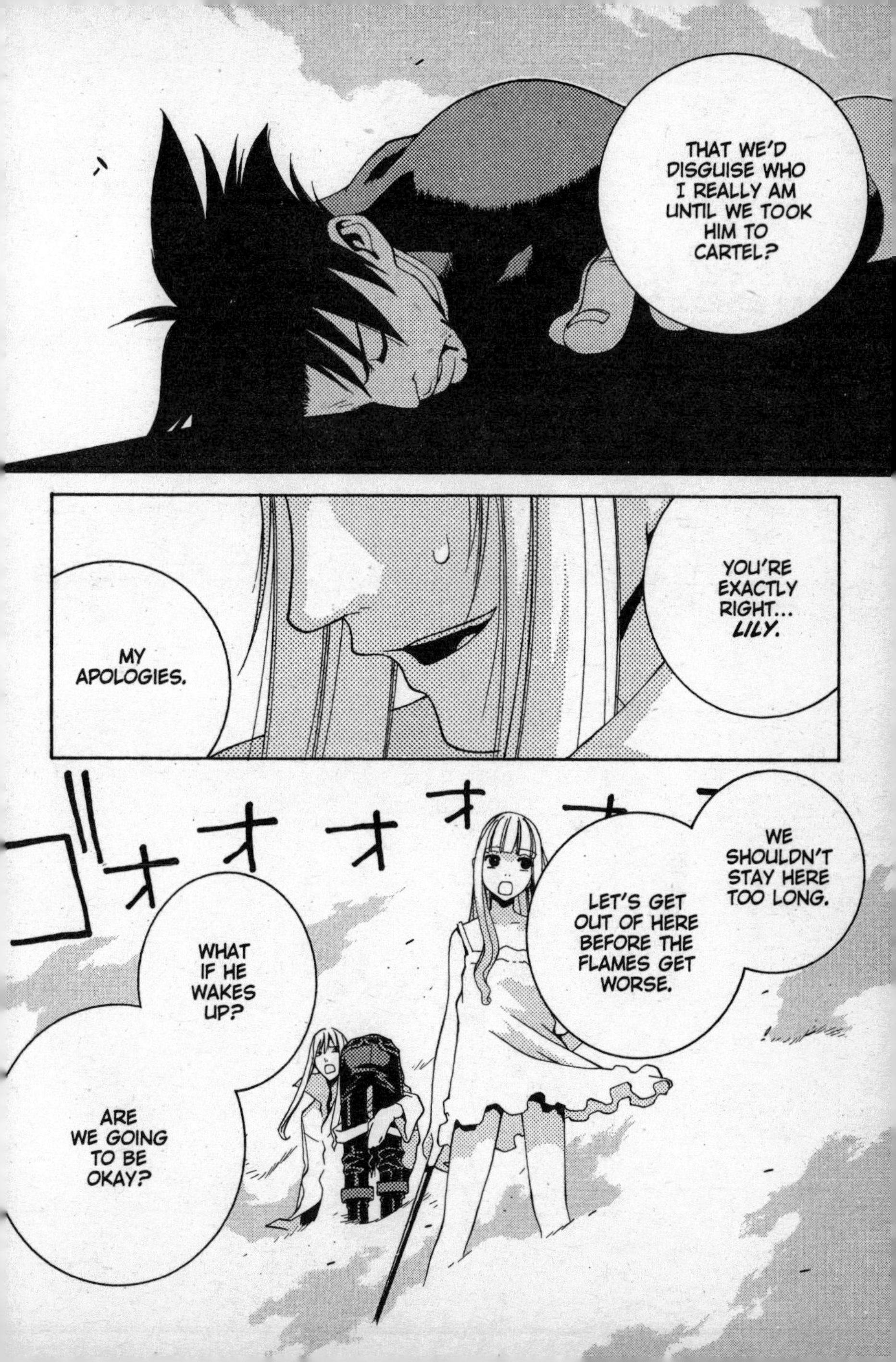
THAT WE'D DISGUISE WHO I REALLY AM UNTIL WE TOOK HIM TO CARTEL?
YOU'RE EXACTLY RIGHT... *LILY.*
MY APOLOGIES.
ゴオオオ
WE SHOULDN'T STAY HERE TOO LONG.
LET'S GET OUT OF HERE BEFORE THE FLAMES GET WORSE.
WHAT IF HE WAKES UP?
ARE WE GOING TO BE OKAY?

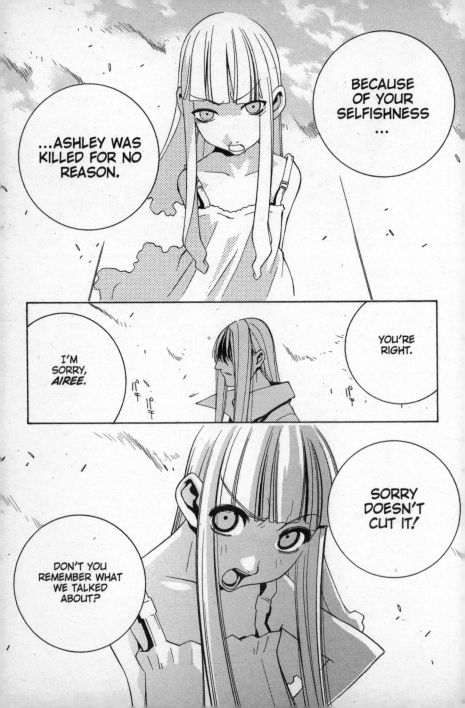

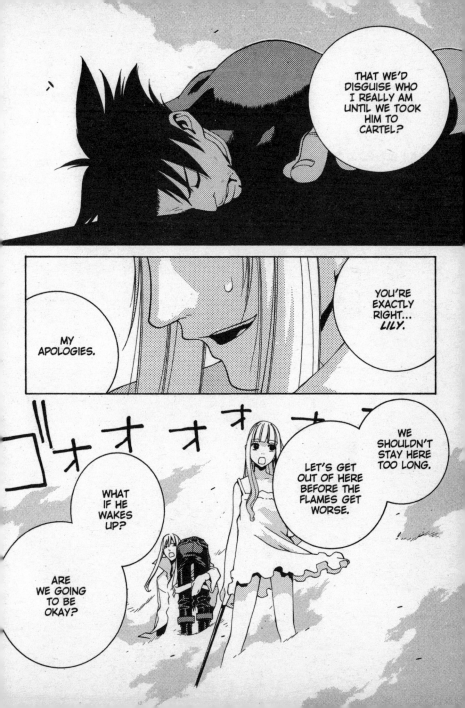

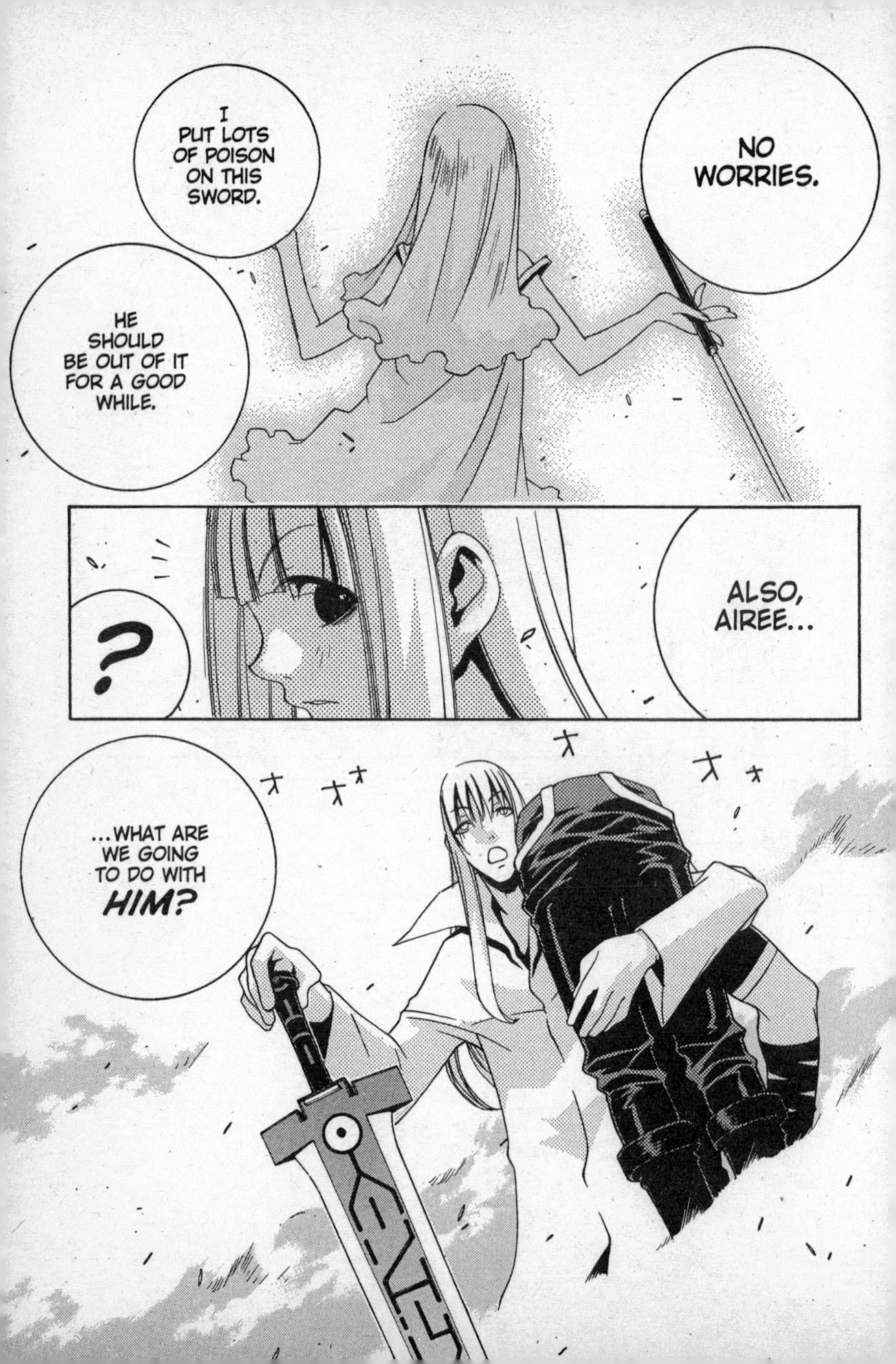
NO WORRIES.
I PUT LOTS OF POISON ON THIS SWORD.
HE SHOULD BE OUT OF IT FOR A GOOD WHILE.
ALSO, AIREE...
?
...WHAT ARE WE GOING TO DO WITH ***HIM?***

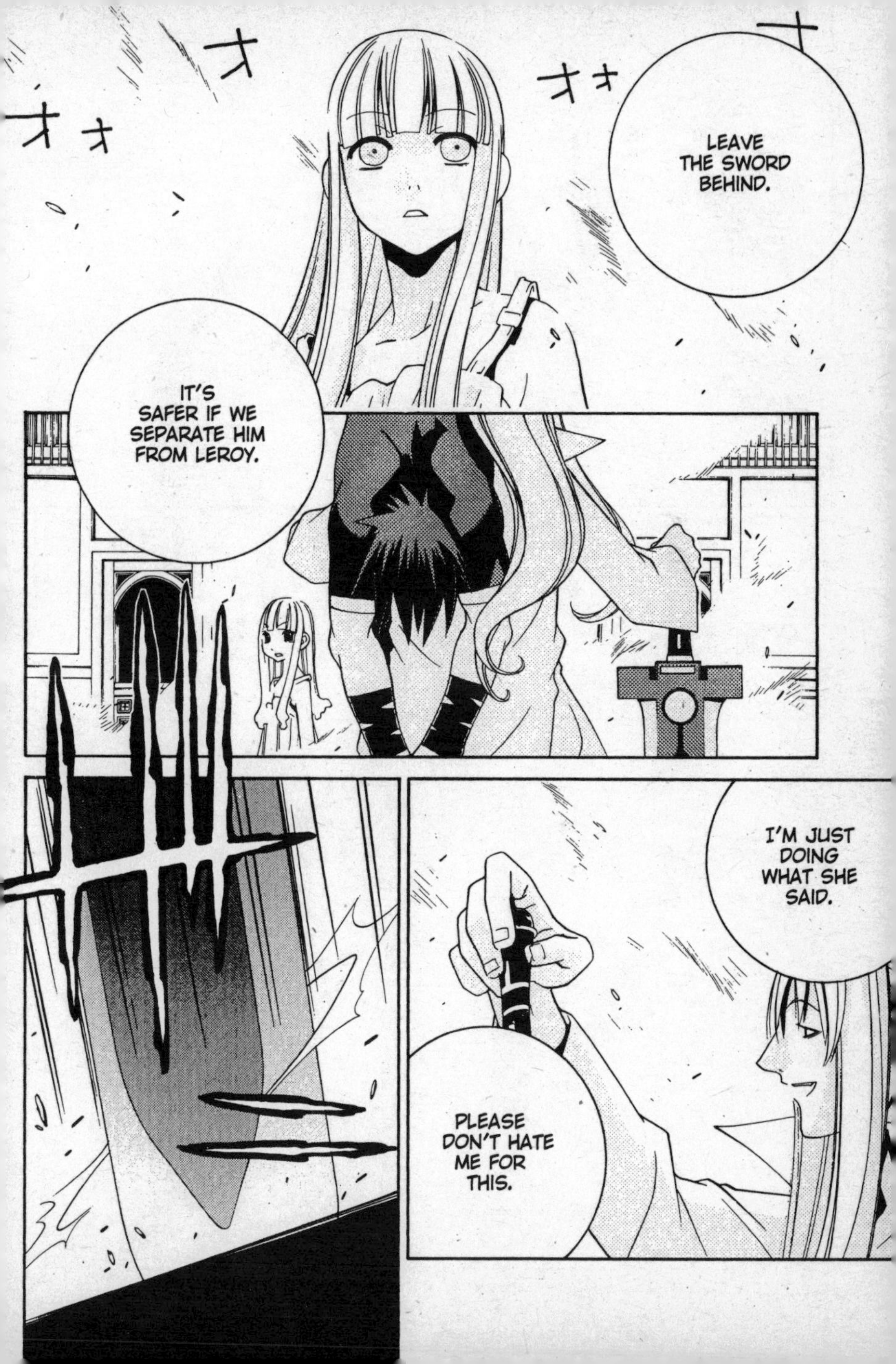
LEAVE THE SWORD BEHIND.
IT'S SAFER IF WE SEPARATE HIM FROM LEROY.
I'M JUST DOING WHAT SHE SAID.
PLEASE DON'T HATE ME FOR THIS.

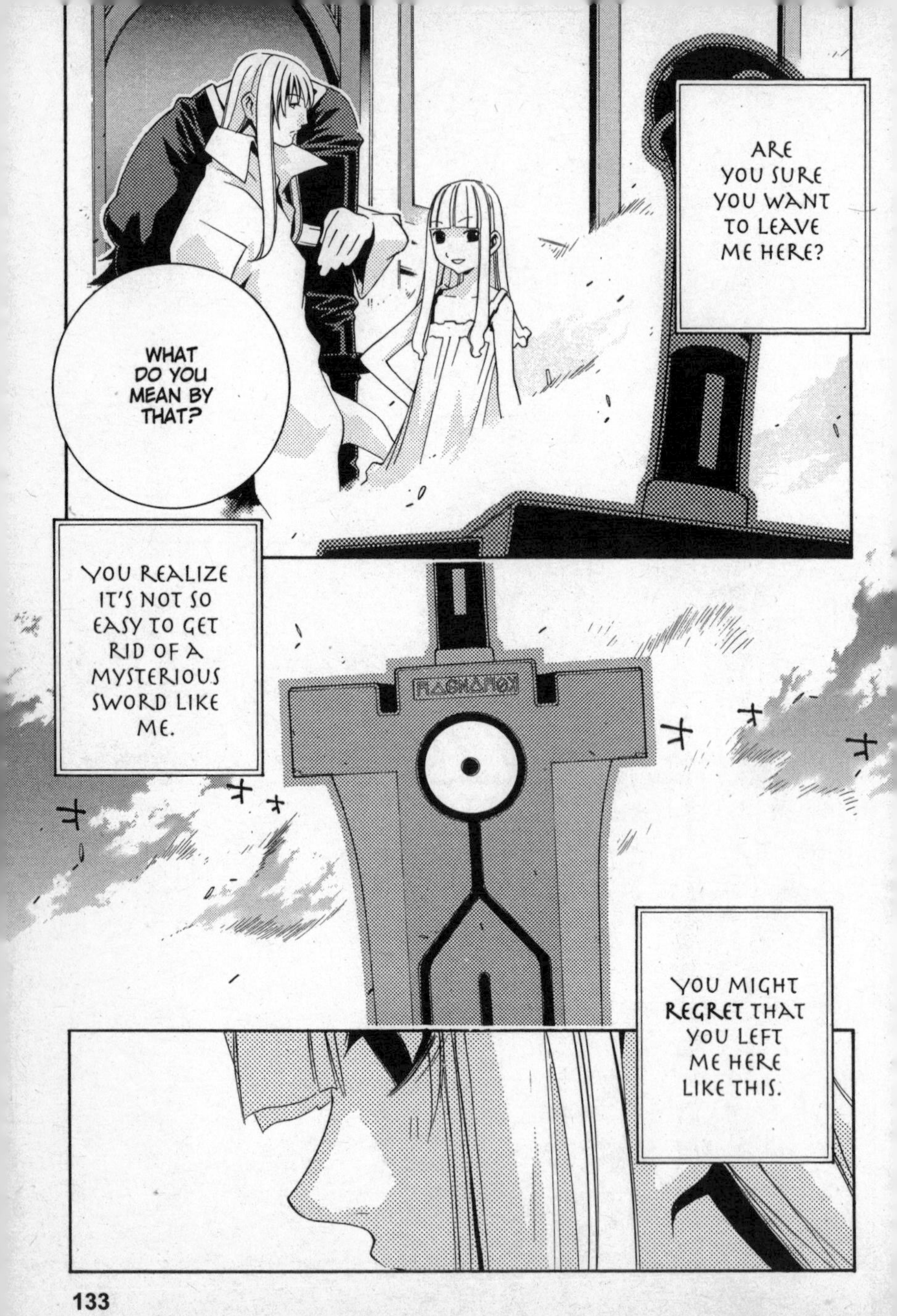
ARE YOU SURE YOU WANT TO LEAVE ME HERE?
WHAT DO YOU MEAN BY THAT?
YOU REALIZE IT'S NOT SO EASY TO GET RID OF A MYSTERIOUS SWORD LIKE ME.
YOU MIGHT **REGRET** THAT YOU LEFT ME HERE LIKE THIS.

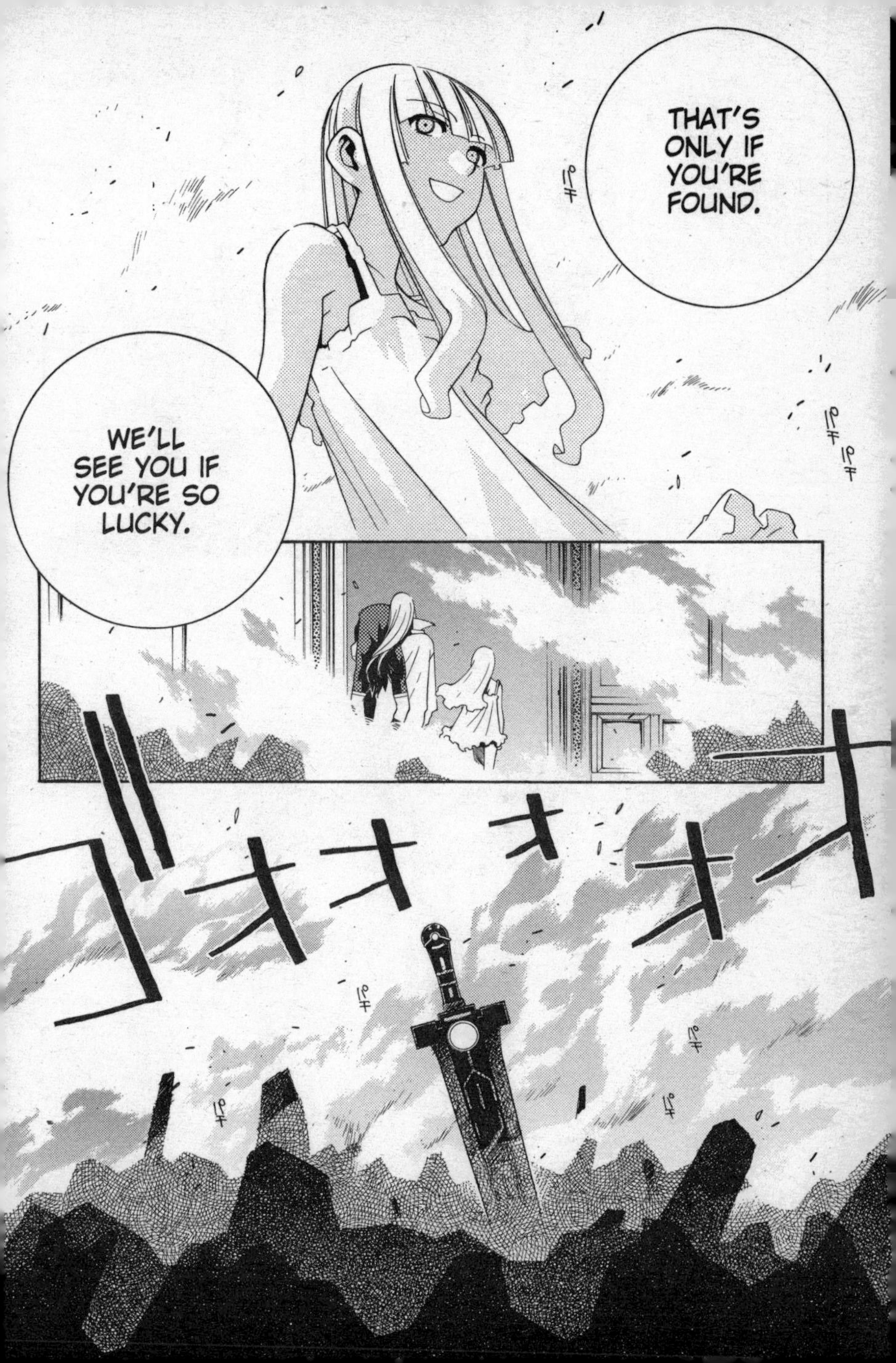
THAT'S ONLY IF YOU'RE FOUND.
WE'LL SEE YOU IF YOU'RE SO LUCKY.

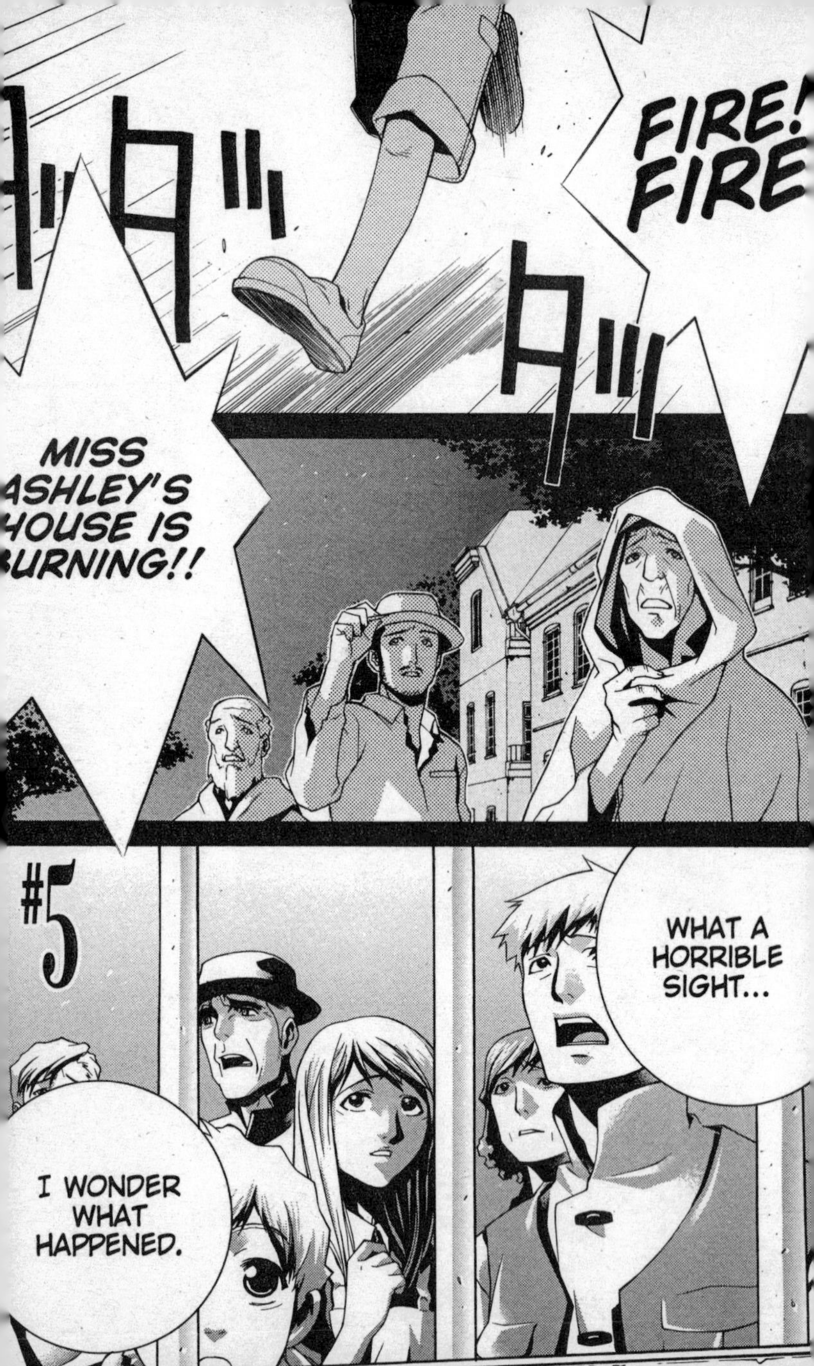
FIRE! FIRE
タッ
タッ
MISS ASHLEY'S HOUSE IS BURNING!!
#5
WHAT A HORRIBLE SIGHT...
I WONDER WHAT HAPPENED.

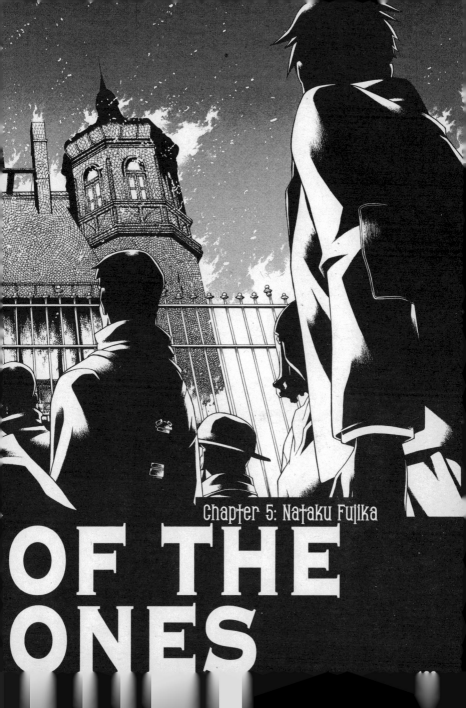

Chapter 5: Nataku Fujika

OF THE
ONES

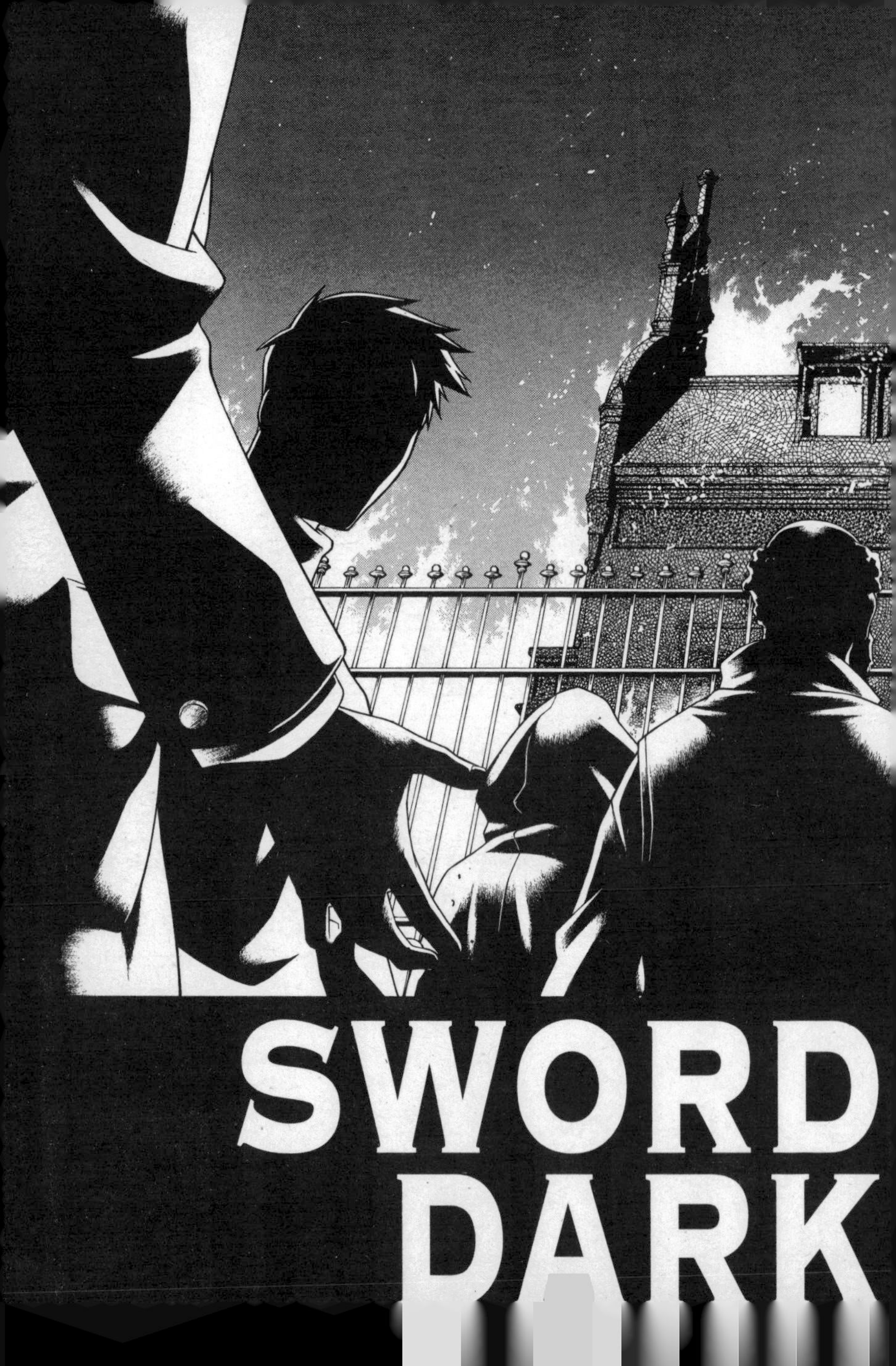
SWORD
DARK

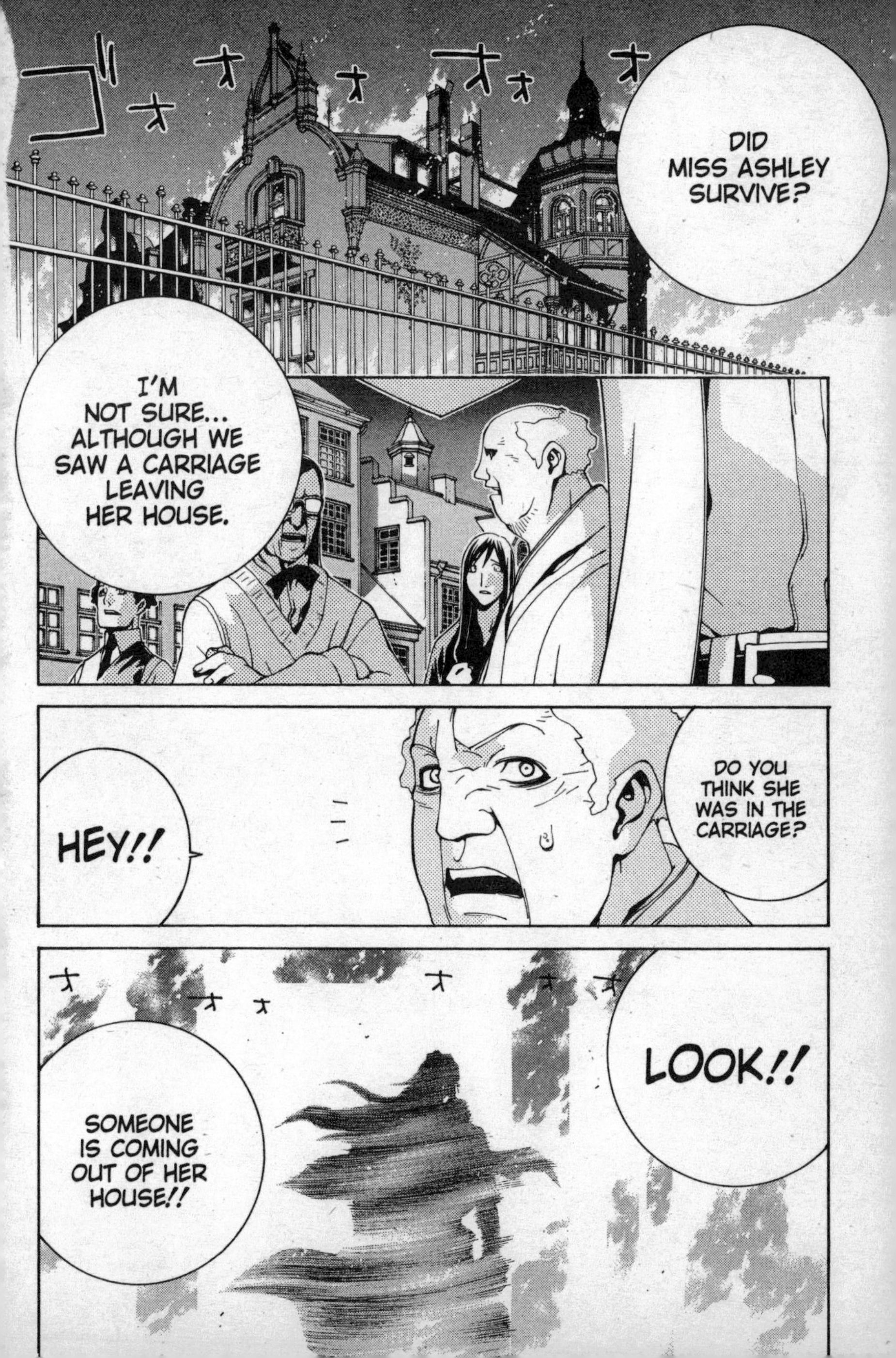
DID MISS ASHLEY SURVIVE?
I'M NOT SURE... ALTHOUGH WE SAW A CARRIAGE LEAVING HER HOUSE.
DO YOU THINK SHE WAS IN THE CARRIAGE?
HEY!!
LOOK!!
SOMEONE IS COMING OUT OF HER HOUSE!!

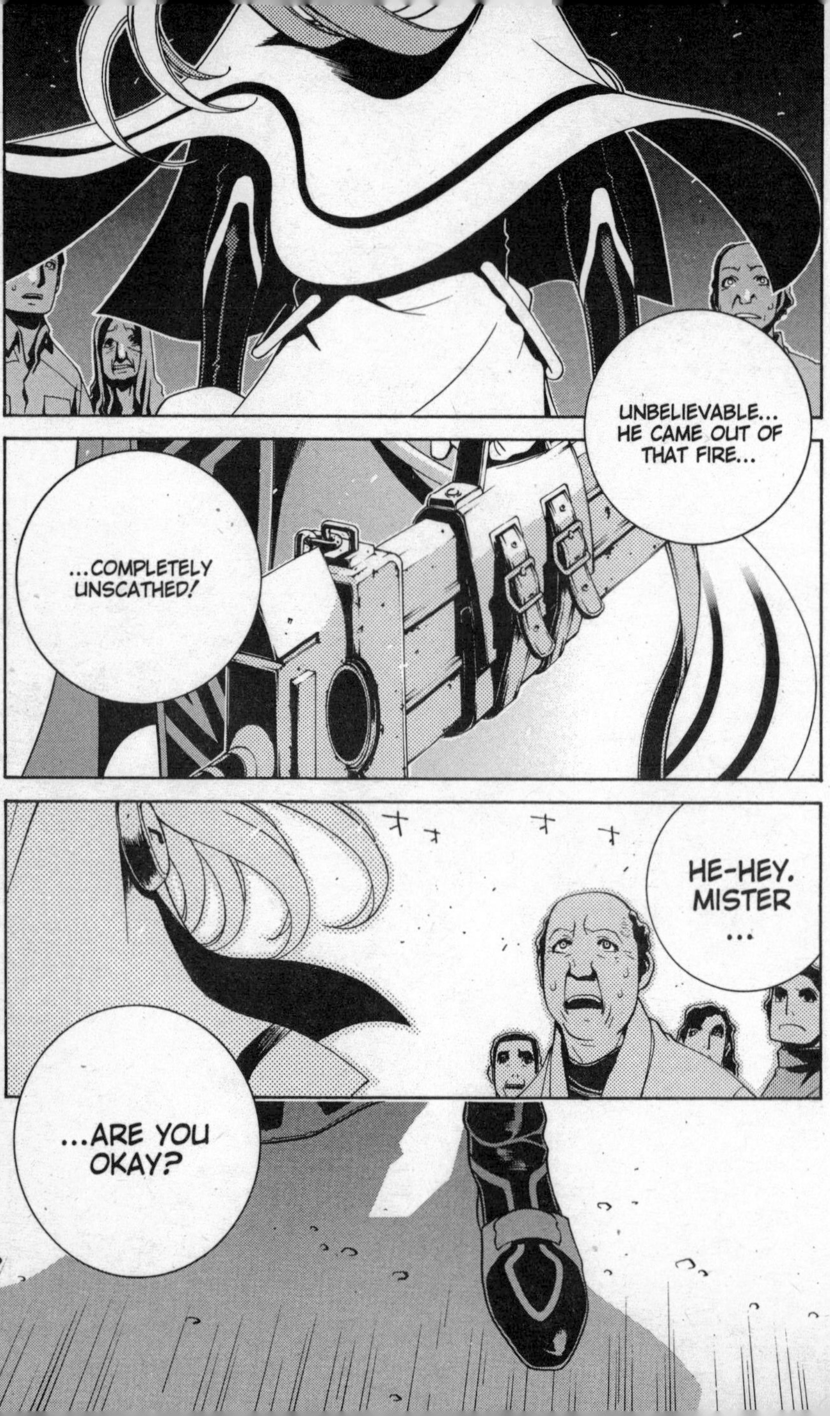
UNBELIEVABLE... HE CAME OUT OF THAT FIRE...
...COMPLETELY UNSCATHED!
HE-HEY. MISTER ...
...ARE YOU OKAY?

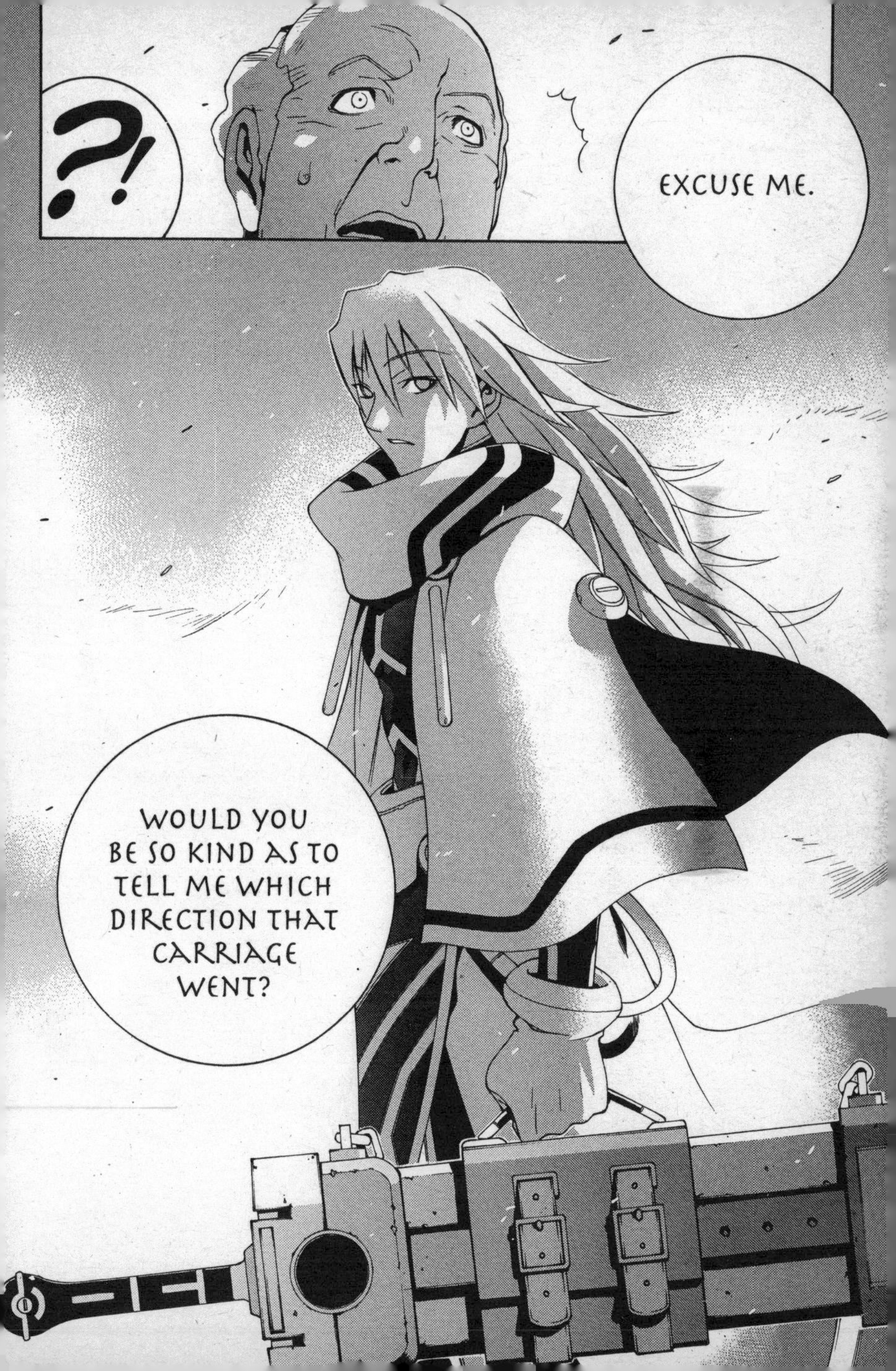
?!
EXCUSE ME.
WOULD YOU BE SO KIND AS TO TELL ME WHICH DIRECTION THAT CARRIAGE WENT?

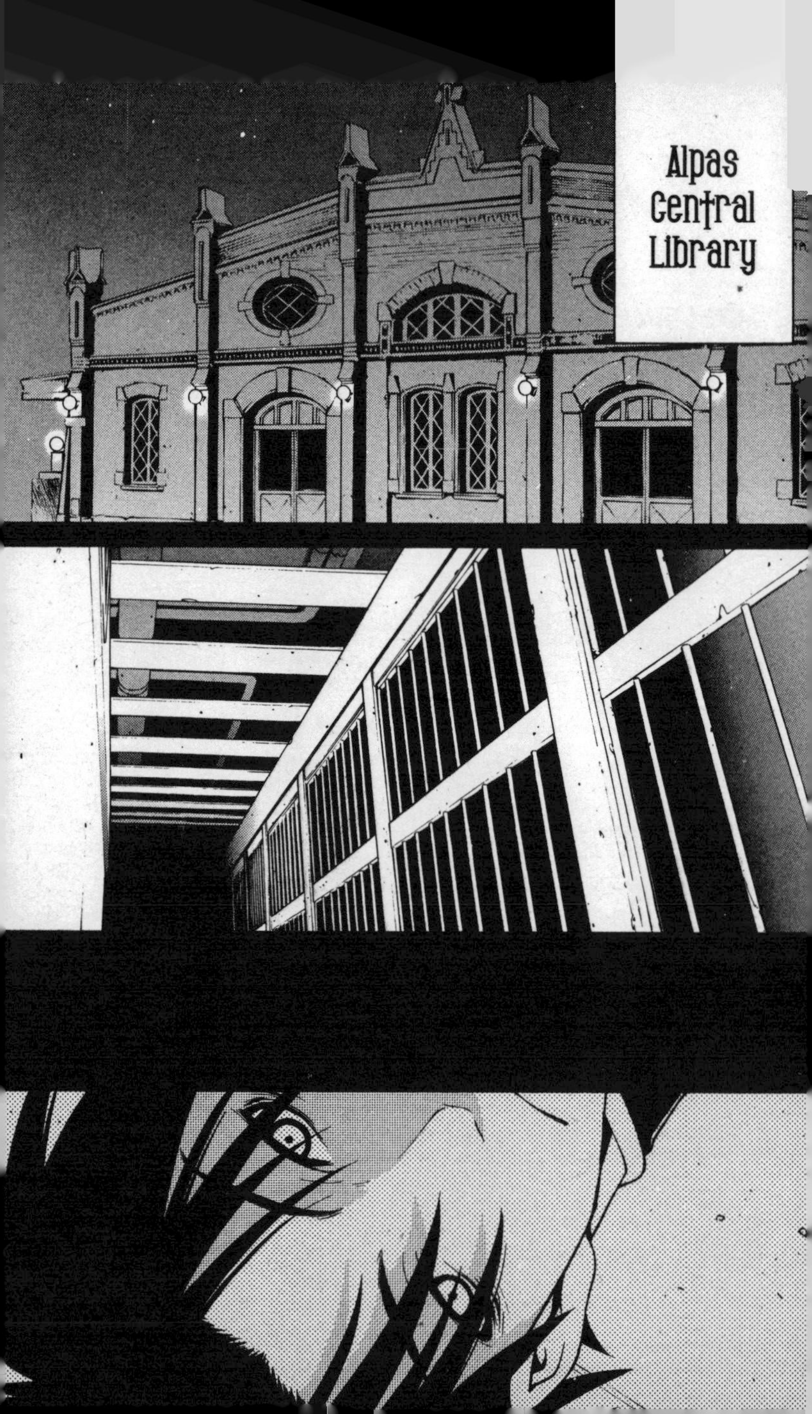
Alpas Central Library

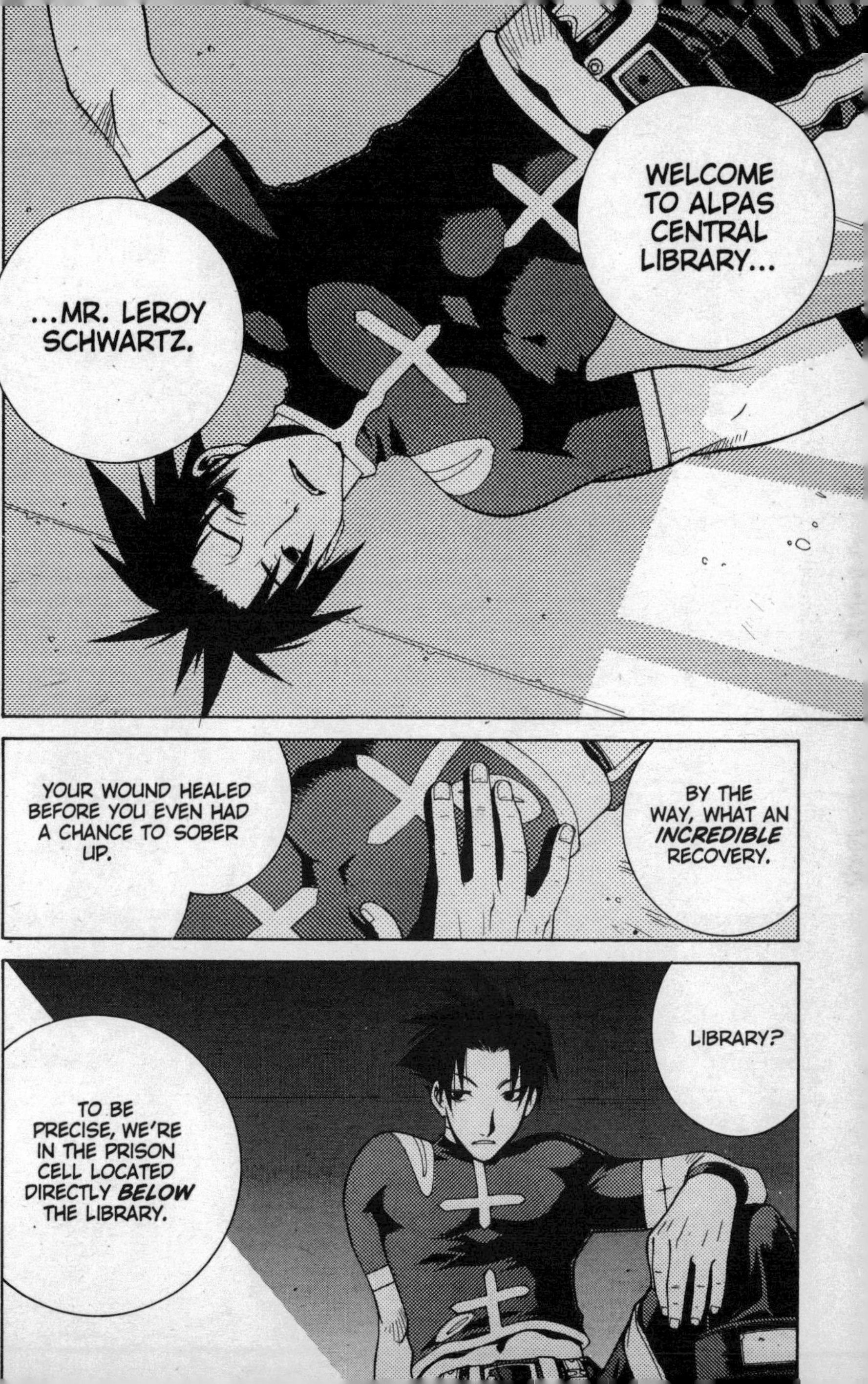
WELCOME TO ALPAS CENTRAL LIBRARY...
...MR. LEROY SCHWARTZ.
BY THE WAY, WHAT AN *INCREDIBLE* RECOVERY.
YOUR WOUND HEALED BEFORE YOU EVEN HAD A CHANCE TO SOBER UP.
LIBRARY?
TO BE PRECISE, WE'RE IN THE PRISON CELL LOCATED DIRECTLY ***BELOW*** THE LIBRARY.

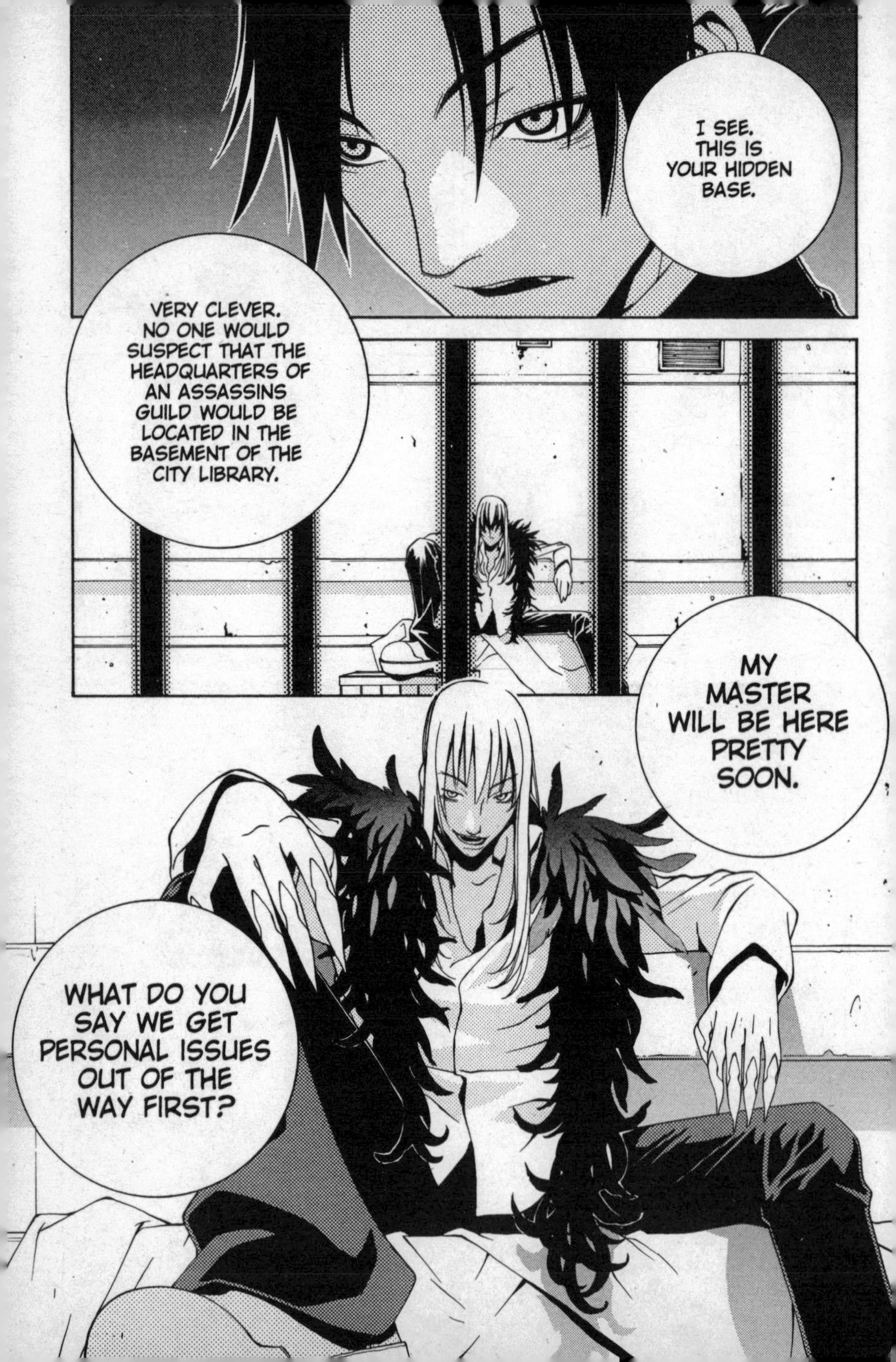
I SEE. THIS IS YOUR HIDDEN BASE.
VERY CLEVER. NO ONE WOULD SUSPECT THAT THE HEADQUARTERS OF AN ASSASSINS GUILD WOULD BE LOCATED IN THE BASEMENT OF THE CITY LIBRARY.
MY MASTER WILL BE HERE PRETTY SOON.
WHAT DO YOU SAY WE GET PERSONAL ISSUES OUT OF THE WAY FIRST?

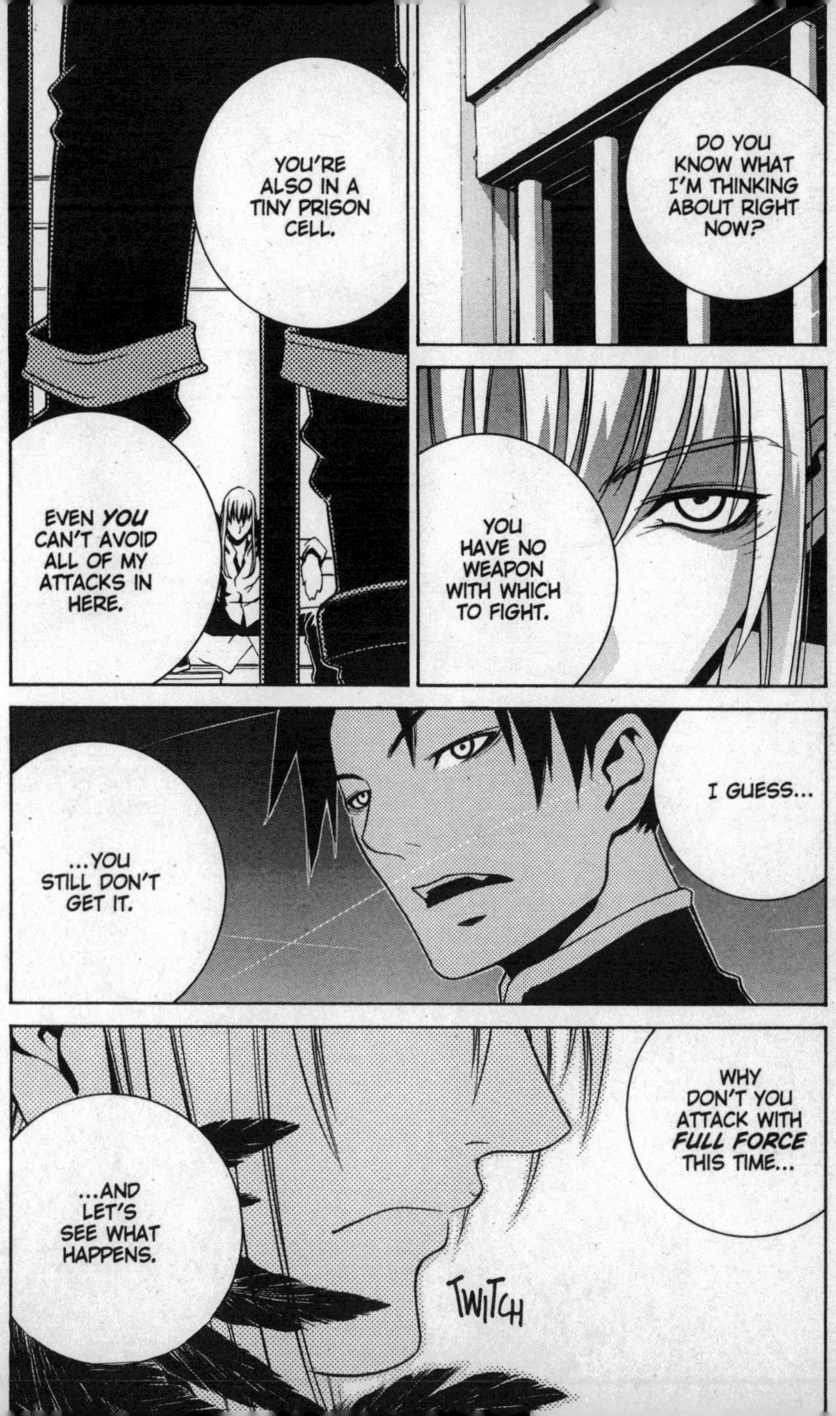
DO YOU KNOW WHAT I'M THINKING ABOUT RIGHT NOW?
YOU HAVE NO WEAPON WITH WHICH TO FIGHT.
YOU'RE ALSO IN A TINY PRISON CELL.
EVEN *YOU* CAN'T AVOID ALL OF MY ATTACKS IN HERE.
I GUESS...
...YOU STILL DON'T GET IT.
WHY DON'T YOU ATTACK WITH ***FULL FORCE*** THIS TIME...
...AND LET'S SEE WHAT HAPPENS.
TWITCH

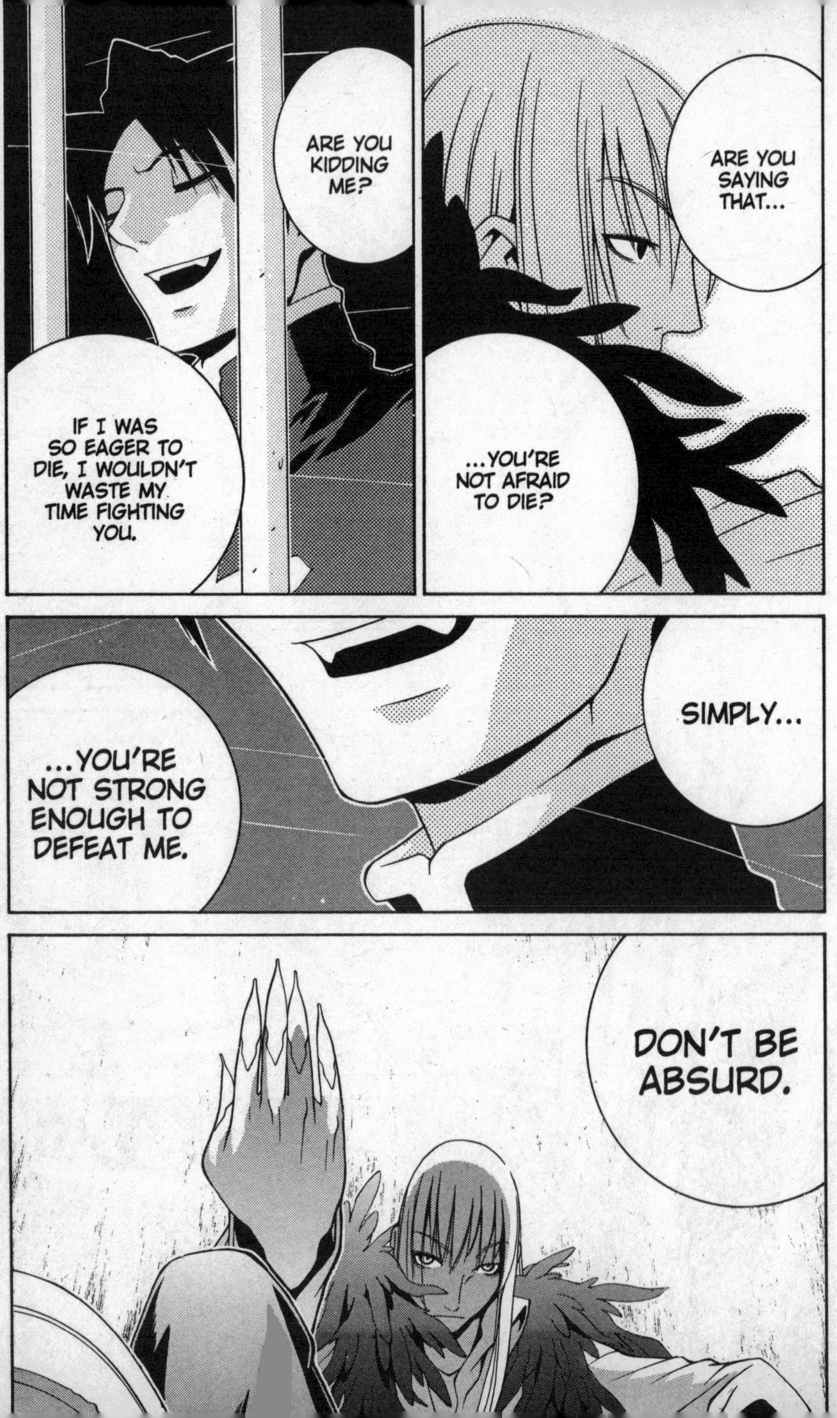
ARE YOU SAYING THAT...
...YOU'RE NOT AFRAID TO DIE?
ARE YOU KIDDING ME?
IF I WAS SO EAGER TO DIE, I WOULDN'T WASTE MY TIME FIGHTING YOU.
SIMPLY...
...YOU'RE NOT STRONG ENOUGH TO DEFEAT ME.
DON'T BE ABSURD.

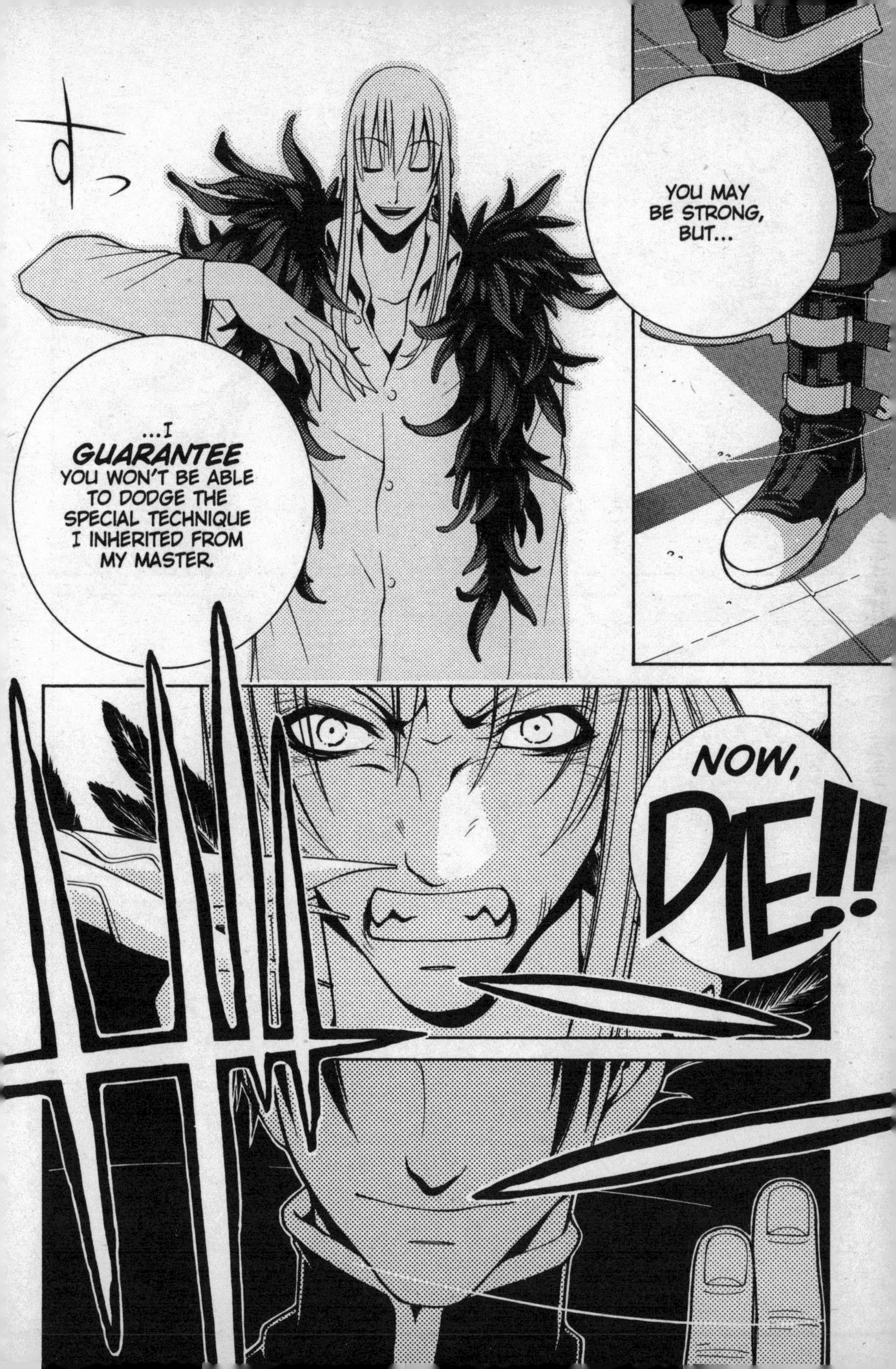
YOU MAY BE STRONG, BUT...
すっ
...I **GUARANTEE** YOU WON'T BE ABLE TO DODGE THE SPECIAL TECHNIQUE I INHERITED FROM MY MASTER.
NOW, DIE!!

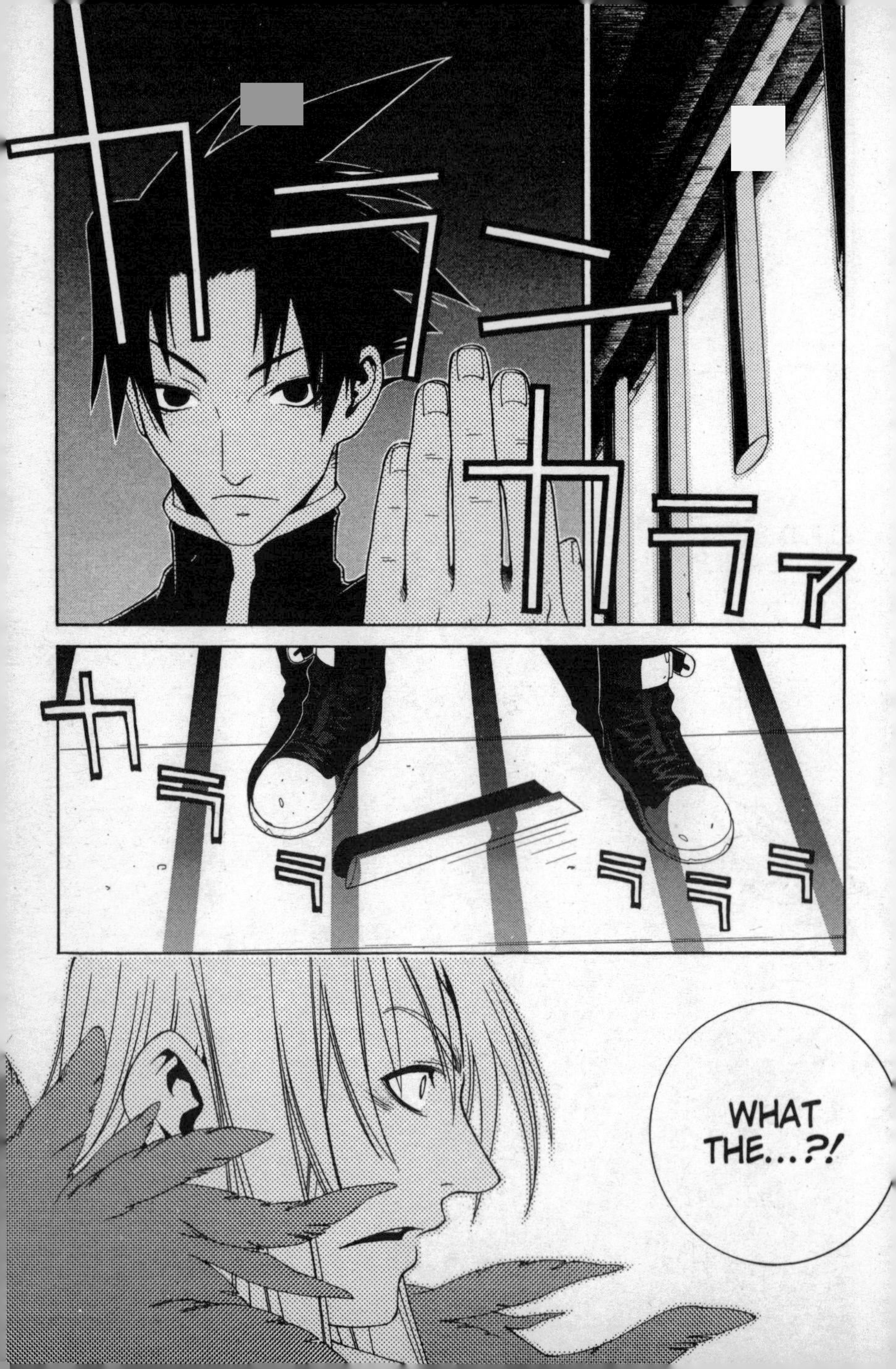
カラン
カララァ
カラララララ
WHAT THE...?!

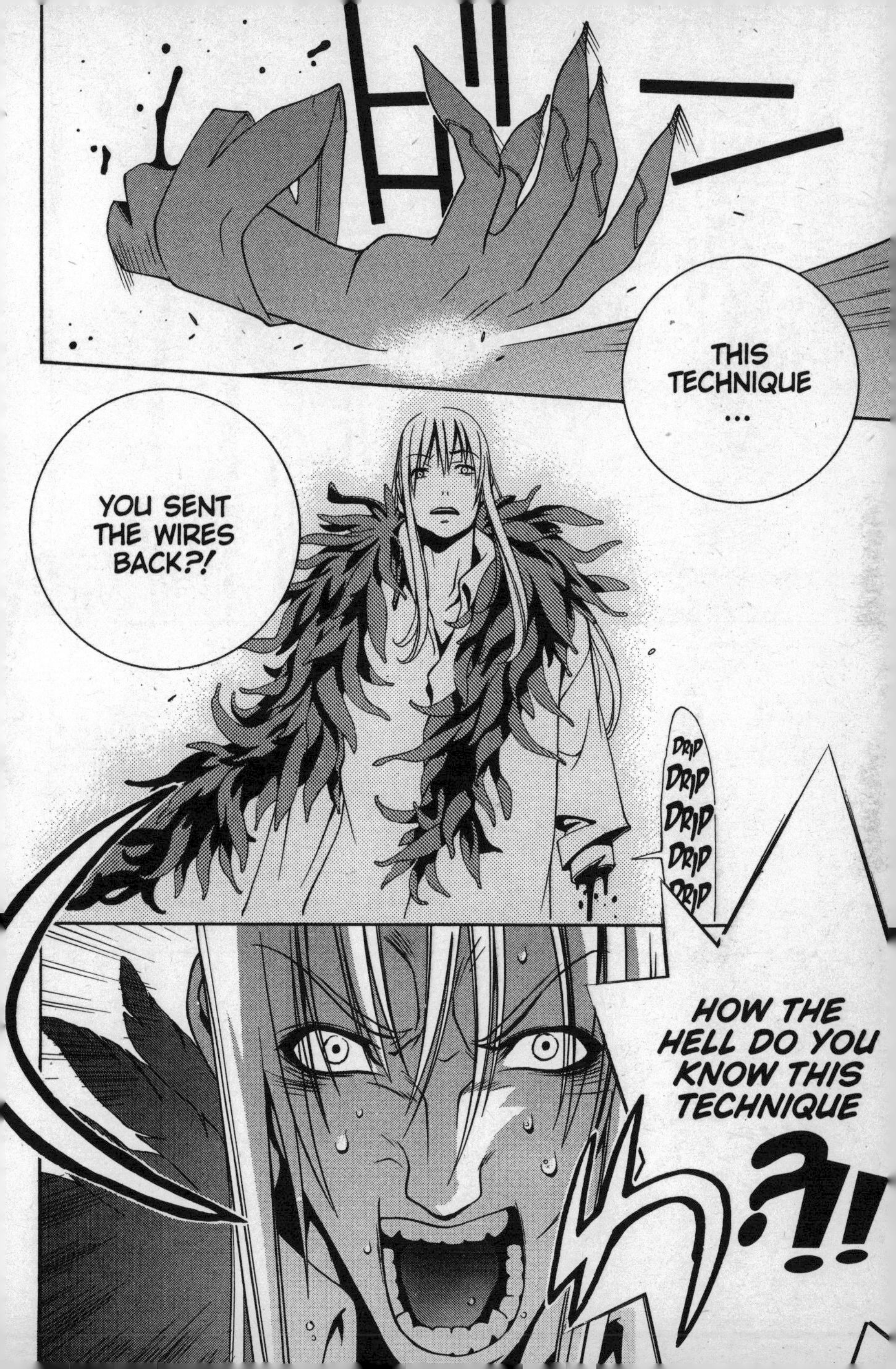
THIS TECHNIQUE ...
YOU SENT THE WIRES BACK?!
DRIP DRIP DRIP DRIP DRIP
HOW THE HELL DO YOU KNOW THIS TECHNIQUE ?!!

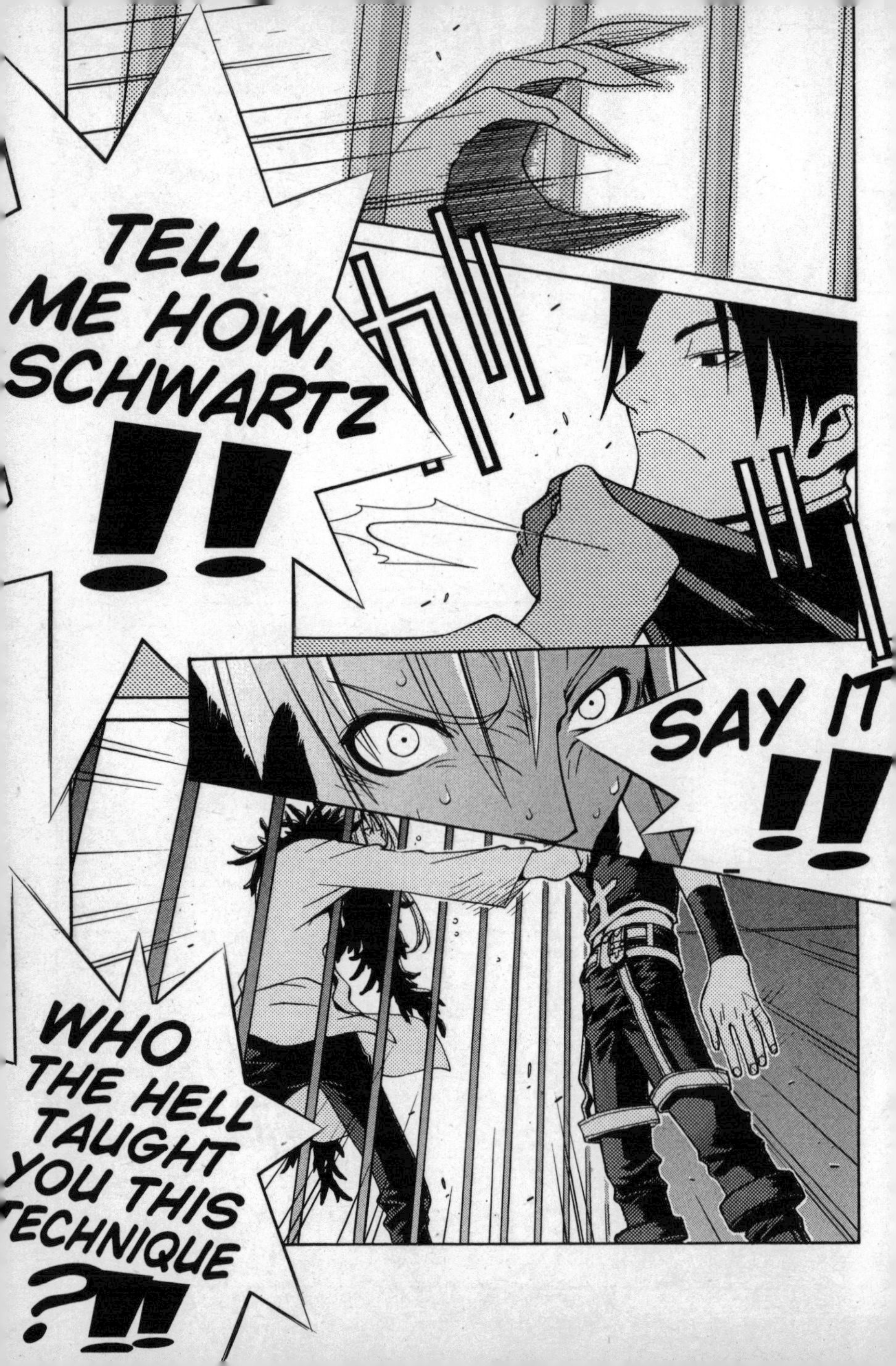
TELL ME HOW, SCHWARTZ!!
SAY IT!!
WHO THE HELL TAUGHT YOU THIS TECHNIQUE?!!

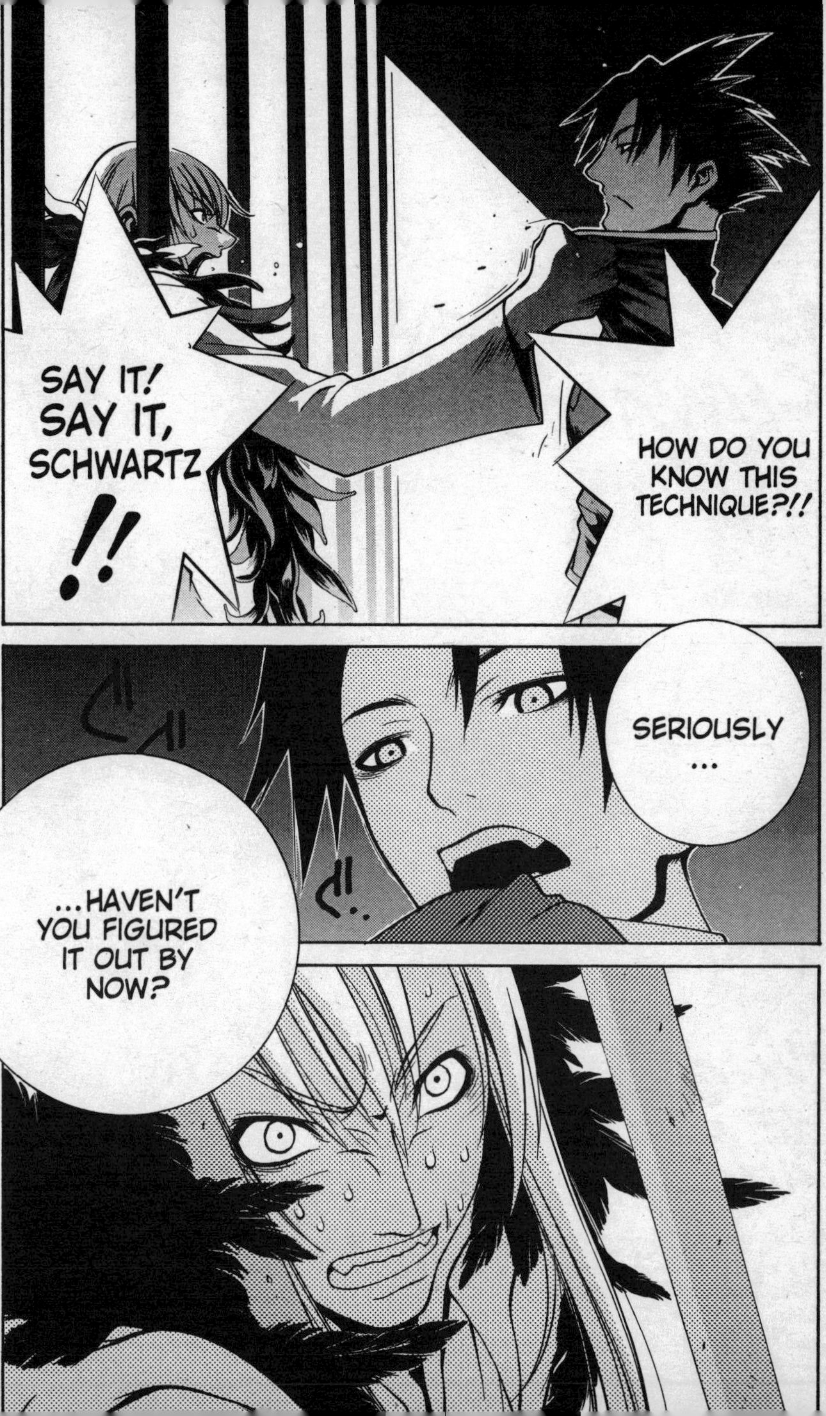
HOW DO YOU KNOW THIS TECHNIQUE?!!
SAY IT! SAY IT, SCHWARTZ!!
SERIOUSLY...
...HAVEN'T YOU FIGURED IT OUT BY NOW?

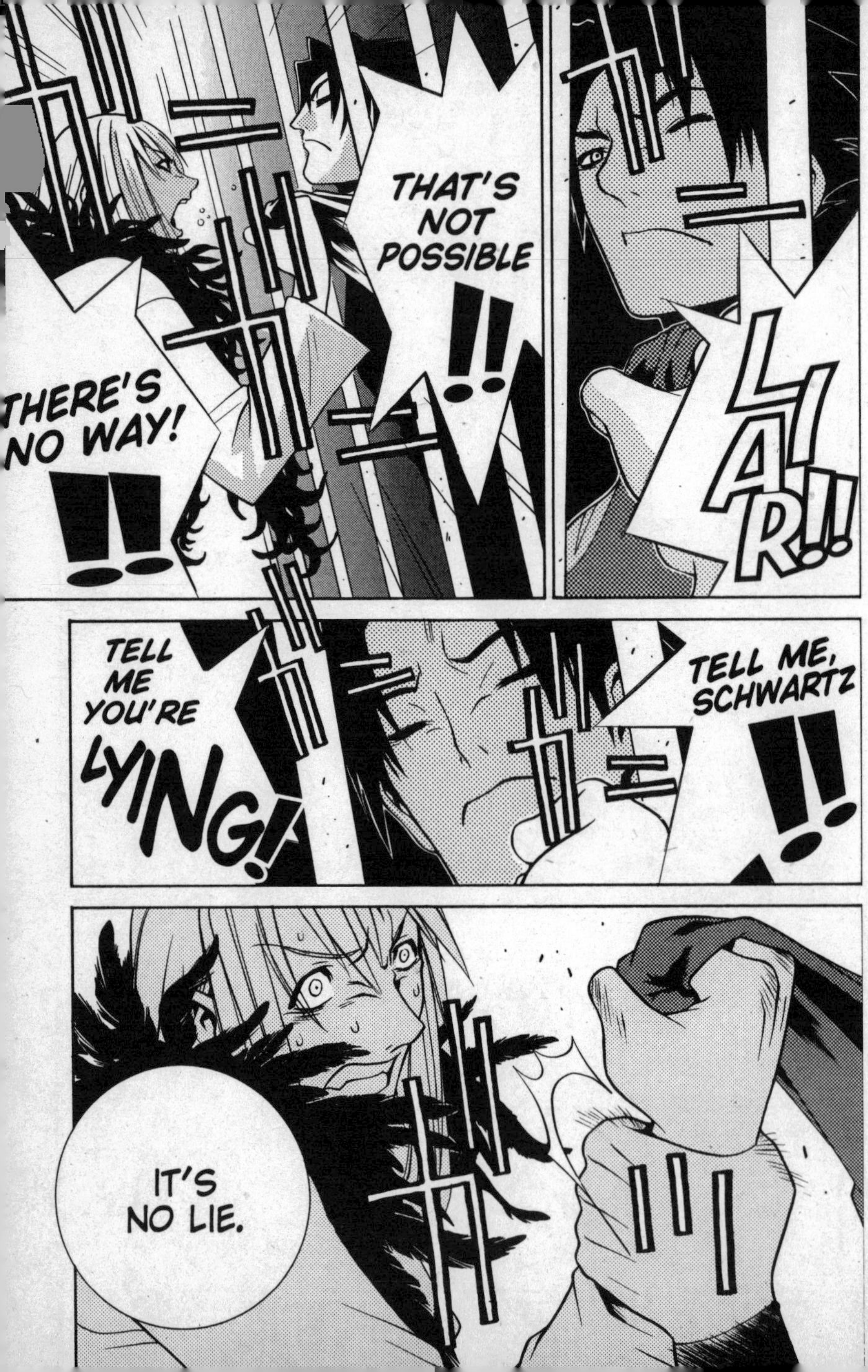
LIAR!!
THAT'S NOT POSSIBLE!!
THERE'S NO WAY!!
TELL ME, SCHWARTZ!!
TELL ME YOU'RE LYING!
IT'S NO LIE.

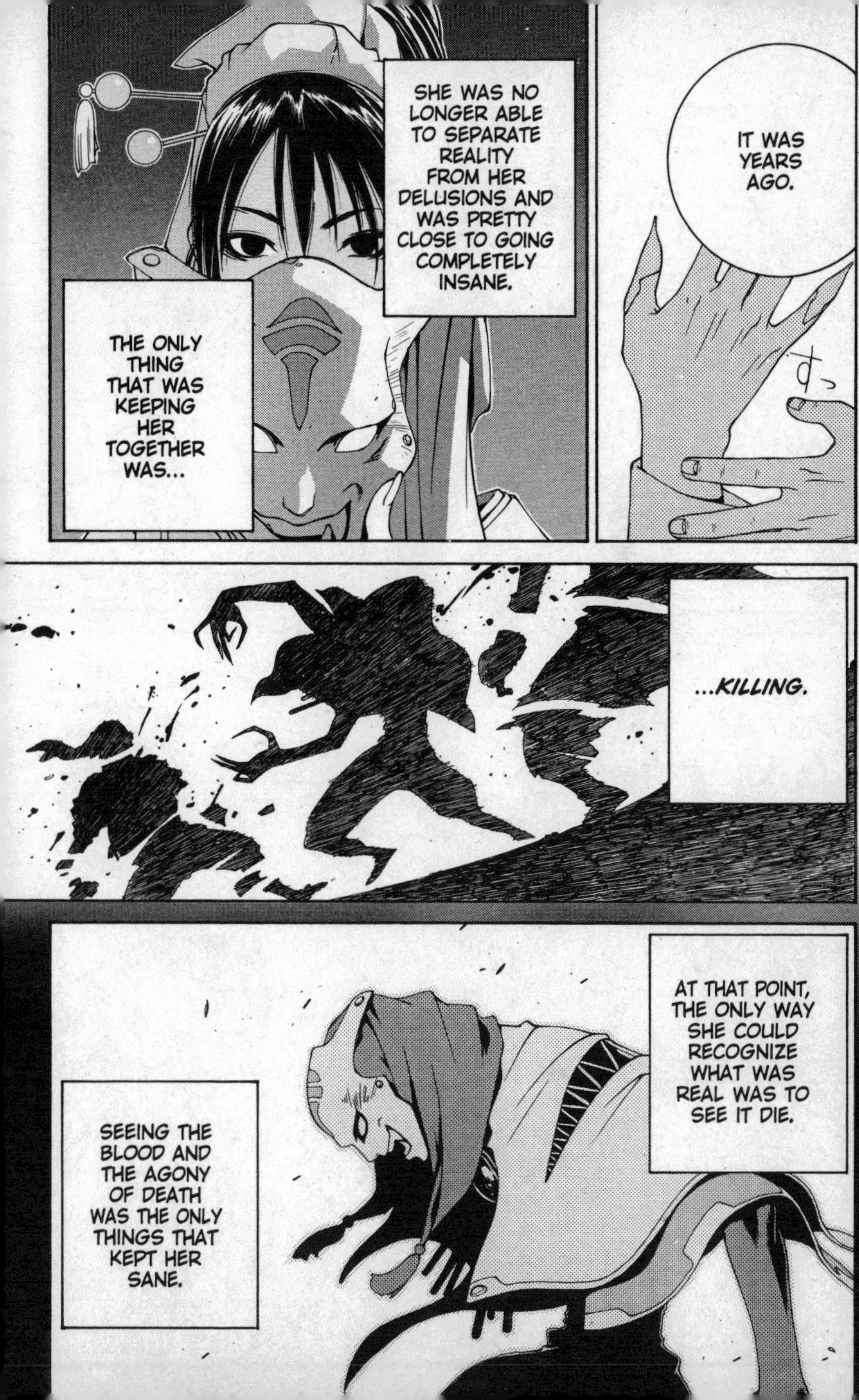
IT WAS YEARS AGO.
すっ
SHE WAS NO LONGER ABLE TO SEPARATE REALITY FROM HER DELUSIONS AND WAS PRETTY CLOSE TO GOING COMPLETELY INSANE.
THE ONLY THING THAT WAS KEEPING HER TOGETHER WAS...
...*KILLING.*
AT THAT POINT, THE ONLY WAY SHE COULD RECOGNIZE WHAT WAS REAL WAS TO SEE IT DIE.
SEEING THE BLOOD AND THE AGONY OF DEATH WAS THE ONLY THINGS THAT KEPT HER SANE.

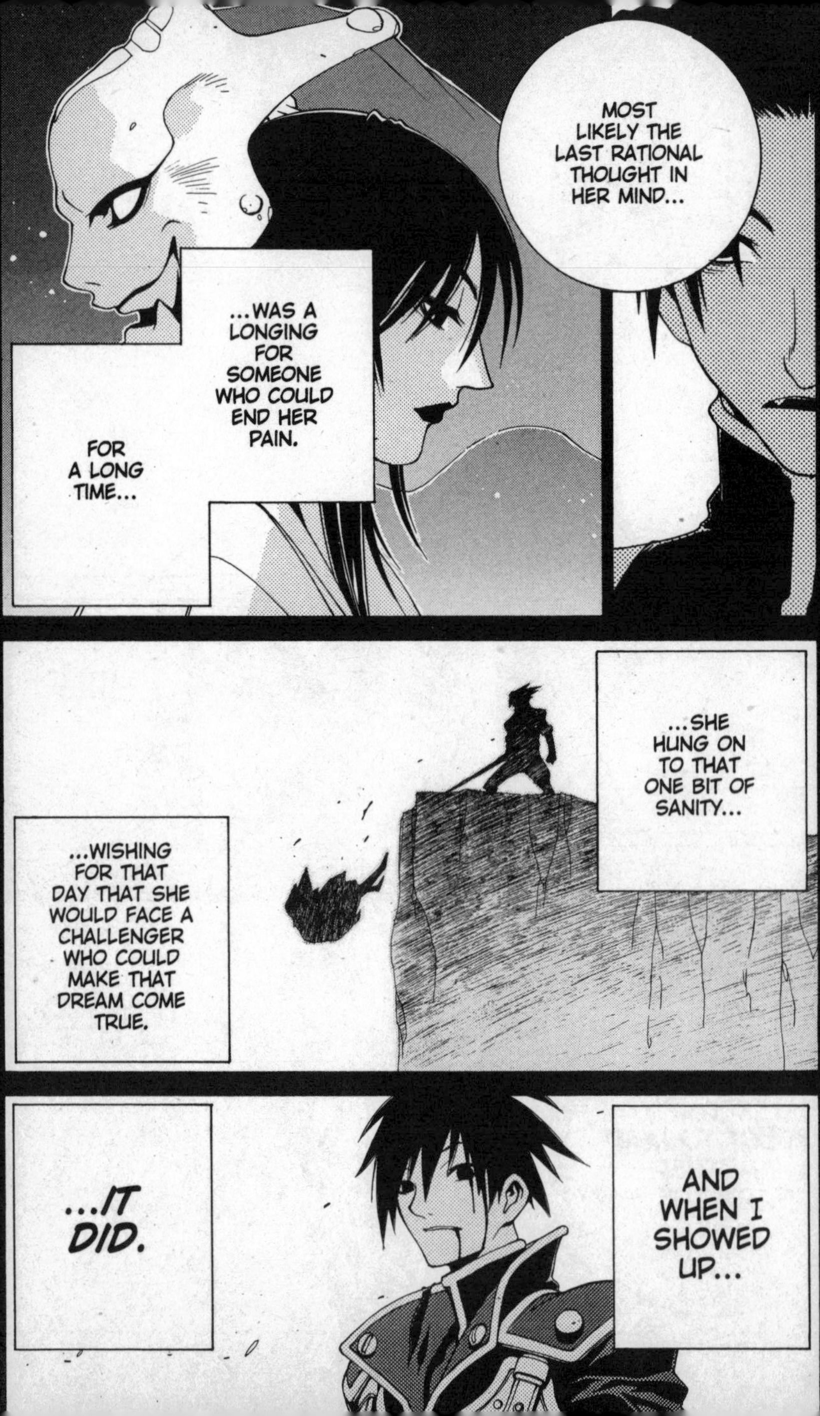
MOST LIKELY THE LAST RATIONAL THOUGHT IN HER MIND...
...WAS A LONGING FOR SOMEONE WHO COULD END HER PAIN.
FOR A LONG TIME...
...SHE HUNG ON TO THAT ONE BIT OF SANITY...
...WISHING FOR THAT DAY THAT SHE WOULD FACE A CHALLENGER WHO COULD MAKE THAT DREAM COME TRUE.
AND WHEN I SHOWED UP...
...IT DID.

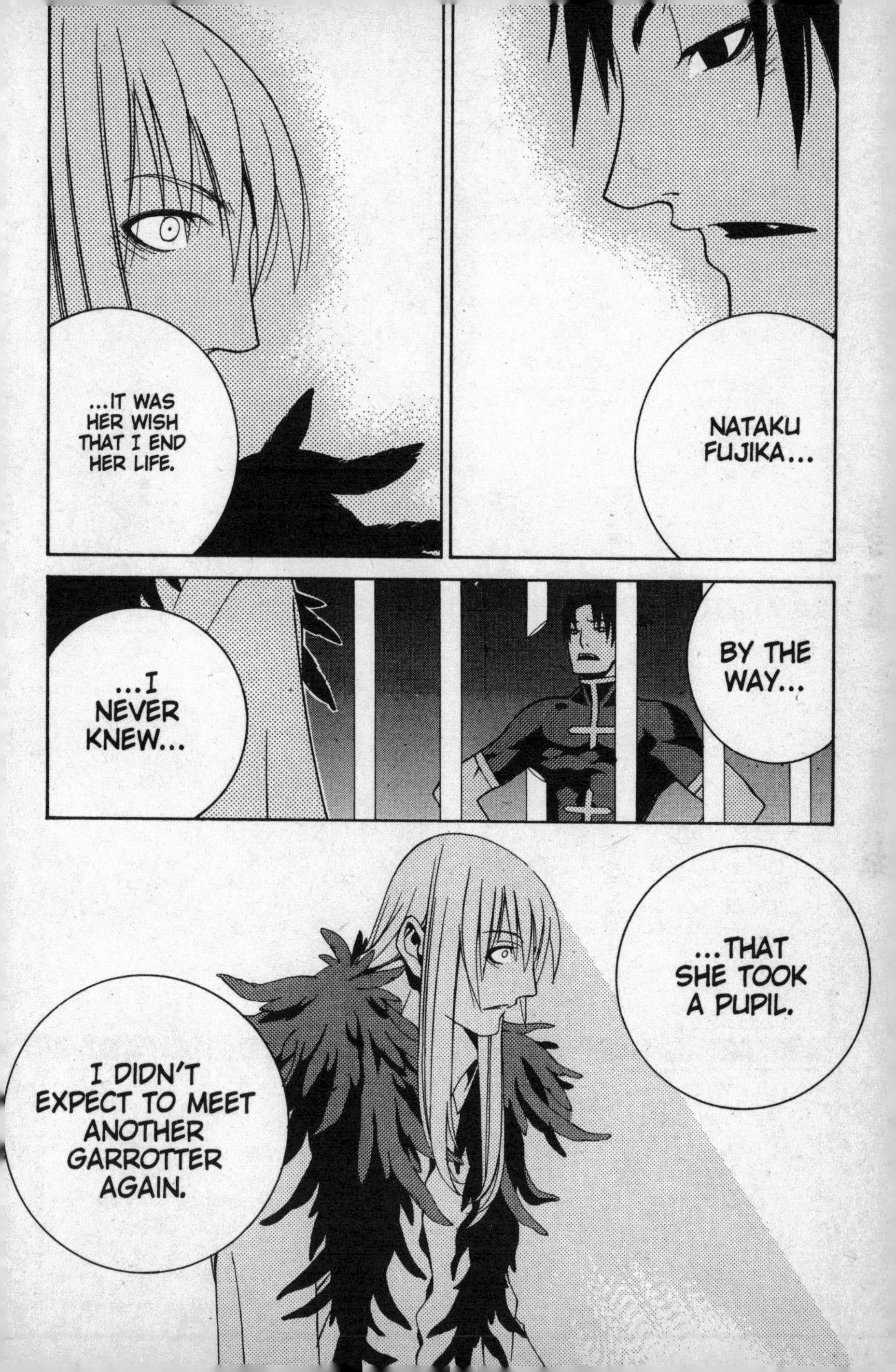
NATAKU FUJIKA...
...IT WAS HER WISH THAT I END HER LIFE.
BY THE WAY...
...I NEVER KNEW...
...THAT SHE TOOK A PUPIL.
I DIDN'T EXPECT TO MEET ANOTHER GARROTTER AGAIN.

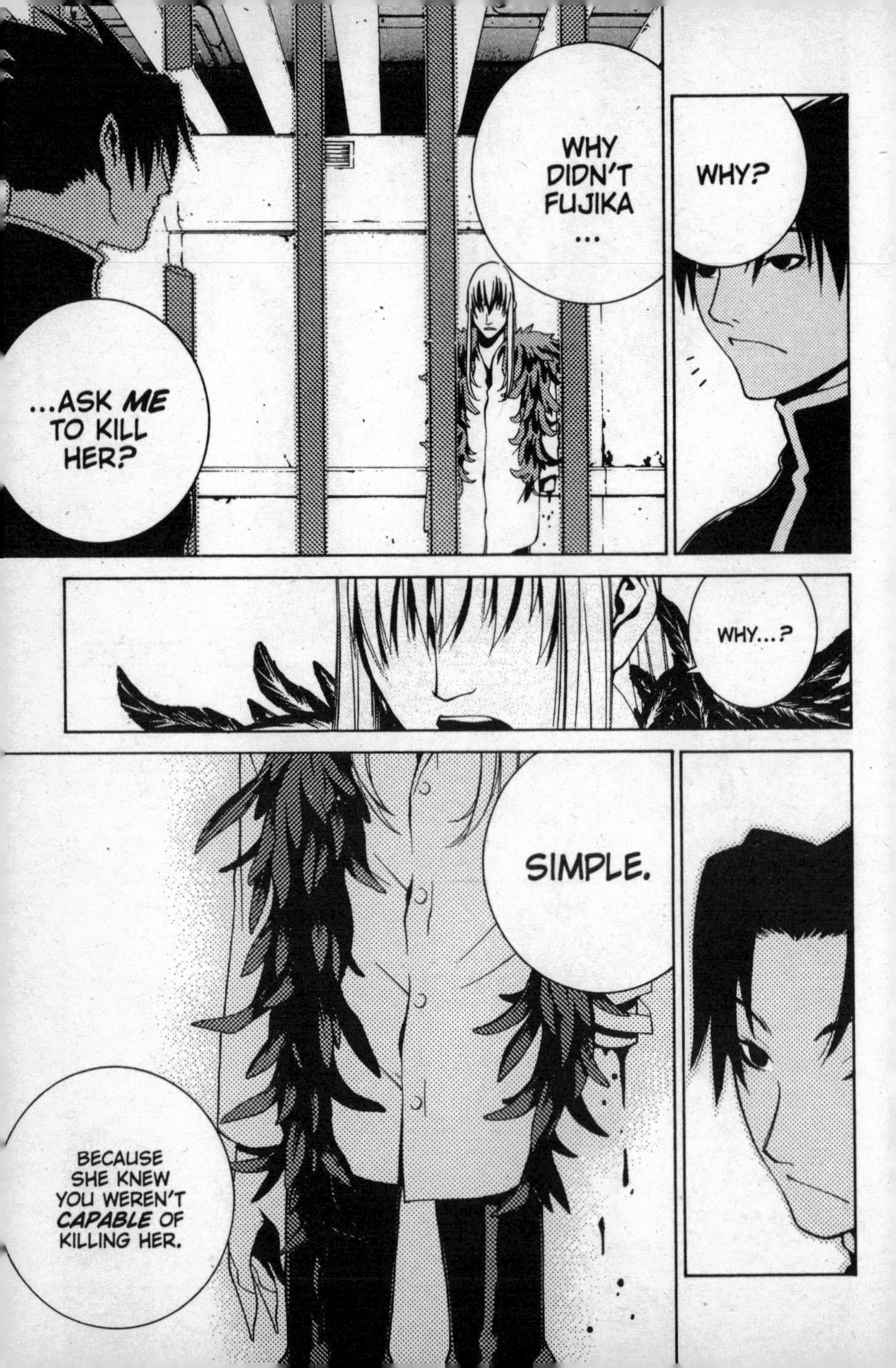
WHY?
WHY DIDN'T FUJIKA ...
...ASK *ME* TO KILL HER?
WHY...?
SIMPLE.
BECAUSE SHE KNEW YOU WEREN'T *CAPABLE* OF KILLING HER.

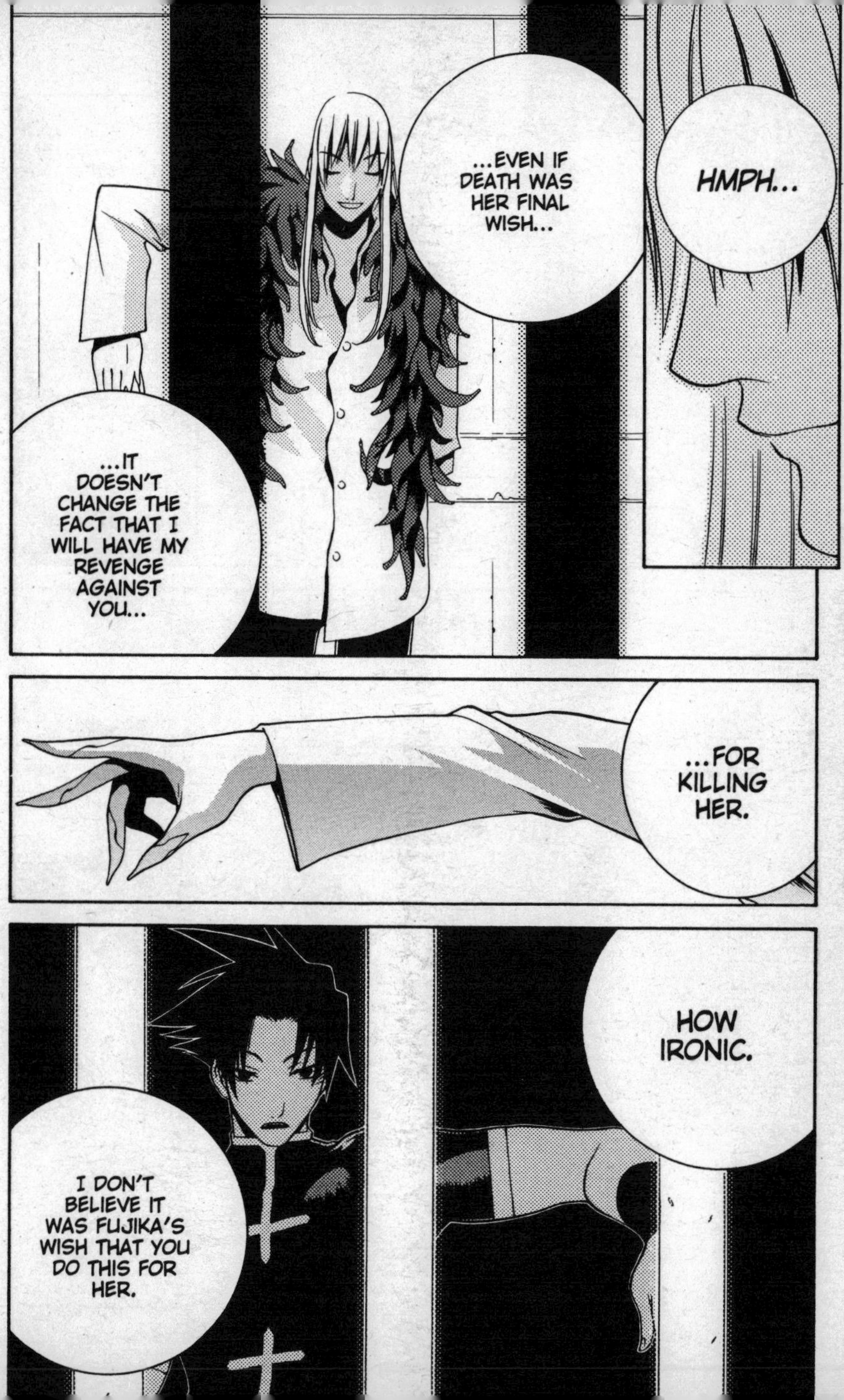
HMPH...
...EVEN IF DEATH WAS HER FINAL WISH...
...IT DOESN'T CHANGE THE FACT THAT I WILL HAVE MY REVENGE AGAINST YOU...
...FOR KILLING HER.
HOW IRONIC.
I DON'T BELIEVE IT WAS FUJIKA'S WISH THAT YOU DO THIS FOR HER.

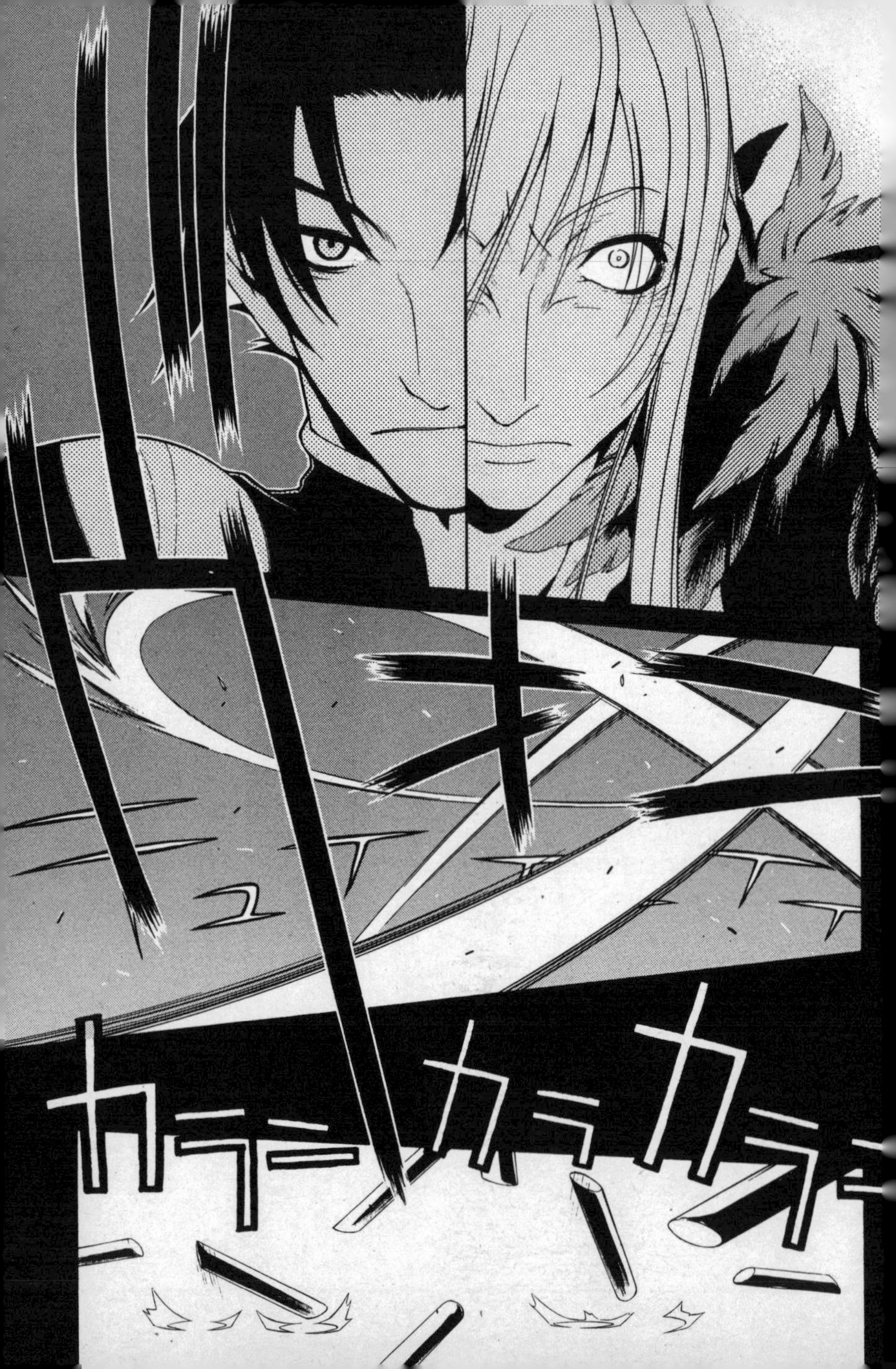

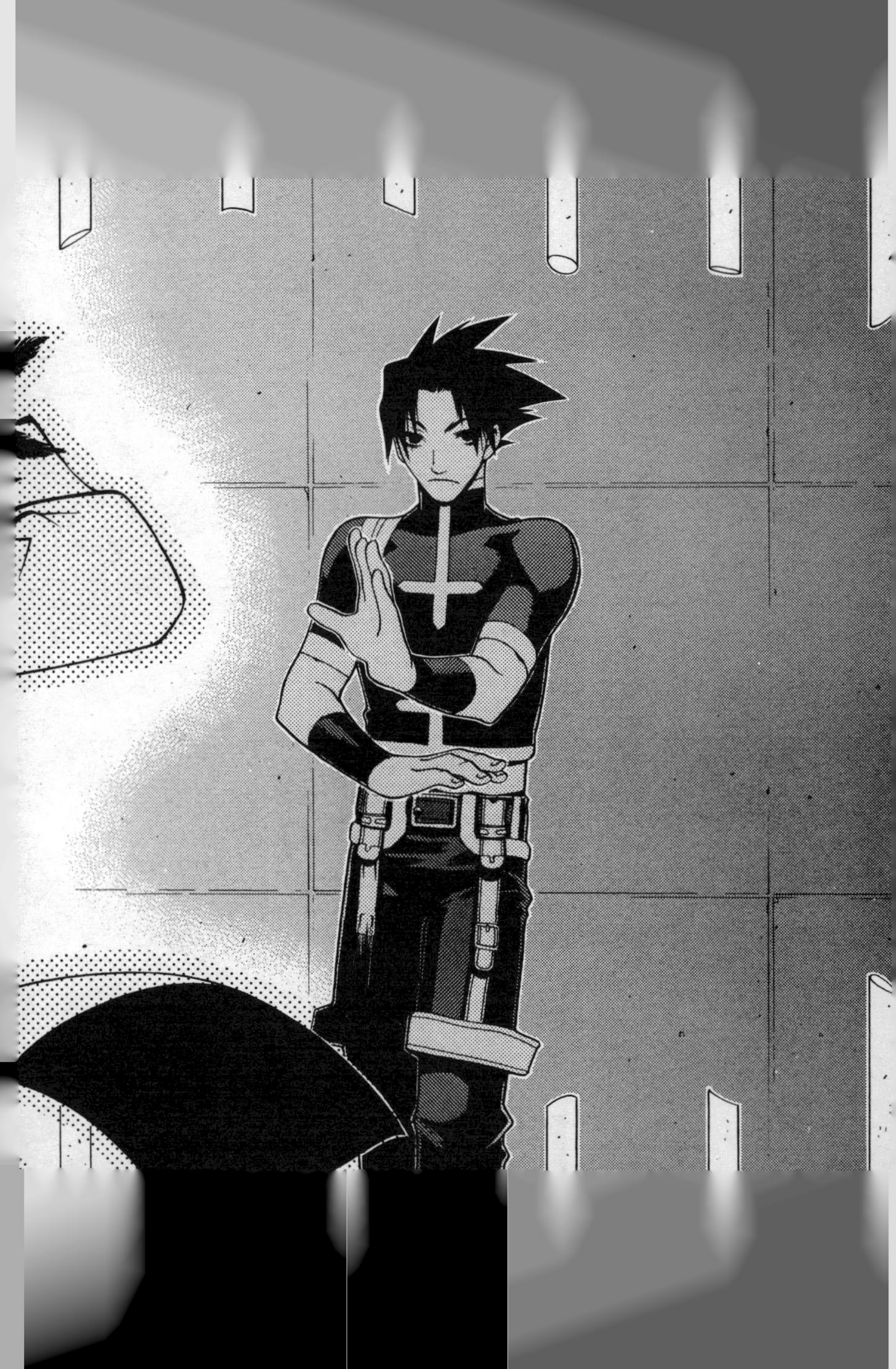

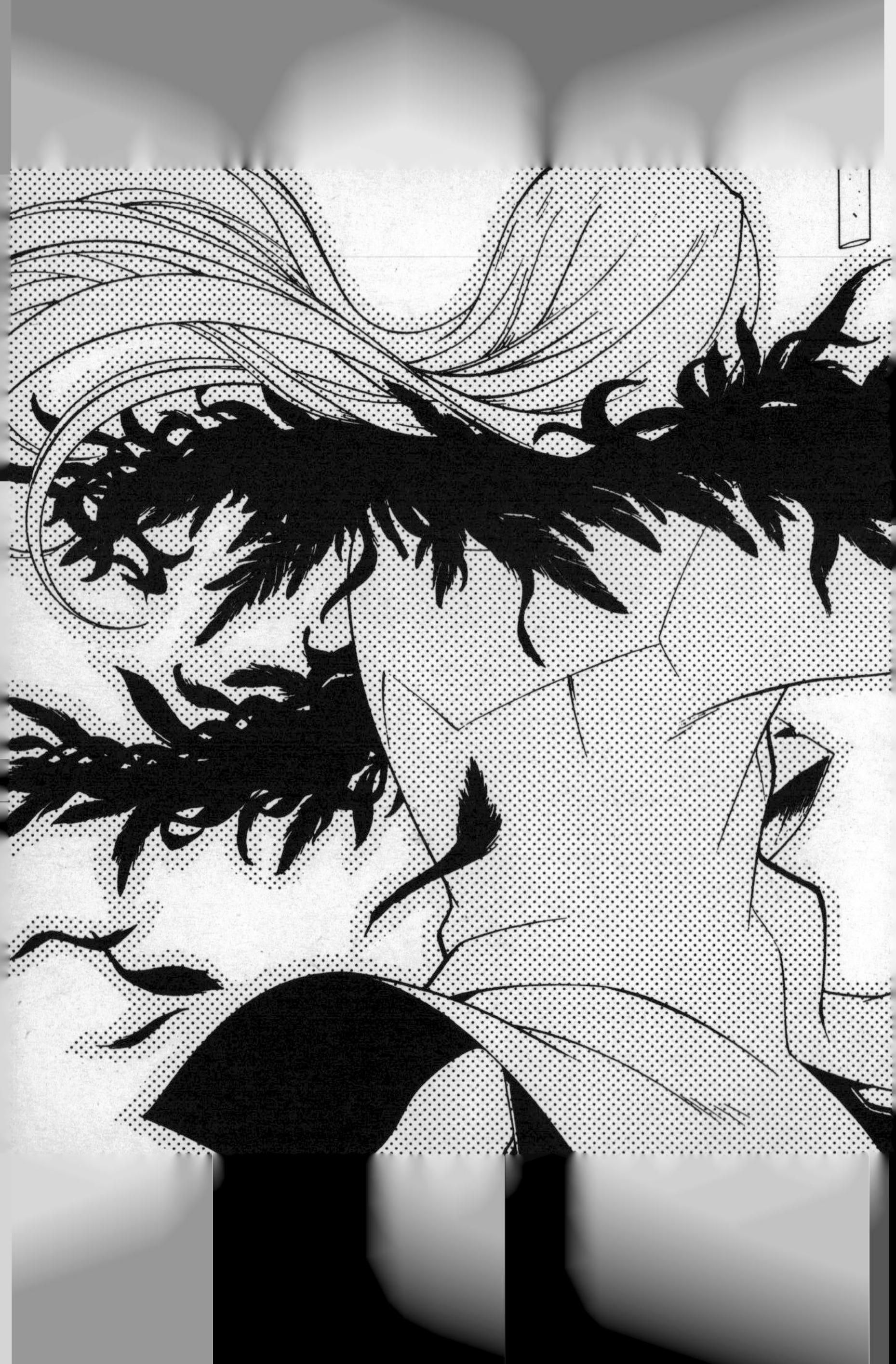

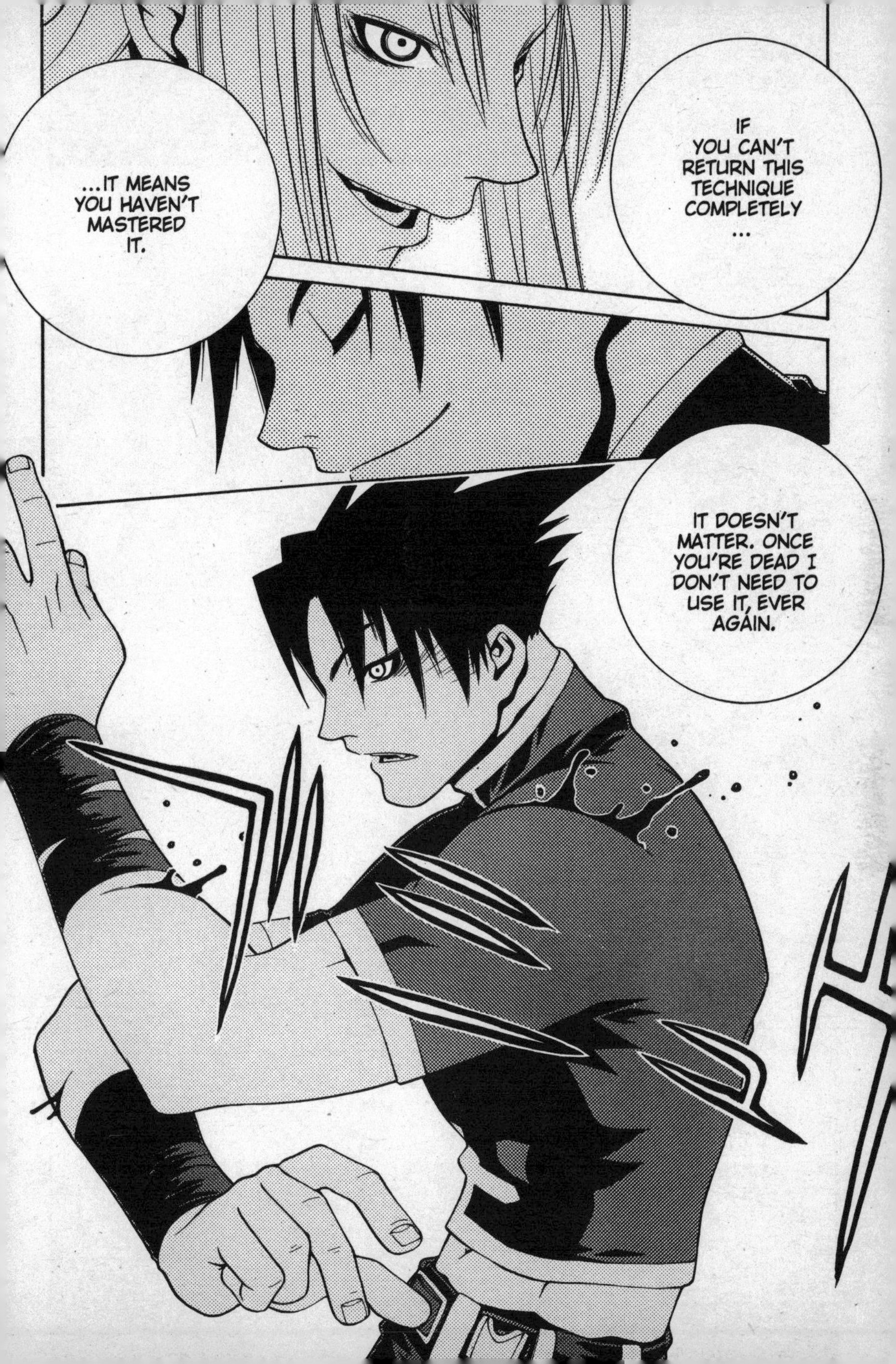
IF YOU CAN'T RETURN THIS TECHNIQUE COMPLETELY ...
...IT MEANS YOU HAVEN'T MASTERED IT.
IT DOESN'T MATTER. ONCE YOU'RE DEAD I DON'T NEED TO USE IT, EVER AGAIN.

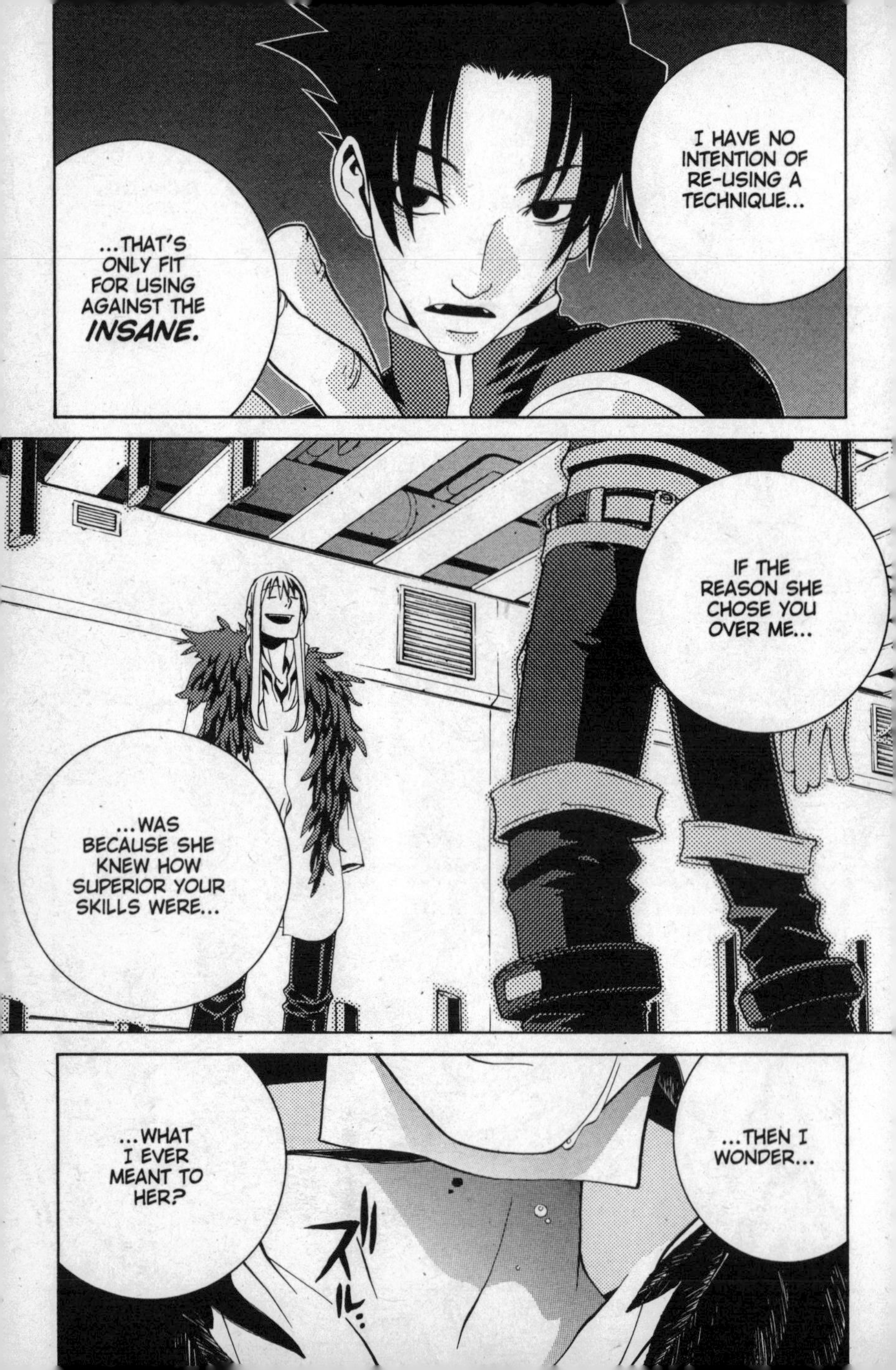
I HAVE NO INTENTION OF RE-USING A TECHNIQUE...
...THAT'S ONLY FIT FOR USING AGAINST THE *INSANE.*
IF THE REASON SHE CHOSE YOU OVER ME...
...WAS BECAUSE SHE KNEW HOW SUPERIOR YOUR SKILLS WERE...
...THEN I WONDER...
...WHAT I EVER MEANT TO HER?
ズル‥

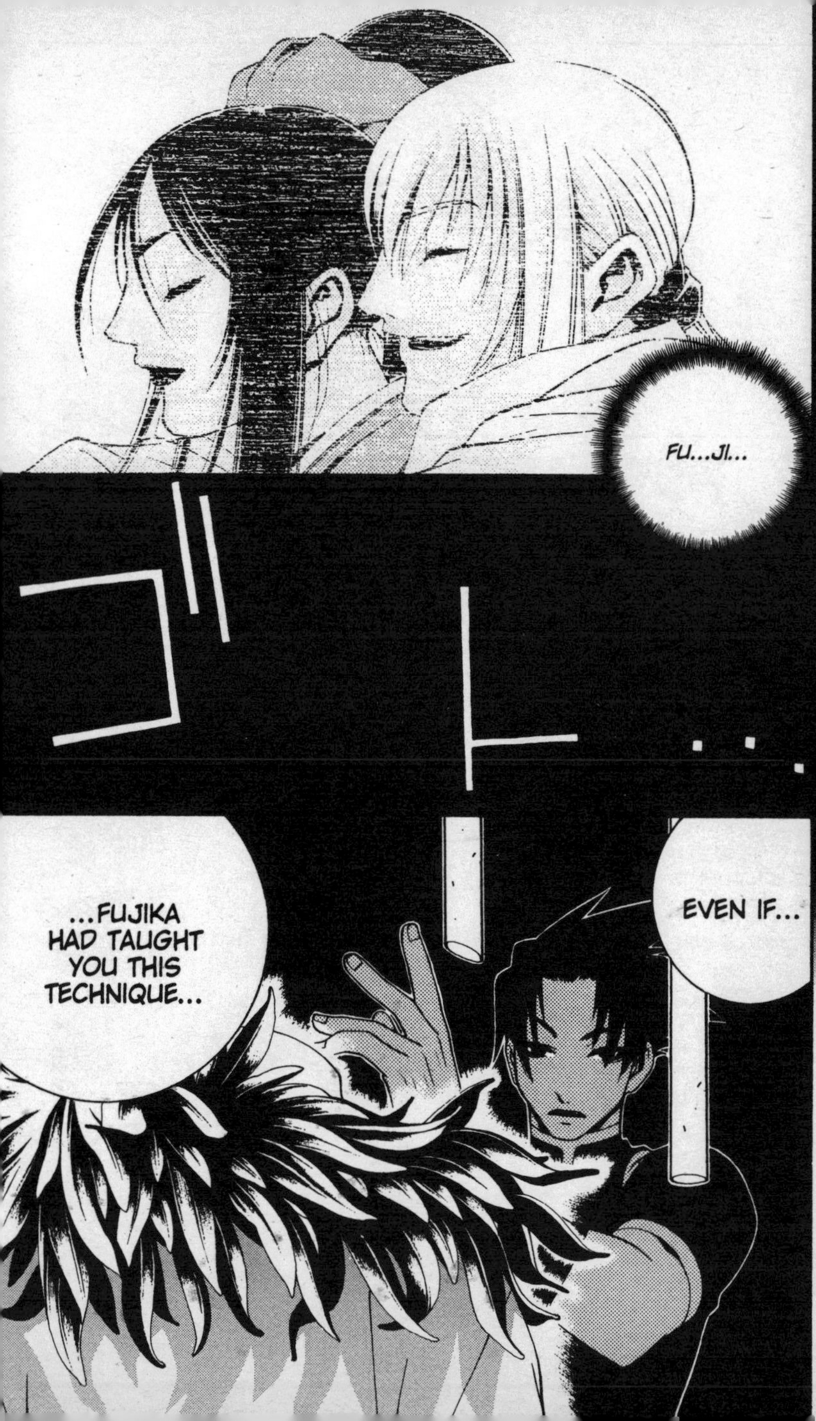
FU...JI...
ゴト...
EVEN IF...
...FUJIKA HAD TAUGHT YOU THIS TECHNIQUE...

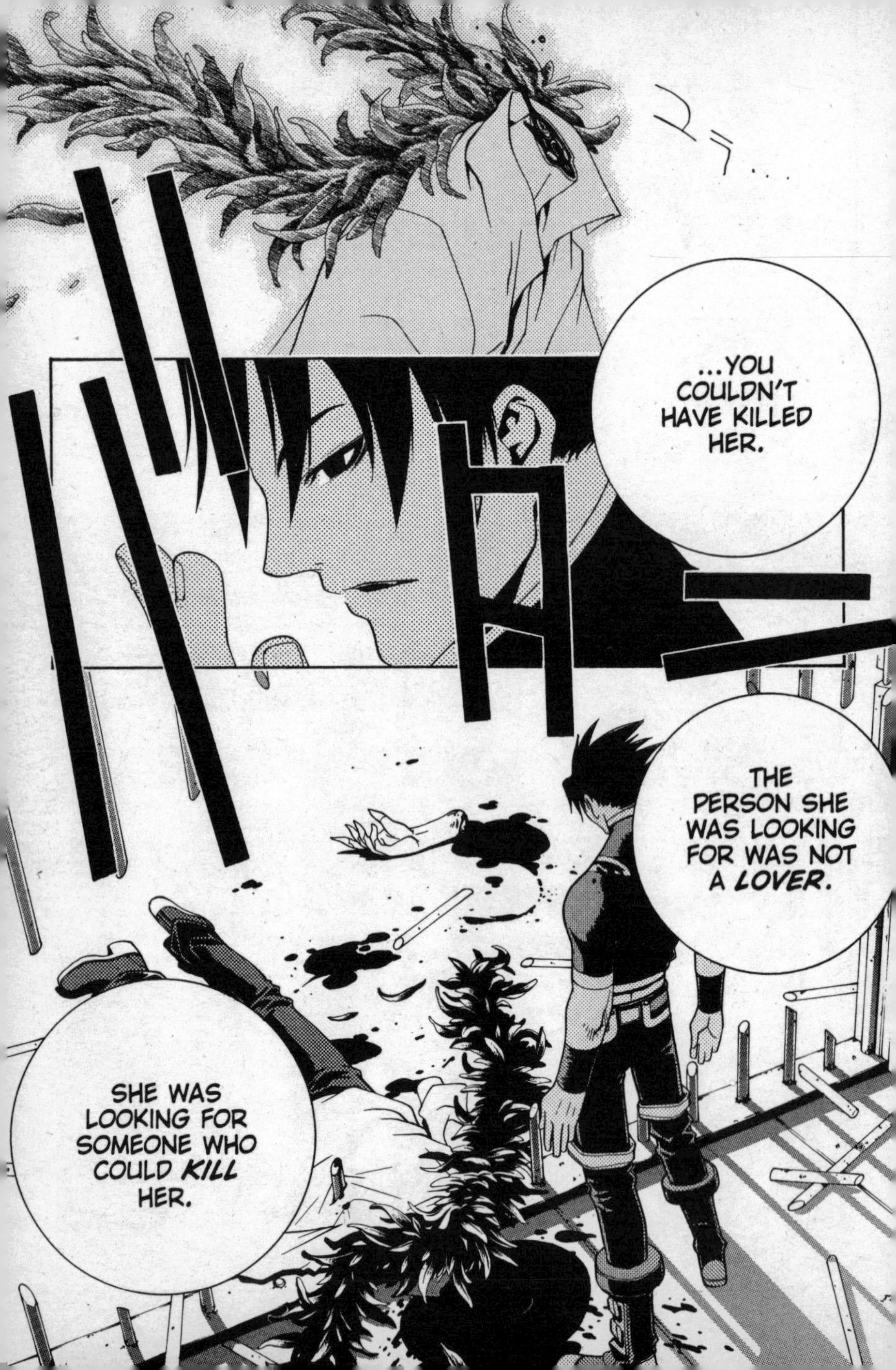
...YOU COULDN'T HAVE KILLED HER.
THE PERSON SHE WAS LOOKING FOR WAS NOT A *LOVER*.
SHE WAS LOOKING FOR SOMEONE WHO COULD *KILL* HER.

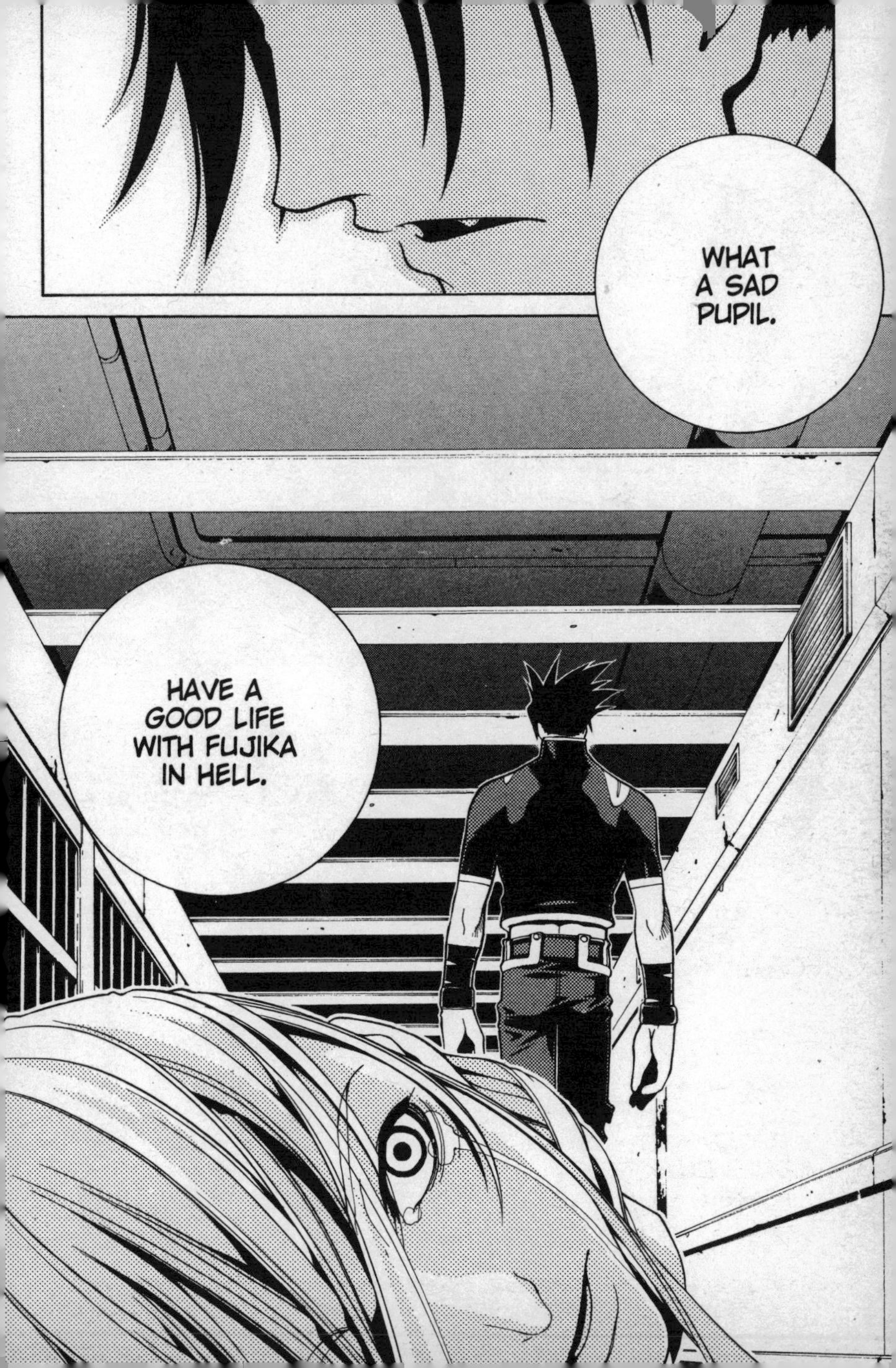
WHAT A SAD PUPIL.
HAVE A GOOD LIFE WITH FUJIKA IN HELL.

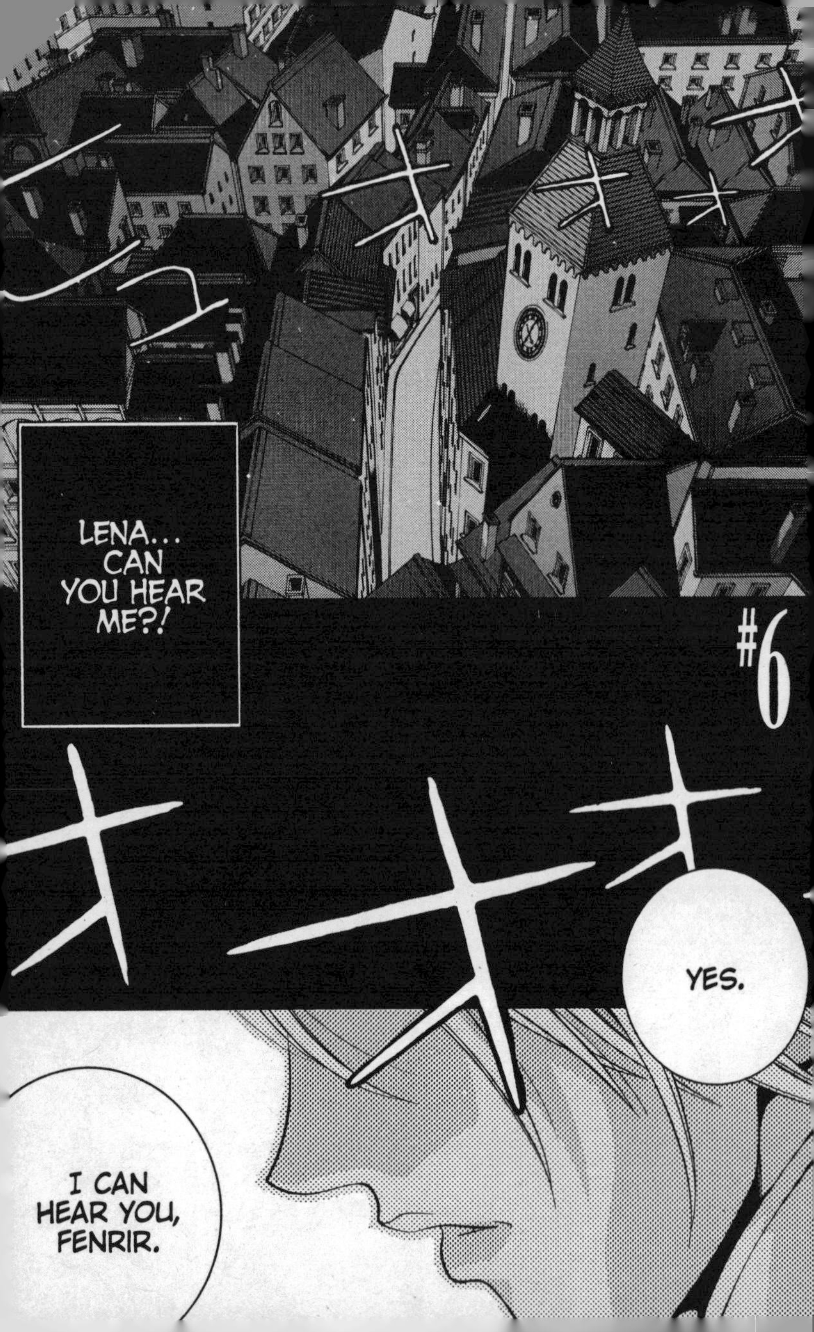
LENA... CAN YOU HEAR ME?!
#6
YES.
I CAN HEAR YOU, FENRIR.

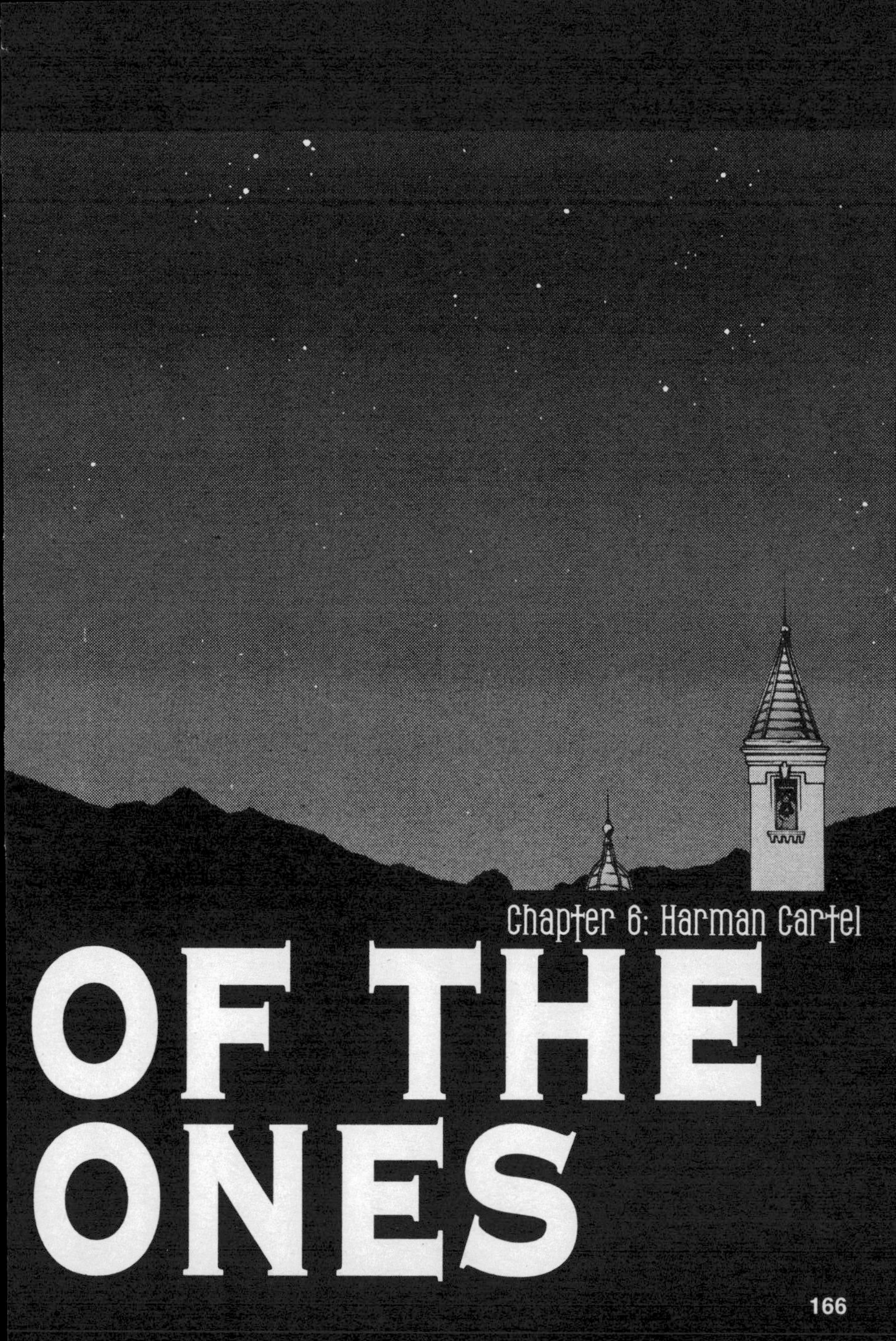
Chapter 6: Harman Cartel
OF THE
ONES

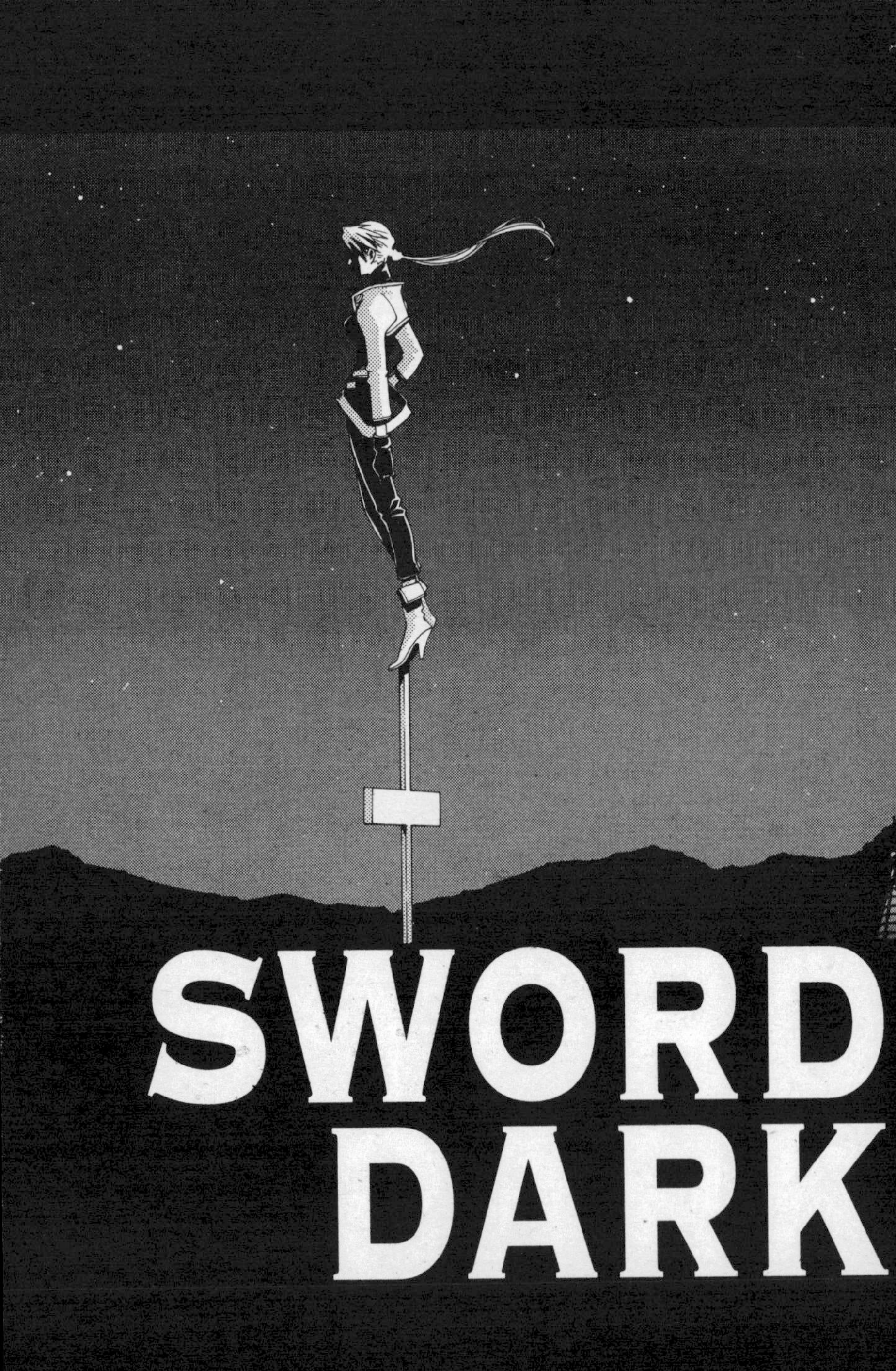
SWORD
DARK

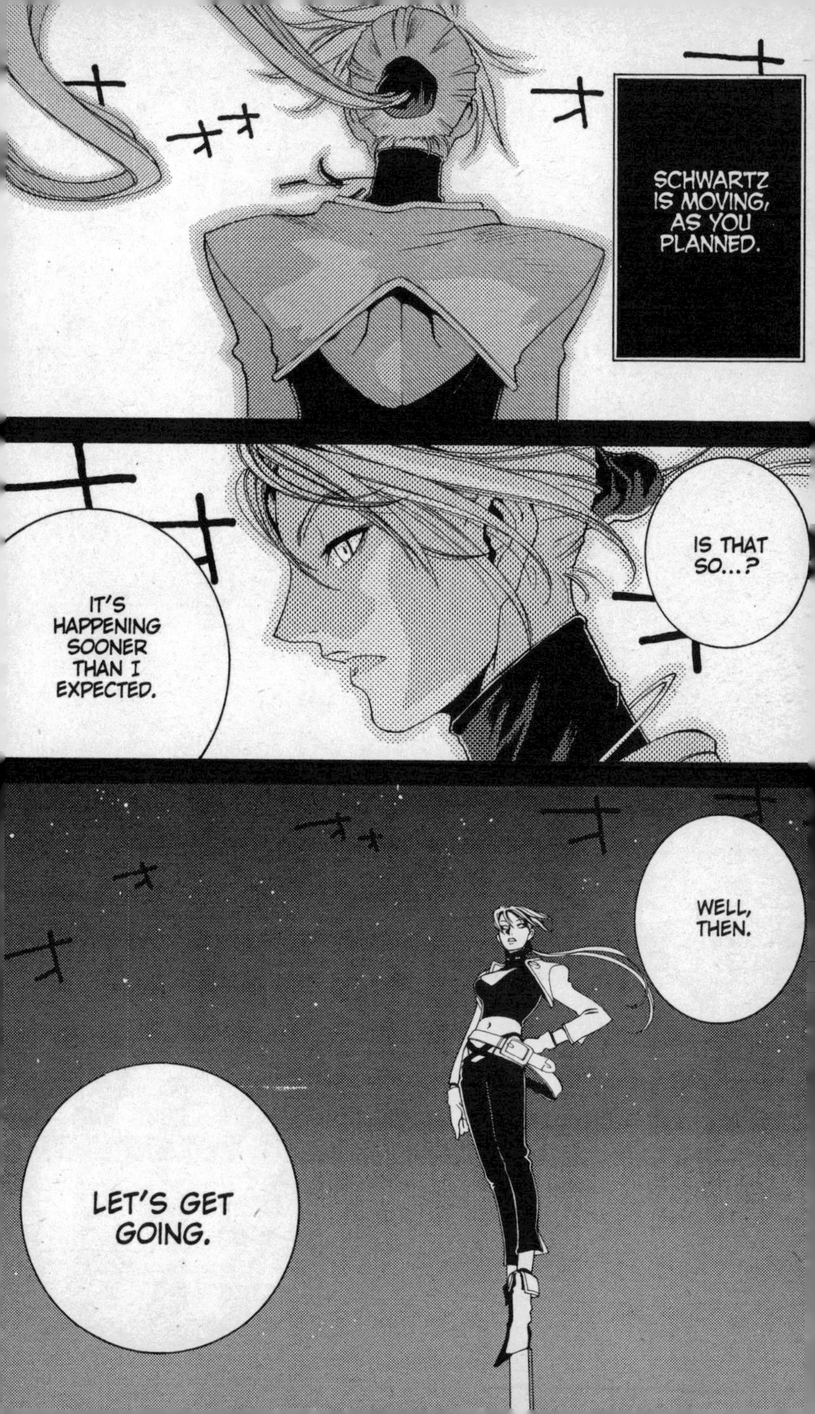
SCHWARTZ IS MOVING, AS YOU PLANNED.
IS THAT SO...?
IT'S HAPPENING SOONER THAN I EXPECTED.
WELL, THEN.
LET'S GET GOING.

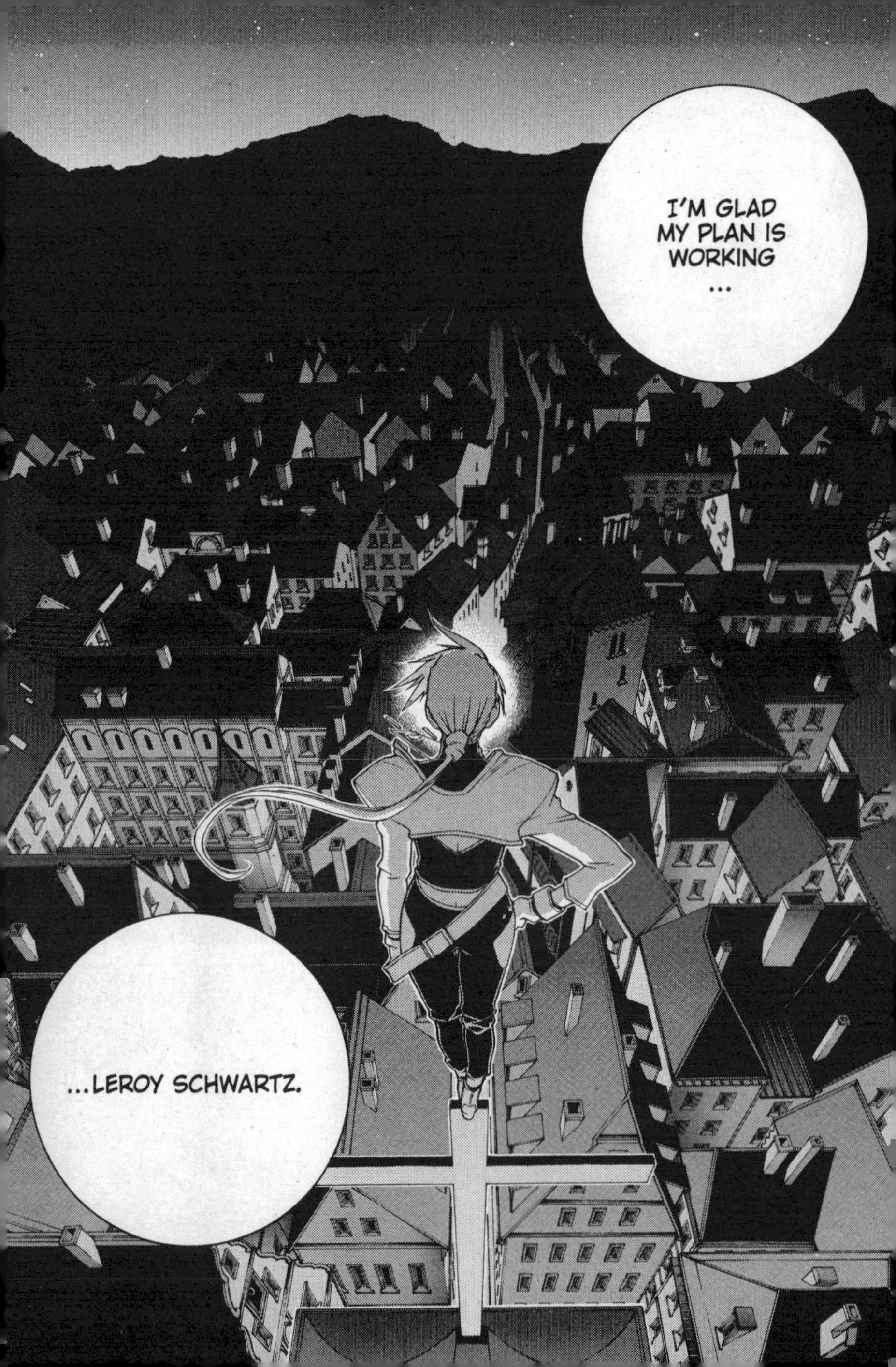
I'M GLAD MY PLAN IS WORKING ...
...LEROY SCHWARTZ.

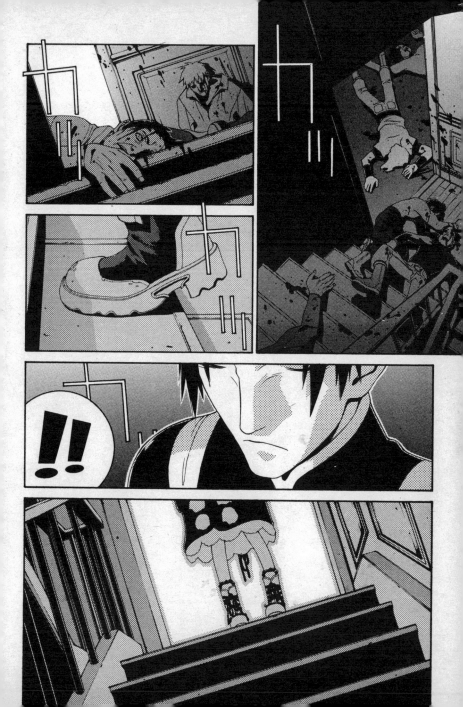

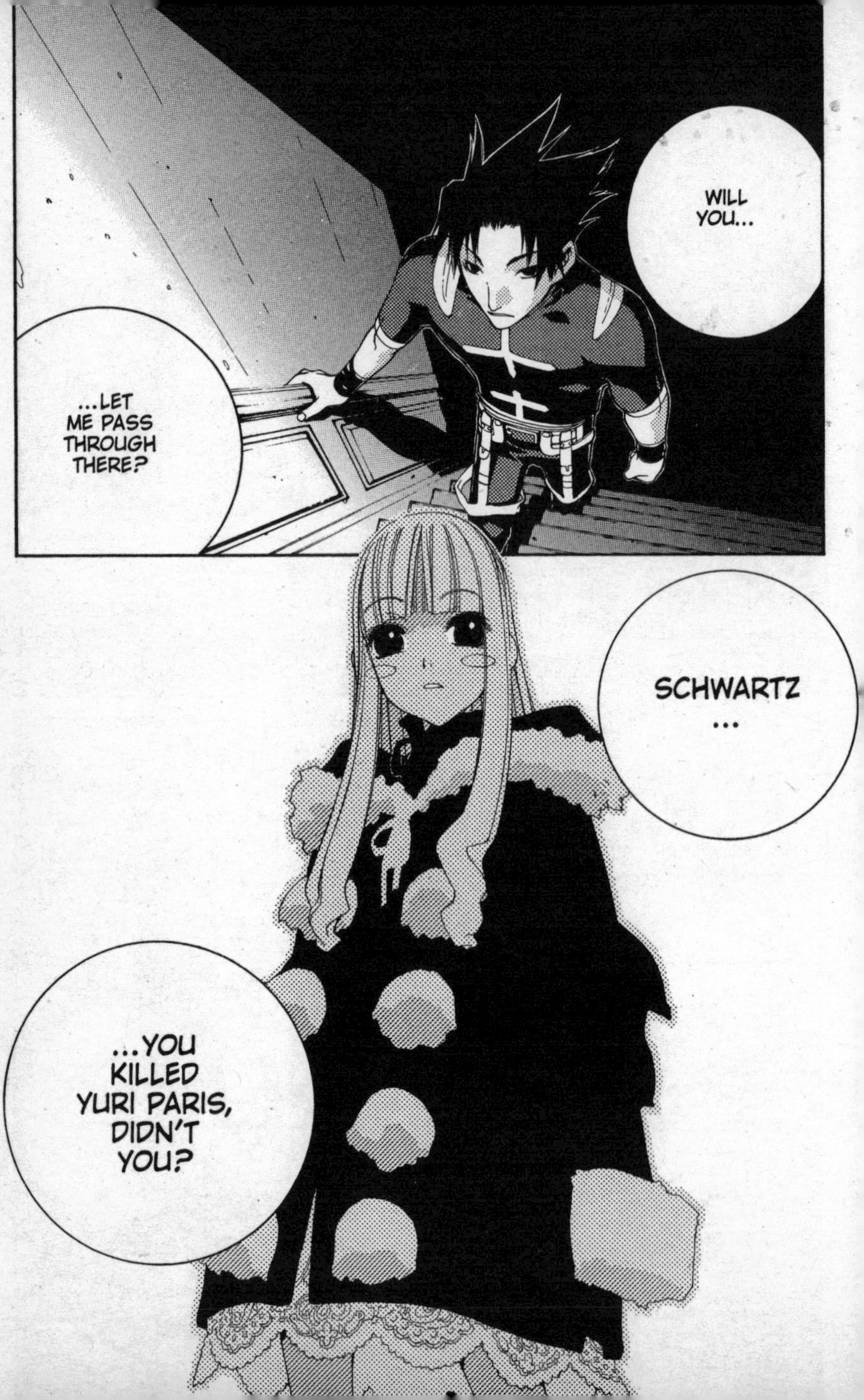
WILL YOU...
...LET ME PASS THROUGH THERE?
SCHWARTZ ...
...YOU KILLED YURI PARIS, DIDN'T YOU?

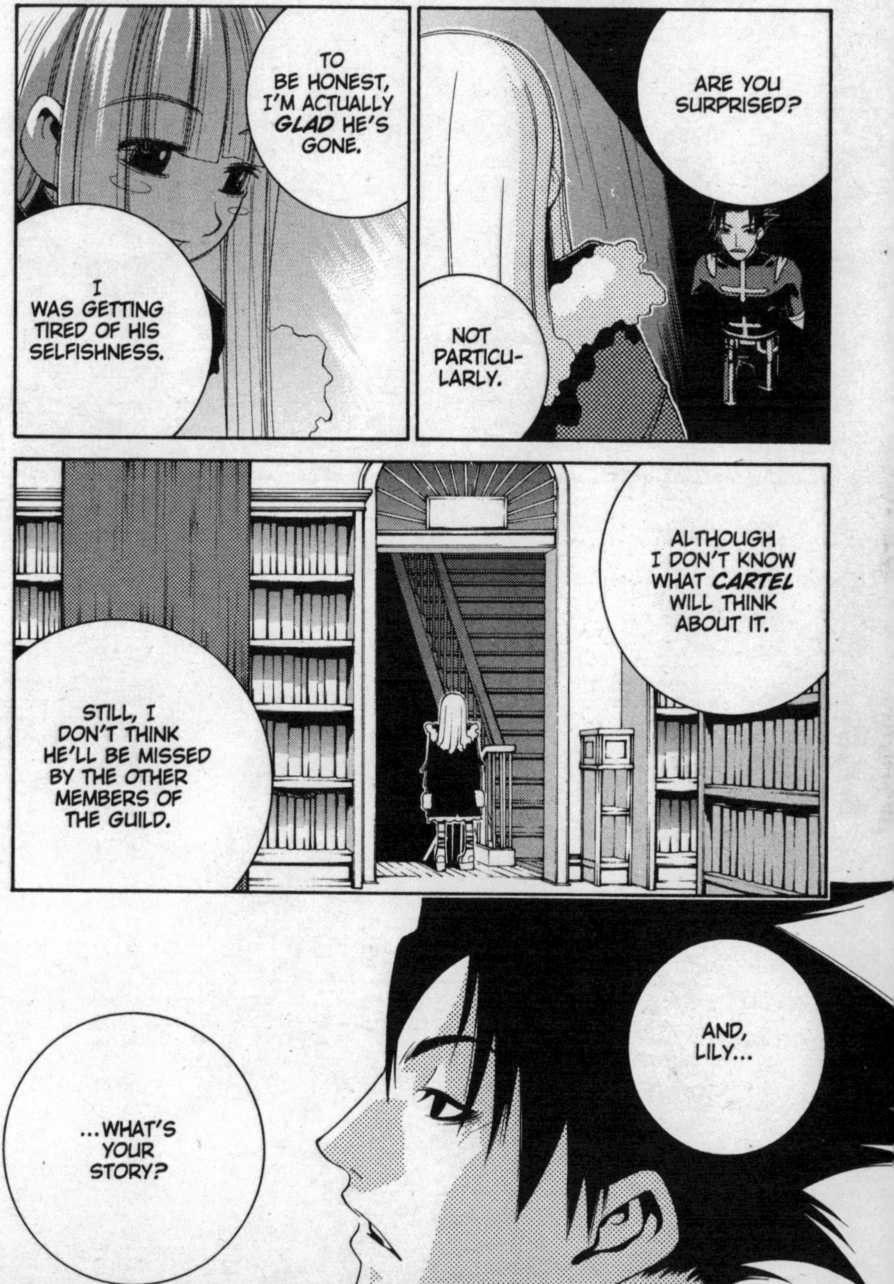
ARE YOU SURPRISED?
NOT PARTICULARLY.
TO BE HONEST, I'M ACTUALLY *GLAD* HE'S GONE.
I WAS GETTING TIRED OF HIS SELFISHNESS.
ALTHOUGH I DON'T KNOW WHAT *CARTEL* WILL THINK ABOUT IT.
STILL, I DON'T THINK HE'LL BE MISSED BY THE OTHER MEMBERS OF THE GUILD.
AND, LILY...
...WHAT'S YOUR STORY?

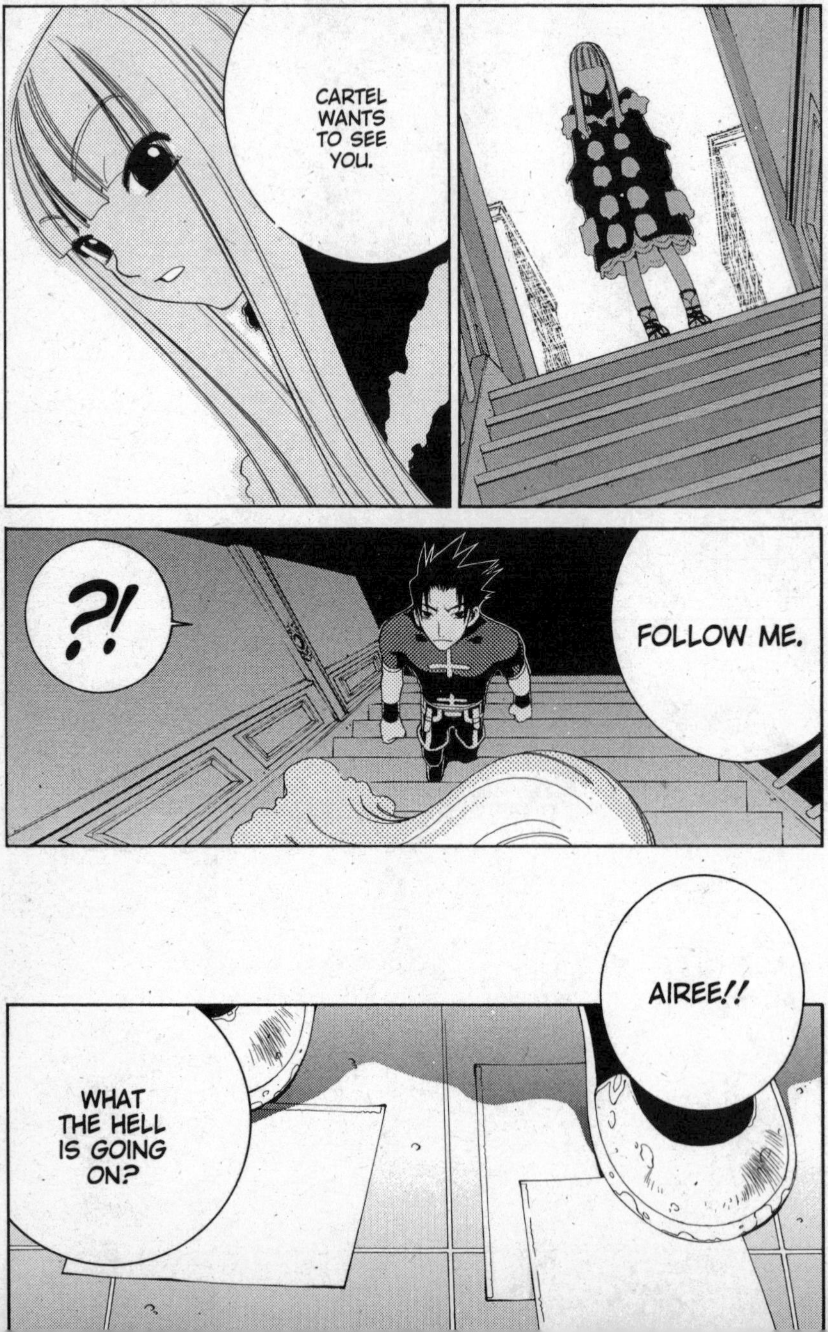
CARTEL WANTS TO SEE YOU.
FOLLOW ME.
?!
AIREE!!
WHAT THE HELL IS GOING ON?

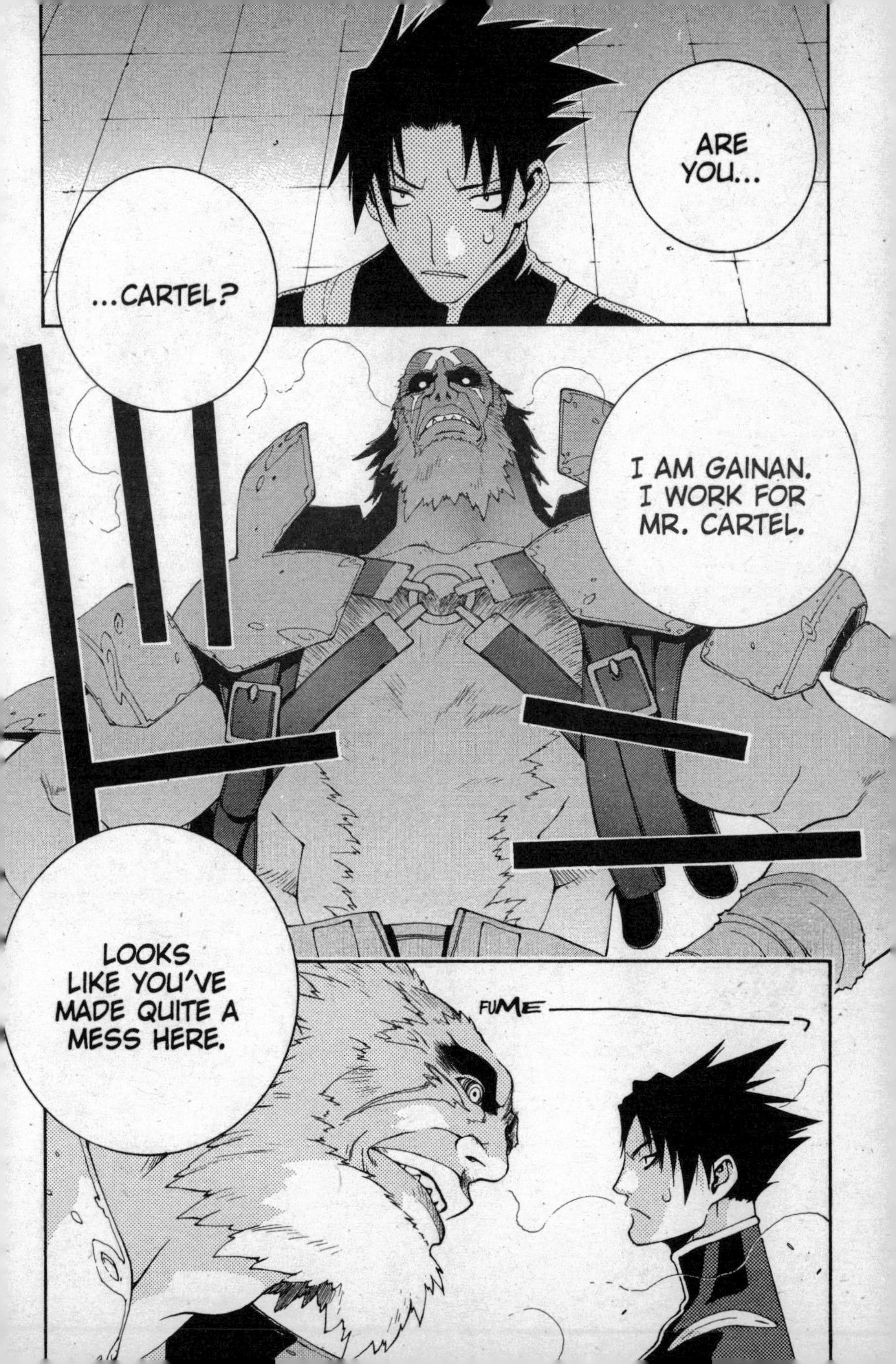
ARE YOU...
...CARTEL?
I AM GAINAN. I WORK FOR MR. CARTEL.
LOOKS LIKE YOU'VE MADE QUITE A MESS HERE.
FUME

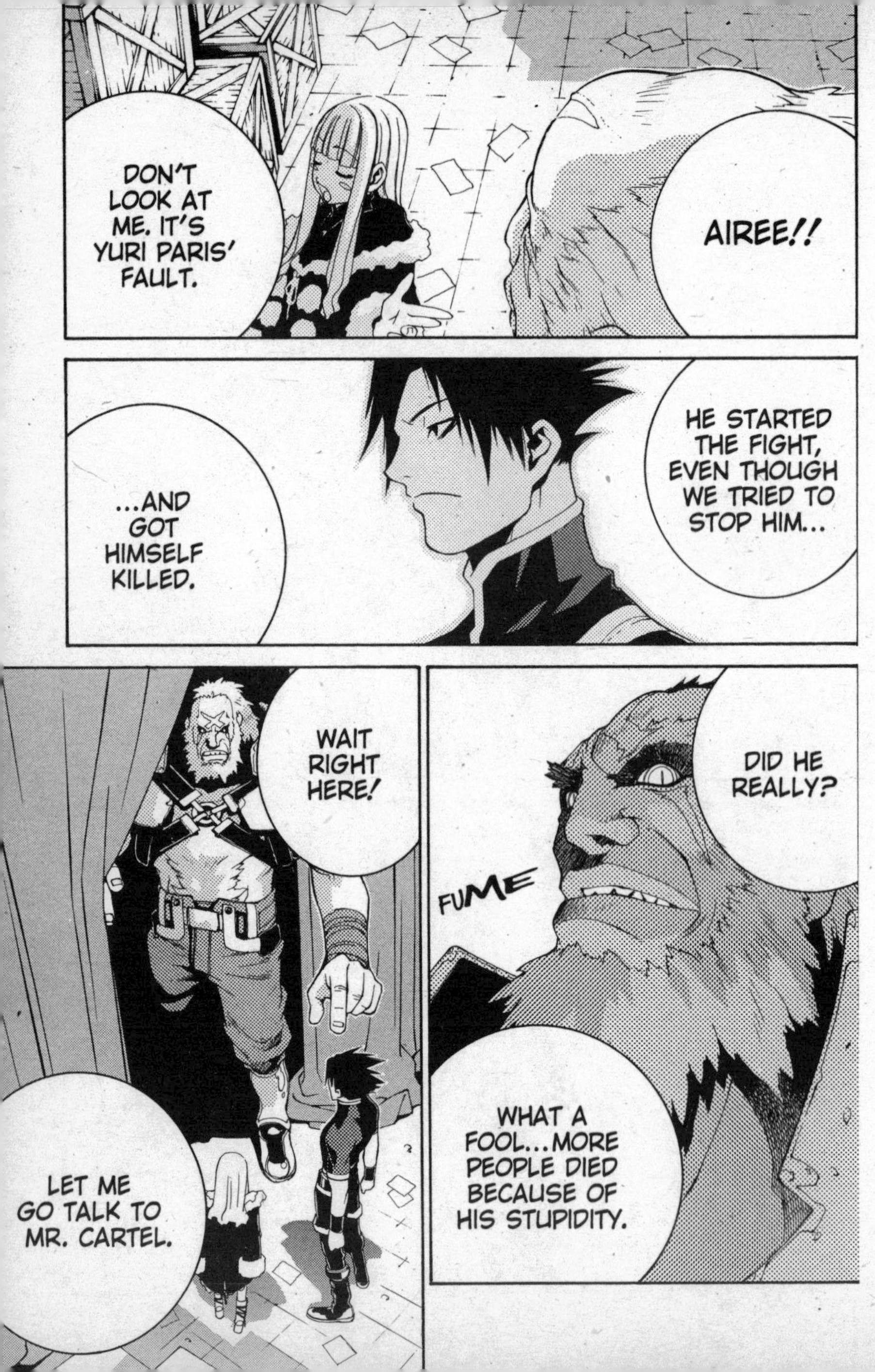
AIREE!!
DON'T LOOK AT ME. IT'S YURI PARIS' FAULT.
HE STARTED THE FIGHT, EVEN THOUGH WE TRIED TO STOP HIM...
...AND GOT HIMSELF KILLED.
DID HE REALLY?
FUME
WHAT A FOOL...MORE PEOPLE DIED BECAUSE OF HIS STUPIDITY.
WAIT RIGHT HERE!
LET ME GO TALK TO MR. CARTEL.

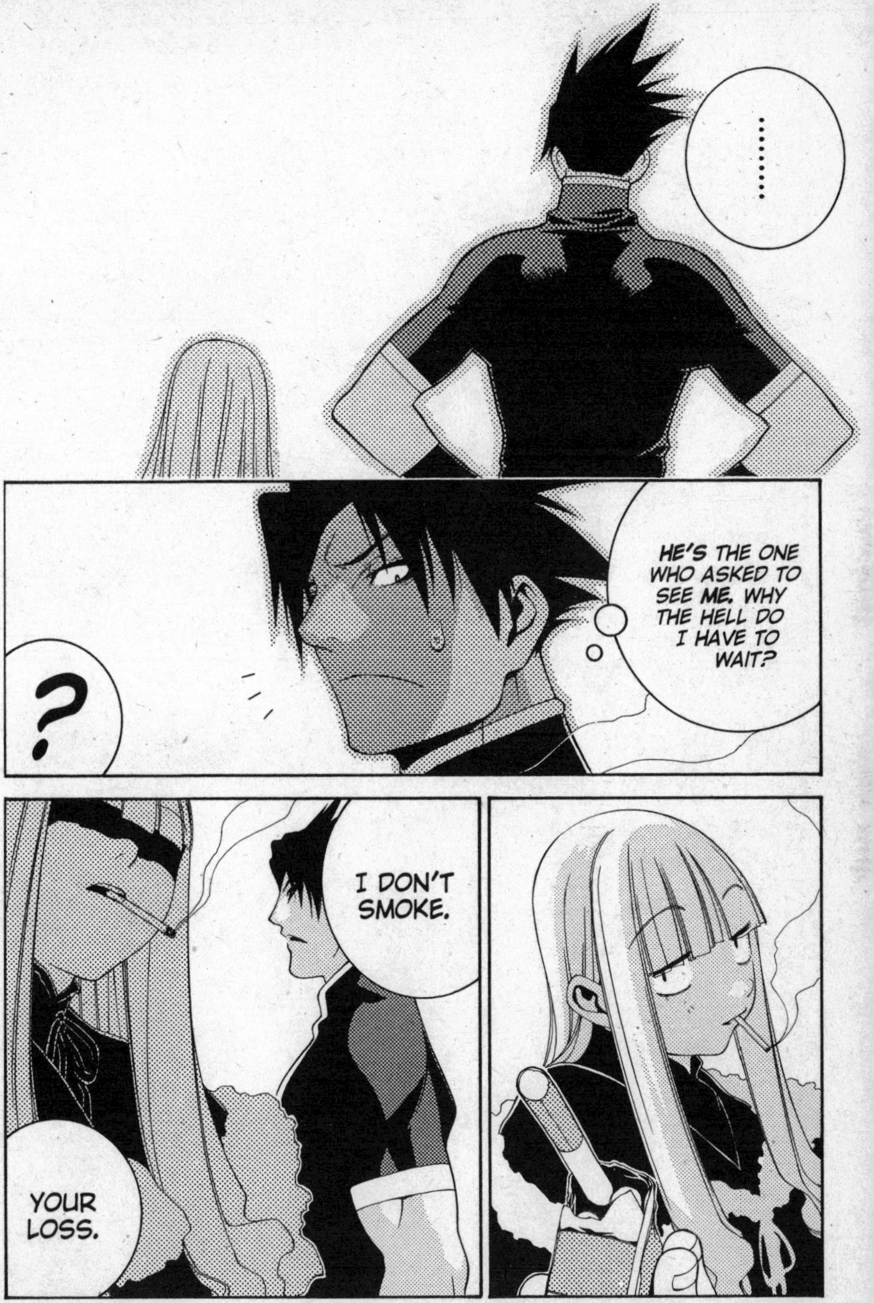
……
HE'S THE ONE WHO ASKED TO SEE ME. WHY THE HELL DO I HAVE TO WAIT?
?
I DON'T SMOKE.
YOUR LOSS.

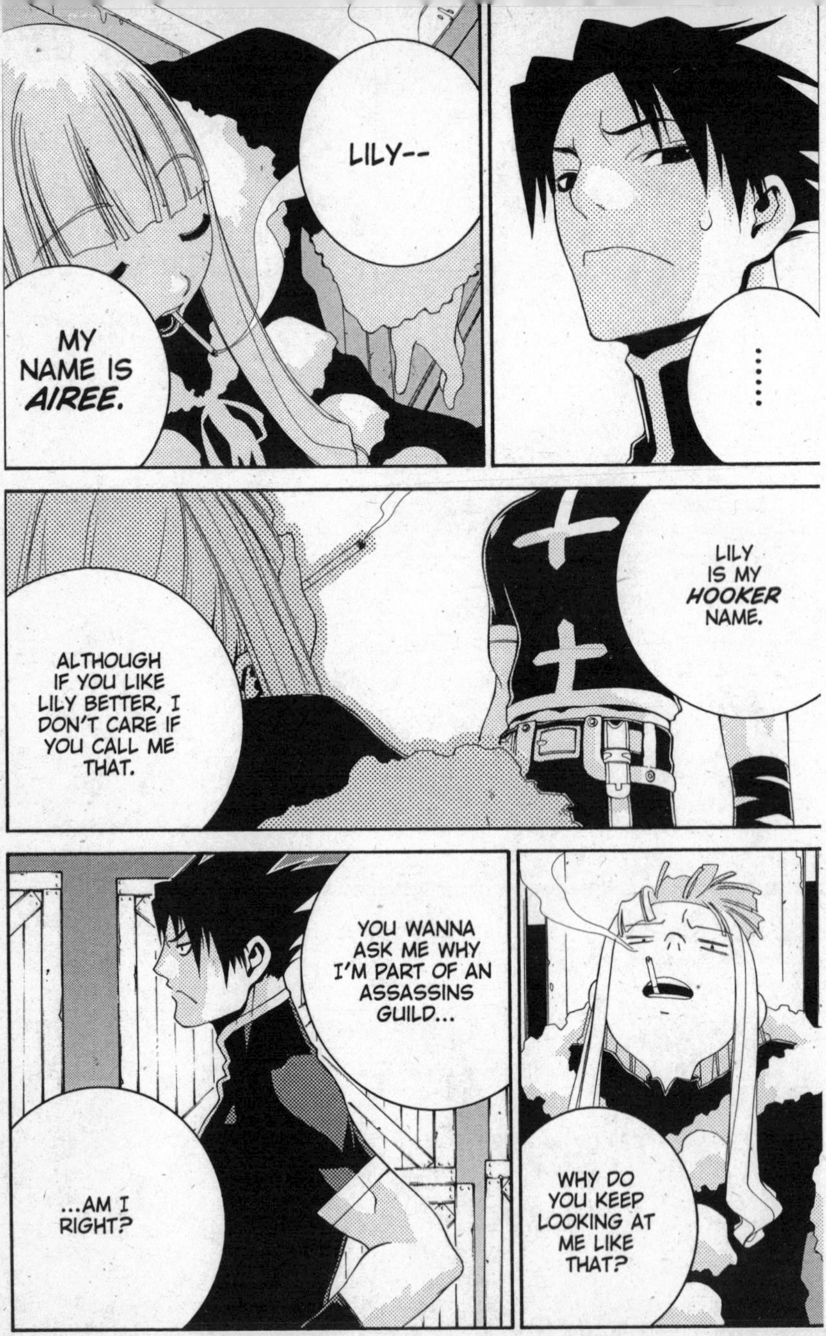
......
LILY--
MY NAME IS *AIREE.*
LILY IS MY *HOOKER* NAME.
ALTHOUGH IF YOU LIKE LILY BETTER, I DON'T CARE IF YOU CALL ME THAT.
WHY DO YOU KEEP LOOKING AT ME LIKE THAT?
YOU WANNA ASK ME WHY I'M PART OF AN ASSASSINS GUILD...
...AM I RIGHT?

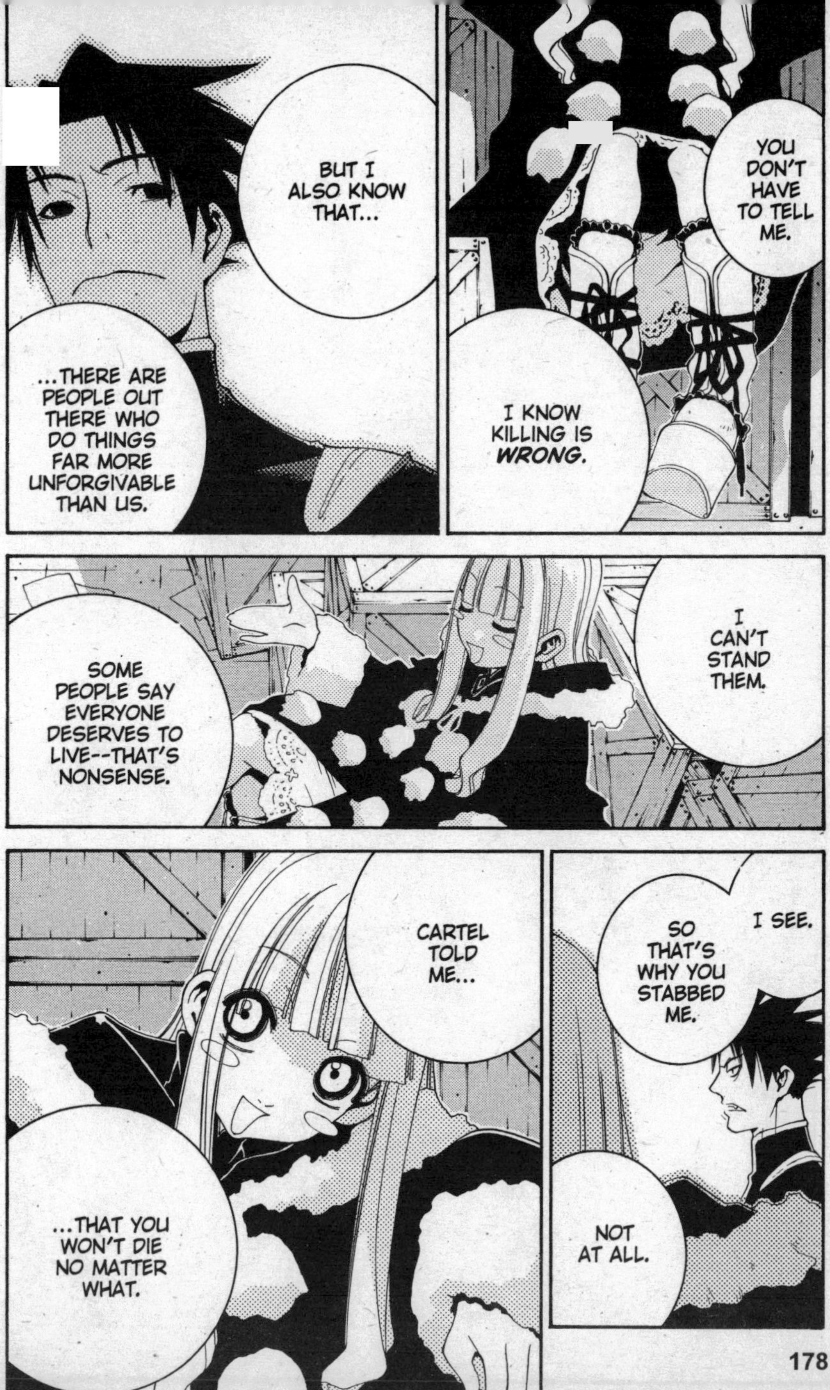
YOU DON'T HAVE TO TELL ME.
I KNOW KILLING IS *WRONG.*
BUT I ALSO KNOW THAT...
...THERE ARE PEOPLE OUT THERE WHO DO THINGS FAR MORE UNFORGIVABLE THAN US.
I CAN'T STAND THEM.
SOME PEOPLE SAY EVERYONE DESERVES TO LIVE--THAT'S NONSENSE.
I SEE.
SO THAT'S WHY YOU STABBED ME.
NOT AT ALL.
CARTEL TOLD ME...
...THAT YOU WON'T DIE NO MATTER WHAT.

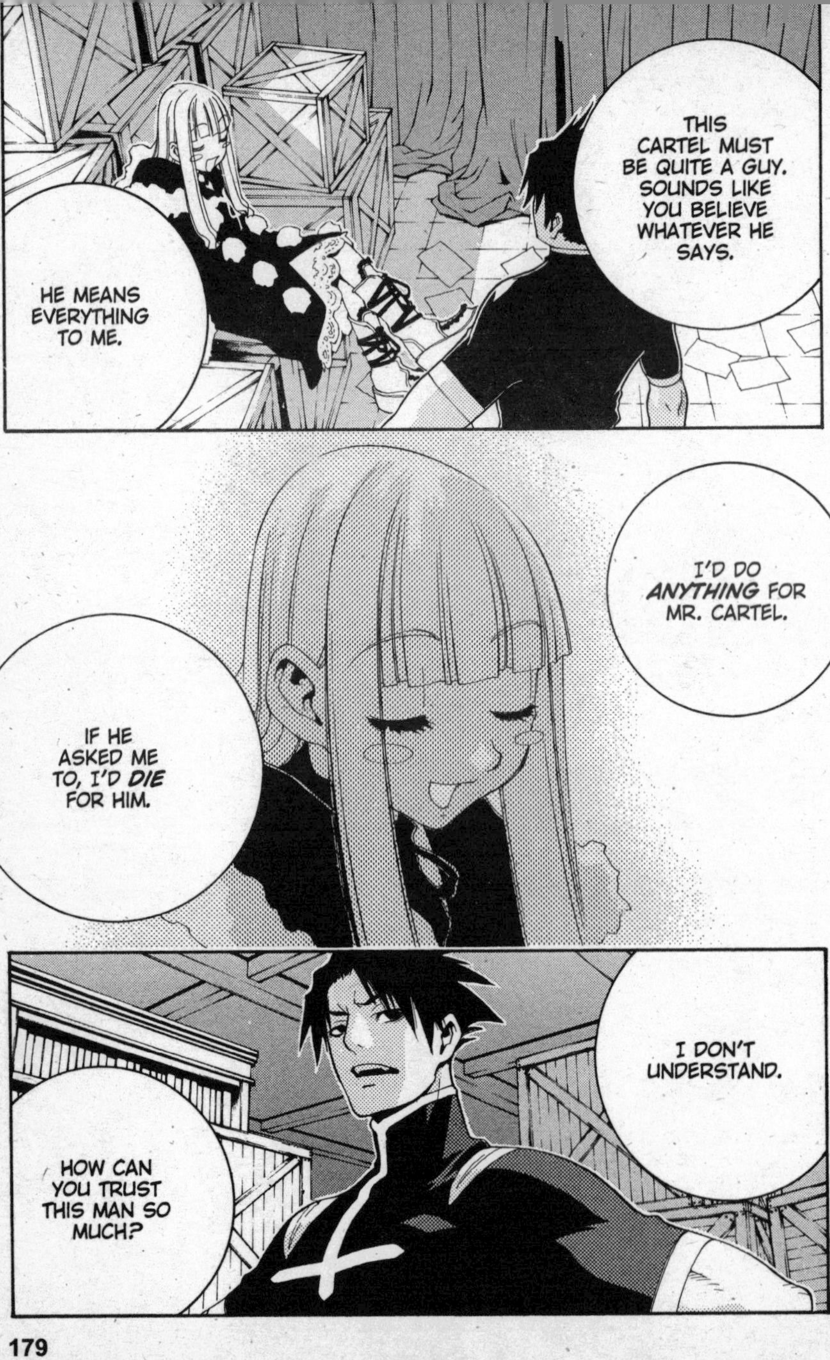
THIS CARTEL MUST BE QUITE A GUY. SOUNDS LIKE YOU BELIEVE WHATEVER HE SAYS.
HE MEANS EVERYTHING TO ME.
I'D DO *ANYTHING* FOR MR. CARTEL.
IF HE ASKED ME TO, I'D *DIE* FOR HIM.
I DON'T UNDERSTAND.
HOW CAN YOU TRUST THIS MAN SO MUCH?

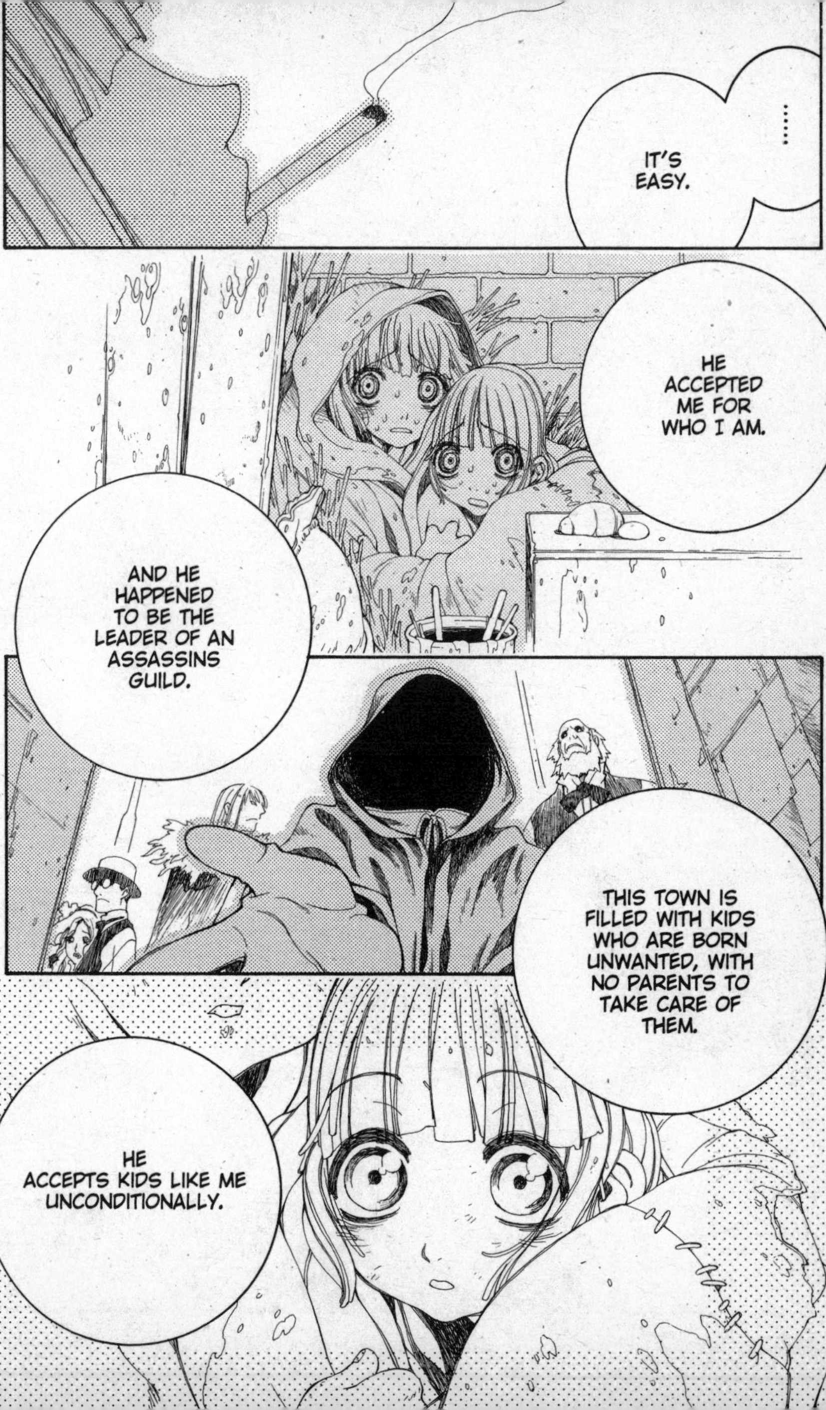
......
IT'S EASY.
HE ACCEPTED ME FOR WHO I AM.
AND HE HAPPENED TO BE THE LEADER OF AN ASSASSINS GUILD.
THIS TOWN IS FILLED WITH KIDS WHO ARE BORN UNWANTED, WITH NO PARENTS TO TAKE CARE OF THEM.
HE ACCEPTS KIDS LIKE ME UNCONDITIONALLY.

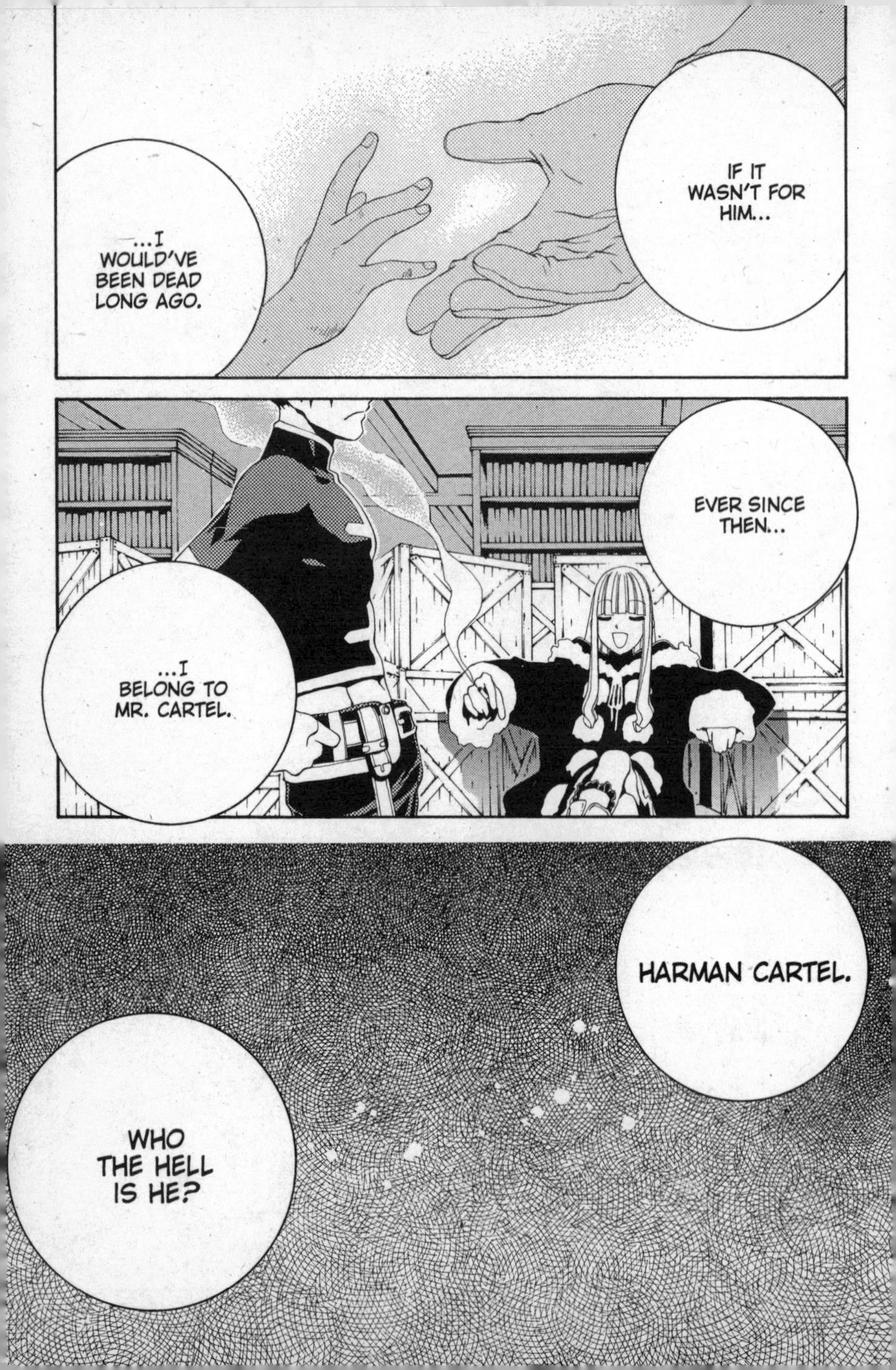
IF IT WASN'T FOR HIM...
...I WOULD'VE BEEN DEAD LONG AGO.
EVER SINCE THEN...
...I BELONG TO MR. CARTEL.
HARMAN CARTEL.
WHO THE HELL IS HE?

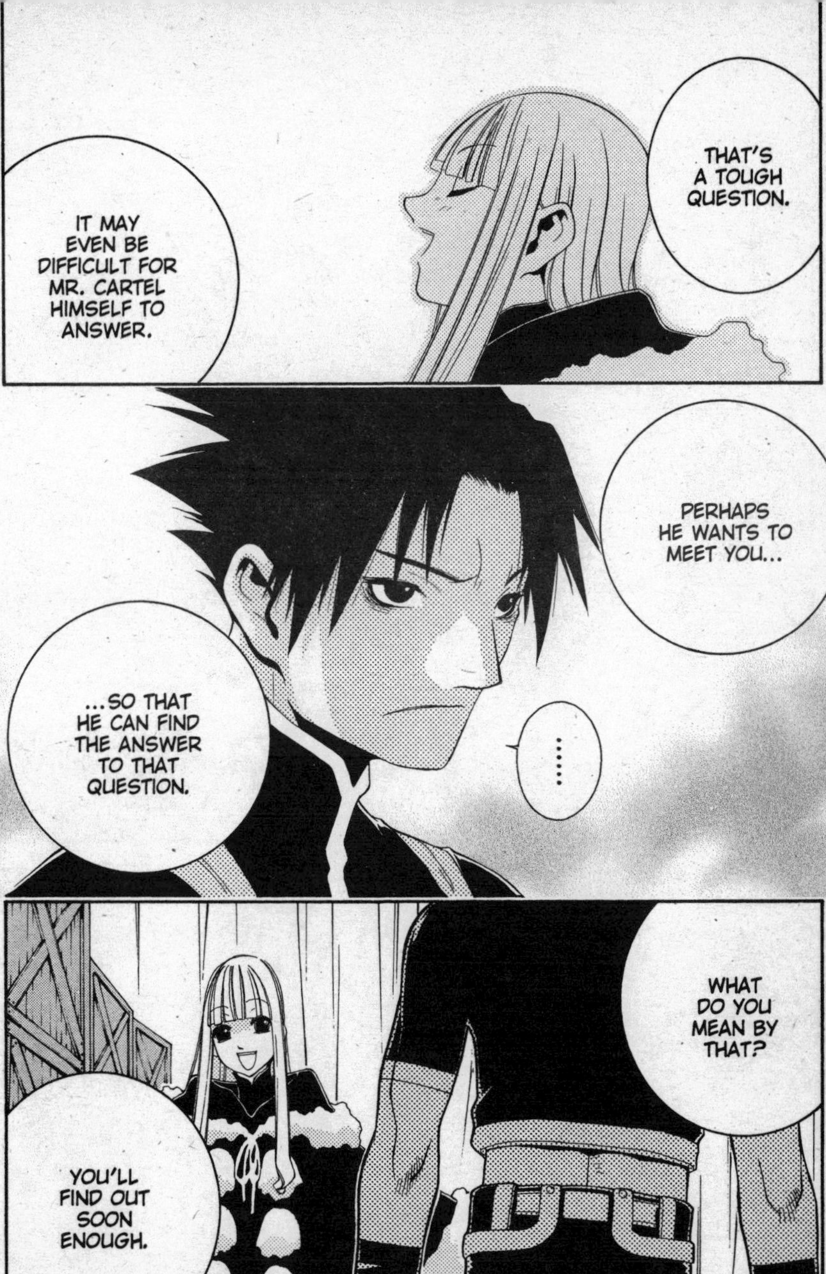
THAT'S A TOUGH QUESTION.
IT MAY EVEN BE DIFFICULT FOR MR. CARTEL HIMSELF TO ANSWER.
PERHAPS HE WANTS TO MEET YOU...
...SO THAT HE CAN FIND THE ANSWER TO THAT QUESTION.
......
WHAT DO YOU MEAN BY THAT?
YOU'LL FIND OUT SOON ENOUGH.

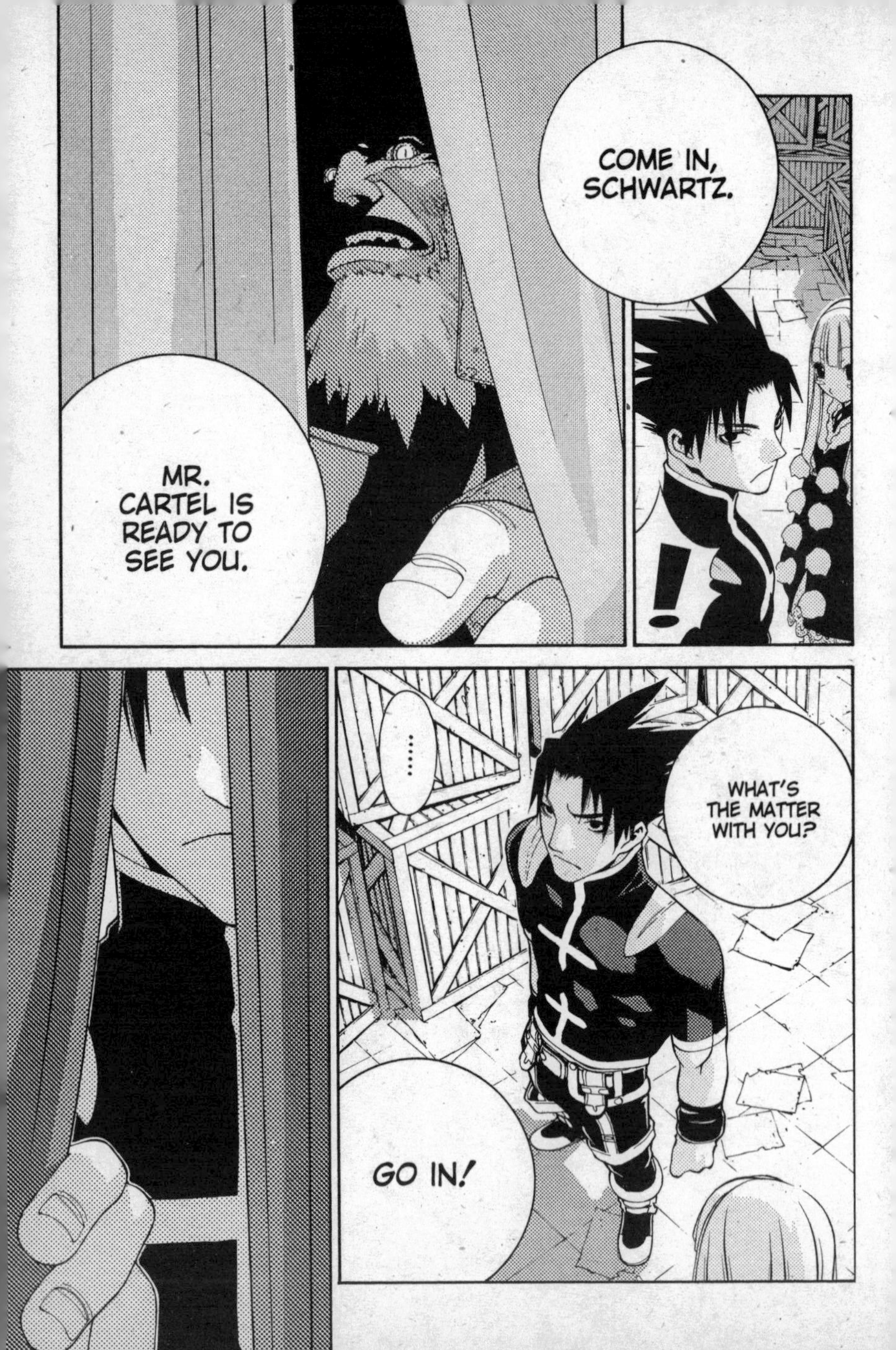
COME IN, SCHWARTZ.
!
MR. CARTEL IS READY TO SEE YOU.
WHAT'S THE MATTER WITH YOU?
......
GO IN!

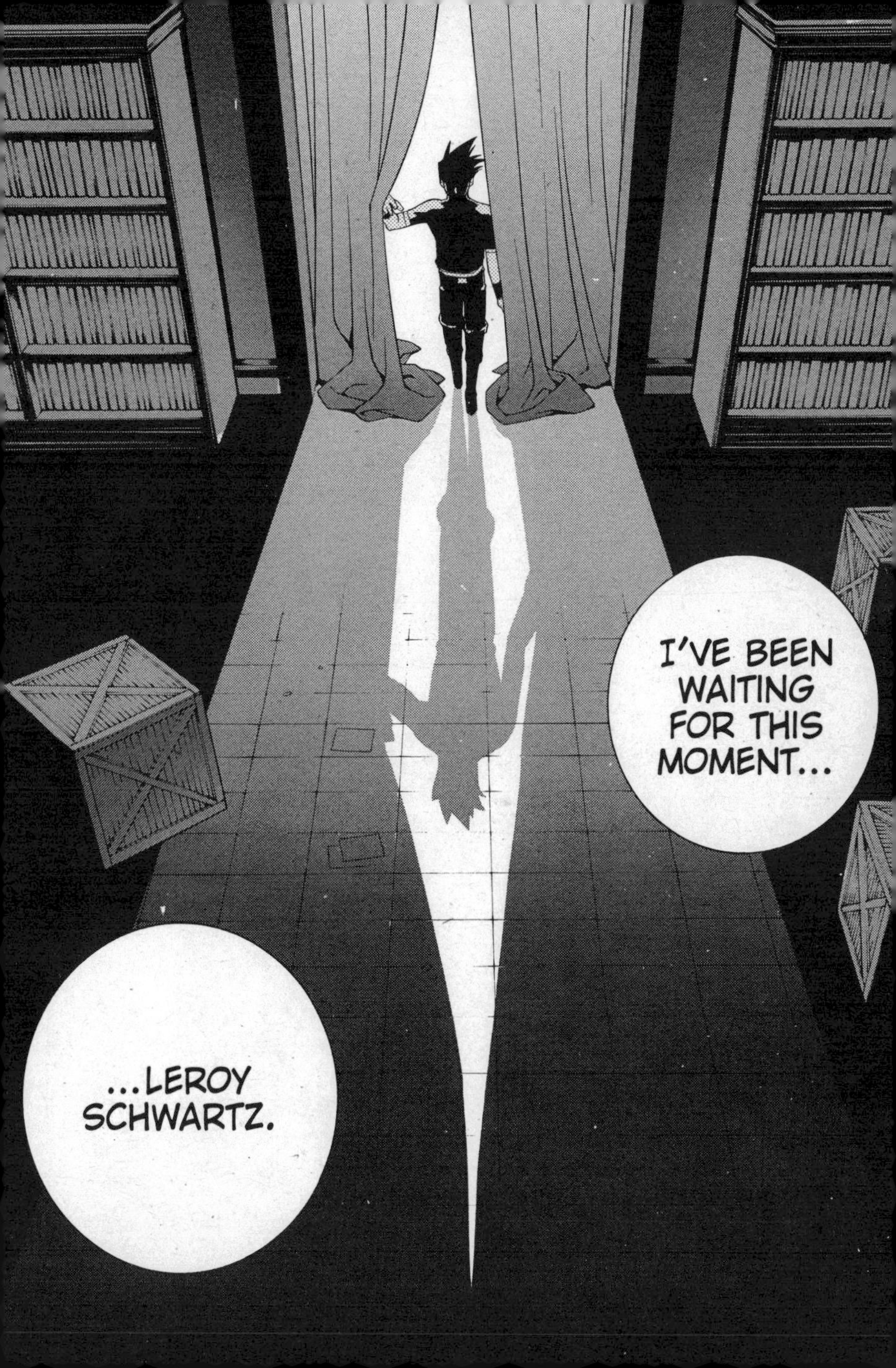
I'VE BEEN WAITING FOR THIS MOMENT...
...LEROY SCHWARTZ.

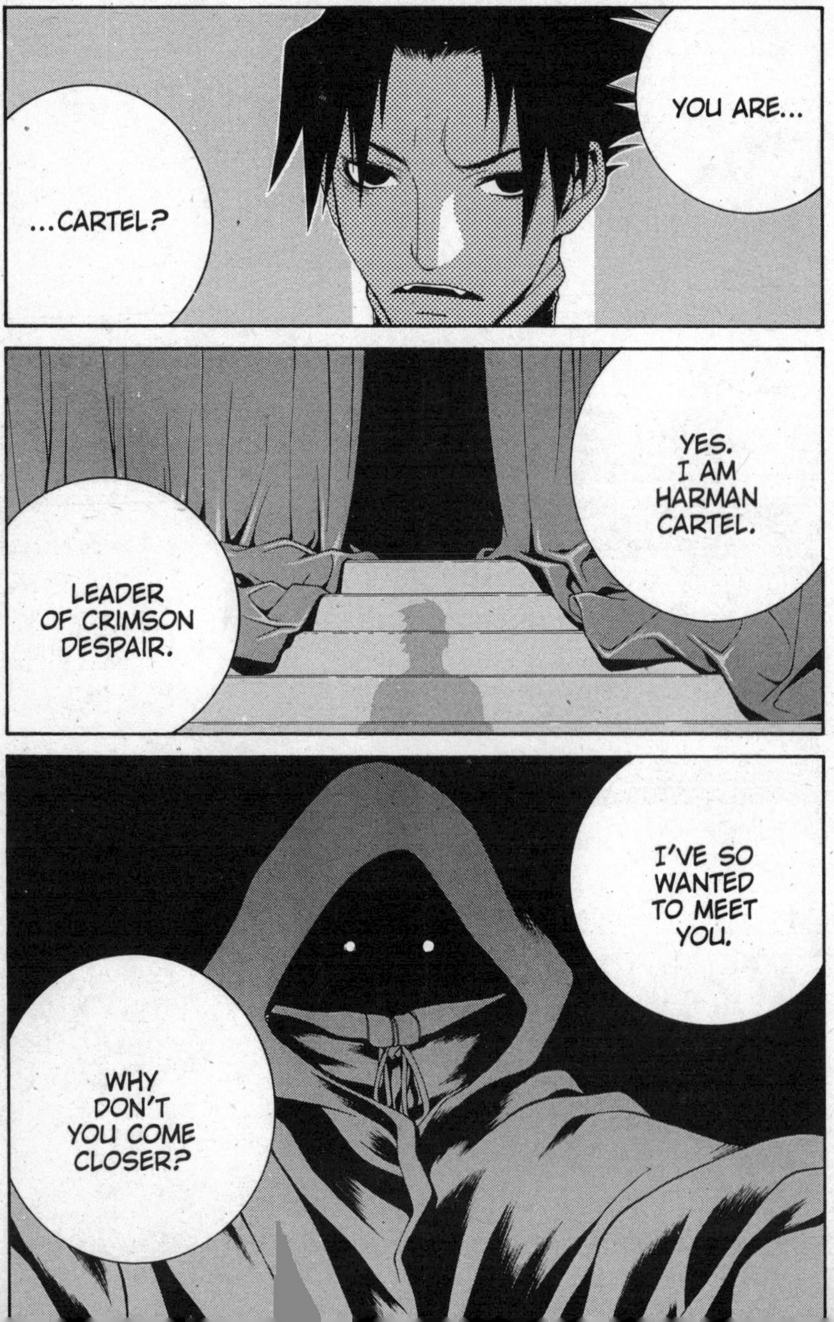
YOU ARE...
...CARTEL?
YES. I AM HARMAN CARTEL.
LEADER OF CRIMSON DESPAIR.
I'VE SO WANTED TO MEET YOU.
WHY DON'T YOU COME CLOSER?

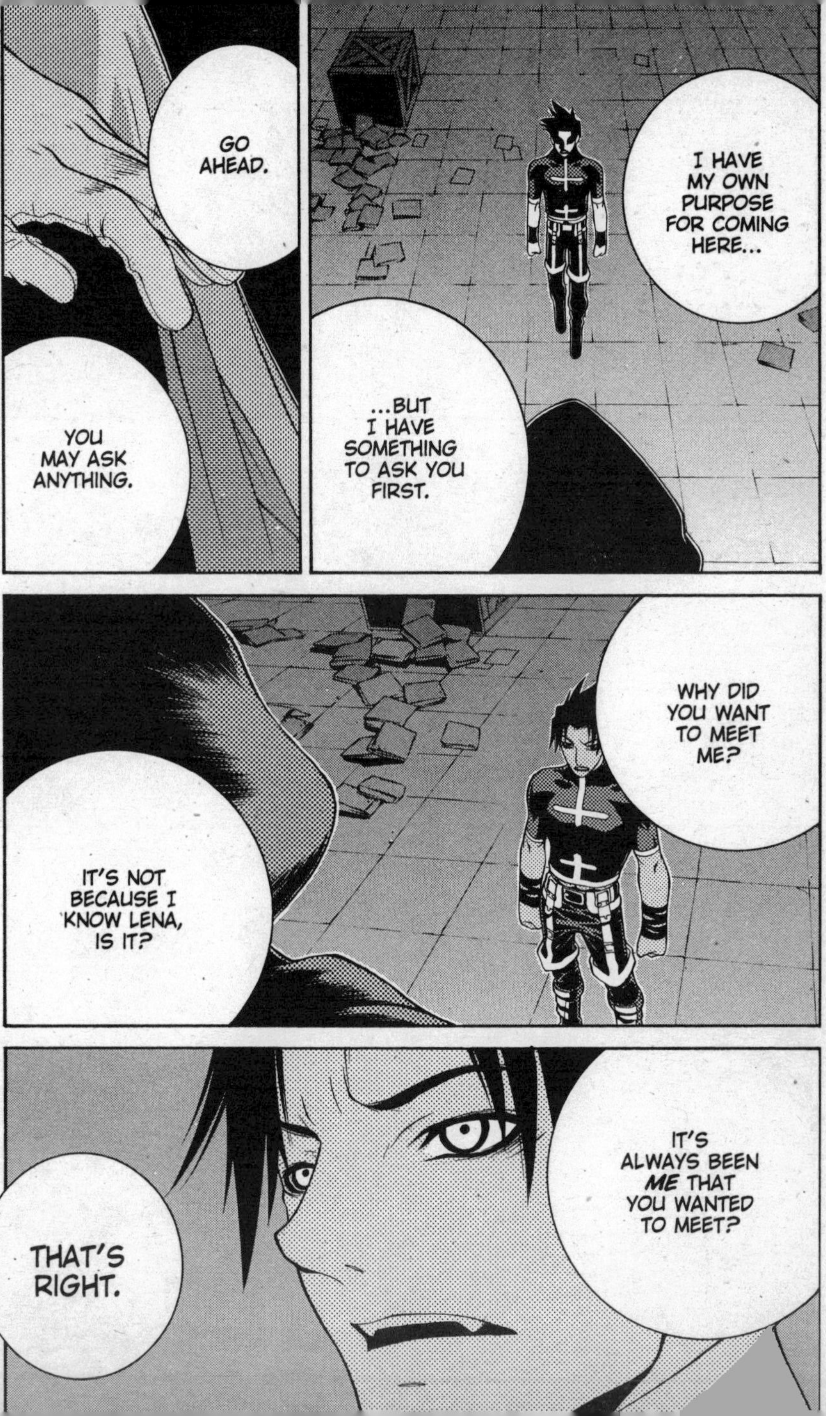
I HAVE MY OWN PURPOSE FOR COMING HERE...
...BUT I HAVE SOMETHING TO ASK YOU FIRST.
GO AHEAD.
YOU MAY ASK ANYTHING.
WHY DID YOU WANT TO MEET ME?
IT'S NOT BECAUSE I KNOW LENA, IS IT?
IT'S ALWAYS BEEN *ME* THAT YOU WANTED TO MEET?
THAT'S RIGHT.

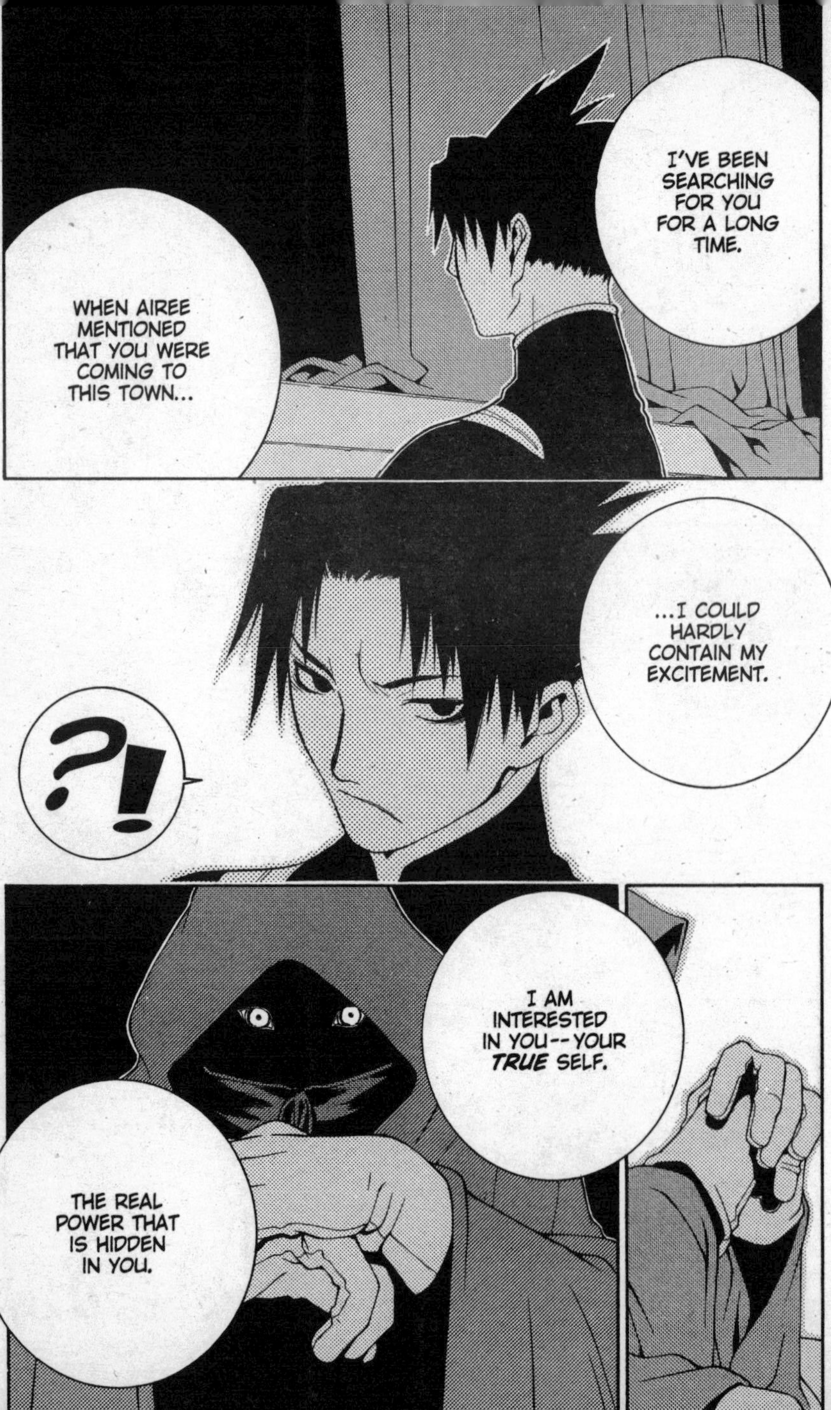
I'VE BEEN SEARCHING FOR YOU FOR A LONG TIME.
WHEN AIREE MENTIONED THAT YOU WERE COMING TO THIS TOWN...
...I COULD HARDLY CONTAIN MY EXCITEMENT.
?!
I AM INTERESTED IN YOU--YOUR TRUE SELF.
THE REAL POWER THAT IS HIDDEN IN YOU.

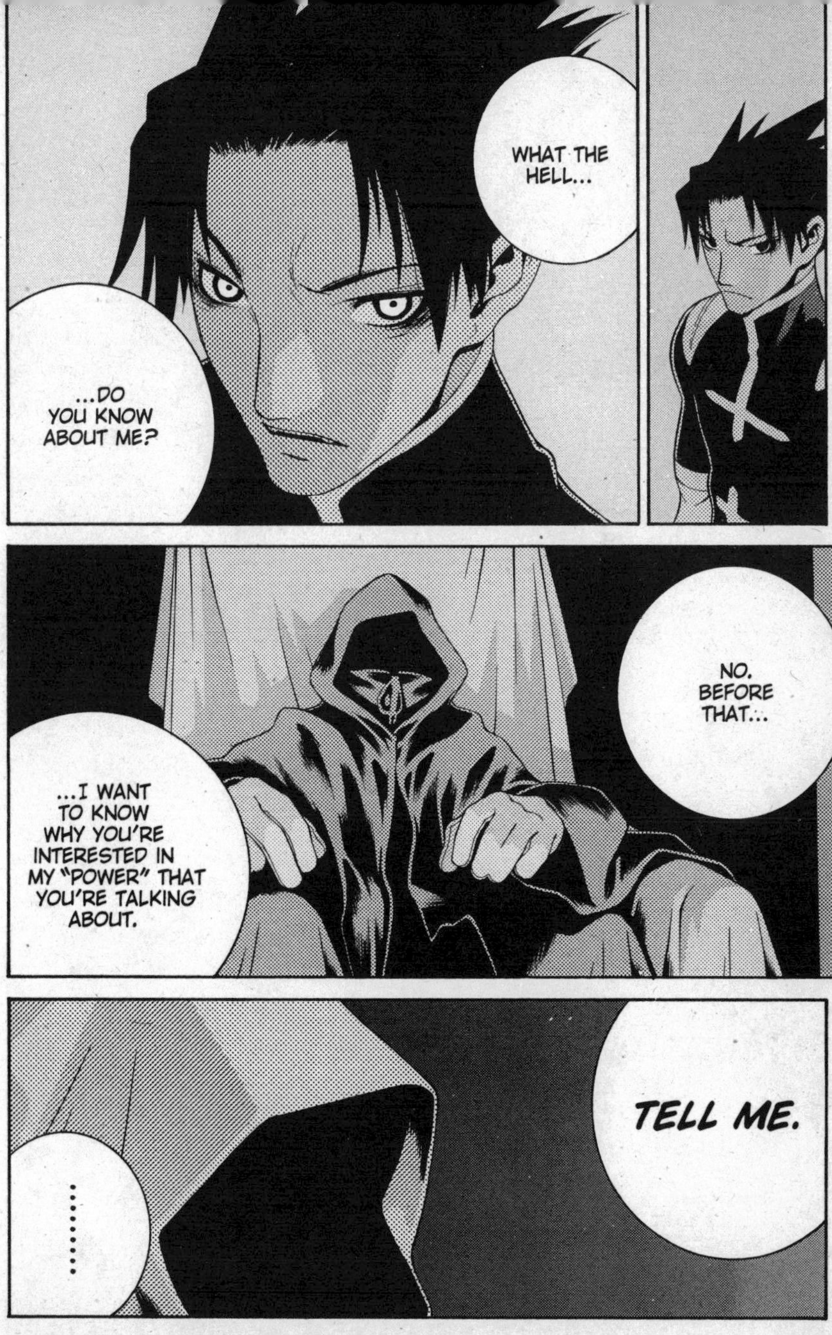
WHAT THE HELL...
...DO YOU KNOW ABOUT ME?
NO. BEFORE THAT...
...I WANT TO KNOW WHY YOU'RE INTERESTED IN MY "POWER" THAT YOU'RE TALKING ABOUT.
TELL ME.
....

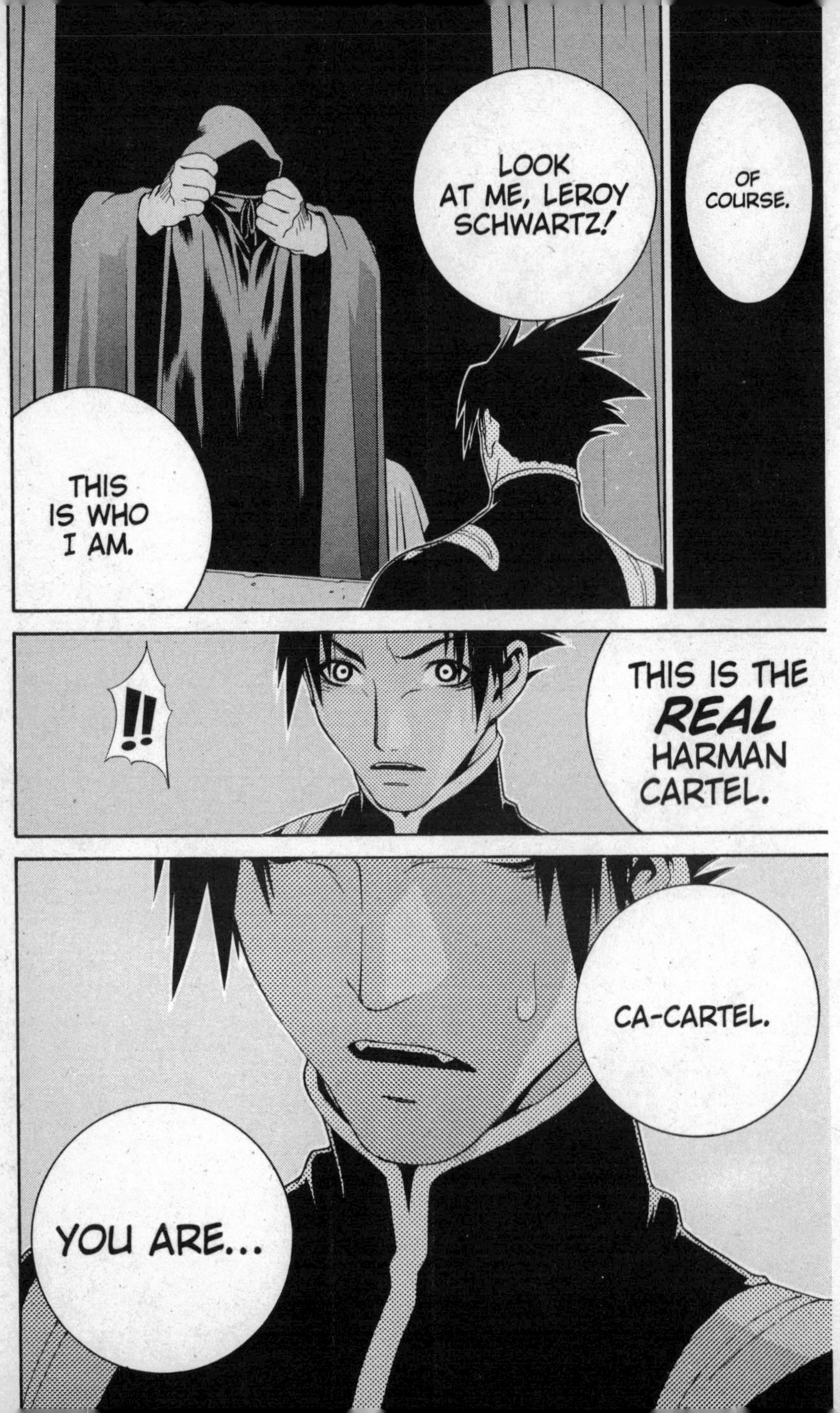
OF COURSE.
LOOK AT ME, LEROY SCHWARTZ!
THIS IS WHO I AM.
THIS IS THE *REAL* HARMAN CARTEL.
!!
CA-CARTEL.
YOU ARE...

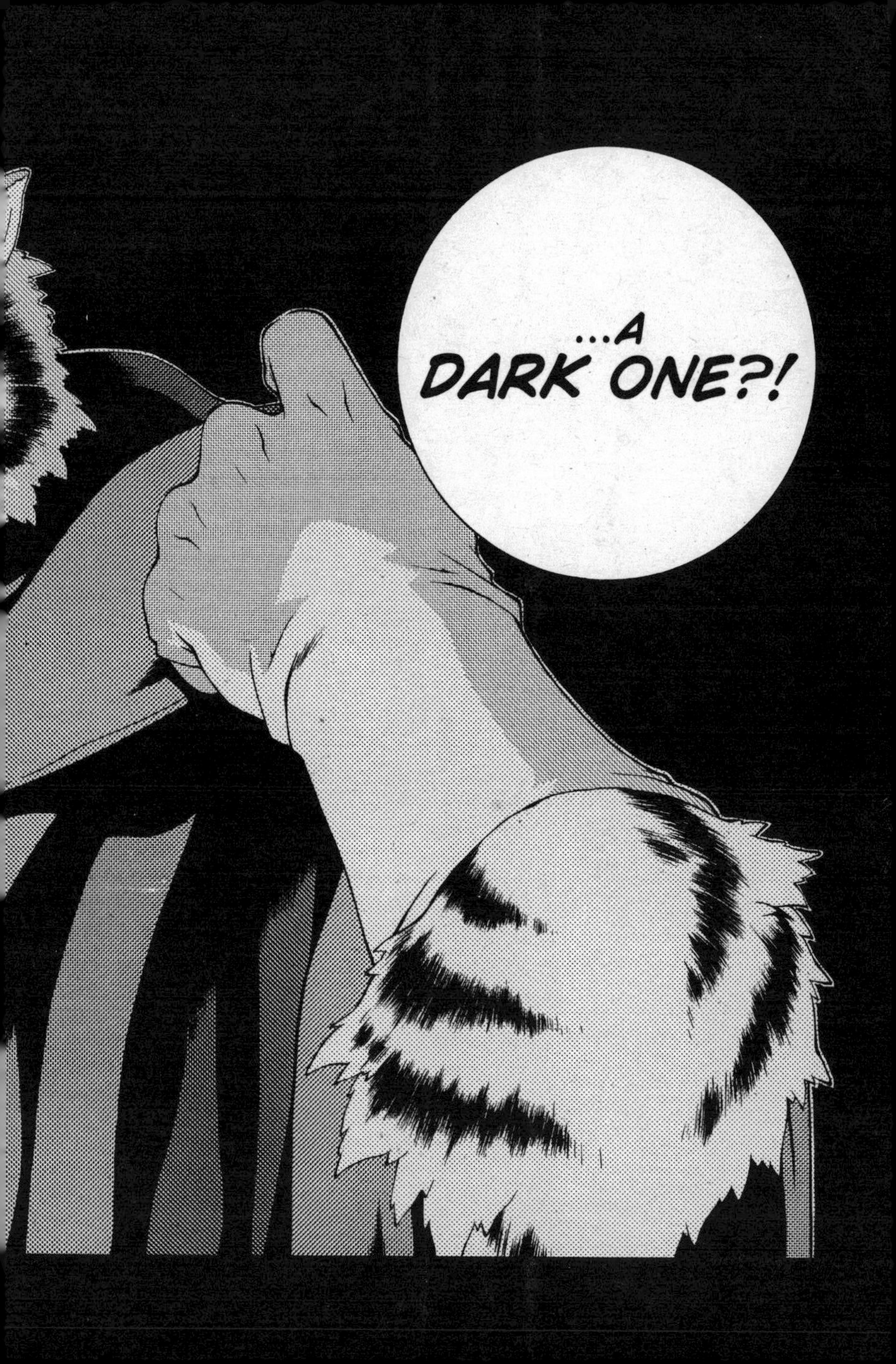
...A DARK ONE?!

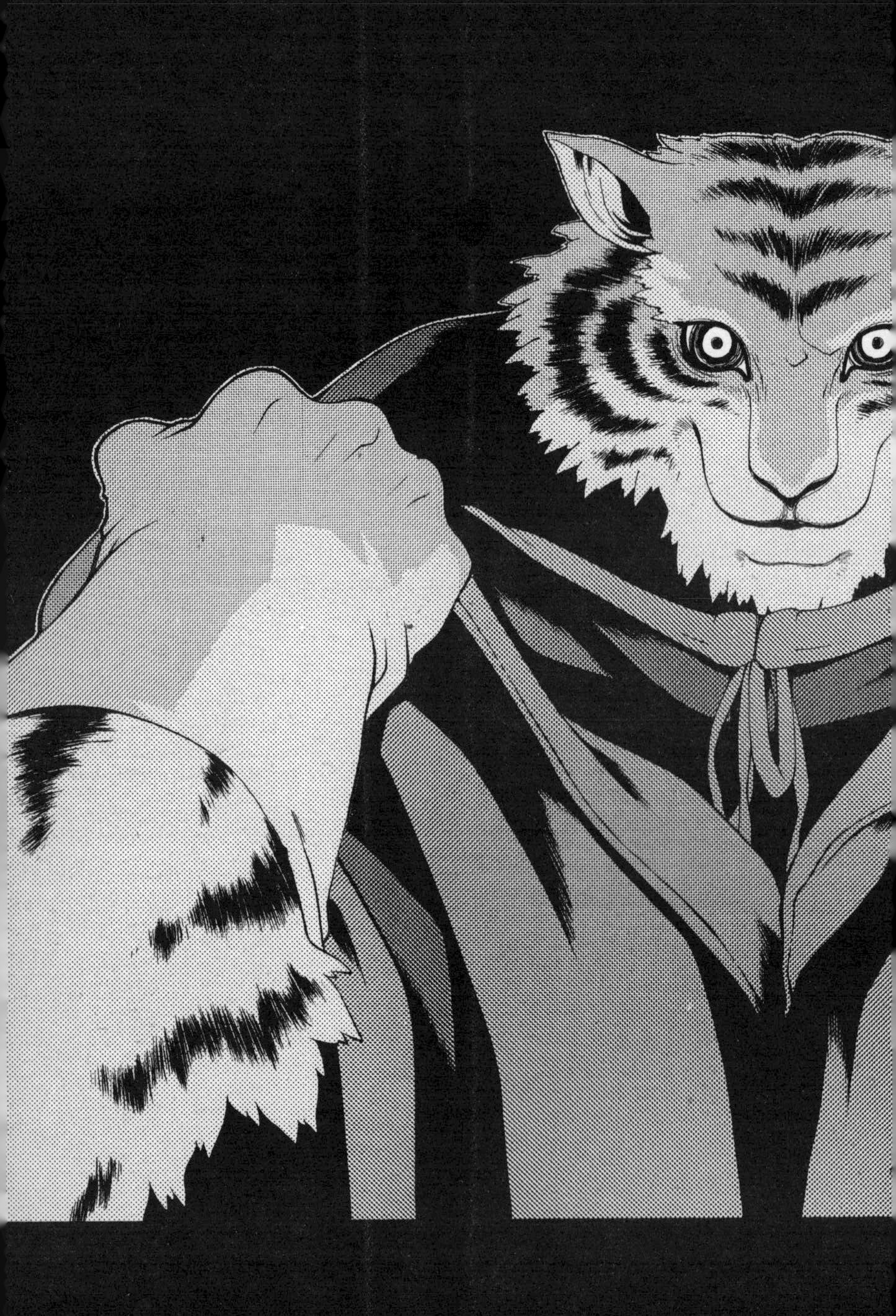

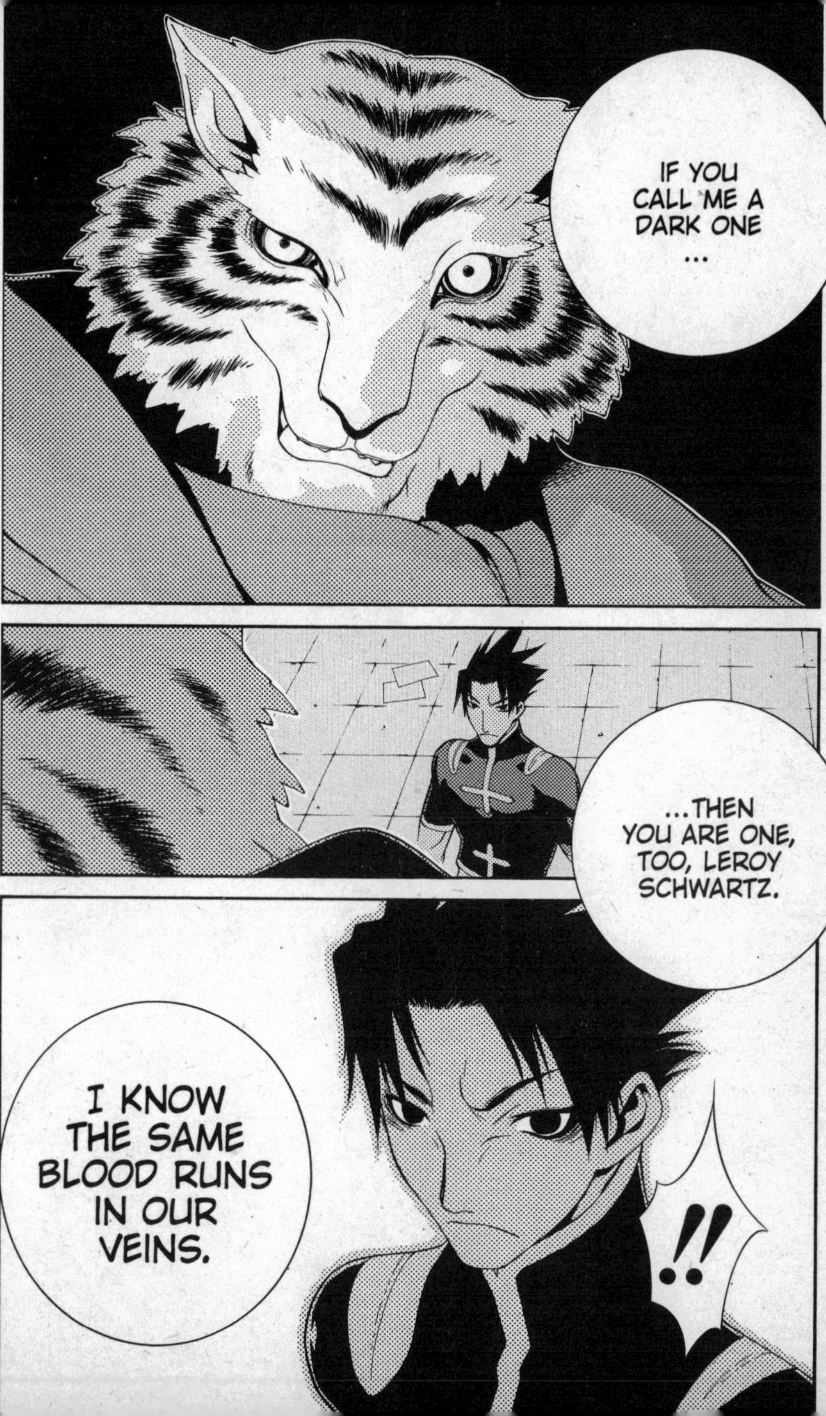
IF YOU CALL ME A DARK ONE ...
...THEN YOU ARE ONE, TOO, LEROY SCHWARTZ.
I KNOW THE SAME BLOOD RUNS IN OUR VEINS.
!!

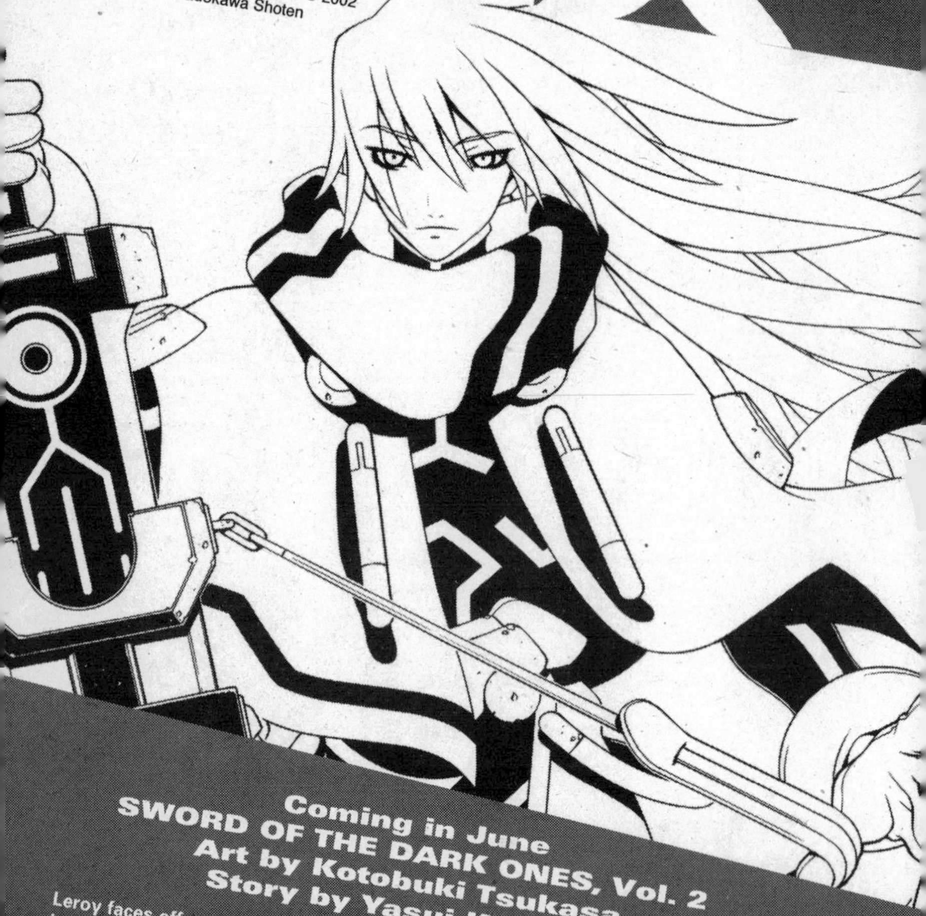

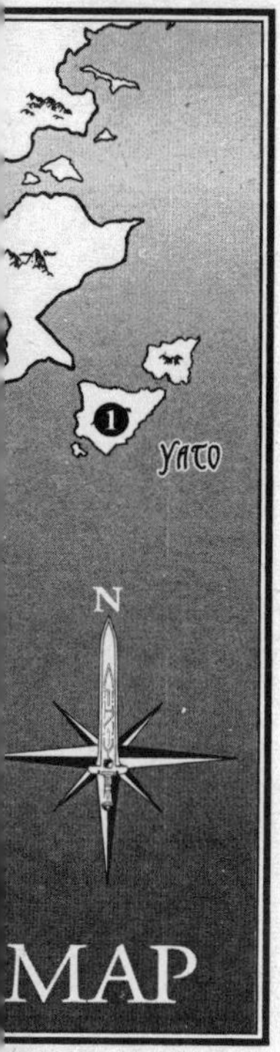
YATO
N
MAP

OVERVIEW

- MAGNIFICENT STAGE OF WAR -

THE VAST RAGNAROK CONTINENT. THIS INCLUDES THE OLDEST AND LARGEST STATE, THE **ASGARD EMPIRE,** WHICH INVENTED THE STEAM ENGINE AND IS THE MOST ADVANCED CIVILIZATION. NEXT TO ASGARD IN SIZE IS THE **VERNERD EMPIRE** WHICH IS IN A CONSTANT STATE OF WAR AGAINST THE ASGARD EMPIRE. IN **EARTHLAND**, A POOR NATION LOCATED IN THE NORTHEAST, THERE'S A GREAT DISPARITY BETWEEN RICH AND POOR DUE TO THE COLD CLIMATE AND BARREN SOIL.

VOLUME 1'S MAIN STAGE, THE TOWN OF ALPAS, IS LOCATED IN THE SOUTH OF THE CONTINENT. A KEY STOP ON THE TRADE ROUTES, ALL PRODUCTS ARRIVING AT THE PORT CITY OF KANAN MUST PASS THROUGH HERE ON THEIR WAY TO THE WALLED CITIES OF AGATO AND ROLAY. WHILE ON THE SURFACE, ALPAS SEEMS A PROSPEROUS, UPSTANDING COMMUNITY, THE TOWN AUTHORITY HAS DEEP TIES TO THE CRIMSON DESPAIR ASSASSINS GUILD.

YATO IS THE EASTERNMOST INHABITED ISLAND AND ITS PEOPLE CHOOSE TO REMAIN CUT OFF FROM THE MAIN CONTINENT. THEY REFUSE TO TRADE WITH THE MAIN CONTINENT. THIS IS WHERE LEROY MET NATAKU FUJIKA. THE HEADQUARTERS OF HAGAKURE, A MASSIVE ASSASSINS GUILD (AS BIG AS CRIMSON DESPAIR) IS LOCATED HERE.

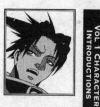

VOL 1 CHARACTER INTRODUCTIONS

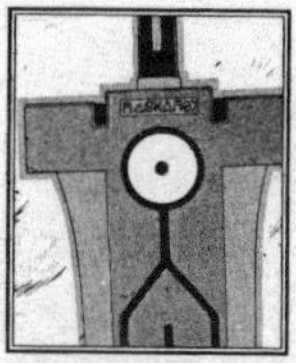

LEROY SCHWARTZ: THE MAIN CHARACTER IN SWORD OF THE DARK ONES. HE HAS SUPERHUMAN STRENGTH, SPEED AND STAMINA. DESPITE HIS TOUGH EXTERIOR, HE LOVES WOMEN AND CAN'T HELP COMING TO THE AID OF THOSE IN NEED. HE SHOWS NO MERCY TO THOSE WHO HURT INNOCENT PEOPLE AS THE DARK ONES DO. WHAT IS HIDDEN BEHIND HIS SUPERHUMAN POWER?

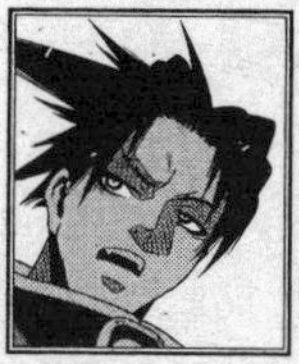

SWORD OF THE DARK ONES

DARK ONES MA

WE'LL GUIDE YOU THR
THE GRAND AND COM
WORLD OF RAGNAROK
EXPLAIN KEY CONCEP
THE MERCENARY GUIL
THE DARK ONES. LET
DEEP INTO THIS DA
WORLD!!!

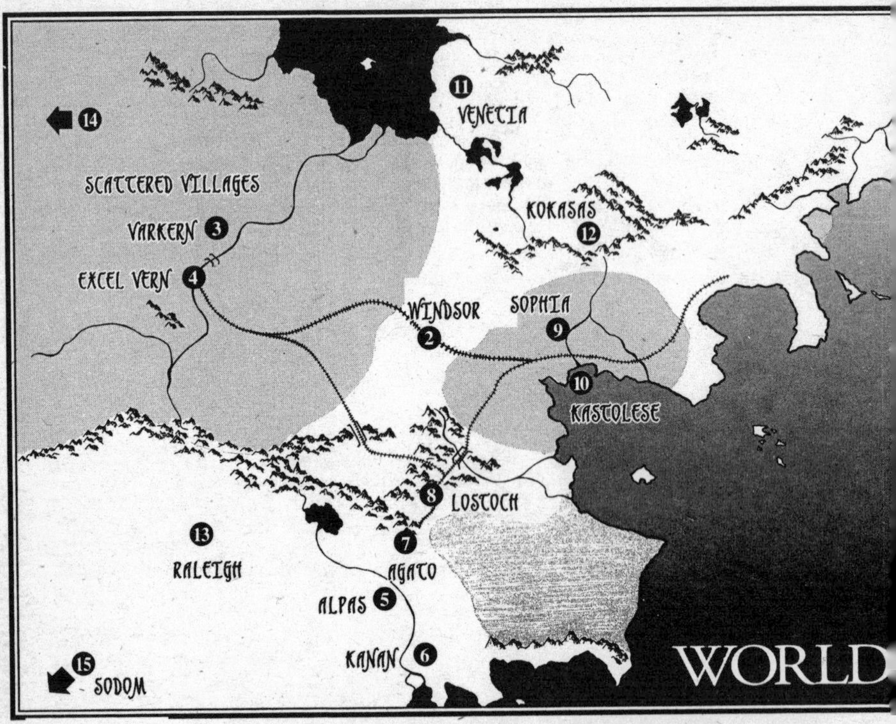
WORLD
14
SCATTERED VILLAGES
VARKERN 3
EXCEL VERN 4
11
VENETIA
KOKASAS
12
WINDSOR
2
SOPHIA
9
10
KASTOLESE
8
LOSTOCH
13
7
RALEIGH
AGATO
ALPAS 5
KANAN 6
15
SODOM

Ashley: Madame of the Scarlet Lady bordello, which is run by the assassins guild Crimson Despair. She failed to capture Leroy when he came to her bedroom. She was tragically killed in the crossfire while Yuri Paris and Leroy were battling.

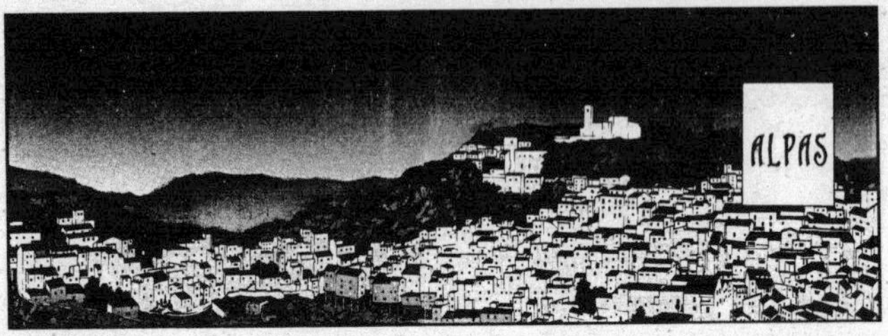
ALPAS

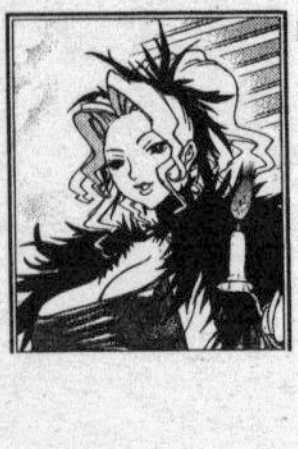

In this volume, she tells Leroy that her little sister was kidnapped and asks him to rescue her, despite the two sharing a dark past. There is a mysterious presence, Fenrir, who accompanies and serves her wherever she goes.

Lena Northlight: A beautiful woman with eyes the color of jade. She is an assassin and when she murders, she does so without hesitation or expression. She doesn't open herself up to anyone — although it appears she is a different person when it comes to her little sister.

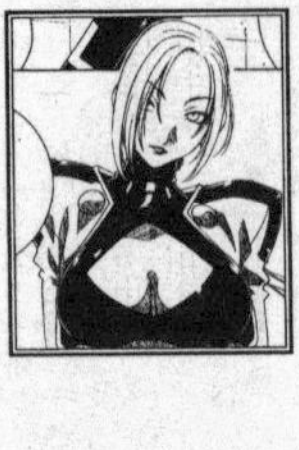

Ragnarok: Leroy's partner in crime, this legendary sword is fully sentient and is able to talk. He is logical and level-headed, the exact opposite of Leroy in every way. He and Leroy trust each other implicitly. His origin is still unknown in the story.

Mercenary Guild–The Saviors

The Mercenary Guild is the largest organization in human society and has branches all over the continent. Leroy used to belong to the Guild, which was established several hundred years ago. A mercenary's chief duty is to defeat Dark Ones who interfere with citizen's peaceful lives, but they also engage in various other duties such as suppressing wars, serving as bodyguards, defeating bandits, etc. Their ranking system starts with E rank and goes through A, then S, with the highest rank being Double S. One's duty and salary are determined by rank. The mercenary ranking system is consistent throughout the continent and rank is given depending on one's performance and accomplishments. Leroy was about to be ranked Double S, but abruptly left the Guild before the promotion was given. His record was erased and he was stripped of his S rank. However, since he was the first one to decline Double S rank he earned quite a reputation on his own. Also in order to have two nicknames, like "Leroy Lightning-Speed" and "Black Lightning", one has to be above A rank mercenary.

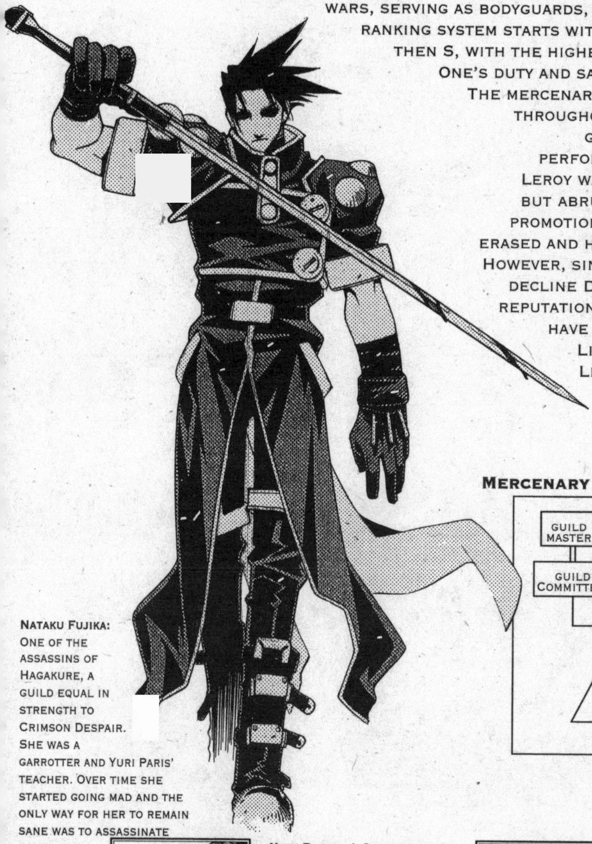

Mercenary Guild Organizational Chart

Guild Master
Guild Committee
S-rank party
S-rank Mercenary
A-rank party
A-rank Mercenary
B-rank party
B-rank Mercenary
C-rank party
C-rank Mercenary
D-rank party
D-rank Mercenary
E-rank party
E-rank Mercenary

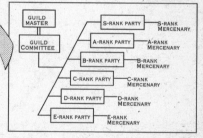

Nataku Fujika: One of the assassins of Hagakure, a guild equal in strength to Crimson Despair. She was a garrotter and Yuri Paris' teacher. Over time she started going mad and the only way for her to remain sane was to assassinate someone. To end her madness, she taught Leroy the secret technique for defeating her and had him kill her. Her appearance is that of a mysterious beauty; however she is really a man.

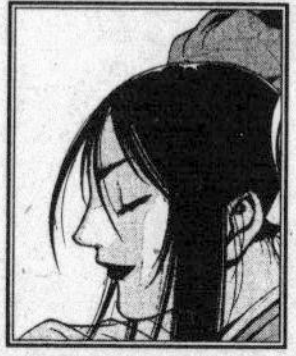

Yuri Paris: A Garrotter. As soon as he found out that Leroy had killed his lover, Nataku Fujika, he was determined to avenge her death and kill Leroy, ignoring his orders to bring the ex-mercenary in alive. Too late, he discovered that Fujika had taught Leroy her secret technique to defeat a garrotter. He lost the battle and was killed.

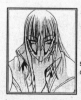

Airee (Lily): This little girl from the Scarlet Lady is actually an assassin for Crimson Despair. She has relied on Cartel ever since he found her on street when she was little.

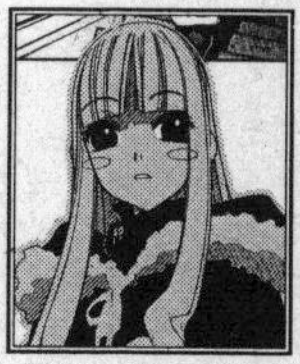

The Dark Ones–Masters of Darkness

Violent and vicious, these are the monsters who have caused humanity to live in fear. Their origin and true nature are still unknown. Depending on their abilities and form, Dark Ones are classified as upper, middle or lower class. Middle and lower-class Dark Ones are generally the only ones seen; so little is known about the upper-class ones that they have become legends. No one has been able to even determine how powerful upper-class ones are. Not that anyone's in a hurry to face them--even lower-class ones are too strong for ordinary humans to defeat.

It is believed that in ancient times humans were once almost wiped out by the Dark Ones, but the historical record is so sparse, no one knows the full story. over the past few decades there have been an increase in attacks by the Dark Ones, and as a result, cities have become the only haven from attacks. It has become customary for people to hire a mercenary escort when traveling to protect themselves from the Dark Ones.

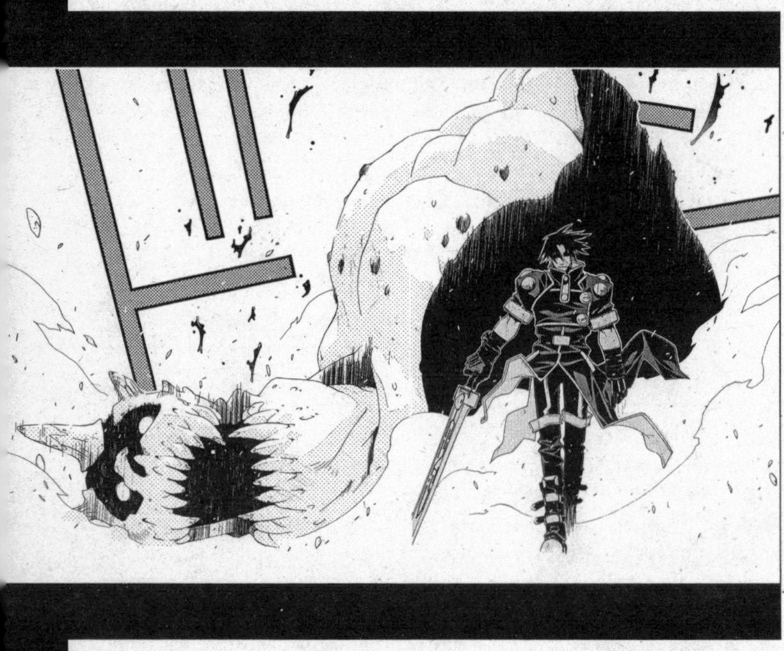

Geinan:
An assassin with Crimson Despair.

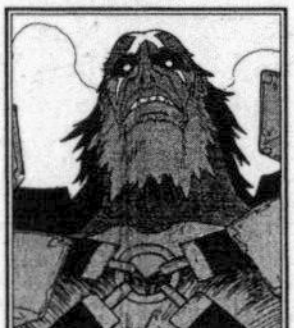

Harman Cartel:
Leader of the largest assassins guild, Crimson Despair. He finally showed his face--but is he a Dark One or something else? Why is he so interested in Leroy's hidden power? You may find the answer in Volume 2!

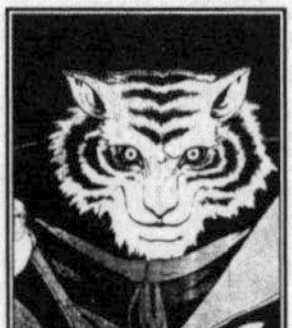

CREATOR'S COMMENTS

THE NOVELS FROM WHICH THIS MANGA IS INSPIRED ARE TOLD IN THE FIRST-PERSON. WHEN WRITING IN THE FIRST-PERSON POINT OF VIEW, YOU CAN'T WRITE FACTS THAT ARE NOT KNOWN OR SEEN BY THE STORYTELLER IN THE STORY.

SO HOW WOULD WE HANDLE ADAPTING THIS STORY TO MANGA?

CLEARLY WE MADE SOME CHANGES. WE WANTED TO GIVE THE WRITER A CHANCE TO SHOW THE STORY FROM MULTIPLE POINTS OF VIEW. IT MIGHT SEEM LIKE AN EASY TRANSITION TO GO FROM NOVEL TO MANGA, BUT WE WANTED TO REALLY EXPAND ON THE WORLD IN MANY WAYS, NOT JUST SHOW READERS WHAT THEY'VE ALREADY READ. SOME SCENES WHICH WOULD HAVE BEEN NEARLY IMPOSSIBLE TO BRING OUT IN THE NOVEL, BECOME POSSIBLE IN THE MANGA VERSION.

BUT THERE'S ANOTHER REASON WHY ADAPTING AN EXISTING NOVEL INTO A MANGA ISN'T EASY—IT'S A VERY DIFFICULT TASK TO MANIPULATE CHARACTERS AND STORIES WRITTEN BY SOMEONE ELSE (ESPECIALLY SOMEONE AS PROTECTIVE OF HIS CHARACTERS AS I AM). EVEN IF THE STORY IS EXACTLY THE SAME, SOME SCENES WHICH SUCCEED IN PROSE FORM JUST DON'T TRANSLATE WELL TO MANGA. FUNNY SCENES IN THE NOVEL MAY LOSE THEIR EFFECTS IN MANGA FORM, AND CONVERSELY, SCENES WHICH SEEMED DRY AND EXPOSITIONAL BECOME TENSE AND EXCITING IN THE MANGA. I AM AMAZED HOW OFTEN THIS HAPPENED.
THROUGH REPEATED TRIAL AND ERROR, MANGA-KA TSUKASA KOTOBUKI HAS SUCCESSFULLY ADAPTED THE STORY THAT I CREATED INTO AN ACTION-PACKED MANGA. NOT ONLY THAT, HE HAS DONE SO WHILE MAINTAINING THE GREATEST RESPECT FOR MY ORIGINAL STORY (AS WELL AS TO TASA'S ORIGINAL ILLUSTRATIONS). TSUKASA KOTOBUKI, MY HAT GOES OFF TO YOU! SEEING HOW YOU'VE OVERCOME THE TRANSITION FROM NOVEL TO MANGA, IT'S LIKE I'M READING THE STORY FOR THE FIRST TIME. I CAN'T WAIT TO SEE HOW THE REST OF IT PANS OUT!

LADIES AND GENTLEMEN, PLEASE JOIN ME IN EXPLORING THE WONDERFUL WORLD OF SWORD OF THE DARK ONES PORTRAYED BY MR. TSUKASA KOTOBUKI.

KENTAROU YASUI

cmx

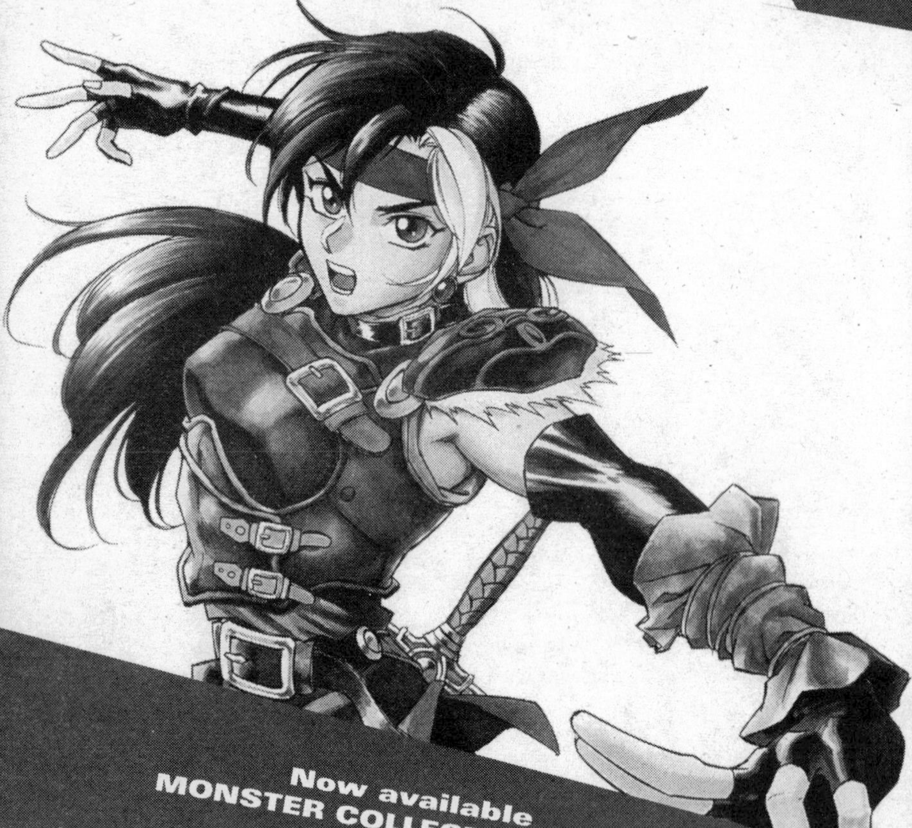

Now available
MONSTER COLLECTION, Vol. 1
By Itoh Sei

Kasche may have a talent for controlling beasts, but she's got a lot to learn about self-control before she can become a full-fledged summoner. Joined by allies both human and not, Kasche must recapture a relic from an evil summoner before he can use it to unlock the Encyclopedia Verum.

cmxmanga.com

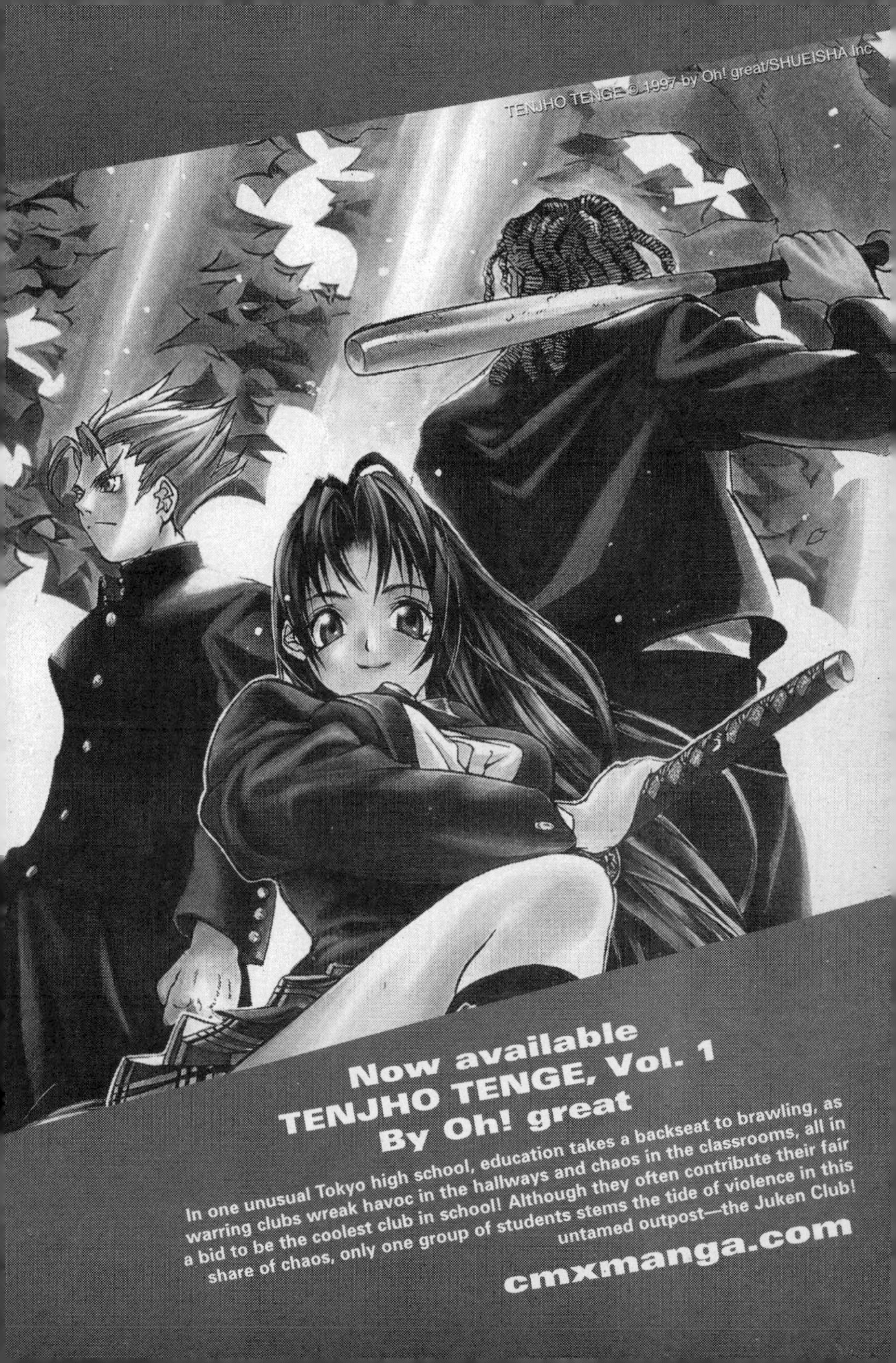
TENJHO TENGE © 1997 by Oh! great/SHUEISHA Inc.
Now available
TENJHO TENGE, Vol. 1
By Oh! great
In one unusual Tokyo high school, education takes a backseat to brawling, as warring clubs wreak havoc in the hallways and chaos in the classrooms, all in a bid to be the coolest club in school! Although they often contribute their fair share of chaos, only one group of students stems the tide of violence in this untamed outpost—the Juken Club!
cmxmanga.com

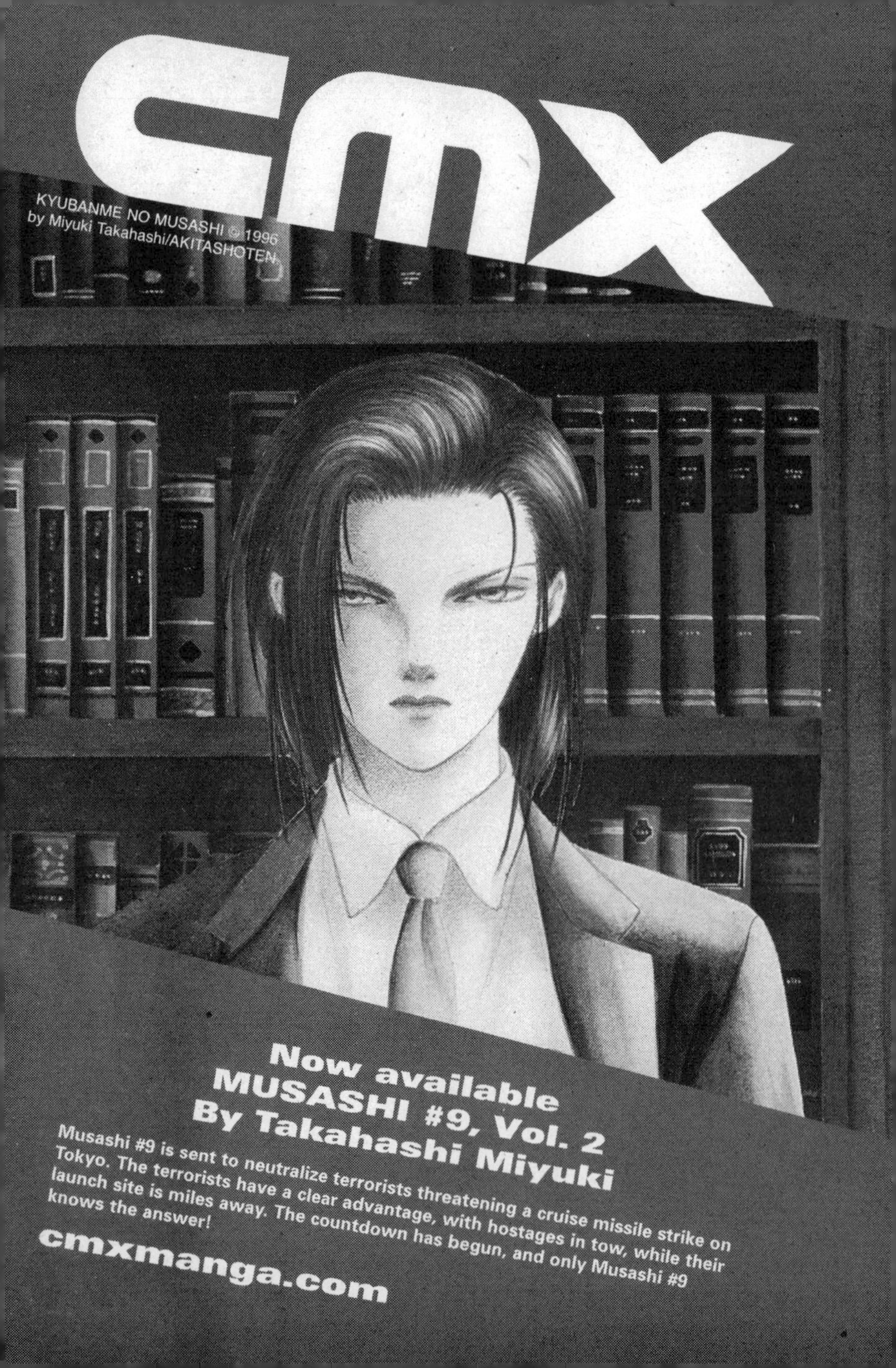
cmx
KYUBANME NO MUSASHI © 1996
by Miyuki Takahashi/AKITASHOTEN
Now available
MUSASHI #9, Vol. 2
By Takahashi Miyuki
Musashi #9 is sent to neutralize terrorists threatening a cruise missile strike on Tokyo. The terrorists have a clear advantage, with hostages in tow, while their launch site is miles away. The countdown has begun, and only Musashi #9 knows the answer!
cmxmanga.com

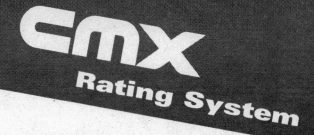

CMX Rating System

Titles with this rating are appropriate for all age readers. They contain no offensive material. They may contain mild violence and/or some comic mischief.

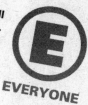

EVERYONE

Titles with this rating are appropriate for a teen audience and older. They may contain some violent content, language, and/or suggestive themes.

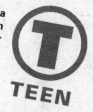

TEEN

Titles with this rating are appropriate for mature readers. They may contain graphic violence, nudity, sex and content suitable only for older readers.

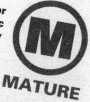

MATURE

CMX

Jim Lee
Editorial Director
John Nee
VP—Business Development
Jonathan Tarbox
Group Editor
Paul Levitz
President & Publisher
Georg Brewer
VP—Design & Retail Product Development
Richard Bruning
Senior VP—Creative Director
Patrick Caldon
Senior VP—Finance & Operations
Chris Caramalis
VP—Finance
Terri Cunningham
VP—Managing Editor
Alison Gill
VP—Manufacturing
Rich Johnson
VP—Book Trade Sales
Hank Kanalz
VP—General Manager, WildStorm
Lillian Laserson
Senior VP & General Counsel
David McKillips
VP—Advertising & Custom Publishing
Gregory Noveck
Senior VP—Creative Affairs
Cheryl Rubin
Senior VP—Brand Management
Bob Wayne
VP—Sales & Marketing

Akilah Tsubasa
Translation

Jake Forbes
Adaptation

Saida Temofonte
Lettering

John J. Hill
CMX Logo & Publication Design

Ed Roeder
Additional Design

ISBN: 1-4012-0647-6

FLIP IT!!

All the pages in this book were created—and are printed here—in Japanese RIGHT-to-LEFT format. No artwork has been reversed or altered, so you can read the stories the way the creators meant for them to be read.

JAPANESE NAMES
Authentic Japanese name order is family name first, given name second. In CMX books we list the names of all characters as well as the manga creators in Japanese order, unless otherwise instructed by the author.

RIGHT TO LEFT?!

Traditional Japanese manga starts at the upper right-hand corner, and moves right-to-left as it goes down the page. Follow this guide for an easy understanding.

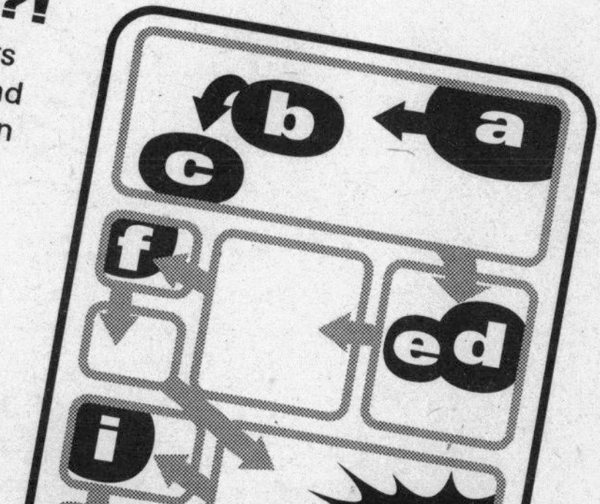

a
b
c
ed
f
g
h
i
j

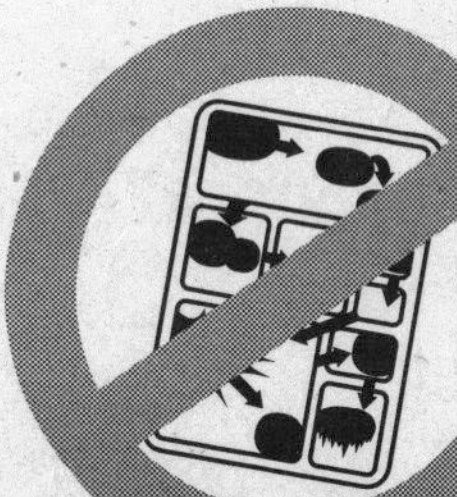

Catch the latest at cmxmanga.com!